POETRY 1900-2000

EDITOR

MEIC STEPHENS

PARTHIAN

LIBRARY OF WALES

Parthian
The Old Surgery
Napier Street
Cardigan SA43 1ED
www.parthianbooks.co.uk

The Library of Wales is a Welsh Assembly Government initiative which highlights and celebrates Wales' literary heritage in the English language.

The publisher acknowledges the financial support of the Welsh Books Council. Contributions to the cost of paying copyright fees for the poems in this anthology have been made by the University of Glamorgan, the Thomas Ellis Memorial Fund and the Guild of Graduates of the University of Wales.

The Library of Wales publishing project is based at Trinity College, Carmarthen, SA31 3EP.
www.libraryofwales.org

Series Editor: Dai Smith

First published in 2007
© The Poets and/or their Estates.

Preface © Dafydd Elis-Thomas
Editor's note © Meic Stephens
All Rights Reserved

ISBN 1-902638-88-3
ISBN 978-1-902638-88-1

Cover design by Marc Jennings
Cover image *Do not go Gentle into that Good Night* by Ceri Richards
© Estate of Ceri Richards/DACS 2007
Typeset by logodædaly

Printed and bound by Gomer Press, Llandysul, Wales

British Library Cataloguing in Publication Data

A cataloguing record for this book is available from the British Library.

LIBRARY OF WALES

PREFACE

A preface is literally that, a saying or writing beforehand. Usually, though, they are written afterwards, after a reading of the contents. The purpose especially of the preface to a book such as this is usually to explain or justify what is in it or even to persuade a potential reader to buy it. In the case of this volume in this series this is hardly necessary. After all, the series itself came about in 2005 when the then Minister for Culture in the Welsh Government, Alun Pugh AM, accepted a recommendation from the Culture Committee of the National Assembly that such a series should be funded and published and placed in all schools and libraries. The series is itself a cultural act, yet another feature of the nation-building that had been going on throughout the twentieth century but has proceeded apace since its turn into the twenty-first. That a volume which is an anthology of a century of poetry should be one in the series called the Library of Wales is in one sense self-evident. It is literally again the flowering of the best offerings of a culture. Perhaps it might be more provocative to assert in this preface that without something called poetry existing and associated with and naming a place called Wales during the last century this very series and the political process which led to it would not have happened. Without poetry, even perhaps without 'Poetry Wales', Wales at least as we now know it would not have come about.

Can poetry or any other art form – drama, films, novels,

music of all kinds, visual art, and dance – be that important? Along with sport of all kinds it is these forms of cultural actions that make us distinctive as human beings. Think how much of our waking time is spent watching, listening, following and supporting all these activities. Every community and society and country does it. We compete around these activities, we celebrate and agonise over them, and we endlessly express criticisms of them. It is through culture or cultures plural that we live. Diversity and difference of cultures and cultural expressions are the very basis of them. If all cultural activities were and looked the same, if everyone sang or danced or played football in the same way, we would have nothing to play or watch or talk about. Differences of form and languages are of the essence of cultures.

As we read poems aloud to ourselves, or better still to each other in a group, it is fascinating to try and work out what kind of speaking or writing occasion the poem might most resemble. Is the poet talking to herself? Or is s/he telling a personal story to a close friend, or addressing a person, often an absent lover or a hero from the past? If the person apparently addressed is dead it becomes an elegy, a very classic genre of poetry indeed. Sometimes the voices in the poem -- never to be confused with that of the poet herself of course as we all have many voices! – may be almost making a public speech or a declaration of protest. The voice-in-the-poem is never as crude or as hectoring as that of a politician, although a poem may well help us to understand an event by interpretation better than a journalist or historian because of the way in which the interpretation is given to us. It is hinted at, gleaned from glints and glimpses, rarely shouting and in-your-face. So too with places and people.

There are as many definitions of Wales as there are people and places in it. This is always as it should be. It is true of all countries and cultures, though there will always be those who try to close down the discussion by insisting their version is somehow right, justified usually by a version of the past, and sometimes more frighteningly by a prescribed version of the future. Wales is an open book with open borders, two and many more languages. English-language Wales at one time had to assert itself in its place in the national rain, as once when the editor of this series, Dai Smith, and the writer of this preface shared a platform asserting that 'English is a Welsh Language'. During that evening the poem entitled 'Ponies, Twynyrodyn' by Meic Stephens, the editor of this anthology, was aptly quoted for its resonating closing line 'exiles all, until the coming thaw'. The coming of that 'thaw' between asserted identities, alleged competing 'heartlands' and Welshness-es, versions of could-have-been, should-have-been national histories in various Wales-es, are all rehearsed in this anthology. When the thaw came many of us saw that it was quite a different country from either the one we had experienced or the one we imagined it to be.

In the making of nations as 'imagined communities' the over-active imagination as found in poetry has its own particular role. It can, however, only work that role effectively within the other forms of cultural life by being poetry. To work it must not only be composed and written as poetry, lyric or otherwise – that is matter that can be safely left to poets – but it must also be read on its own terms. Making sure that it is read as poetry and not expected to be something else is a matter for all of us as readers and critics – and all of us as readers are potentially both! I still think that however much emphasis we quite rightly put on biographical and socio-economic context in our reading there is no substitute for that practice of the close reading of the text of each poem, teasing out the meanings we collectively find there as a group of readers, always reading-out and hopefully not too much reading-in!

I hope that this method of teaching poetry as part of the humanities curriculum which I learned as a young teacher from the so-called American New Criticism when it was still relatively new will find its place whenever this hugely broad canvas of an anthology is used as a teaching resource.

But I also hope that this anthology, despite its size, will be read in bed by those subjects of one of my favourite Dylan Thomas poems 'In my Craft or Sullen Art':

> '... the lovers, their arms
> Round the griefs of the ages,
> Who pay no praise or wages
> Nor heed my craft or art.'

I am certain that its readers, both national and international, will pay more than heed to the poetry of this volume of twentieth-century Wales.

Dafydd Elis-Thomas

Editor's Note

This anthology consists of representative selections from the work of one hundred Welsh poets, and poets living in Wales, written during the 20th century. It includes 554 poems and is therefore the most capacious compendium of Welsh verse in English ever compiled. Most of the poets were either born in Wales or to Welsh parents living elsewhere. About twenty others (two Americans among them) are included because they have been domiciled in Wales for long periods and, an even more crucial qualification, have made significant contributions to our country's literature.

Every decade of the century is represented, as is almost every part of Wales – urban, industrial and rural. Our country's history is also reflected here, from Edwardian times to the age of the internet and global warming. English, long established as one of the languages of Wales, has by now a rich, vibrant and multi-faceted literature and it is heartening to know that the National Assembly wishes to promote it by sponsoring the Library of Wales, the series to which this anthology belongs. It is to be hoped that Welsh writing in English will soon take its place with Welsh-language literature in the curriculum of our schools.

Many of the poems chosen also reflect the landscape and people of Wales. This was not the over-riding consideration, for surely it must be desirable for Welsh poets to write about countries other than their own. Yet it still seems to me (as it has since the 1960s when I was editor of *Poetry Wales*) that to have a body of English verse which can properly be called Welsh there must be some reference to the land and people, to the past as well as the present – otherwise, we shall produce merely a regional or provincial literature indistinguishable from that produced in parts of England. Like Irish and Scottish poetry, Welsh poetry in English should speak to the world, but it should also be rooted in the Welsh experience and have something to say about the country in which it is written. Even so, there is a healthy range of attitudes towards things Welsh in this book: how poets think of Wales is as pluralistic today as it has always been, and long may it be so.

The biographical notes on our hundred poets (of whom 34 are dead and 66 alive, 24 female and 76 male) are meant to give some plain facts about them and are briefer for those still in the land of the living than for those no longer with us; fuller details about most of them will be found in my *New Companion to the Literature of Wales*.

No poet born after 1975 has been included. This closing date may well seem arbitrary but a line had to be drawn if the book, already Gargantuan in scope, was to be kept to a manageable size. Another ground for eligibility was that all poets should have published at least one book – or a substantial number of poems in the magazines – before the end of 2000. This requirement may have had the effect of excluding a few poets still in their thirties, but they are only a very few. If they do not appear here, at least they have the consolation of knowing that their century is the twenty-first.

As an old hand at anthologies I am aware that I am bound to surprise, baffle, disappoint or infuriate some readers by my choice of poets and poems. But if I also stimulate fresh thinking about the course of Welsh writing in English over the last hundred years, and the reputations of certain poets, I shall be content. Many of my choices were made in the light of the growing number of critical studies and collected editions which have appeared in recent years and my selection made, in every case, after re-reading the poet's entire oeuvre. A few poets have been included to suggest continuity and the changing literary scene. In short, by casting my net widely but selectively I have tried to produce a comprehensive, authoritative and lively anthology which still leaves room in the republic of Welsh letters for discussion and dissent.

I am grateful to the University of Glamorgan, the Thomas Ellis Memorial Fund and the Guild of Graduates of the University of Wales for the confidence they showed in me as Editor by making financial contributions to the cost of paying copyright fees.

In the task of compilation I have sought the opinions of a number of friends and colleagues. They include Dr Sam Adams, Dr John Barnie, Professor Tony Brown, Mrs Gillian Clarke, Mr Tony Conran, Professor Tony Curtis, Mr Don Dale-Jones, Mr John Davies, Dr Richard Davies, Dr Moira Dearnley, Mr Mick Felton, Mr Peter Finch, Dr John Harris, Mr Paul Henry, Mr Nigel Jenkins, Dr Patrick McGuinness, Mr Robert Minhinnick, the late Professor Leslie Norris, Dr Francesca Rhydderch, Professor Dai Smith, Professor M. Wynn Thomas, and the Reverend Cynwil Williams. I have not always taken their advice, however, and they should not be held responsible for any of the book's shortcomings. I have put aside the traditional niceties of editorial etiquette by including, at the insistence of the series editor, a few poems of my own.

I should like to thank John Tomlinson for his expertise in setting the text and my wife Ruth for her help in reading the proofs.

I am grateful to all the poets, or their estates, for so readily giving permission for poems to be used. That I have been personally acquainted with almost all the contributors – the exceptions are fewer than a dozen – has brought to my task an additional pleasure at spending even more time in the company of their work. Having been involved in the Welsh literary scene for close on half a century, I hope this book will be seen as a valedictory salute to old friends and an avuncular nod in the direction of younger men and women now making names for themselves.

Meic Stephens

POETRY 1900-2000

CONTENTS

xxiii

xxix

xxxiii

W. H. DAVIES

William Henry Davies was born in Newport, Monmouth-
shire, on 3 July 1871. His father died three years later and,
after his mother's second marriage, the boy was adopted by
his father's parents and brought up in their public house in
Newport's docklands. Apprenticed to a picture-framer at
the age of fourteen, he acquired a love of art and, a
wanderer from an early age, discovered a keen interest in
nature on walks in rural Gwent. In 1893, with a small
income left him by his grandmother, he set out for America
where, unable to find regular employment, he became a
hobo. In Ontario in 1899, on his way to the Klondyke
goldfields, he fell from a train on which he was trying to
hitch a ride, and his right leg had to be amputated below
the knee. Having returned to London, he was fired with
ambition to be a poet and in 1905, at his own expense,
published his first book, *The Soul's Destroyer*. His first
income from writing came from *The Autobiography of a
Super-Tramp* (1908) which, with a preface by George
Bernard Shaw, brought him immediate fame. In 1911,
largely through the offices of Edward Thomas, he was
awarded a Civil List pension and some of his work was
included in the anthology *Georgian Poetry*. Now keenly
aware of his calling as a man of letters, he began
frequenting literary and artistic circles in London. His
marriage in 1923 to a former prostitute brought him a new
source of inspiration; the story of their extraordinary
courtship and happy marriage is told in *Young Emma*,

published posthumously in 1980. The couple settled in the village of Nailsworth in Gloucestershire, where, at his home 'Glendower', on 26 September 1940, the poet died. He had published some two dozen books between 1905 and 1939. The first edition of his *Collected Poems* (1928), although it contained 431 poems, was by no means complete; in the 1963 edition there were 749. His *Selected Poems*, chosen by Jonathan Barker, appeared in 1985. While most of his poems celebrate the beauty of nature, some touch on social injustice and the suffering of marginal people: there is a darker side to W. H. Davies than those who know only 'Leisure', one of the most famous poems ever written in English, care to think.

THE KINGFISHER

It was the Rainbow gave thee birth,
    And left thee all her lovely hues;
And, as her mother's name was Tears,
    So runs it in my blood to choose
For haunts the lonely pools, and keep
In company with trees that weep.

Go you and, with such glorious hues,
    Live with proud Peacocks in green parks;
On lawns as smooth as shining glass,
    Let every feather show its marks;
Get thee on boughs and clap thy wings
    Before the windows of proud kings.

Nay, lovely Bird, thou art not vain;
    Thou hast no proud, ambitious mind;
I also love a quiet place
    That's green, away from all mankind;
A lonely pool, and let a tree
Sigh with her bosom over me.

LEISURE

What is this life if, full of care,
We have no time to stand and stare.

No time to stand beneath the boughs
And stare as long as sheep or cows.

No time to see, when woods we pass,
Where squirrels hide their nuts in grass.

No time to see, in broad daylight,
Streams full of stars like skies at night.

No time to turn at Beauty's glance,
And watch her feet, how they can dance.

No time to wait till her mouth can
Enrich that smile her eyes began.

A poor life this if, full of care,
We have no time to stand and stare.

DAYS THAT HAVE BEEN

Can I forget the sweet days that have been,
  When poetry first began to warm my blood;
When from the hills of Gwent I saw the earth
  Burned into two by Severn's silver flood:

When I would go alone at night to see
  The moonlight, like a big white butterfly,
Dreaming on that old castle near Caerleon,
  While at its side the Usk went softly by:

When I would stare at lovely clouds in Heaven,
  Or watch them when reported by deep streams;
When feeling pressed like thunder, but would not
  Break into that grand music of my dreams?

Can I forget the sweet days that have been,
  The villages so green I have been in:
Llantarnam, Magor, Malpas, and Llanwern,
  Liswery, old Caerleon, and Alteryn?

Can I forget the banks of Malpas Brook,
  Or Ebbw's voice in such a wild delight,
As on he dashed with pebbles in his throat,
  Gurgling towards the sea with all his might?

Ah, when I see a leafy village now,
  I sigh and ask it for Llantarnam's green;
I ask each river where is Ebbw's voice –
  In memory of the sweet days that have been.

4

A GREAT TIME

Sweet Chance, that led my steps abroad,
  Beyond the town, where wild flowers grow –
A rainbow and a cuckoo, Lord,
  How rich and great the times are now!
    Know, all ye sheep
    And cows, that keep
On staring that I stand so long
  In grass that's wet from heavy rain –
A rainbow and a cuckoo's song
  May never come together again;
    May never come
    This side the tomb.

THE COLLIER'S WIFE

The collier's wife had four tall sons
  Brought from the pit's mouth dead,
  And crushed from foot to head;
When others brought her husband home,
Had five dead bodies in her room.

Had five dead bodies in her house –
  All in a row they lay –
  To bury in one day:
Such sorrow in the valley has
Made kindness grow like grass.

Oh, collier, collier, underground,
  In fear of fire and gas,

What life more danger has?
Who fears more danger in this life?
There is but one – thy wife!

THE INQUEST

I took my oath I would inquire,
   Without affection, hate, or wrath,
Into the death of Ada Wright –
   So help me God! I took that oath.

When I went out to see the corpse,
   The four months' babe that died so young,
I judged it was seven pounds in weight,
   And little more than one foot long.

One eye, that had a yellow lid,
   Was shut – so was the mouth, that smiled;
The left eye open, shining bright –
   It seemed a knowing little child.

For as I looked at that one eye,
   It seemed to laugh, and say with glee:
'What caused my death you'll never know –
   Perhaps my mother murdered me.'

When I went into court again,
   To hear the mother's evidence –
It was a love-child, she explained.
   And smiled, for our intelligence.

'Now, Gentlemen of the Jury,' said
    The coroner – 'this woman's child
By misadventure met its death.'
    'Aye, aye,' said we.The mother smiled.

And I could see that child's one eye
    Which seemed to laugh, and say with glee:
'What caused my death you'll never know –
    Perhaps my mother murdered me.'

THE VILLAIN

While joy gave clouds the light of stars,
    That beamed where'er they looked;
And calves and lambs had tottering knees,
    Excited, while they sucked;
While every bird enjoyed his song,
Without one thought of harm or wrong –
I turned my head and saw the wind,
    Not far from where I stood,
Dragging the corn by her golden hair,
    Into a dark and lonely wood.

THE POET

When I went down past Charing Cross,
    A plain and simple man was I:
I might have been no more than air,
    Unseen by any mortal eye.

But, Lord in Heaven, had I the power
　To show my inward spirit there,
Then what a pack of human hounds
　Had hunted me, to strip me bare.

A human pack, ten thousand strong,
　All in full cry to bring me down;
All greedy for my magic robe,
　All crazy for my burning crown.

A WOMAN'S HISTORY

When Mary Price was five years old,
　And had a bird that died,
She laid its body under flowers;
　And called her friends to pray to God,
And sing sad hymns for hours.

When she, before her fifteenth year,
　Was ruined by a man,
The neighbours sought him out, and said –
　'You'll come along and marry her,
Or hang till you are dead.'

When they had found the child he wronged,
　And playing with her doll,
'I'll come along with you,' said she –
　'But I'll not marry anyone
Unless my doll's with me.'

With no more love's heat in her than
　　The wax upon her arm;
With no more love-light in her eyes
　　Than in the glass eyes of her doll –
Nor wonder, nor surprise.

When Mary Price was thirty-five,
　　And he was lying dead,
She wept as though her heart would break:
　　But neighbours winked to see her tears
Fall on a lover's neck.

Now Mary Price is seventy-five,
　　And skinning eels alive:
She, active, strong, and full of breath,
　　Has caught the cat that stole an eel,
And beaten it to death.

LET US LIE CLOSE

Let us lie close, as lovers should,
　　That, if I wake when barn-cocks crow –
I'll feel your body at my side,
　　And hear your breathing come and go.

When dreams, one night, had moved our bodies,
　　I, waking, listened for your breath;
I feared to reach and touch your face,
　　That it was icy-cold in death.

Let us lie close, as lovers should,
    And count our breaths, as some count sheep;
Until we say 'Good night', at last
    And with one kiss prepare for sleep.

HUW MENAI

Hugh Owen Williams, who wrote as Huw Menai, was born in Caernarfon on 13 July 1888. Leaving school at the age of twelve, he followed his father into the mines of South Wales, finding employment at a pit in Merthyr Vale in 1906, where he soon became politically active. Although his mother-tongue was Welsh, he chose to write in English for left-wing newspapers. Sacked on account of his political views, he was later given a job as a weigher, and therefore 'a company man' as opposed to a check-weigher who worked for the colliers. He lived for many years, unworldly, confident in his calling as a poet, often unemployed and the father of eight children, first in Gilfach Goch and then in Pen-y-graig in the Rhondda Fawr, and there he died on 28 June 1961. He published four books of verse: *Through the Upcast Shaft* (1920), *The Passing of Guto* (1929), *Back in the Return* (1933) and *The Simple Vision* (1945). Although he spent most of his life in the industrial valleys of Glamorgan, and wrote sometimes about the miner's lot, his work lacks the power and passion of Idris Davies. His simple lyrics, often in archaic language, have rather homespun qualities; for this reason, perhaps, he was taken up in fashionable, left-wing, middle-class London circles and, for a while, enjoyed a reputation as 'the Poet of the South Wales Coalfield'.

THE OLD PEASANT IN THE BILLIARD SALOON

Stretched out full length, his eighty years too ripe
    For upright posture, on the bench each day
Sleeping aloud, or tugging at his pipe,

Or one eye open on the billiard play.
A sufferer from old age too wise for tears!
    And does he see, in that smoke-ridden place,
Th' Almighty Cueist sending the different spheres
    Upon their business spinning through all space?
Or does it make for a more homely scene,
    With him a lusty youth in Somerset
Bringing the cattle home through fields of green?
    Muttering of something that he has not met!
Muttering to himself, his later sense
Having found none worthier of his confidence!

CWM FARM NEAR CAPEL CURIG

Some cool medieval calm hath settled here
    On this lone farmstead, wherein humble folk
    Still speak the tongue that Owain Glyndŵr spoke,
And worship in it, too, the God they fear.
For to these perilous Ways, where rocks rise sheer,
    Their kinsmen came to curse the tyrant yoke;
    And here the proud invader's heart was broke
By brave and stubborn men year after year.
Unconquerable still! Here birds but know
    The Cymric speech; the very mountains brood
O'er consonants that, rugged streamlets, flow
    Into deep vowel lakes... and by this wood,
    Where Prince Llywelyn might himself have stood,
Forget-me-nots in wild profusion grow!

A . G . P R Y S – J O N E S

Arthur Glyn Prys-Jones, the son of shoolteachers, was born in Denbigh on 7 March 1888, but the family moved to Pontypridd when he was nine years old. Educated at Llandovery College and Jesus College, Oxford, he began his career as a teacher of History and English; in 1919 he was appointed Staff Inspector for Secondary Education in Wales, after which he made his home in Cardiff. He played a prominent role in the city's cultural life as one of the founders of the Little Theatre and served as Secretary of the Welsh Committee of the Festival of Britain in 1951. His anthology *Welsh Poets* (1917) was the first of its kind. For long the doyen of Welsh writers in English, he was elected President of the English-language section of Yr Academi Gymreig in 1970. His last years were spent in Kingston-upon-Thames, where he died on 21 February 1987. He may be properly regarded as the first poet writing in English in the twentieth century for whom Welsh nationality was a source of pride and inspiration. Usually intended to be read aloud, many of his poems are in the simpler metrical styles of Welsh lyrical poetry, while others, written in freer forms, are concerned with the history, people and landscape of Wales; he was also one of the few Welsh poets writing in English to have written comic verse. He published six volumes of his own poems and his *Collected Poems*, edited by Don Dale-Jones, appeared in 1988.

A BALLAD OF GLYN DŴR'S RISING

My son, the moon is crimson, and a mist is in the sky:
Oh can't you hear the thudding feet, the horsemen speeding by?
Oh can't you hear the muttering that swells upon the breeze,
And the whispers that are stealing through the chancel of the trees?
Tonight we two go riding, for the threads of fate are spun,
And we muster far at Corwen at the rising of the sun.

My son, the winds are calling, and the mountains and the flood
With a wail of deep oppression that wakes havoc in my blood.
And I have waited, waited long through the bitter years
For this hour of freedom's challenge and the flashing of the spears:
So we two go riding, riding, through the meshes of the night,
That we hail Glyn Dŵr at Corwen at the breaking of the light.

My son, go kiss your mother, kiss her gently, she'll not wake,
For a greater mother calls you, though you perish for her sake:
Lo! the Dragon flag is floating out across the silver Dee,
And the soul of Wales is crying at the very heart of me –
Crying justice, crying vengeance: pray, my son, for strength anew,
For many will be sleeping at the falling of the dew.

SALT MARSHES

These marsh-lands evoke sorrow:
I can feel
The ancient grief of grass, the gloom of water,
And sense the lurking terror
Which haunts the landscape here,

14

The menace of those potent, unseen powers
That ride their wings of dread to hag the dark.
See how that witch, the twilight, hastening near
Makes sharp her sickle-edge to mow the day;
And how the ragged mendicants of mist
Rise up in shrouded garb from stealthy lairs
Thrusting their shapeless hands round one's face,
Obtruding, clammy, obdurate and clinging.

The sun has set: the tide creeps trembling in,
Muting its rhythmic cadences:
The black dykes gurgle like small children choking
In quick convulsions, speechless and afraid,
And the grey flock of frightened sheep
Moves in a huddled mob to shelter.

This is no place for mortals,
It is anguished ground, and, maybe, Cain-accursed,
Through violent deeds of darkness long ago:
Boorish and barren in its eldritch days
And pagan in its vows of vengeful evil;
Unhallowed grave for seamen's flotsam bones
Picked white by plucking seas,
And sepulchre of shreds of winnowed ships
That once wove heraldry upon the waves
In full-sailed beauty, free from silting sands.

Yet I was comforted when I discerned
The blessed candle of a gentle spirit,
Like a white nun within a lazar-house,

Drawn to this shore by some strong cord of love:
And knew, with her oblations made and ended,
Redemption pouring in on shriven tides.

SPRING COMES TO GLAMORGAN

Today I saw Spring's footprints in the Vale,
Small snowdrops glistening in a dawn-green dell
Beyond Llysworney:
And then, towards the sea,
Below St. Hilary, where thrush-song rings,
I heard her trysting call fall through the trees
Within the primrose wood where Merlin flings
His saffron mantle to the daffodils.

Today, I saw grey tombstones hoar with moss
In deep St. Donat's where the Stradlings sleep
Between their rock-fast castle-keep
And the soft lowland.
And there I saw the carven Crucified
Upon His Calvary Cross:
He did not stir, for all His suffering;
Nor moved the marble angels from their places
To quench His endless agony.

But they that lay so long with upturned faces,
Each in his narrow niche of this rich earth
Within the sanctuary of the lichened wall,
These all
Had heard Spring's call,
And woken from their oaken sleeping.

And so they pass
Along the old, familiar pathways of the grass
Towards the woods where birds are music making,
Where crocuses are breaking:
They come, these visitants, with arms outspread;
No bonds of wood and clay
Can keep them captive here on such a day:
On such a day as this along the Vale
There are no dead.

QUITE SO

Within the whispering gallery of St. Paul's
The merest whisper travels round the walls:
But in the parts where I was born and bred
Folk hear things long before they're even said.

ELEVATED

A baker whose bread you could trust
Was known in Taff Vale as Dai Crust:
    But now, ever since
    He sold buns to a prince,
He's known as Sir Dai Upper Crust.

BUSINESS AS USUAL

When Gabriel's starting trumpet rends the skies
And all arise for that last race of man,
Dai Jones, the bookie, glasses to his eyes,
Will spot the winners, and the also-ran.

17

WYN GRIFFITH

Llewelyn Wyn Griffith was born at Llandrillo-yn-Rhos, then in Caernarfonshire, on 30 August 1890. His childhood was spent in various small towns in North Wales, including Blaenau Ffestiniog and Dolgellau, where his father was a headteacher. In 1909 he left Wales to enter the Civil Service and was to make his career with the Inland Revenue, of which he was Assistant Secretary from 1945 to 1952. During the First World War he served with the Royal Welsh Fusiliers, witnessing the slaughter at Mametz Wood and winning the *Croix de guerre*. The rest of his career was spent as a civil servant in England. Despite removal from his homeland, he made a distinguished contribution to Welsh life, notably as a prominent member of the Honourable Society of Cymmrodorion. A frequent broadcaster in both Welsh and English, he was for many years a member of the Welsh team in the popular radio programme *Round Britain Quiz*. He died in a nursing home in Bowdon, Cheshire, on 27 September 1977. Most of his prose works were intended to interpret Welsh culture and his own background for the sake of his children, who were brought up in England and knew no Welsh, and for that of the English reader. They include *Up to Mametz* (1931), *Spring of Youth* (1935), *The Wooden Spoon* (1937) and *The Way Lies West* (1945). He published only one book of verse, *The Barren Tree* (1945), which contains a verse-play for radio, 'Branwen'. These books are the work of a Welshman of fine sensibility faced with the horrors of modern warfare and the rise of totalitarianism in Europe.

18

IF THERE BE TIME

If there be time enough before the slaughter
let us consider our heritage
of wisdom, remembering the coil of laughter
girdled our youth, wine of bright vintage
carrying short sorrows into oblivion;
some talk of love in smooth meadows
where dusk brings quiet and night a vision
of daylight joys freed from their shadows.
Above all, wisdom: for years are shrinking
into a huddle of days and the world a parish
where neighbours bolt their doors and lights are dimming.
Soon there will be nothing left for us to cherish
but the grave words of the last statesmen
before the battle starts and the air is darkened:
fast fall the night upon the frightened children
and on the wombs where once they quickened.
What towered land of man's endeavour
will first be desert, with all our learning
a burnt page trodden in the dust of error?
Farewell to wisdom and to all remembering.

SILVER JUBILEE 1939

Faint now in the evening pallor
answering nothing but old cries,
a troop of men shouldering their way
with a new tune I recognise

as something near to Flanders, but far
from the dragon years we killed
to no purpose, scattered seed
on land none but the devil tilled.

That a poet sings as his heart beats
is no new word, but an ancient tale.
Grey shadows on the pavement
and Europe sick of its own bale.

I have no answer, no rising song
to the young in years who are old
with our arrogance, our failure.
Let it be silence: the world is cold.

DAVID JONES

David Jones was born in Brockley in Kent on 1 November 1895. His mother was English and his father Welsh, a native of Holywell in Flintshire. He received little formal education but was encouraged to draw and entered the Camberwell Art School at the age of fourteen, later studying at the Westminster School of Art. The event that shaped him as a writer was the First World War, during which he served as a private with the Royal Welsh Fusiliers on the Western Front. In 1921 he was received into the Roman Catholic Church and, during the mid-1920s, lived with Eric Gill's community of artist-craftsmen at Capel-y-ffin in the Black Mountains, where his vision of the Welsh landscape was intensified. Having suffered a nervous breakdown in 1933, he lived for a while with his parents and later in a convent at Harrow-on-the-Hill in Middlesex, from where, confined to his room by ill health and looked after by the Order of Blue Nuns, he maintained a voluminous correspondence with artists, writers and scholars (including several in Wales), refining his ideas of Christian order in a secular world. Although he disclaimed any aptitude for scholarship, he was in fact a scholar-poet who drew not only on his experience of war but also on archaeology, history, mythology and anthropology, and particularly on 'the Matter of Britain', which have shaped these islands since pre-Roman times. He also had a concept of Man as maker, *homo faber*, and an acute sense of the cultural and spiritual crisis caused by centralizing forces in the modern world; for him, the anglicization of Wales was part of this baneful process. David Jones died at Harrow-on-the-Hill on 28 October 1974.

His first writing, published as *In Parenthesis* in 1937, centres on the figure of Private John Ball and a group of Royal Welsh Fusiliers, Welshmen and Londoners in about equal proportions and so representing the two traditions to which David Jones felt he belonged. It follows them from the parade ground deep into the world of the trenches, ending with their assault on Mametz Wood where most of them are killed. Realistic in its portrayal of the horrors of warfare, and of the humour, comradeship and suffering of 'the essential foot-mob', it uses a wealth of historical, mythological and literary allusions, especially to Malory and the *Gododdin*, to set the conflict in the context of past wars involving men of the Island of Britain. David Jones's second long work, *The Anathémata* (1952), has an even wider canvas, and greater verbal richness: it is a celebration of the Christian mysteries, a recalling of the making, both geological and cultural, of Britain from Celtic, Latin and Teutonic 'deposits' relating to London and Wales, and is concerned with the validity of sacrament and symbol in the age of the machine. David Jones is generally regarded as one of the great figures of modern English literature and one for whom Wales had a crucial and abiding significance. Among other books essential for an understanding of his work are his collections of essays, *Epoch and Artist* (1959) and *The Dying Gaul* (1978). A number of sequences and fragments can be found in *The Tribune's Visitation* (1969), *The Sleeping Lord* (1974), *The Kensington Mass* (1975) and *The Roman Quarry* (1981).

from IN PARENTHESIS

This Dai adjusts his slipping shoulder-straps, wraps close
his misfit outsize greatcoat – he articulates his English with
an alien care.
    My fathers were with the Black Prinse of Wales
at the passion of
the blind Bohemian king.
They served in these fields,
it is in the histories that you can read it, Corporal – boys
Gower, they were – it is writ down – yes.
    Wot about Methuselum, Taffy?
I was with Abel when his brother found him,
under the green tree.
I built a shit-house for Ataxerxes.
I was a spear in Balin's hand
           that made waste King Pellam's land.
I took the smooth stones of the brook,
I was with Saul
playing before him.
I saw him armed like Derfel Gatheren.
I the fox-run fire
         consuming in the wheat-lands;
and in the standing wheat in Cantium made some attempt
to form – (between dun August oaks their pied bodies
darting). And I the south air, tossed from high projections
by his Olifant; (the arid marcher-slopes echoing –
should they lose
Clere Espaigne la bele).
    I am '62 Socrates, my feet are colder than you think

on this
Potidaean duck-board.
        I the adder in the little bush
whose hibernation-end
undid,
unmade victorious toil:
In ostium fluminis.
At the four actions in regione Linnuis
                by the black waters.
At Bassas in the shallows.
At Cat Coit Celidon.
At Guinnion redoubt, where he carried the Image.
In urbe Legionis.
By the vallum Antonini, at the place of boundaries, at the
toiling estuary and strong flow called Tribruit.
By Agned mountain.
On Badon hill, where he bore the Tree.
        I am the Loricated Legions.
Helen Camulodunum is ours;
she's the toast of the Rig'ment,
she is in an especial way our Mediatrix.
        She's clement and loving, she's Friday's child, she's
loving and giving;
O dulcis
imperatrix.
        Her ample bosom holds:
Pontifex maximus,
Comes Litoris Saxonici,
Comes Britanniarum,
Gwledig,

Bretwalda, as these square-heads say.
    She's the girl with the sparkling eyes,
she's the Bracelet Giver,
she's a regular draw with the labour companies,
whereby
the paved army-paths are hers that grid the island which is
    her dower.
Elen Luyddawc she is – more she is than
Helen Argive.
    My mob digged the outer vallum,
we furnished picquets;
we staked trip-wire as a precaution at
Troy Novaunt.
    I saw the blessèd head set under
        that kept the narrow sea inviolate.
To keep the Land,
to give the yield:
    under the White Tower
        I trowelled the inhuming mortar.
    They learned me well the proportions due –
by water
by sand
by slacked lime.
    I drest the cist –
the beneficent artisans knew well how to keep
the king's head to keep
the land inviolate.
    The Bear of the Island: he broke it in his huge pride,
and over-reach of his imperium.
The Island Dragon.

The Bull of Battle
           (this is the third woeful uncovering).
Let maimed kings lie – let be
O let the guardian head
keep back – bind savage sails, lock the shield-wall, nourish
the sowing.
The War Duke
The Director of Toil –
        he burst the balm-cloth, unbricked the barrow
(cruel feet march because of this
              ungainly men sprawl over us).
O Land! – O Brân lie under.
The chrism'd eye that watches the French-men
that wards under
that keeps us
that brings the furrow-fruit,
keep the land, keep us
keep the islands adjacent.

I marched, sixty thousand and one thousand marched,
because of the brightness of Flur, because of the keeper of
promises
           (we came no more again)
who depleted the Island
           (and this is the first emigrant host)
and the land was bare for our going.
        O blessèd head hold the striplings from the narrow sea.
        I marched, sixty thousand marched who marched for
Kynan and Elen because of foreign machinations,
           (we came no more again)

who left the land without harness
              (and this is the second emigrant host).
O Brân confound the counsel of the councillors, O blessèd
head, hold the striplings from the narrow sea.

In the baized chamber confuse his tongue:
that Lord Agravaine.
He urges with repulsive lips, he counsels: he nets us into
expeditionary war.
              O blessèd head hold the striplings from the narrow sea.

I knew the smart on Branwen's cheek and the
turbulence in Ireland
              (and this was the third grievous blow).

I served Longinus that Dux bat-blind and bent;
the Dandy Xth are my regiment;
who diced
Crown and Mud-hook
under the Tree,
whose Five Sufficient Blossoms
yield for us.

I kept the boding raven
              from the Dish.
With my long pilum
I beat the crow
from that heavy bough.

But I held the tunics of these –
I watched them work the terrible embroidery that He put on.
I heard there, sighing for the Feet so shod.
I saw cock-robin gain
              his rosy breast.
I heard Him cry:

Apples ben ripe in my gardayne

I saw Him die.

     I was in Michael's trench when bright Lucifer bulged
his primal salient out.
That caused it,
that upset the joy-cart,
and three parts waste.

     You ought to ask: Why,
What is this,
what's the meaning of this.
Because you don't ask,
although the spear-shaft
drips,
there's neither steading – not a roof-tree.

     I am the Single Horn thrusting
by night-stream margin
in Helyon.

     Cripes-a-mighty-strike-me-stone-cold – you don't say.

     Where's that birth-mark, young 'un.

     Wot the Melchizzydix! – and still fading – jump to it
Rotherhithe.

          Never die never die
          Never die never die
          Old soljers never die
          Never die never die
          Old soljers never die they never die
          Never die
          Old soljers never die they
          Simply fade away.

from THE TUTELAR OF THE PLACE

Now sleep on, little children, sleep on now, while I tell out the greater suffrages, not yet for young heads to understand:

Queen of the differentiated sites, administratix of the demarcations, let our cry come unto you.
>   In all times of imperium save us when the *mercatores* come save us
>   from the guile of the *negotiatores* save us from the *missi*, from the agents
>   who think no shame
by inquest to audit what is shameful to tell
>   deliver us.
When they check their capitularies in their curias
>   confuse their reckonings.
When they narrowly assess the *trefydd*
>   by hide and rod
>   by *pentan* and pent
by impost and fee on beast-head
>   and roof-tree
and number the souls of men
>   notch their tallies false
disorder what they have collated.
When they proscribe the diverse uses and impose the rootless uniformities, pray for us.
>   When they sit in *Consilium*
to liquidate the holy diversities
>   mother of particular perfections

                        queen of otherness
                        mistress of asymmetry
patroness of things counter, parti, pied, several
protectress of things known and handled
help of things familiar and small
                        wardress of the secret crevices
                        of things wrapped and hidden
mediatrix of all the deposits
                        margravine of the troia
empress of the labyrinth
                        receive our prayers.
When they escheat to the Ram
                        in the Ram's curia
the seisin where the naiad sings
                        above where the forked rod bends
or where the dark outcrop
                        tells on the hidden seam
pray for the green valley.
When they come with writs of oyer and terminer
                        to hear the false and
                        determine the evil
according to the advices of the Ram's magnates who serve
the Ram's wife, who write in the Ram's book of Death.
In the bland megapolitan light
        where no shadow is by day or by night
be our shadow.
Remember the mound-kin, the kith of the *tarren* gone from
this mountain because of the exorbitance of the Ram...
remember them in the rectangular tenements, in the houses
of the engines that fabricate the ingenuities of the Ram...

Mother of Flowers save them then where no flower blows.

Though they shall not come again because of the requirements of the Ram with respect to the world plan, remember them where the dead forms multiply, where no stamen leans, where the carried pollen falls to the adamant surfaces, where is no crevice.

In all times of *Gleichschaltung*, in the days of the central economies, set up the hedges of illusion round some remnant of us, twine the wattles of mist, white-web a Gwydion-hedge

      like fog on the *bryniau*

      against the commissioners

and assessors bearing the writs of the Ram to square the world-floor and number the tribes and write down the secret things and take away the diversities by which we are, by which we call on your name, sweet Jill of the demarcations

      arc of differences

      tower of individuation

queen of the minivers

laughing in the mantle of variety

belle of the mound

      for Jac o'the mound

our belle and donnabelle

      on all the world-mountain.

In the December of our culture ward somewhere the secret seed, under the mountain, under and between, between the grids of the Ram's survey when he squares the world-circle.

Sweet Mair devise a mazy-guard

in and out and round about

31

double-dance defences
countermure and echelon meanders round
the holy mound
                fence within the fence
pile the dun ash for the bright seed
                (within the curtained wood the canister
within the canister the budding rod)
troia in depth the shifting wattles of illusion for the ancilia
for the palladia for the kept memorials, because of the
commissioners of the Ram and the Ram's decree
concerning the utility of the hidden things.

When the technicians manipulate the dead limbs of our
culture as though it yet had life, have mercy on us.Open
unto us, let us enter a second time within your stola-folds
in those days – ventricle and refuge both, *hendref* for
world-winter, asylum from world-storm. Womb of the Lamb
the spoiler of the Ram.

from THE SLEEPING LORD

Tawny-black sky-scurries
                low over
Ysgyrid hill
and over the level-topped heights
                of Mynydd Pen-y-fal
                cold is wind
                grey is rain, but
                BRIGHT IS CANDELA
where this lord is in slumber.

Are his wounded ankles
                         lapped with the ferric waters
that all through the night
                         hear the song
from the night-dark seams
                         where the narrow-skulled *caethion*
labour the changing shifts
                         for the cosmocrats of alien lips
in all the fair lands
                         of the dark measures under
(from about Afon Lwyd
                         in the confines of green Siluria
westward to where the naiad of the *fons*-head
                         pours out the Lesser Gwendraeth
high in the uplands
                         above Ystrad Tywi
and indeed further
                         west & south of Merlin's Caer
even in the lost cantrevs
                         of spell-held Demetia
where was Gorsedd Arberth, where the *palas* was
                         where the prince who hunted
met the Prince of Hunters
                         in his woof of grey
and gleam-pale dogs
                         not kennelled on earth-floor
lit the dim chase.)

Is the Usk a drain for his gleaming tears

who weeps for the land
     who dreams his bitter dream
for the folk of the land
does Tawe clog for his sorrows
do the parallel dark-seam drainers
     mingle his anguish-stream
with the scored valleys' tilted refuse.
Does his freight of woe
     flood South by East
on Sirhywi and Ebwy
     is it southly bourn
on double Rhondda's fall to Taff?

   Do the stripped boughs grapple
above the troubled streams
     when he dream-fights
his nine day's fight
     which he fought alone
with the hog in the Irish wilderness
     when the eighteen twilights
     and the ten midnights
and the equal light of the nine mid-mornings
were equally lit
     with the light of the saviour's fury
and the dark fires of the hog's eye
which encounter availed him nothing.

    Is his royal anger ferriaged
where black-rimed Rhymni
     soils her Marcher-banks
     Do the bells of St.Mellon's

toll his dolour
                                   are his sighs canalled
where the mountain ash
                                   droops her bright head
for the black pall of Merthyr?...

But yet he sleeps:
                                   when he shifts a little in his fitfull
slumber does a covering stone dislodge
                                   and roll to Reynoldstone?
When he fretfully turns
                                   and crying out in a great voice
                                   in his fierce sleep-anger
does the habergeon'd sentinel
                                   alert himself sudden
from his middle-watch doze
                                   in the crenelled traverse-bay
of the outer bailey-wall
                                   of the *castell* these Eingl-Ffrancwyr
call in their lingua La Haie Taillée
that the Saeson other ranks
                                   call The Hay
(which place is in the tongue of the men of the land,
Y Gelli Gandryll, or, for short, Y Gelli) ...

Yet he sleeps on
                                   very deep is his slumber:
how long has he been the sleeping lord?
are the clammy ferns
                                   his rustling vallance
does the buried rowan

                    ward him from evil, or
does he ward the tanglewood
                    and the denizens of the wood
are the stunted oaks his gnarled guard
                    or are their knarred limbs
strong with his sap?
Do the small black horses
                    grass on the hunch of his shoulders?
are the hills his couch
                    or is he the couchant hills?
Are the slumbering valleys
                    him in slumber
                    are the still undulations
the still limbs of him sleeping?
Is the configuration of the land
                    the furrowed body of the lord
are the scarred ridges
                    his dented greaves
do the trickling gullies
                    yet drain his hog-wounds?
Does the land wait the sleeping lord
                    or is the wasted land
that very lord who sleeps?

EILUNED LEWIS

Eiluned Lewis was born in 1900 at Glan Hafren, a large house set in parkland near Newtown in Montgomeryshire. Educated at boarding school and then at Westfield College in the University of London, she became a journalist in Fleet Street where, from 1931 to 1936, she was assistant to the managing director of the *Daily News*, and later a drama critic for *The Sunday Times*. After her marriage in 1937 she lived in Surrey, and there she died in 1979. Her first novel, *Dew on the Grass* (1934), is based on her childhood in Wales while *The Captain's Wife* (1943) is set in Pembrokeshire among the seagoing, farming community from which her mother's people had sprung. *In Country Places* (1951) is a collection of her essays and *Honey Pots and Brandy Bottles* (1954) the record of a countrywoman's year. With her brother Peter Lewis she wrote *The Land of Wales* (1937); she also edited the selected letters of the novelist Charles Morgan. Her two books of poems are *December Apples* (1935) and *Morning Songs* (1944). Although she wrote only a little verse, her work has kept its charm for those who admire her delicacy and love of the natural world.

THE BIRTHRIGHT

We who were born
In country places,
Far from cities
And shifting faces,

We have a birthright
No man can sell,
And a secret joy
No man can tell.

For we are kindred
To lordly things,
The wild duck's flight
And the white owl's wings;
To pike and salmon,
To bull and horse,
The curlew's cry
And the smell of gorse.

Pride of trees,
Swiftness of streams,
Magic of frost
Have shaped our dreams:
No baser vision
Their spirit fills
Who walk by right
On the naked hills.

THE BRIDE CHEST

The bride chest stands in the room, the little room
Up the winding stair,
The light from the window falls on the kneeling girl
And her yellow hair.
Here voices and feet are forgotten.

Here peace begins,
The mouth of the house is muffled
And silence wins.

Old and cool is the linen she sorts and smooths,
And fine the thread;
Dust are the hands that wove, and dust the lovers,
Still wide their bed.
Fortunate lovers who lived before
The coming of fears;
Their children, begotten in plenty,
Are nourished with tears.

Below on river and garden whispering falls
The summer rain;
The frosts of May have found the trees in their spring,
Will they flower again?
Blackbirds chuckle, low on the lawn
The swallows glide,
Pale hangs the lilac, and pale the face
Of the kneeling bride.

SHIPS' SIRENS

Often I've thought of you on foggy nights
When spectre vessels booming seaward creep,
How you, who loved the sea, would love this sound,
Till, thinking of you thus, I'd fall asleep,
Indifferent to the ghostly-footed night,
Like some glad mariner when port's in sight.

Now that's all over, all our cargo lost,
Our ship of dreams gone to the breaker's yard,
I shall no more repine, but say with you
That our joint voyage was from the first ill-starred.
Only when sirens cry their midnight fears
Shall memory return in tide of tears.

GWYN WILLIAMS

Gwyn Williams was born in Port Talbot on 24 August 1904. Educated at the University College of Wales, Aberystwyth and Jesus College, Oxford, from 1935 to 1969 he taught at the Universities of Cairo, Alexandria, Libya and Istanbul, latterly as Professor of English Literature. On his return to Wales he settled with his second wife at Treweithan, a house built by his forebears near Trefenter in Cardiganshire, but in 1983 moved to Aberystwyth; he died there on 24 December 1990. During the years he spent in the Near East he translated a good deal of Welsh poetry into English; his translations, for long considered to be the best available, were collected under the title *To Look for a Word* in 1976. He published, among other books, three novels, four travel-books, a history of Wales, and *An Introduction to Welsh Literature* in the *Writers of Wales* series (1978). His four books of poems in English are *Inns of Love* (1970), *Foundation Stock* (1974), *Choose Your Stranger* (1979) and, posthumously, *Flyting in Egypt* (1991); his *Collected Poems* appeared in 1987. An account of this highly sophisticated writer's life, especially in relation to the places in which he lived, is to be found in his autobiography, *ABC of (D)GW* (1981), which explores the personality and opinions of a Welsh patriot the springs of whose culture were intensely local, whether inspired by the rigours of upland Wales or by the more exotic experiences of such places as Anatolia. A pagan by conviction, he faced his own mortality with stoicism and humour.

INNS OF LOVE: FOR D.

You are my Anchor and my Ship,
my Porto Bello, my Welcome to Town,
my Swan, my Angel, my White Hart,
my Bunch of Grapes, my Salutation.

May I be Crown to your fresh Rose,
the falcon for your Crystal Palace,
a leaping dolphin to your Star
and to your Albion, Prince of Wales.

A Unicorn to your World's End,
in your sweet Valley I'll be Trout,
Hound to your Hare, I'm the Green Man
will hold you in his Western Arms.

BELLY DANCER

She begins diffidently
with eyes to the earth and hands
torn upwards, with breasts
barely quivering till the hips
take a rhythm from the drums;

then up from the earth pulses
(the feet are best bare with no
insulation from sand or grass)
movement, an outward surge
tidal to the shores of skin.

42

Earth escapes now flowers
in flesh, the passion rock
root and worm is stated
is limned to visible symbol
stirs in haunch and nipple and thigh;

until earth is forgotten
and the body incorporates
(still touching the earth –
this must hold) all energy
seasonal and extra-seasonal, all;

becomes the briefest of flowers
a trembling astrolabe
veined and plotted with all
axis all equator all orbit
lucent now with dissociated lust.

Until the planets recede,
the earth takes back its blood,
body resumes flesh, the knees
sag to the asking earth, the writhing
girl gives a new birth to the god.

WILD NIGHT AT TREWEITHAN

The evening's late November, clouds hump and streak,
the starlings are swept off-course in a black spray,
the gale howls and rattles in my wide chimney,
whistles in a nasty searching hurry.

The ponies can hardly believe it and face it
instead of turning their backsides as they usually do.
Is it drink makes me silly enough to think there's a force
that wants to get rid of something here before day?

The mountain's still black, the great chimneys
aren't rocked, the singing wires hold, we're
still linked to those others, I think of the farmhouse
as a hill-fort of stone with lines out over the moor.

No, there's no power to fear out there in the darkness,
only the idiot unpathed swirl of air belting
over this earth's face as we swing through hidden
stars. I have confidence in my grandfather's building.

LAME FOX

I was passing Bron-yr-hydd on my way home
when a fox slipped out of my shadowed
larches. The dog

had put him up. He didn't pause with raised paw,
like Williams Parry's fox, nor sit wickedly
grinning at me

like the one that distracted Dafydd ap Gwilym on his way
to a girl. He never noticed me. Yet
only ten yards away

he crossed the road in front of me, slowly
making for a gap and dragging
a stricken leg.

No question of speed though the dog was near
and in daylight. The torch of his tail,
the lighted dart

Dafydd saw in his backside, the explosion
of autumnal firework, was guttering out
with no longer sparks

above the stubble. A fugitive from
a fox shoot? There had been one yesterday
in a woodland

over the hill. Had he sought my quiet
trees for refuge over night, a place to die in
or to nurse back

his strength and lust? No, he was done for,
a great dog-fox on his last journey, as I called
his last enemy off.

Old swift harrier of hens now limping,
the pride of his body shrinking to his rib case,
lead shot in his belly,

to the lower spruces, where once he ruled
unchallenged and easily, to lose all,
his terrain,

the occasional heat of his sleek mates, his shining
pelt, his polished rutting, his sensuous
awareness of

what was about him, his speed, his guile,
his sharp ruthlessness, his redness, all
his legendary

qualities. Into sudden oblivion with
no bang of gun or doom. Me too, I thought.
Does it fit me?

What loss will be my greatest? To lose sureness
and lightness of foot, memory, mother,
father, children,

darling, since I've rejected the old easy promise
of meeting again beyond. (How old
would I be

in heaven, which would be my wife there?
Nasty questions not to be asked. Cut back
to the palpable.

May he vulpinize me rather than I
make a human of him.) Does he sense
the despair

of his last hour? Can he avoid the waste
of groans, tears, prayers and teach me
how to die?

Is that why I was beyond his notice today?
It was I who stood to observe the likeness,
though farthest of the three,

I hope, from the end, with de Vigny's words
alive on my tongue and his wolf's end a cry
into the silence.

SAINT URSULA OF LLANGWYRYFON

Picked offhand by the angels to demonstrate
for Christ; little she-bear Ursula, saint
perhaps of some monstrous forgotten faith,
mother-goddess turned virgin or just a girl

afraid to marry a handsome pagan?
In Claude's picture you are already crowned
in thin gold, you stand calm, your girls
shoulder each other eagerly out of church

down the stone steps (what are those bows and arrows
for if not to foretell your martyrdom
by a brute's arrow in splendid Cologne?)
to the fine-sparred ships, the unregarding

stevedores, to the classic water and
the trip to death. Your bones lie abroad
and here where I think you lisped Latin
where you feared marriage and rough Saxon ways

where my forebears trimmed stone in your honour
and an arch by one of them is a local wonder,
does anyone else think of you as the cracked peal
of the bell of your Church of the Virgins

twists and dies up the pilgrim route through the still
Sunday air past the abandoned houses
to a ridge that looks over to Enlli
from old stones over the bear-god's valley?

EASTER POEM

It's night. I stroke the cotoneaster
above my head in the hedge
as I used to stroke a girl's hair.
Am I falling in love with the earth
I'll be mated with before long
or is it an easy urge to belong
more to the things about me? From birth
we drift away from the lair
of rank nature, cadge
a brief freedom, but this Easter
catches me with its quick switch
from sun to snow. Earth, you bitch!

DRAWING A LINE

Prunus explodes pink is still barracks
at Gobowen; the high church gates at Wrex-
ham are locked; Cartrefle, barracks of alien
teacher training with sullen (for Dylan)
yet soothing names on hideous shacks, Cemaes,
Afan, Gwynedd, Powys, till one comes
to a flower of a new library, all light
and soft colour of growth. A frontier district
with beauty behind wire. Streams running from green
mountains have cut the valleys that let in
the English. A sad area where the Welsh now
are caught looking over their shoulders when
they're moved to speak their language, like the reapers
trousered on Leominster porch. The Shrewsbury
refreshment room was easy and confident
in Englishness but the line up the border didn't
carry so much as disturb me with its faithless
winding from plain to bastion. Surely ruthless
passport control and pale customs officers
would be better than this wavering, this farce
of union. So let's have a clear line set
and be safely ourselves on either side of it.

IDRIS DAVIES

Idris Davies was born on 6 January 1905 in Rhymney, Monmouthshire. He was brought up in a Welsh-speaking home but his schooling was through the medium of English. At the age of 14 he became a miner in Abertysswg where his father was chief winding-engine man. Early in 1926 he lost a finger while working underground at the Maerdy Pit, Pontlottyn, and had barely restarted work when the General Strike began and the mine was closed. Having been introduced to the work of Shelley by a fellow-miner, he quickly saw that poetry could relate to politics, especially Socialism and the cause of the working class. After taking a correspondence course, he studied at Loughborough College and the University of Nottingham, where he qualified as a teacher. He taught at schools in England and then in Wales, latterly at Llandysul in Cardiganshire and Treherbert in the Rhondda Fawr. After many unsuccessful attempts to find a post in Monmouthshire, in 1947 he joined the staff of Cwmsyfiog Primary School in the Rhymney Valley but, four years later, was found to be suffering from cancer; he died at his mother's house in Rhymney on 6 April 1953. His first volume, *Gwalia Deserta* (1938), took as its theme the dereliction of South Wales during the economic depression of the inter-war years. His second, *The Angry Summer* (1943), is a loosely chronological record, with interludes, of the General Strike (3-12 May 1926) and the seven-month lock-out of the miners which followed, from the high spirits of its beginning to the ignominious return to work. The main focus of its 50 short untitled sections is on the plight of the mining communities, especially their womenfolk, but also on Dai, the archetypal miner who becomes the poet's *alter ego*. Both books are long, unified, dramatic poems which amount to eloquent denunciations of the capitalist system and a passionate statement of the poet's profound sympathy with his own people. His third book, *Tonypandy and other poems* (1945), a more varied collection finished while he was in Treherbert, includes the long autobiographical poem 'I was born in Rhymney'. Early critics of Idris Davies's verse tended to emphasize his integrity while pointing to the narrow range of his subject-matter. It has become clear, however, that he worked within limitations of his own making in order to give sharper focus to his chosen themes. Most of the poems in all three of his books are cast either as short lyrics or in the accumulative, long-line form which he learned from the rhetoric of the Welsh pulpit. His *Selected Poems* appeared a few weeks before his death; the standard edition of his work is Dafydd Johnston (ed.), *The Complete Poems of Idris Davies* (1994); a small selection of his poems is to be found in *A Carol for the Coalfield* (2002).

from GWALIA DESERTA

II

My fathers in the mining valleys
Were slaves who bled for beer,
Who had no Saviour to acclaim
And whose god was Fear.

And they sold the fern and flower
And the groves of pine

For a hovel and a tankard,
    And the dregs are mine.

So in these rain-swept graveyards
    Where my fathers sleep,
Shall I sulk, and curse them
    Who made their lives so cheap?

Or shall I pause, and pity
    Those luckless lads of old,
Those sullen slaves whipped onward
    To load my lords with gold?

IV

O timbers from Norway and muscles from Wales,
Be ready for another shift and believe in co-operation,
Though pit-wheels are frowning at old misfortunes
And girders remember disasters of old;
O what is man that coal should be so careless of him,
And what is coal that so much blood should be upon it?

VIII

Do you remember 1926? That summer of soups and speeches,
The sunlight on the idle wheels and the deserted crossings,
And the laughter and the cursing in the moonlit streets?
Do you remember 1926? The slogans and the penny concerts,
The jazz-bands and the moorland picnics,
And the slanderous tongues of famous cities?

Do you remember 1926? The great dream and the swift
                                                    disaster,
The fanatic and the traitor, and more than all,
The bravery of the simple, faithful folk?
'Ay, ay, we remember 1926,' said Dai and Shinkin,
As they stood on the kerb in Charing Cross Road,
'And we shall remember 1926 until our blood is dry.'

XII

There's a concert in the village to buy us boots and bread,
There's a service in the chapel to make us meek and mild,
And in the valley town the draper's shop is shut.
The brown dogs snap at the stranger in silk,
And the winter ponies nose the buckets in the street.
The 'Miners' Arms' is quiet, the barman half afraid,
And the heroes of newspaper columns on explosion day
Are nearly tired of being proud.
But the widow on the hillside remembers a bitterer day,
The rap at the door and the corpse and the crowd,
And the parson's powerless words.
And her daughters are in London serving dinner to my lord,
And her single son, so quiet, broods on his luck in the queue.

XV

O what can you give me?
Say the sad bells of Rhymney.

Is there hope for the future?
Cry the brown bells of Merthyr.

Who made the mineowner?
Say the black bells of Rhondda.

And who robbed the miner?
Cry the grim bells of Blaina.

They will plunder willy-nilly,
Say the bells of Caerphilly.

They have fangs, they have teeth!
Shout the loud bells of Neath.

To the south, things are sullen,
Say the pink bells of Brecon.

Even God is uneasy,
Say the moist bells of Swansea.

Put the vandals in court!
Cry the bells of Newport.

All would be well if – if – if –
Say the green bells of Cardiff.

Why so worried, sisters, why?
Sing the silver bells of Wye.

XXIV

Because I was sceptical in our Sunday School
And tried to picture Jesus crawling in the local mine,
The dozen deacons bred on the milk of Spurgeon
Told me I was dangerous and in danger,
That I would be roasted and pronged and tossed like a pancake;
And then they would frown and go apart to pray.
On Sabbath evenings when I yawned in grandmother's pew,
When the parson roused himself with his raised arms,
And the elders cried out 'Amen, Amen',
And Jenkins the Joiner nudged his wife with a caramel,
And tired mothers were musing on carpets and insurance agents,
And young fathers coaxed tiny boys to sleep,
I remember I used to stare through the chapel windows
Watching the sun like a perfect tomato touching the hill,
And a swarthy young man wandering on a purple ridge,
And his body was bent and his smile was compassionate.
And sometimes in mid-week I would see him again,
And we would smile and understand.

XXVI

The village of Fochriw grunts among the higher hills;
The dwellings of miners and pigeons and pigs
Cluster around the little grey war memorial.
The sun brings glitter to the long street roofs
And the crawling promontories of slag,
The sun makes the pitwheels to shine,
And praise be to the sun, the great unselfish sun,

The sun that shone on Plato's shoulders,
That dazzles with light the Taj Mahal.
The same sun shone on the first mineowner,
On the vigorous builder of this brown village,
And praise be to the impartial sun.
He had no hand in the bruising of valleys,
He had no line in the vigorous builder's plan,
He had no voice in the fixing of wages,
He was the blameless one.
And he smiles on the village this morning,
He smiles on the far-off grave of the vigorous builder,
On the ivied mansion of the first mineowner,
On the pigeon lofts and the Labour Exchange,
And he smiles as only the innocent can.

XXXI

Consider famous men, Dai bach, consider famous men,
All their slogans, all their deeds,
And follow the funerals to the grave.
Consider the charlatans, the shepherds of the sheep!
Consider the grease upon the tongue, the hunger of the
                                                    purse!
Consider the fury of the easy words,
The vulgarity behind the brass,
The dirty hands that shook the air, that stained the sky!

Yet some there were who lived for you,
Who lay to die remembering you.

Mabon was your champion once upon a time
And his portrait's on the milk-jug yet.
The world has bred no champions for a long time now,
Except the boxing, tennis, golf and Fascist kind,
And the kind that democracy breeds and feeds for
                                        Harringay.
And perhaps the world has grown too bitter or too wise
To breed a prophet or a poet ever again.

XXXIV

When we walked to Merthyr Tydfil, in the moonlight long ago,
When the mountain tracks were frozen and the crests were
                                        capped with snow,
We had tales and songs between us, and souls too young to fret,
And we had hopes and visions which the heart remembers yet.

The winds from the farthest mountains blew about us as we
                                        strode,
But we were warm and merry on the crooked freezing road,
And there were lamp-lit homesteads to south and east and
                                        west
And we watched the round moon smiling on those little lights
                                        of rest.

The moon is still as radiant and the homely hills remain,
But the magic of those evenings we shall not meet again,
For we were boyish dreamers in a world we did not know
When we walked to Merthyr Tydfil in the moonlight long ago.

from THE ANGRY SUMMER

1

Now it is May among the mountains,
Days for speeches in the valley towns,
Days of dream and days of struggle,
Days of bitter denunciation.

Now it is May in all the valleys,
Days of the cuckoo and the hawthorn,
Days for splashing in the mountain ponds,
Days for love in crowded parks.

Now it is May in little gardens,
In square allotments across the railway,
Days for song and dance and roaming,
Days for action and achievement.

Now it is May in the minds of men,
Days for vision and for marching,
Days for banners and for music,
And beauty born of sacrifice.

7

Mrs Evans, fach, you want butter again.
How will you pay for it now, little woman
With your husband out on strike, and full
Of the fiery language? Ay, I know him,

His head is full of fire and brimstone
And a lot of palaver about communism,
And me, little Dan the Grocer
Depending so much on private enterprise.

What, depending on the miners and their
Money too? O yes, in a way, Mrs Evans,
Yes, in a way I do, mind you.
Come tomorrow, little woman, and I'll tell you then
What I have decided overnight.
Go home now and tell that rash red husband of yours
That your grocer cannot afford to go on strike
Or what would happen to the butter from Carmarthen?
Good day for now, Mrs Evans fach.

15

In the square brown chapel below the hill
Dai's frail mother is deep in prayer,
A broken old mother who bears no ill
To anyone anywhere.

'Please God have blessings for us all
And comfort them who mourn,
And have mercy on me in my humble shawl
And melt the hearts of stone.'

The sun's last light is passing away,
And a moth flits to and fro,

And out in the street the children play
And the echoes softly go.

'O Brother who came from Nazareth
To help and heal and save,
O Lord of life and Lord of death,
Help my old heart to be brave.'

24

Cow-parsley and hawthorn blossom
And a cottage among trees,
A thrush and a skylark singing,
And a gypsy lying at ease.

Roses in gentlemen's gardens
Smile as we pass by the way,
And the swans of my lord are sleeping
Out of the heat of the day.

And here we come tramping and singing
Out of the valleys of strife,
Into the sunlit cornlands,
Begging the bread of life.

31

Let's go to Barry Island, Maggie fach,
And give all the kids one day by the sea,
And sherbert and buns and paper hats,
And a rattling ride on the Figure Eight;

We'll have tea on the sands, and rides on the donkeys,
And sit in the evening with the folk of Cwm Rhondda,
Singing the sweet old hymns of Pantycelyn
When the sun goes down beyond the rocky islands.
Come on, Maggie fach, or the train will be gone
Then the kids will be howling at home all day,
Sticky with dirt and gooseberry jam.
Leave the washing alone for today, Maggie fach,
And put on your best and come out to the sun
And down to the holiday sea.
We'll carry the sandwiches in a big brown bag
And leave our troubles behind for a day
With the chickens and the big black tips
And the rival soup-kitchens, quarrelling like hell.
Come, Maggie fach, with a rose on your breast
And an old Welsh tune on your little red lips,
And we'll all sing together in the Cardiff train
Down to the holiday sea.

37

Send out your homing pigeons, Dai,
Your blue-grey pigeons, hard as nails,
Send them with messages tied to their wings,
Words of your anger, words of your love.
Send them to Dover, to Glasgow, to Cork,
Send them to the wharves of Hull and Belfast,
To the harbours of Liverpool and Dublin and Leith,
Send them to the islands and out to the oceans,
To the wild wet islands of the northern sea
Where little grey women go out in heavy shawls

At the hour of dusk to gaze on the merciless waters,
And send them to the decorated islands of the south
Where the mineowner and his tall stiff lady
Walk round and round the rose-pink hotel, day after day
after day.
Send out your pigeons, Dai, send them out
With words of your anger and your love and your pride,
With stern little sentences wrought in your heart,
Send out your pigeons, flashing and dazzling towards the
sun.

Go out, pigeons bach, and do what Dai tells you.

43

O rain of July pouring down from the heavens,
Pouring and pelting from the vaults of the sky,
Pelting and slashing and lashing the trees,
Lashing the gardens behind the streets,
Sweeping the dust from the cabbage leaves,
And bringing Mrs Hughes' pet geranium out to the garden wall,
Sweep away, thunder-rain, the dross from our valleys,
Carry the rubbish to the seas and the oceans,
Wash away the slag-heaps of our troubles and sorrows,
Sweep away, thunder-rain, the slime from our valleys,
And let our streets, our home, our visions
Be cleansed and be shining when the evening comes
With its rainbow arching the smiling uplands,
With its glittering trees and laughing flowers,
And its mountains bright with the setting sun.

from TONYPANDY

III

The dusk deepens into the autumn night,
The cold drizzle spreads across the valleys,
The rubbish heaps are lost among the mists,
And where will you go for the evening, Dai,
For the evening in Tonypandy?
Will you count your coppers and join
The cinema queue where the tired women
Huddle like sheep, and comfort one another
With signs and sentimental phrases,
And where some folk blame the local councillors
For all the evils of the day and night?
O in the little queue, what tales are told
When we have shuffled off the burdens of the day –
What rancour, what compassion, what relief!
Or perhaps you will go to the prayer meeting down the chapel,
Where the newest member can pray for an hour without
stopping,
The one converted at the last Big Meeting.
Or will you go to the pub at the corner
Where tongues come loose and hearts grow soft,
Where politics are so easy to understand,
Where the Irish labourer explains the constitution of de Valera,
And the Tory Working Man snarls behind his beer
At those who do not worship Winston Churchill,
And those who vaguely praise the Beveridge Report.
Or perhaps you will go back to your fireside this evening

And talk with your Martha of the children abroad,
The son out in Italy, the quick-tongued Ifor,
And the young quiet Emrys in the R.A.F.,
And Mair, with her roses and her laughing eyes,
So sprightly in her khaki uniform;
And you will be proud and you will be sad,
And you will be brave for Martha's sake,
And you will be Dai the great of heart.

CAPEL CALVIN

There's holy holy people
They are in capel bach –
They don't like surpliced choirs,
They don't like Sospan Fach.

They don't like Sunday concerts,
Or women playing ball,
They don't like Williams Parry much
Or Shakespeare at all.

They don't like beer or bishops,
Or pictures without texts,
They don't like any other
Of the nonconformist sects.

And when they go to Heaven
They won't like that too well,
For the music will be sweeter
Than the music played in Hell.

A CAROL FOR THE COALFIELD

From the moors of Blaen Rhymni down to the leaning wall
Of Caerphilly Castle you shall hear the same accents
Of sorrow and mirth and pride, and a vague belief
That the future shall be greater than the past.

The man in the Rhondda Valley and the man in Abertillery
Have shared the same years, the same days of hope and
desolation,
And in Ogmore Vale and in Ammanford both old and young
dream
That the future shall be greater than the past.

On the ragged hills and by the shallow polluted rivers,
The pious young man and the old rascal of many sins,
The idealists and the wasters, all sometimes believe and say
That the future shall be greater than the past.

Mothers praying for sons away in the wars, and mothers
waiting
On doorsteps and by firesides for men coming home from the
pits,
And the old folk bent and scarred with years of toil, all some-
times hope
That the future shall be greater than the past.

Last night the moon was full above the slag heaps and the
grave-yards
And the towns among the hills, and a man arose from his
dream

And cried out: Let this day be sufficient, and worthy of my
people
And let the night winds go on wailing of the future and the
past.

A STAR IN THE EAST

When Christmastide to Rhymney came
And I was six or seven
I thought the stars in the eastern sky
Were the brightest stars of heaven.

I chose the star that glittered most
To the east of Rhymney town
To be the star above the byre
Where Mary's babe lay down.

And nineteen hundred years would meet
Beneath a magic light,
And Rhymney share with Bethlehem
A star on Christmas night.

LAND OF MY MOTHERS

Land of my mothers, how shall my brothers praise you?
With timbrels or rattles or tins?
With fire.
How shall we praise you on the banks of the rhymneying waters,
On the smoky shores and the glittering shores of Glamorgan,

On wet mornings in the bare fields behind the Newport docks,
On fine evenings when lovers walk by Bedwellty Church,
When the cuckoo calls to miners coming home to Rhymney Bridge,
When the wild rose defies the Industrial Revolution
And when the dear old drunken lady sings of Jesus and a
                                                    little shilling.

Come down, O girls of song, to the bank of the coal canal
At twilight, at twilight
When mongrels fight
And long rats bite
Under the shadows of pit-head light,
And dance, you daughters of Gwenllian,
Dance in the dust in the lust of delight.

And you who have prayed in golden pastures
And oiled the wheels of the Western Tradition
And trod where bards have danced to church,
Pay a penny for this fragment of a burning torch.
It will never go out.
It will gather unto itself all the fires
That blaze between the heavens above and the earth beneath
Until the flame shall frighten each mud-hearted hypocrite
And scatter the beetles fattened on the cream of corruption,
The beetles that riddle the ramparts of Man.

Pay a penny for my singing torch,
O my sisters, my brothers of the land of my mothers,
The land of our fathers, our troubles, our dreams,

The land of Llewellyn and Shoni bach Shinkin,
The land of the sermons that pebble the streams,
The land of the englyn and Crawshay's old engine,
The land that is sometimes as proud as she seems.

And sons of the mountains and sons of the valleys
O lift up your hearts, and then
Lift up your feet.

GLYN JONES

Glyn Jones was born in Merthyr Tydfil on 28 February 1905. His parents were left-wing in politics, Nonconformist in religious practice, and Welsh-speaking. Educated at St. Paul's College, Cheltenham, he became a teacher at a school in a slum area of Cardiff, where his experience of the pupils' poverty affected him deeply. In 1942, despite his being too old for call-up, he registered as a conscientious objector on Christian pacifist grounds, and was immediately dismissed from his post. Moved to a school in Bridgend, he found that most of the staff there would not speak to him; two years later, he was given a post at a school in Caerphilly, where he was much happier. In 1952 he joined the staff of Glan-taf County School in Cardiff and there he remained until his retirement in 1965. He died at his home in Whitchurch on 10 April 1995. He had begun his literary career as a prose-writer with the publication of two collections of short stories, *The Blue Bed* (1937) and *The Water Music* (1944); the most important of his three novels are *The Valley, The City, The Village* (1956) and *The Island of Apples* (1965). Lyrical, mysterious, comic and often grotesque, these books, like his verse, deal with life in Merthyr or rural Carmarthenshire where his family had its roots. His lifelong Christianity was fundamental to his vision as a writer: his stories and poems abound with characters who, for all their shortcomings, are drawn with compassion. Although he spoke Welsh, he was unable to write creatively in the language because, as he pointed out in his richly anecdotal book *The Dragon Has Two Tongues*

(1968), he had received a wholly English education. As an adult, however, he read a great deal of Welsh poetry, translated folk-verses and saga literature into English and allowed Welsh prosody to influence his own writing. His first book of verse, *Poems* (1939), displays his delight in music and colour, while *The Dream of Jake Hopkins* (1954) shows his technical virtuosity and sense of humour. He continued to write verse well into old age and his *Selected Poems: Fragments and Fictions* (1988) includes some of his finest work. His *Collected Poems* appeared posthumously under the editorship of Meic Stephens in 1996 and his *Collected Stories*, edited by Tony Brown, in 1999; a small selection of his poems and a story are to be found in *The Common Path* (2005).

ESYLLT FERCH BRYCHAN

As he climbs down our hill, my kestrel rises,
Steering in silence up from five empty fields,
A smooth sun brushed brown across his shoulders,
Floating in wide circles, his warm wings stiff.
Their shadows cut; in new soft orange hunting-boots
My lover crashes through the snapping bracken.

The still gorse-hissing hill burns, brags gold broom's
Outcropping quartz; each touched bush spills dew.
Strangely last moment's parting was never sad,
But unreal, like my promised years; less felt
Than this intense and silver snail calligraphy
Scrawled here in the sun across these stones.

70

Why have I often wanted to cry out
More against his going when he has left my flesh
Only for the night? When he has gone out
Hot from my mother's kitchen, and my combs
Were on the table under the lamp, and the wind
Was banging the doors of the shed in the yard.

SCENE

This is the scene, let me unload my tongue,
Discharge perhaps some dirty water from my chest.

The north swells, bunioned with Pumlumon, whose
Side leaks water like some rusty old
Boiler's brickwork; his bleeding plait; cars at spring-tides
Line the river roads, switch headlights on, stroke
The stopped tide with car beams, finger the night bore.
That's Severn. Southward, beyond the bottled Channel,
England, Somerset, like foreign parts, and west,
John Masefield's notchy water, Cardigan Bay.

Circuited thus my crumbled country lies.

The flat eyes of the Pembroke hawks discern
Zigzag coast-cliffs, three-ply islands, black rocks
Stuck bad-toothed and edgy from blue-bag sea.
(One night not pinholed by a single star,
I lay half-frozen in the light-house field
And heard the fighting gulls, the prow-wash tide,
My body swept with big beams swung from Strumble Head;)
Vine-veins of rivers flourish everywhere;

Some plains, paint-blistered into bolt-head hills;
The cloud-clawed mountains; prick-lark, a darkened star,
Drops, sees like a batter Beacon peaks,
Stiff, rough, stirred, gone solid-hard, rush up,
Fan Lleia, Fan Gihirich, Pen y Fan
A wool road winding white along each pass.

You men who bus or walk for mart-day towns,
Bear baskets full containing fish or rabbits,
Are river-limers, clubbers of salmon,
I might have been, and liked it, born like you
Westward, or north, beyond the crooked coalfields.
But night on the Valleys and my first star stood
Voluble above those Beacon peaks,
Gesticulating like a tick-tack man.

Standing now where that birth-star was eloquent
I see my bitter county dawn between
My hands, I grieve above five valleys leaning
Suppliant against my unstruck rock.
The cream rose blushing sweet and scarlet stares
Back along the barren pink-hooked stem.
I hear my heart speak to the bleaky sky,
Coal and the Valleys were my lucky egg,
As though some bird should scribble his short song.
I feel the mobbing flowers hug my feet;
The winds descend about my body, hoarse
As a garment, and my lonely burning flesh
Smokes up this sky-hook like a plunging fish.
Proudly I hail this pale past-sailing sun.

EASTER

Morning in the honey-months, the star
Of annunciation still lit in the sky,
Upon me fell the heavy unpinned hair
Of apple, perfumed almond, pear,
With dawn-chorus, dewfall, and the incarnate
Promise of the primrose flesh in bloom.
Leaving the morning garden, I sought the room,
The bedside of a woman winsome to me
Once, though old, clean in her white cap, comely
In candle-light, or the green shine of stars.

In death's stink now, with tears I watch her, old
And hideous in her dying – bitterly
She moans, her face death-dark, her tangled hair
Tortured behind her little rolling head.
She wakes a moment, calming our kindling room,
Opens untroubled eyes and lifting up
Bone arms like glistening sticks, prays for the droll
Child of her weeping sailor. Anguish returns;
Again she moans – it is the grave-bound flesh
That grieves – but soon now must remission come
Upon the agony of this endured embrace,
Soon must the flesh rot in its stony bed.

Now, with a burning in the east, the breeze
Curves across the young cheek of the day;
Soon shall the thrush be at his crowing point,
Frailer than filigree the stems begin to bud;
Soon over grooved fields shall grow the soft

Plush-pile of the grass-like wheat, the green
Velvety nap of springing corn burst forth –
Soon, soon, the doors of every grave shall open
And the light of dawn shall shine upon the dead.

MERTHYR

Lord, when they kill me, let the job be thorough
And carried out behind that county borough
Known as Merthyr, in Glamorganshire.
It would be best if it could happen, Sir,
Upon some great green roof, some Beacon slope
Those monstrous clouds of childhood slid their soap
Snouts over, into the valley. The season,
Sir, for shooting, summer; and love the reason.
On that hill, varnished in the glazing tide
Of evening, stand me, with the petrified
Plantations, the long blue spoonful of the lake,
The gold stook-tufted acres without break
Below me, and the distant corduroy
Glass of the river – which, a mitching boy,
I fished – flowing as though to quench
The smouldering coalfield in its open trench
Of steamy valley, fifteen miles away.
Here, Sir, are more arrangements for that day:
Lay me, lead-loaded, below the mourning satin
Of some burnt-out oak; the skylark's chirpy Latin
Be my 'Daeth yr awr'; gather the black
Flocks for bleaters – sweet grass their ham – upon the back
Of lonely Fan Gihirych; let night's branchy tree
Glow with silver-coated planets over me.

74

And yet, sometimes, I can't help wondering;
Is this rather posh poetic death the thing,
After all, for somebody like me? I realize
I have a knack for telling bardic lies,
To say I see in some protean hill
A green roof, ship's prow or an eagle's bill;
To claim the mountain stream for me's as clear
As flowing gin, and yet as brown as beer.
I fancy words, some critics praise me for
A talent copious in metaphor.
But this my gift for logopœic dance
Brothers, I know, a certain arrogance
Of spirit, a love of grandeur, style and dash,
Even vain-glory, the gaudiest panache,
Which might impel to great rascality
A heedless heart. This glorying in all
Created things, the golden sun, the small
Rain riding in the wind, the silvery shiver
Of the dawn-touched birches, and the chromium river,
Innocent itself, has yet calamitous
And wilful pride for child and famulus.
And thus I see the point when puritan
Or mystic poet harried under ban
Sensual nature, earth, sea and firmament;
I apprehend some strain of what they meant,
And look at nature with a wary eye.
Sir, that death I sought was pure effrontery.

Lord, when they kill me, let the job be thorough
And carried out *inside* that county borough

Known as Merthyr, in Glamorganshire,
A town easy enough to cast a slur
Upon, I grant. Some cyclopean ball
Or barn-dance, some gigantic free-for-all,
You'd guess, had caused her ruins, and those slums –
Frightening enough, I've heard, to daunt the bums --
Seem battered wreckage in some ghastly myth,
Some nightmare of the busting aerolith.
In short, were she a horse, so her attackers
Claim, her kindest destination were the knackers.
Yet, though I've been in Dublin, Paris, Brussels,
London, of course, too, I find what rustles
Oftenest and scentiest through the torpid trees
Of my brain-pan, is some Merthyr-mothered breeze,
Not dreams of them – a zephyr at its best
Acting on arrogance like the alkahest.

An object has significance or meaning
Only to the extent that human feeling
And intellect bestow them. All that sensational news
The heart hears, before she starts to bruise
Herself against the universe's rocky rind,
Is what she treasures most – the sight of wind
Fretting a great beech like an anchored breaker;
The vale, pink-roofed at sunset, a heavenly acre
Of tufted and irradiated toothpaste; the moon
Glistening sticky as snail-slime in the afternoon;
Street-papers hurdling, like some frantic foal,
The crystal barriers of squalls; the liquid coal
Of rivers; the hooter's loud liturgic boom;

Pit-clothes and rosin fragrant in a warm room –
Such sensations deck a ruinous scene
(To strangers) with tinsel, scarlet, spangles, green,
Gold, ribbons, and the glare of pantomime's
Brilliancy in full floods, foots and limes.

But far more than the scene, the legendary
Walkers and actors of it, the memory
Of neighbours, worthies, relatives,
Their free tripudiation, is what gives
That lump of coal that Shelley talks about
Oftenest a puff before it quite goes out.
My grandfather's fantastic friends, old Siôn
O Ferthyr, occultist, meddler with the unknown –
(The spirits in malevolence one night
Nigh strangled him, but sobered Siôn showed fight!)
My grandfather himself, musician, bard,
Pit-sinker, joker, whom the Paddys starred
As basser for their choir – so broken out!
My undersized great granny, that devout
Calvinist, with mind and tongue like knives;
The tall boys from Incline Top, and those boys' wives;
The tailor we believed a Mexican,
A rider of the prairies; Dr Pan
Jones (he it was who gave my father
The snowy barn-owl) Bishop – *soi-disant* rather;
Refined Miss Rees; Miss Thomas ditto; Evan
Davies, and the Williamses from Cefn.
Sir, where memories, dense as elephant
Grass, of these swarm round, in some common *pant*

Or hilltop lay me down; may the ghostly breeze
Of their presence be all my obsequies;
Not sheep and birds about me, but lively men,
And dead men's histories, O Lord. Amen.

CWMCELYN

His wings blissful in a silent drumming
Of beautiful sunlight, the buzzard. Below him,
The estuary; below him the hills,
Green fields with the hay gone; the cornfields,
Silent and sunburnt encampments
Of wheat-stooks; below him the tranquil
River, gently heaving the mirrors
Afloat on her surface; below him
These woods, where flashes the grey pigeon,
White in the paint of her flying.
Below him Cwmcelyn, the farm.

Now the griefs of that homestead are mine.
Drunken, in anger, or passion,
Dejected, trampling this warm web-work of trees
Between village and farm, my blood,
Through long generations, bore their flesh.
Let me not, in the repose of this sunlight,
Tranquil on fields and on heaving estuary, see
Their symbol and image; or falsify
Toiling and poverty, rebellion
And bitterness of theirs to pastoral

Heaven. Defilement was theirs, and folly,
        Suffering, questioning and death. And yet
        Between them and the Eternal, a harmony.

Soon shall I leave these swarthy cornfields,
        The dawdling gull, and the grave river, for
        The acrid city, where the body of the burnt
Saint smoked in its unavailing martyrdom;
Where now the sacrifice of love is not enjoined;
        For the talk, for the belittling fool,
        For the annihilation, for no God,
No king, no shrine, no sanctuary.
Whose is the name to which every knee
        In that city's empty-hearted wilderness
        Shall bow? Ghostly reapers of Cwmcelyn,
You arraign them the demoniac folly,
The soul's dissonance, and the despair.

MORNING

On the night beach, quiet beside the blue
Bivouac of sea-wood, and fresh loaves, and the
Fish baking, the broken ghost, whose flesh burns
Blessing the dark bay and the still mast-light,
Shouts, 'Come'.
        A naked man on deck who heard
Also cockrow, turning to the pebbles, sees
A dawn explode among the golden boats,
Pulls on his sea-plaid, leaps into the sea.

Wading the hoarfrost meadows of that fiord's
Daybreak, he, hungering fisherman, forgets
Cockrow tears, dark noon, dead god, empty cave,
All those mountains of miraculous green
Light that swamped the landing-punt, and kneels,
Shivering, in a soaked blouse, eating by the
Blue blaze the sweet breakfast of forgiveness.

BINDWEED

Suddenly the scent of bindweed in the warm lane
And the smoking sea of remembering him bursts open
Upon its rocks, its snow-dust wets the sun.

The heavy scent of bindweed brings only sorrow.
Grey gull-flocks puffed over waves disintegrate like gunsmoke.
Storm-sodden crags are not colder than my heart.

Bindweed is the scent of heavy remembering.
Beyond the window – the great ocean in its bed.
I am alone. In the past Gwynn was with me.

The scent of bindweed drifts like childhood remembered.
Meshed white on green is the great wave's polished incurve.
Bullets that took Gwynn were already in flight.

Cruel the sweet scent of innocent bindweed.
Winds tear off the tide's skin in one brandished fleece.
Gwynn died. Happiness is irrational.

Bindweed now in this lane, then in that sea-garden.
Waves everywhere throw anguished arms around rocks.
The comforter in his comforting is not comforted.

Sweet bindweed was heavy in that August garden.
The grey sea stiffens and sinks to a slab of iron.
How is it the heart dead at its quick can suffer?

GOODBYE, WHAT WERE YOU?

At the voice of the mother on a warm hearth,
        Dark and firelit, where the hobbed kettle crinkled
In the creak and shudder of the rained-on window,
        This world had its beginning
And was here redeemed.

All in that kitchen's warmth, that mother's glow,
        Was blessèd, nothing was abandoned.
There God's boy was born, loving, by lantern light,
        His church built of the breathing of cattle;
Before nightfall all lost in prowling woods were home;
        To the dying in cactus land a hand came full of rain;
Here a child wept repentant into a Father's breast,
        Warm for his childish tears, not bright with stars,
Or filled with his suffering that mother's arms
        And in the shawls of her prayers and kisses slept.

In the kitchen shadow and flicker and warmth,
        And the deafening storm, thickening hair by hair
Its blinding pelt of tempest on the window panes.

THE COMMON PATH

On one side the hedge, on the other the brook:
   Each afternoon I passed, unnoticed,
The middle-aged schoolmistress, grey-haired,
   Gay, loving, who went home along the path.

That spring she walked briskly, carrying her bag
   With the long ledger, the ruler, the catkin twigs,
Two excited little girls from her class
   Chattering around their smiling teacher.

Summer returned, each day then she approached slowly,
   Alone, wholly absorbed, as though in defeat
Between water and hazels, her eyes heedless,
   Her grey face deeply cast down. Could it be
Grief at the great universal agony had begun
   To feed upon her heart – war, imbecility,
Old age, starving, children's deaths, deformities?
   I, free, white, gentile, born neither
Dwarf nor idiot, passed her by, drawing in
   The skirts of my satisfaction, on the other side.

One day, at the last instant of our passing,
   She became, suddenly, aware of me
And, as her withdrawn glance met my eyes,
   Her whole face kindled into life, I heard
From large brown eyes a blare of terror, anguished
   Supplication, her cry of doom, death, despair.
And in the warmth of that path's sunshine

And of my small and manageable success
I felt at once repelled, affronted by her suffering,
The naked shamelessness of that wild despair.

Troubled, I avoided the common until I heard
Soon, very soon, the schoolmistress, not from
Any agony of remote and universal suffering
Or unendurable grief for others, but
Private, middle-aged, rectal cancer, was dead.

What I remember, and in twenty years have
Never expiated, is that my impatience,
That one glance of my intolerance,
Rejected her, and so rejected all
The sufferings of wars, imprisonments,
Deformities, starvation, idiocy, old age –
Because fortune, sunlight, meaningless success,
Comforted an instant what must not be comforted.

THE MEANING OF FUCHSIAS

The lush valley, the two golden mares loving in the apple
orchard,
The golden-maned for Gwilym, the milky one for me,
And through those dark boughs the vast white mansion-
walls of heaven.
Why did we not hear, in that treachery of sun-varnished
windows,
Of handsome clouds, of the fragrant flesh of pears, of gull-
white moons in their eternal blue,

And pastures cast out of morning fire everywhere
                                        brilliant as enamels,
The creeping by of our days, of time, of change –
    Only the thrush's hammering of morning in the dapples
                                        of that sunlight,
And the cupboards of the trees around us creaking,
                                        creaking.

On the slope the still bushes stood in the sun, staring
                        down in silence at their shadows.
    'Fuchsias,' said Gwilym, 'wild fuchsias' – each bush
                                        of flowers
The dark glow in my mind still of lit lanterns burning
                crimson through transparencies of wine,
    A new delight then, inextinguishable, a heart's enduring
                                        wonder.
In these sleek gardens, where only meaning has no root or
                                        blossoming,
    What is it within me stares through its bars at fuchsias,
So that I bear again the sudden burden of my many dead,
    And you, and all our darkened suns, possess me through
                                the doorways of my tears,
You, sanctified listener, who rode by night your golden pony
    Through the graveyard, listening, and hearing nothing.

VERNON WATKINS

Vernon Watkins was born on 27 June 1906 in Maesteg, Glamorgan, the son of a bank manager who was to settle with his family in Swansea seven years later. After a year at Swansea Grammar School the boy was sent to public schools in England, latterly to Repton in Derbyshire. The family was Welsh-speaking but the poet neither spoke nor learned the language. The only Welsh sources he was able to use in his poetry were the figure of Taliesin, sometimes in poems set in Gower, where his parents had made their home in 1931, and the folklore of the Mari Lwyd, about which he had heard in his father's home village of Taff's Well near Cardiff. At Magdalene College, Cambridge, he found the French and German courses uncongenial and, despite having passed his examinations, left at the end of his first year. At his father's insistence he became a junior clerk in the Butetown branch of Lloyds Bank in Cardiff. Associating poetry with the idyllic experience of his last years at Repton, he was unable to adjust to the realities of working life and suffered a nervous breakdown, after which he was removed to the Bank's branch in St. Helen's, Swansea, where he was to remain, without the slightest professional ambition, for the rest of his working life; after his marriage, he made his home at Pennard in Gower. He always spoke of his breakdown as 'a revolution of sensibility' and his poetry was to be devoted to 'the conquest of time', by which he meant the recreation of the Eden-like ambience he had known at Repton. Two other crises from which he drew inspiration were the destruction of Swansea by German bombs in 1941 and the death of Dylan Thomas whom he loved. At the time of his death in Seattle on 8 October 1967, during a second visit as Professor of Poetry at the University of Washington, his name was being canvassed, with others, for the Poet Laureateship. He published six volumes of verse during his lifetime: *Ballad of the Mari Lwyd* (1941), *The Lamp and the Veil* (1945), *The Lady with the Unicorn* (1948), *The Death Bell* (1954), *Cypress and Acacia* (1959), and *Affinities* (1962). After his death there appeared another four volumes: *Fidelities* (1968), *Uncollected Poems* (1969), *The Ballad of the Outer Dark* (1979), and *The Breaking of the Wave* (1979), as well as compilations such as *I That Was Born in Wales* (1976) and *Unity of the Stream* (1978). His *Collected Poems*, a book containing more than 350 poems, many of them long, appeared in 1986 under the editorship of Ruth Pryor, and his *New Selected Poems*, edited by Richard Ramsbotham, in 2006. Long overshadowed by his friend Dylan Thomas, Vernon Watkins became a very different poet – a modern metaphysical Christian concerned with eternal truths. Sometimes obscure, but always with formal excellence, he wrote out of that 'grief' into which he had fallen as a young man. Innocent, unworldly, refusing to believe ill of anyone, but tenacious in his commitment to the poet's art, he ploughed his own furrow and was never diverted from it.

GRIEFS OF THE SEA

It is fitting to mourn dead sailors,
To crown the sea with some wild wreath of foam
On some steep promontory, some cornercliff of Wales
Though the deaf wave hear nothing.

It is fitting to fling off clothing,
To enter the sea with plunge of seawreaths white
Broken by limbs that love the waters, fear the stars,
Though the blind wave grope under eyes that see, limbs
                                        that wonder,
Though the blind wave grope forward to the sand
With a greedy, silvered hand.

It is a horrible sound, the low wind's whistle
Across the seaweeds on the beach at night.
From stone to stone through hissing caves it passes
Up the curved cliff and shakes the prickly thistle
And spreads its hatred through the grasses.

In spite of that wicked sound
Of the wind that follows us like a scenting hound,
It is fitting on the curved cliff to remember the drowned,
To imagine them clearly for whom the sea no longer cares,
To deny the language of the thistle, to meet their foot-firm
                                        tread
Across the dark-sown tares
Who were skilful and erect, magnificent types of godhead,
To resist the dogging wind, to accuse the sea-god;

Yet in that gesture of anger we must admit
We were quarrelling with a phantom unawares.

For the sea turns whose every drop is counted
And the sand turns whose every grain a holy hour-glass holds
And the weeds turn beneath the sea, the sifted life slips free,
And the wave turns surrendering from its folds
All things that are not sea, and thrown off is the spirit
By the sea, the riderless horse which they once mounted.

PORTRAIT OF A FRIEND

He has sent me this
Late and early page
Caught in the emphasis
Of last night's cartonnage,
Crumpled in the post,
Bringing to lamplight
Breath's abatement,
Over- and under-statement,
Mute as a mummy's pamphlet
Long cherished by a ghost.

Who for annunciation has
The white wings of the sheldrake,
Labouring water's praise,
The blind shriek of the mandrake,
Broken shells for story,
Torn earth for love's near head
Raised from time's estuary,

Fed by the raven's bread;
A trespasser in tombs,
He bids the grey dust fall,
Groans in the shaping limbs:
'All stars are in my shawl.'
Who feels the deathbound sighs,
Mocks the Winged Horse's fake,
Toiling, as with closed eyes,
Love's language to remake,
To draw from their dumb wall
The saints to a worldly brothel
That a sinner's tongue may toll
And call the place Bethel.

Trusting a creaking house,
His roof is ruinous,
So mortal. A real wind
Beats on this house of sand
Two tides like ages buffet.
The superhuman, crowned
Saints must enter this drowned
Tide-race of the mind
To guess or understand
The face of this cracked prophet,
Which from its patient pall
I slowly take,
Drop the envelope,
Compel his disturbing shape,
And write these words on a wall
Maybe for a third man's sake.

MUSIC OF COLOURS: WHITE BLOSSOM

White blossom, white, white shell; the Nazarene
Walking in the ear; white touched by souls
Who know the music by which white is seen,
Blinding white, from strings and aureoles,
Until that is not white, seen at the two poles,
Nor white the Scythian hills, nor Marlowe's queen.

The spray looked white until this snowfall.
Now the foam is grey, the wave is dull.
Call nothing white again, we were deceived.
The flood of Noah dies, the rainbow is lived.
Yet from the deluge of illusions an unknown colour is saved.

White must die black, to be born white again
From the womb of sounds, the inscrutable grain,
From the crushed, dark fibre, breaking in pain.

The bud of the apple is already forming there.
The cherry-bud, too, is firm, and behind it the pear
Conspires with the racing cloud. I shall not look.
The rainbow is diving through the wide-open book
Past the rustling paper of birch, the sorceries of bark.

Buds in April, on the waiting branch,
Starrily opening, light raindrops drench,
Swinging from world to world when starlings sweep,
Where they alight in air, are white asleep.
They will not break, not break, until you say
White is not white again, nor may may.

White flowers die soonest, die into that chaste
Bride-bed of the moon, their lives laid waste.
Lilies of Solomom, taken by the gust,
Sigh, make way. And the dark forest
Haunts the lowly crib near Solomon's dust,
Rocked to the end of majesty, warmed by the low beast,
Locked in the liberty of his tremendous rest.

If there is white, or has been white, it must have been
When His eyes looked down and made the leper clean.
White will not be, apart, though the trees try
Spirals of blossom, their green conspiracy.
She who touched His garment saw no white tree.

Lovers speak of Venus, and the white doves,
Jubilant, the white girl, myth's whiteness, Jove's,
Of Leda, the swan, whitest of his loves.
Lust imagines him, web-footed Jupiter, great down
Of thundering light; love's yearning pulls him down
On the white swan-breast, the magical lawn,
Involved in plumage, mastered by the veins of dawn.

In the churchyard the yew is neither green nor black.
I know nothing of Earth or colour until I know I lack
Original white, by which the ravishing bird looks wan.
The mound of dust is nearer, white of mute dust that dies
In the soundfall's great light, the music in the eyes,
Transfiguring whiteness into shadows gone,
Utterly secret. I know you, black swan.

RETURNING TO GOLEUFRYN

Returning to my grandfather's house, after this exile
From the coracle-river, long left with a coin to be good,
Returning with husks of those venturing ears for food
To lovely Carmarthen, I touch and remember the turnstile
Of this death-bound river. Fresh grass. Here I find that crown
In the shadow of dripping river-wood; then look up to the
                                                  burning mile
Of windows. It is Goleufryn, the house on the hill;
And picking a child's path in a turn of the Towy I meet the
                                               prodigal town.

Sing, little house, clap hands: shut, like a book of the Psalms,
On the leaves and pressed flowers of a journey. All is sunny
In the garden behind you. The soil is alive with blind-petalled
                                                  blooms
Plundered by bees. Gooseberries and currants are gay
With tranquil, unsettled light. Breathless light begging alms
Of the breathing grasses bent over the river of tombs
Flashes. A salmon has swallowed the tribute-money
Of the path. On the farther bank I see ragged urchins play

With thread and pin. O lead me that I may drown
In those earlier cobbles, reflected; a street that is strewn with
                                                  palms,
Rustling with blouses and velvet. Yet I alone
By the light in the sunflower deepening, here stand, my eyes
                                                cast down
To the footprint of accusations, and hear the faint, leavening

Music of first Welsh words; that gust of plumes
'They shall mount up like eagles', dark-throated assumes,
Cold-sunned, low thunder and gentleness of the authentic
Throne.

Yet now I am lost, lost in the water-wound looms
Where brief, square windows break on a garden's decay.
Gold butter is shining, the tablecloth speckled with crumbs.
The kettle throbs. In the calendar harvest is shown,
Standing in sheaves. Which way would I do you wrong?
Low, crumbling doorway of the infirm to the mansions of
evening,
And poor, shrunken furrow where the potatoes are sown,
I shall not unnumber one soul I have stood with and known
To regain your stars struck by horses, your sons of God
breaking in song.

TALIESIN IN GOWER

Late I return, O violent, colossal, reverberant, eavesdropping
sea.
My country is here. I am foal and violet. Hawthorn breaks
from my hands.
I watch the inquisitive cormorant pry from the praying rock
of Pwlldu,
Then skim to the gulls' white colony, to Oxwich's cockle-
strewn sands.

I have seen the curlew's triangular print, I know every inch
of his way.

I have gone through the door of the foundered ship, I have
slept in the winch of the cave
With pine-log and unicorn-spiral shell secreting the colours
of day;
I have been taught the script of the stones, and I know the
tongue of the wave.

I witness here in a vision the landscape to which I was born,
Three smouldering bushes of willow, like trees of fire, and
the course
Of the river under the stones of death, carrying the ear of
corn
Withdrawn from the moon-dead chaos of rocks overlooking
its secret force.

I see, a marvel in Winter's marshes, the iris break from its
sheath
And the dripping branch in the ache of sunrise frost and
shadow redeem
With wonder of patient, living leaf, while Winter, season of
death,
Rebukes the sun, and grinds out men's groans in the voice
of its underground stream.

Yet now my task is to weigh the rocks on the level wings of
a bird,
To relate these undulations of time to a kestrel's motionless
poise.
I speak, and the soft-running hour-glass answers; the core
of the rock is a third:

Landscape survives, and these holy creatures proclaim
                                    their regenerate joys.

I know this mighty theatre, my footsole knows it for mine.
I am nearer the rising peewit's call than the shiver of her
                                    own wing.
I ascend in the loud waves' thunder, I am under the last of
                                    the nine.
In a hundred dramatic shapes I perish, in the last I live and
                                    sing.

All that I see with my sea-changed eyes is a vision too great
                                    for the brain.
The luminous country of auk and eagle rocks and shivers
                                    to earth.
In the hunter's quarry this landscape died; my vision
                                    restores it again.
These stones are prayers; every boulder is hung on a
                                    breath's miraculous birth.

Gorse breaks on the steep cliff-side, clings earth, in patches
                                    blackened for sheep,
For grazing fired; now the fair weather comes to the ravens'
                                    pinnacled knoll.
Larks break heaven from the thyme-breathing turf; far
                                    under, flying through sleep,
Their black fins cutting the rainbow surf, the porpoises
                                    follow the shoal.

They are gone where the river runs out, there where the
                                    breakers divide

The lacework of Three Cliffs Bay in a music of two seas;
A heron flaps where the sandbank holds a dyke to the
twofold tide,
A wave-encircled isthmus of sound which the white bird-
parliament flees.

Rhinoceros, bear and reindeer haunt the crawling glaciers
of age
Beheld in the eye of the rock, where a javelin'd arm held
stiff,
Withdrawn from the vision of flying colours, reveals, like
script on a page,
The unpassing moment's arrested glory, a life locked fast in
the cliff.

Now let the great rock turn. I am safe with an ear of corn,
A repository of light once plucked, from all men hidden
away.
I have passed through a million changes. In a butterfly
coracle borne,
My faith surmounting the Titan, I greet the prodigious bay.

I celebrate you, marvellous forms. But first I must cut the
wood,
Exactly measure the strings, to make manifest what shall be.
All earth being weighed by an ear of corn, all heaven by a
drop of blood.
How shall I loosen this music to the listening,
eavesdropping sea?

THE MARE

The mare lies down in the grass where the nest of the
skylark is hidden.
Her eyes drink the delicate horizon moving behind the song.
Deep sink the skies, a well of voices. Her sleep is the vessel
of Summer.
That climbing music requires the hidden music at rest.

Her body is utterly given to the light, surrendered in
perfect abandon
To the heaven above her shadow, still as her first-born day.
Softly the wind runs over her. Circling the meadow, her
hooves
Rest in a race of daisies, halted where butterflies stand.

Do not pass her too close. It is easy to break the circle
And lose that indolent fullness rounded under the ray
Falling on light-eared grasses your footstep must not yet
wake.
It is easy to darken the sun of her unborn foal at play.

PEACE IN THE WELSH HILLS

Calm is the landscape when the storm has passed,
Brighter the fields, and fresh with fallen rain.
Where gales beat out new colour from the hills
Rivers fly faster, and upon their banks
Birds preen their wings, and irises revive.

Not so the cities burnt alive with fire
Of man's destruction: when their smoke is spent,
No phoenix rises from the ruined walls.

I ponder now the grief of many rooms.
Was it a dream, that age, when fingers found
A satisfaction sleeping in dumb stone,
When walls were built responding to the touch
In whose high gables, in the lengthening days,
Martins would nest? Though crops, though lives, would
fail,
Though friends dispersed, unchanged the walls would stay,
And still those wings return to build in Spring.

Here, where the earth is green, where heaven is true
Opening the windows, touched with earliest dawn,
In the first frost of cool September days,
Chrysanthemum weather, presaging great birth,
Who in his heart could murmur or complain:
'The light we look for is not in this land'?
That light is present, and that distant time
Is always here, continually redeemed.

There is a city we must build with joy
Exactly where the fallen city sleeps.
There is one road through village, town and field,
On whose robust foundation Chaucer dreamed
A ride could wed the opposites in man.
There proud walls may endure, and low walls feed

The imagination if they have a vine
Or shadowy barn made rich with gathered corn.

Great mansions fear from their surrounding trees
The invasion of a wintry desolation
Filling their rooms with leaves. And cottages
Bring the sky down as flickering candles do,
Leaning on their own shadows. I have seen
Vases and polished brass reflect black windows
And draw the ceiling down to their vibrations,
Thick, deep, and white-washed, like a bank of snow.

To live entwined in pastoral loveliness
May rest the eyes, throw pictures on the mind,
But most we need a metaphor of stone
Such as those painters had whose mountain-cities
Cast long, low shadows on the Umbrian hills.
There, in some courtyard on the cobbled stone,
A fountain plays, and through a cherub's mouth,
Ages are linked by water in the sunlight.

All of good faith that fountain may recall,
Woman, musician, boy, or else a scholar
Reading a Latin book. They seem distinct,
And yet are one, because tranquillity
Affirms the Judgment. So, in these Welsh hills,
I marvel, waking from a dream of stone,
That such a peace surrounds me, while the city
For which all long has never yet been built.

GREAT NIGHTS RETURNING

Great nights returning, midnight's constellations
Gather from groundfrost that unnatural brilliance.
Night now transfigures, walking in the starred ways,
Tears for the living.

Earth now takes back the secret of her changes.
All the wood's dropped leaves listen to your footfall.
Night has no tears, no sound among the branches;
Stopped is the swift stream.

Spirits were joined when hazel leaves were falling.
Then the stream hurrying told of separation.
This is the fires' world, and the voice of Autumn
Stilled by the death-wand.

Under your heels the icy breath of Winter
Hardens all roots. The Leonids are flying.
Now the crisp stars, the circle of beginning;
Death, birth, united.

Nothing declines here. Energy is fire-born.
Twigs catch like stars or serve for your divining.
Lean down and hear the subterranean water
Crossed by the quick dead.

Now the soul knows the fire that first composed it
Sinks not with time but its renewed hereafter.
Death cannot steal the light which love has kindled
Nor the years change it.

WATERFALLS

Always in that valley in Wales I hear the noise
    Of waters falling.
                    There is a clump of trees
  We climbed for nuts; and high in the trees the boys
    Lost in the rookery's cries
      Would cross, and branches cracking under their knees

Would break, and make in the winter wood new gaps.
  The leafmould covering the ground was almost black,
    But speckled and striped were the nuts we threw
                    in our caps,
    Milked from split shells and cups,
      Secret as chestnuts when they are tipped from a sack,

Glossy and new.
               Always in that valley in Wales
  I hear that sound, those voices. They keep fresh
    What ripens, falls, drops into darkness, fails,
      Gone when dawn shines on scales,
      And glides from village memory, slips through
                  the mesh,

And is not, when we come again.
              I look:
  Voices are under the bridge, and that voice calls,
    Now late, and answers;
            then, as the light twigs break
    Back, there is only the brook reminding the stones
           where, under a breath, it falls.

ODE TO SWANSEA

Bright town, tossed by waves of time to a hill,
Leaning Ark of the world, dense-windowed, perched
High on the slope of morning,
Taking fire from the kindling East:

Look where merchants, traders, and builders move
Through your streets, while above your chandlers' walls
Herring gulls wheel, and pigeons,
Mocking man and the wheelwright's art.

Prouder cities rise through the haze of time,
Yet, unenvious, all men have found is here.
Here is the loitering marvel
Feeding artists with all they know.

There, where sunlight catches a passing sail,
Stretch your shell-brittle sands where children play,
Shielded from hammering dockyards
Launching strange, equatorial ships.

Would they know you, could the returning ships
Find the pictured bay of the port they left
Changed by a murmuration,
Stained by ores in a nighthawk's wing?

Yes. Through changes your myth seems anchored here.
Staked in mud, the forsaken oyster beds
Loom; and the Mumbles lighthouse
Turns through gales like a seabird's egg.

Lundy sets the course of the painted ships.
Fishers dropping nets off the Gower coast
Watch them, where shag and cormorant
Perch like shades on the limestone rocks.

You I know, yet who from a different land
Truly finds the town of a native child
Nurtured under a rainbow,
Pitched at last on Mount Pleasant hill?

Stone-runged streets ascending to that crow's nest
Swinging East and West over Swansea Bay
Guard in their walls Cwmdonkin's
Gates of light for a bell to close.

Praise, but do not disturb, heaven's dreaming man
Not awakened yet from his sleep of wine.
Pray, while the starry midnight
Broods on Singleton's elms and swans.

FIDELITIES

The fountain gathers, in a single jet,
Fidelities where beams together run,
Thrives upon loss, enriches us with debt.

Nothing will match the day's full unison.
I love to see light break; and yet, and yet,
The final arbiter is not the sun.

Bounteous that brother, but he will forget
Others whose eyes the hand of death has closed,
Nor touch, nor seek them, when their light has set.

Seeing of what compound splendour life's composed,
Who could believe it now a part once played,
With so much owing to so many a ghost?

Of love's stern language noblest lives are made.
The shell of speech by many a voice is shot
Whose light, once kindled, cannot be betrayed.

A certain cadence underlies the plot;
However fatally the thread is spun,
The dying man can rise above his lot.

For me neglect and world-wide fame were one.
I was concerned with those the world forgot.
In the tale's ending saw its life begun;

And I was with them still when time was not.

MARGIAD EVANS

Margiad Evans was born Peggy Eileen Whistler in Uxbridge, London, on 17 March 1909, to parents whose forebears may have included a family from South Wales named Evans. They moved to Ross-on-Wye, Herefordshire, in 1920 and it was with the Border counties that she and her sister Nancy (who wrote short stories under the pseudonym Siân Evans) chose to identify as writers. After her marriage in 1940, she lived for eight years at Llangarron, near Ross, and later in Gloucestershire and Sussex. Having suffered from epilepsy from about 1950, she died of a brain tumour in hospital in Tunbridge Wells on 17 March 1958. She is best-known and widely admired as a prose-writer. Her novels are *Country Dance* (1932), *The Wooden Doctor* (1933), *Turf or Stone* (1934) and *Creed* (1936), while *The Old and the Young* is a volume of short stories; her journal and a selection of her essays are to be found in *Autobiography* (1943) and *A Ray of Darkness* (1952). Her two books of verse are *Poems from Obscurity* (1947) and *A Candle Ahead* (1956). Despite her ill health, borne with great fortitude, she managed to maintain a note of optimism in her poems.

THE NIGHTINGALE

The orchard in the valley first
the green infection took,
the birds forgot their brown highways,
the leaf forgot the root.

The butterflies on breathing wings
went by like sighs of light –
trembled the air's transparency –
articulated flight.

The mountains in the faded mists
with opening souls rejoice.
All night they heard the nightingale
in his full-moon of voice.

A LARK SONNET

Are you widowed? So am I;
earth's laden ring that once was marriage gold
divides us: your coldness makes me cold,
who should not feel the weather where I lie
within the heart's cooled climate. Eternity
is now my mood; and our name is enrolled
with other dead names in the mason's fold
of wrinkled stone. I had to die
while youth was young enough for youth to end
and old enough companion to befriend!
All, all was taken while complete in strength
the hopeful life, its love, its living dream
of joyousness: *that* is the frozen stream –
all passion is short voiced, all love lark-length.

TO MY SISTER SIAN

'Do you remember Sian? How dearly do you remember?'

(Autobiography)

Nature and Time are against us now:
no more we leap up the river like salmon,
nor dive through its fishy holes
sliding along its summer corridor
with all the water from Wales, nor tear it to silver
shreds with our childish arms when it bolted our path for
the day,
nor wade wearing our bindings
of string weed, white-flowering from our nakedness;
nor lie in the hot yellow fields with the cows.

We go home separately, Sian.
Strangest of all changes, that you have one door,
I another! Dreamily I write to our childhood,
sisters with a brotherly friendship, one loyal to both.
There hang the black woods still with candles of daffodils
lighting the draught of the wind, and our parted language
speaks to each of us of the keepers' cot in the brackeny corner
and the stream bed where the water had faded to rock –
Easily we keep our secrets now, for no-one cares
if we dare the red floods together, two little fools in the
darkness
whose souls flew high above danger, whose bodies
death had a hundred times in its reach.

Forever we
did not end, but passed over our paths,

I following you, dabbling our hands in the birds' nests,
darting through ghost walk and haunted graveyard
when the year was dead in the church tower.
We had one home together. That put us beyond all danger:
that set us forever, that and our unfathomable friend-
                                        ship with trees,
fields and horizons. Two children
solitary, pilgrimy, silent, inscrutably wishing
forever dallying with lostness, whether our choice
was through the jay woods, or over mushroom mountains,
or the old cider orchards.

Our secrets
were eternal and will always be. Forever dallying
with lostness, at last we were lost and all paths
were the path of our unforgettable double childhood.
All our secrets were one – secrecy.
The memory of what we kept secret is gone, but the secret
                                        is true.
All the places were us, we were all the places,
and the inscrutable innocent altars of nature.
I see two children slipping into a wood
speechlessly happy. Two lives lived have not changed it.
For our ways, our fields, our river, our lostness
were children. So we were our country.

LYNETTE ROBERTS

Lynette Roberts was born on 4 July 1909 in Buenos Aires, where her father was Director of Argentina's Western Railways, and christened Evelyn Beatrice; her parents, who were of Welsh descent, had emigrated to Argentina from Australia. Educated at the Central School of Arts and Crafts in London, she married Keidrych Rhys in 1939 and they made their home at Llan-y-bri in Carmarthenshire. She was to be dogged by mental and physical ill health for the rest of her life. After her divorce in 1948 she moved with her two children to live in England, but there, in 1955, suffered a breakdown marked by paranoia and hallucinations. In 1969 she returned to Llan-y-bri, moving a few years later to Carmarthen, where she devoted herself to evangelizing as a Jehovah's Witness. The last years of her life were spent at a residential home in Ferryside, on the Tywi estuary, and there she died on 26 September 1995. She published, besides a booklet about the language of Llan-y-bri entitled *Village Dialect* (1944), and *The Endeavour* (1954), an account of Captain Cook's first voyage of exploration to Australia, two books of poetry, namely *Poems* (1944) and *Gods with Stainless Ears* (1951); her *Collected Poems,* edited by Patrick McGuinness, were published in 2005. Most of her poems were written during the Second World War while her husband was away on military service and she was living at Llan-y-bri in a whitewashed, two-roomed cottage without amenities; there she suffered a miscarriage, and was treated with suspicion by villagers on account of her foreign birth – despite her close identification with the district. Many of her later poems are written in a packed, even congested style, and employ recondite vocabulary and references which have inevitably attracted charges of obscurity. But she was also capable of a simpler, more direct lyricism which moves between the domestic and the mythic in haunting ways, as in 'Poem from Llanybri', which was addressed to Alun Lewis.

POEM FROM LLANYBRI

If you come my way that is...
Between now and then, I will offer you
A fist full of rock cress fresh from the bank
The valley tips of garlic red with dew
Cooler than shallots, a breath you can swank

In the village when you come. At ncon-day
I will offer you a choice bowl of cawl
Served with a 'lover's' spoon and a chopped spray
Of leeks or savori fach, not used now,

In the old way you'll understand. The din
Of children singing through the eyelet sheds
Ringing smith hoops, chasing the butt of hens;
Or I can offer you Cwmcelyn spread

With quartz stones from the wild scratchings of men:
You will have to go carefully with clogs
Or thick shoes for it's treacherous the fen,
The East and West Marshes also have bogs.

110

Then I'll do the lights, fill the lamp with oil,
Get coal from the shed, water from the well;
Pluck and draw pigeon with crop of green foil
This your good supper from the lime-tree fell.

A sit by the hearth with blue flames rising,
No talk. Just a stare at 'Time' gathering
Healed thoughts, pool insight, like swan sailing
Peace and sound around the home, offering

You a night's rest and my day's energy.
You must come – start this pilgrimage
Can you come? Send an ode or elegy
In the old way and raise our heritage.

LAMENTATION

To the village of lace and stone
Came strangers. I was one of these
Always observant and slightly obscure.
I roamed the hills of bird and bone
Rescuing bees from under the storm:
Five hills rocked and four homes fell
The day I remember the raid so well.
Eyes shone like cups chipped and stiff
The living bled the dead lay in their grief
Cows, sheep, horses, all had got struck
Black as bird wounds, red as wild duck.

Dead as icebone breaking the hedge
Dead as soil failing of good heart.
Dead as trees quivering with shock
At the hot death from the plane.

O the cold loss of cattle
With their lovely big eyes.
The emptiness of sheds,
The rick stacked high.
The breast of the hills
Will soon turn grey
As the dogs that grieve
And I that fetched them in:
For the good gates are closed
In the yard down our way.

'But my loss. My loss is deeper
Than Rosie's of Chapel House farm
For I met death before birth:
Fought for life and in reply lost
My own with a cold despair.
I hugged the fire around the hearth
To warm the beat and wing
Yet knew the symbol when it came
Lawrence had found the same.
I threw the starling hard as stone
Into the breaking earth....'

Dead as icebone breaking the hedge.
Dead as soil failing of good heart.

Dead as trees quivering with shock
At the hot death from the plane.

O the salt loss of life
Her lovely green ways.
The emptiness of crib
And big stare of night.
The breast of the hills
Yield a bucket of milk:
But the crane no longer cries
With the round birds at dawn
For the home has been shadowed
A storm of sorrow drowned the way.

EARTHBOUND

I, in my dressing gown,
At the dressing table with mirror in hand
Suggest my lips with accustomed air, see
The reflected van like lipstick enter the village
When Laura came, and asked me if I knew.

We had known him a little, yet long enough:
Drinking in all rooms, mild and bitter,
Laughing and careless under the washing-line tree.

The day so icy when we gathered the moss,
The frame made from our own wire and cane;
Ivy in perfect scale, roped with fruit from the same root:
And from the Pen of Flowers those which had survived the
                                                    frost.

We made the wreath standing on the white floor;
Bent each to our purpose wire to rose-wire;
Pinning each leaf smooth,
Polishing the outer edge with the warmth of our hands.

The circle finished and note thought out,
We carried the ring through the attentive eyes of the street:
Then slowly drove by Butcher's Van to the 'Union Hall'.

We walked the greaving room alone,
Saw him lying in his upholstered box,
Violet ribbon carefully crossed,
And about his sides bunches of wild thyme.
No one stirred as we offered the gift. No one drank there
                                                                                    again.

MOORHEN

That this, so common an event
In so deplorable a State
Should draw a wreath of joy
From our pale reeded hearts:
That she, without interference
Or compound political tags,
Can, so easily, paddle out
Her freshest brood of sleek black hens:
Stealing the water's shine with elm-
Webbed stretch, the ribbons of sun
Winding around their necks:

Timely jerks purling through
Grisailles of rain – shocking the air
With scarlet bill and garter.
A bank rat sharpening his teeth
Might up on his haunches to listen;
A wise owl with rabbit ears
Could hardly frown at all this fuss.

THE SEASONS

Spring which has its appeal in ghosts,
Youth, resurrection, cleansing of the soil,
And in dormant roots already considered,
Stirs, with the sharpening of branches
Challenges heart to do that which it cannot,
Sustain overwork, overthought, overlove.
It clears a path for hope: reinstates
Faith, which we had too easily omitted
With death, in the caustic months of the year.

Summer proclaims joy, laughter before its
Arrival: and deceives us into malice
With its non appearance. It suggests
A romance that we have not received
Sunny balconies in the mind: the seldom
Forgotten perfect island summer with its
Warm haze on flesh, flower, and hide:
The blossoming of their structure, fragrance
And appeal, from their own root recorded.

Autumn comes strutting in like a cockerel,
Red, blue, yellow and brown. It disintegrates
Our purpose of singular thought; destroys
Relationships: and cuts the sap of pride
Ruthlessly. Those who survive retain one heart
And voice. Yet autumn with contrawise motion
Shields the creative mind with covering of leaves,
Settles and matures dormant growth which will
Reappear, under the hard skies of spring.

Winter exceeds the year with impunity:
Devours us of all greed: and freezes
That residue. It upholds that which is not:
Which is, the blaze of summer biting
Into our nature for a future reappeal.
Winter intones loss of all things:
Is the next step to death which is loneliness:
Comfort and warmth to be found around our own
Heart and grate, within the steel ribs of this age.

from GODS WITH STAINLESS EARS

We must upprise O my people. Though
Secretly trenched in sorrel, we must
Upshine, outshine the day's sun. And day
Intensified by the falling haggard
Of rain shall curve our smile with straw.

Bring plimsole plover to the tensile sand
And with cuprite crest and petulant feet
Distil our notes into febrile weeds
Crisply starched at the water-rail of tides:
On gault and green stone a gramophone stands,

In zebeline stripes strike out the pilotless
Age: from saxophone towns brass out the dead:
Disinter futility that we entombing men
Might curb our runaway hearts. –
On tamarisk; on seafield pools shivering

With water-cats, ring out the square slate notes
Shape the birdbox trees with neumes, wind sound
Singular into cool and simple corners
Round pale bittern grass and all unseen
Unknown places of sheltered rubble

Where whimbrels, redshanks, sandpipers ripple
For the wing of the living. Under tin of earth,
From wooden boles where owls break music;
From this killing world against humanity
Upprise against, – outshine the day's sun.

Corymb of coriander: each ray frosted
Incandescent: by square stem held, hispid,
And purple spotted. Twice pinnate with fronds
Of chrome. Laid higher than the exulted hedge;
By pure collated disc of daisy glittering

White on a red powdered stem. By cusp of leaves
Held low to ground; this coriander cane,
Colonnade of angelica, chevril, fennel,
Parsley, aniseed, caraway, yarrow,
All kitchen's frescade culled and tied away;

By this eyelet and low fieldfare herbs are
Accentuated; engraved and brought to light:
To green cymes of guelder rose and flax blue
Meadows of Pembrey sedge. To men allergic,
Gunners: Bogrush, Pricklesedge, Stinking Goosefoot,

Foetid Hawk's-beard, Black Horehound, Bloody-veined
Dock, Blue Broomrape, and Bastard Toadflax on dank
Plain of mud cough like Kerberus in midsummer lanes.
Food chyles constricted in their stomach,
Twisting, knotting, and deflexed, rats bolt

Between their teeth. All day the ghosts of ulcer
Hover in front of their paths. With unhealthy
Custom the MO turns a page, lays them aside,
Apart from communication, into pruned
Shuttered wards, curing each for the wrong event!

The MO turns a head. – Long necked in
Achillean sky, geese sleeve their own
Shadows through pools of air. Sailing downstream
Downfast to earth. Hydroplanes splash like
Zinnias on inrushing tides; fussy as moorhens

118

With tarnished back; whose legs of peeled elm
Trail scarlet garters into the shaking tips
Of reeds. To their aid. To his aid. To my lover.
Under tincture of Myddfai Hills, west of
Bristol glass, gold with bracken dust and black

Cattle notes and all chemical paradox:
XEBO 7011 camouflaged in naval oilskin
In all the gorgeous shades of Hades; –
By seiriol cat with greenfield eyes.
By kitchen rilled with distemper and grass.

By coat stained and saddlestitched by my flowering
Hands. By neighbours like Byzantine Waterspouts; leaning
Out of bedroom windows. By damn tin-blower.
Leaf feathers of the white-eyed woodpecker
Spangled with lime leaves, wearing the

Chuckling red hat! By 7. With magic and craft
To heel. Without abbreviation or contraction
Take thou my lover 4 pints from the 'Farmers' Arms'
Or, if flat, 6 glass tankards from Jones
'Black Horse'. Not supplying either sip homeward

Sloe-gin from Merlin's desk or board 'Cow and Gate'
Lorry. Up to Carmarthen: to the wine merchant's; mention
Vicar's name, demand whiskey 'Old Parr',
Mix. Let a mixture be made. Let him my lover
Take one silver tablespoonful out of IN

A little water each fourth hour and the
Acridity of his mind shall be as the crimson
Heart on our fresco wall. – To perfect eyestrain
For your wedgwood eyes, collyrium of well water
From the Ffyn-on-ol-bri springs.

JEAN EARLE

Jean Earle was born Jean Smith in Bristol on 28 August 1909 and brought up in Ton Pentre in the Rhondda Fawr, where her father worked as an architect and surveyor with the Crawshay Bailey estate; Earle was her grandmother's surname. After taking a secretarial course in Cardiff, and marrying in 1937, she lived in Colwyn Bay, Plymouth, Prestatyn, Solfa in Pembrokeshire, and Edwardsville near Merthyr Tydfil. From 1958 to 1990 she was employed as a secretary in the office of the Bishop of St. David's at Abergwili in Carmarthenshire. She died in Shrewsbury on 8 April 2002. In her seventies when she published her first book, *A Trial of Strength* (1980), she went on to publish *The Intent Look* (1984), *Visiting Light* (1987), *The Sun in the West* (1995) and *The Bed of Memory* (2001); her *Selected Poems* appeared in 1990.

WALKING HOME

A room in a bishop's palace,
Diocesan matters
Discreetly filed, stencils.

In winter, sometimes,
Sunset pouring through an oak – so old,
Arms are chained to head. It flares indignant,
Glinting its bonds. The typewriter answers,
Simmering red.

Why not such fancies? Machine and I
Have done the work, meticulous –
No less efficient
Because sunsets change us.

It is, that lonely tasks
Breed fantasies. Years of walking home
Through the great garden have enriched,
Saved – perhaps from losing 'strangeness',
Delicate lens
Tinting the common sight, quickly mislaid
Among computers, systems,
But in a musty room
Facing the freedom of birds and squirrels,
Become an intuition; grace to see
Natural lambency about the creatures.

Some say that people emanate
This shining, also. I never saw it outline
Any that I know....

Therefore, it follows – walking home,
I am not luminous to birds and animals
As they to me. My passing means no more
Than the shadows of firs
Brushing out a cold evening coming.
Fir shadow too, in the brown room,
Very sweet all day. One must ignore it
For the work's sake. But afterwards, what harm
If the shadow perceive a sudden flush
Between unhuman things –

The oak, the typewriter
In its business mask –
Were not its steely vitals drawn
Native as oak, from the hot earth?

A thousand blackbirds roost
In the drive bushes. Garden and churchyard
Are one great round, steeped in ceremonial
Long before Christ. Often I feel the rites
Quilling like blackbirds...

This is an old, holy place,
Waging perpetual wars. I side with them –
But am unsure under what rising powers
I walk home.

VISITING LIGHT

A single rose-red tile
On an opposite roof
Comes and goes among adjacent slates,
According to light, weather.
Rain, blown off the spring river,
Brings it up proud
Of surrounding greys –
Like an expected face, flushing.

Roofs fascinate –
How they straddle families,
Equal across the too-many

123

As over the so-lonely,
Giving nothing away.
Discreet above violent stoves,
Cold or much-tumbled beds –
The small saucepan with one furtive egg,
All he can or all he will
Allow himself – which?

Here broods a latent poetry
Nobody reads.
The weed that has managed flowers,
Pinched in a crack,
Lays its thin shadow down
In the afternoons; as a new mother will,
In the room below.

Jackdaws are in these chimneys,
Their difficult lives
Reflect our own; but who will be awake
For the luminous dawn
When the young fly for the first time?

Jackdaws seem inimical
To the mosses, disrupt them down
To me, as I clean my step,
Rubbing with bluestone in the old way.
My scour against the world's indifference
To important symbols – the common roof,
Likeness of patterns.
How warm this moss is,
In my cross hand! A miniscule forest

Full of see-through deaths
That should have had wings...

'Under one roof'
Is such an old expression,
Steady and parental –
Yet life beneath,
Hidden by the roof, changes pace
Daring and malicious as jackdaws,
Unpredictable
As visiting light: or the one rose-red tile
Flushing up – vanishing.

STILLBORN

There was a child born dead.

Time has bleached out the shocking insult,
Ageing has cicatrised the body's wound.

Still I do not like to prune bushes
That push to the sun ...
Nor put my brush into the spider's house
Where she keeps her children,
Darting with terrible life.

With reluctance, I gouge potatoes
Sprouting intently in a dark bag.

Furtive, I slip one into the earth.
'Grow!' I say. 'Grow, if you must ...'

JUGGED HARE

She mourned the long-ears
Hung in the pantry, his shot fur
Softly dishevelled. She smoothed that,
Before gutting – yet she would rather
Sicken herself, than cheat my father
Of his jugged hare.

A tender lady, freakish as the creature –
But resolute. She peeled it to its tail.
Oh, fortitude! Her rings sparked in and out
Of newspaper wipes. Blood in a bowl,
Sacrificial gravy. A rarely afforded
Bottle of port.

She sustained marriage
On high events, as a child plays house.
Dramas, conciliations –
Today, the hare. She sent me out
To bury the skin,
Tossed the heart to the cat.

She was in full spate.

Fragrance of wine and herbs
Blessed our kitchen; like the hare's dessert
Of wild thyme; or like his thighs
As though braised by God. She smiled

And dished up on willow,
Having a nice touch in framing
One-off scenarios.

After the feast, my father was a lover
Deeply enhanced.
I heard them go to bed,
Kissing – still inside her picture.
Later, I heard her sob
And guessed it was the hare
Troubled her. My father slept,
Stunned with tribute. She lay now
Outside her frame, in the hare's dark

Hating her marital skills
And her lady-hands, that could flense a hare
Because she wooed a man.
In years to come,
I understood.

TOM EARLEY

Tom Earley was born at Mountain Ash in the Cynon Valley on 13 September 1911; his father was a pit-head blacksmith. Educated at Trinity College, Carmarthen, he spent most of his life in London as a teacher of English, latterly at St. Dunstan's College in Catford. A lifelong pacifist and libertarian socialist, he joined the Peace Pledge Union in 1937 and was closely involved with the Campaign for Nuclear Disarmament and the Committee of 100. He was also a member of Plaid Cymru, took a keen interest in Welsh affairs, and learned to speak the language while following a course at the City Literary Institute in London. He died in Bloomsbury on 30 October 1998. His four books of poems are *Welshman in Bloomsbury* (1966), *The Sad Mountain* (1970), *Rebel's Progress* (1979), and *All These Trees* (1992). Almost all his poems refer to his upbringing in South Wales and are, for the most part, wry comments on life in the industrial valleys.

TIDDLERS

Here where the road now runs to Aberdare
the old canal lay stagnant in its bed
of reeds and rushes housing dragonflies
which flashed from sunshine into willow shade.

Beneath this very bridge we came to fish
for roach and perch and other smaller fry
like minnows, sticklebacks, and tiny frogs
and all these smelt peculiarly of pits.

A smell of stinkhorn-fungus, coal and damp
still clung to them as though they had swum up
some subterranean passage from the mine.

They smelt the house out when we got them home
and, when we changed the water, always died:
clean water killed them.

REBEL'S PROGRESS

When idle in a poor Welsh mining valley,
Dissatisfied with two pounds five a week,
I got invited to a marxist rally
And found to my amazement I could speak.

I soon could spout about the proletariat,
The bourgeoisie and strikes and lockouts too,
Could run an AGM or commissariat
As well as boss-class secretaries do.

At first I joined Aneurin Bevan's party
But soon got disillusioned with all that,
Joined Harry Pollitt and became a commy.
They turned down all my pacifism flat.

The hungry thirties found me hunger marching
To squat with Hannington inside the Ritz.
Then PPU. For just this I'd been searching
Before the war and long before the blitz.

I liked the people in the Peace Pledge meeting
But found that they were holier than me
So marched with Collins and quite soon was greeting
My former comrades in the CND.

To sit with Russell next became my hobby,
Vanessa Redgrave's fame I hoped to share.
Got thrown around in Whitehall by a bobby
And then a broken arm in Grosvenor Square.

So now I'll leave the politics to others
And not be an outsider any more.
I'll go back to the valley, to my mother's,
And never set my foot outside the door.

Except to go to chapel on Bryn Sion
And maybe join the Cwmbach male voice choir,
I'll sit at home and watch the television
And talk about the rugby by the fire.

BRENDA CHAMBERLAIN

Brenda Chamberlain was born in Bangor on 17 March 1912. In 1931 she went to train as a painter at the Royal Academy Schools in London and five years later, after marrying the artist-craftsman John Petts, settled at Tŷ'r Mynydd, above the village of Llanllechid, near Bethesda in Caernarfonshire. During the Second World War, while working as a guide searching Snowdonia for lost aircraft, she temporarily gave up painting in favour of poetry and worked, with her husband, on the production of the *Caseg Broadsheets*, a series of six which included poems by Dylan Thomas, Alun Lewis, and Lynette Roberts. In 1947, her marriage ended, she went to live on Bardsey (Ynys Enlli), a small island off the tip of the Llŷn peninsula, where she remained until 1961. After six years on the Greek island of Ydra, she returned to Bangor; it was there, depressed and with financial problems, she died from an overdose of sleeping tablets on 11 July 1971. She described the rigours and excitements of her life on Bardsey in *Tide Race* (1962) and the island also inspired many of her paintings, which are now highly prized. Her only book of verse, *The Green Heart* (1958), contains fifty-two poems reflecting her life in Llanllechid, on Bardsey and in Germany where she had an unhappy relationship with a man she had met before the war. Her poems are intensely passionate in their response to life and death, painterly in their imagery, and at the same time simple and utterly confident.

TO DAFYDD COED MOURNING HIS
MOUNTAIN-BROKEN DOG

Tears that you spill, clown David, crouched by rock,
Have changed to nightmare quartzite, chips of granite.
The valley chokes with grief-stones wept from eyes
New-taught that death-scythes flash in the riven block
To reap warm entrails for a raven-harvest.
Withdrawn in the stone-shot gully of the barren ground;
You mourn, baffled by crevice and goat height
Proving tricksy as dog-fox run to earth on the scree,
For one who lies in company of beetle-shard and sheep,
For him whose loose dropped brain and lungs hang coldly
Trembling from the flowered ledge down iceplant ways to
                                                    silence.
The tears you shed are stone. So leave the dead to stand as
                                                    monument.
Be shepherd friend again, clown grinning under wet eyes,
Stopping your ears to sound the valley breeds;
A corpse-man's cry for succour, a dead dog's howl.

YOU, WHO IN APRIL LAUGHED

You, who in April laughed, a green god in the sun;
Sang in the bowel-rock below me
Words unknown: but how familiar-strange
Your voice and presence. Other quests
But led to this; to lie unseen and watch,
From cloud-ascending rib and slab of stone
Your downward passage, greendrake-garmented:
A blade of wheat, watered in desolation.

O love in exile now,
I keep the hill paths open for you; call
The shifting screes, warm rock, the corniced snows
To witness, that no wall
Precipitous, ice-tongued, shall ever stand
Between us, though we rot to feed the crow.

TALYSARN

Bone-aged is my white horse;
Blunted is the share;
Broken the man who through sad land
Broods on the plough.

Bone-bright was my gelding once;
Burnished was the blade;
Beautiful the youth who in green Spring
Broke earth with song.

ISLANDMAN

Full of years and seasoned like a salt timber
The island fisherman has come to terms with death.
His crabbed fingers are coldly afire with phosphorus
From the night-sea he fishes for bright-armoured herring.

Lifting his lobster pots at sunrise,
He is not surprised when drowned sailors
Wearing ropes of pearl round green throats,
Nod their heads at him from underwater forests.

His black-browed wife who sits at home
Before the red hearth, does not guess
That only a fishscale breastplate protects him
When he sets out across ranges of winter sea.

DEAD PONIES

There is death enough in Europe without these
Dead ponies on the mountain.
They are the underlining, the emphasis of death.
It is not wonderful that when they live
Their eyes are shadowed under mats of hair.
Despair and famine do not gripe so hard
When the bound earth and sky are kept remote
Behind clogged hairs.

The snows engulfed them, pressed their withered haunches
flat,
Filled up their nostrils, burdened the cage of their ribs.
The snow retreated. Their bodies stink to heaven,
Potently crying out to raven hawk and dog:
Come! Pick us clean; cleanse our fine bones of blood.

They were never lovely save as foals,
Before their necks grew long, uncrested;
But the wildness of the mountain was in their stepping,
The pride of Spring burnt in their haunches,
They were tawny as the rushes of the marsh.

The prey-birds have had their fill, and preen their feathers:
Soft entrails have gone to make the hawk arrogant.

R. S. THOMAS

Ronald Thomas was born in Cardiff on 29 March 1913; he later added Stuart to his name in deference to his snobbish mother. Since his father was in the Merchant Navy, the family had to move from place to place before settling in Holyhead when the only child was five. After reading Classics at the University College of North Wales, Bangor, he received his theological training at St. Michael's College in Llandaf, in Cardiff. Ordained deacon in the Church in Wales in 1936 and priest in the year following, he held two curacies in north-east Wales, first at Chirk in Denbighshire and then at Hanmer in Flintshire. According to his auto-biography, it was while gazing westward at the hills of North Wales that he first found himself attracted to the notion that he might be Welsh. He became rector of Manafon in Montgomeryshire in 1942, and there began to learn Welsh, taking it to be the *sine qua non* of Welsh nationality, though it was not the language of most of his parishioners. In Manafon he wrote the poems in *The Stones of the Field* (1946), *An Acre of Land* (1952) and *The Minister* (1955), which were collected in his first substantial book, *Song at the Year's Turning* (1955). Here the peasant Iago Prytherch makes his first appearances, a complex persona who is, by turns, the poet's confidant, spokesman, protagonist and *alter ego*. Here, too, are the poems lamenting the passing of the upland way of life as the attraction of towns, depopulation and the influx of English settlers take their toll. In 1954, partly to draw closer to Welsh-speaking Wales, R. S. Thomas moved to Eglwys-fach, a village in northern Cardiganshire a few miles south of Machynlleth. There too he found more English people than Welsh in his congregation, though the district provided him with ample opportunity to watch wild birds. Many of the poems he wrote at this time were caustically anti-English, but also unsparingly bitter in their condemnation of the anglicised Welsh. A lifelong pacifist and member of the Campaign for Nuclear Disarmament, he nevertheless lent moral support to several ultra-Nationalist groups such as Meibion Glyndŵr who burned English holiday homes in Welsh-speaking areas. His poems about Wales began to diminish in number after his move, in 1967, to St Hywyn's, Aberdaron, at the furthermost tip of the Llŷn peninsula. There he found what he had been searching for – a parish where most people spoke Welsh and, having found it, he no longer needed to write about it. Instead he resumed the exploration of those religious and philosophical themes which he had read in the work of philosophers such as Kierkegaard. Many of the poems in *Not That He Brought Flowers* (1968), *H'm* (1972), *Laboratories of the Spirit* (1975), *The Way of It* (1977) and *Frequencies* (1978) are among the finest ever written on religious themes in the English language. Retiring from the Anglican priesthood in 1978, the poet went to live in a cottage at Y Rhiw, near Pwllheli, where he entered his last prolific phase. His *Collected Poems 1945-1990* appeared in 1993. In 1996, his first wife having died five years before, he remarried and went to live at Pentre-felin in Gwynedd, and it was there he died on 25 September 2000. R. S. Thomas shares with Dylan Thomas the distinction of being one of the two greatest Welsh poets writing in English during the 20th century. His poems on specifically Welsh subjects are harsh and unremitting in their 'winnowing of the people', as he once described his function as a poet, but those of his later phase written out of his discourse with God – 'that great absence in our lives' – command the admiration of a wide readership. Their language, clipped and pared, draws on a variety of elements, including metaphysical conceits, contradictory propositions, and imagery drawn from physics and cosmological science, ending in an angst mitigated only by his tenacious, questioning and sometimes unorthodox religious belief.

A PEASANT

Iago Prytherch his name, though, be it allowed,
Just an ordinary man of the bald Welsh hills,
Who pens a few sheep in a gap of cloud.
Docking mangels, chipping the green skin
From the yellow bones with a half-witted grin
Of satisfaction, or churning the crude earth
To a stiff sea of clouds that glint in the wind –
So are his days spent, his spittled mirth
Rarer than the sun that cracks the cheeks
Of the gaunt sky perhaps once in a week.
And then at night see him fixed in his chair
Motionless, except when he leans to gob in the fire.
There is something frightening in the vacancy of his mind.
His clothes, sour with years of sweat
And animal contact, shock the refined,
But affected, sense with their stark naturalness.

Yet this is your prototype, who, season by season
Against siege of rain and the wind's attrition,
Preserves his stock, an impregnable fortress
Not to be stormed even in death's confusion.
Remember him, then, for he, too, is a winner of wars,
Enduring like a tree under the curious stars.

THE WELSH HILL COUNTRY

Too far for you to see
The fluke and the foot-rot and the fat maggot
Gnawing the skin from the small bones,
The sheep are grazing at Bwlch-y-Fedwen,
Arranged romantically in the usual manner
On a bleak background of bald stone.

Too far for you to see
The moss and the mould on the cold chimneys,
The nettles growing through the cracked doors,
The houses stand empty at Nant-yr-Eira,
There are holes in the roofs that are thatched with sunlight,
And the fields are reverting to the bare moor.

Too far, too far to see
The set of his eyes and the slow pthisis
Wasting his frame under the ripped coat,
There's a man still farming at Ty'n-y-Fawnog,
Contributing grimly to the accepted pattern,
The embryo music dead in his throat.

CYNDDYLAN ON A TRACTOR

Ah, you should see Cynddylan on a tractor.
Gone the old look that yoked him to the soil;
He's a new man now, part of the machine,
His nerves of metal and his blood oil.
The clutch curses, but the gears obey
His least bidding, and lo, he's away
Out of the farmyard, scattering hens.
Riding to work as a great man should,
He is the knight at arms breaking the fields'
Mirror of silence, emptying the wood
Of foxes and squirrels and bright jays.
The sun comes over the tall trees
Kindling all the hedges, but not for him
Who runs his engine on a different fuel.
And all the birds are singing, bills wide in vain,
As Cynddylan passes proudly up the lane.

WELSH HISTORY

We were a people taut for war: the hills
Were no harder, the thin grass
Clothed them more warmly than the coarse
Shirts our small bones.
We fought, and were always in retreat,
Like snow thawing upon the slopes
Of Mynydd Mawr; and yet the stranger
Never found our ultimate stand
In the thick woods, declaiming verse
To the sharp prompting of the harp.

Our kings died, or they were slain
By the old treachery at the ford.
Our bards perished, driven from the halls
Of nobles by the thorn and bramble.

We were a people bred on legends,
Warming our hands at the red past.
The great were ashamed of our loose rags
Clinging stubbornly to the proud tree
Of blood and birth, our lean bellies
And mud houses were a proof
Of our ineptitude for life.

We were a people wasting ourselves
In fruitless battles for our masters,
In lands to which we had no claim,
With men for whom we felt no hatred.

We were a people, and are so yet.
When we have finished quarrelling for crumbs
Under the table, or gnawing the bones
Of a dead culture, we will arise
And greet each other in a new dawn.

WELSH LANDSCAPE

To live in Wales is to be conscious
At dusk of the spilled blood
That went to the making of the wild sky,
Dyeing the immaculate rivers

In all their courses.
It is to be aware,
Above the noisy tractor
And hum of the machine
Of strife in the strung woods,
Vibrant with sped arrows.
You cannot live in the present,
At least not in Wales.
There is the language for instance,
The soft consonants
Strange to the ear.
There are cries in the dark at night
As owls answer the moon,
And thick ambush of shadows,
Hushed at the fields' corners.
There is no present in Wales,
And no future;
There is only the past,
Brittle with relics,
Wind-bitten towers and castles
With sham ghosts;
Mouldering quarries and mines;
And an impotent people,
Sick with inbreeding,
Worrying the carcase of an old song.

EVANS

Evans? Yes, many a time
I came down his bare flight
Of stairs into the gaunt kitchen

With its wood fire, where crickets sang
Accompaniment to the black kettle's
Whine, and so into the cold
Dark to smother in the thick tide
Of night that drifted about the walls
Of his stark farm on the hill ridge.

It was not the dark filling my eyes
And mouth appalled me; not even the drip
Of rain like blood from the one tree
Weather-tortured. It was the dark
Silting the veins of that sick man
I left stranded upon the vast
And lonely shore of his bleak bed.

A BLACKBIRD SINGING

It seems wrong that out of this bird,
Black, bold, a suggestion of dark
Places about it, there yet should come
Such rich music, as though the notes'
Ore were changed to a rare metal
At one touch of that bright bill.

You have heard it often, alone at your desk
In a green April, your mind drawn
Away from its work by sweet disturbance
Of the mild evening outside your room.

A slow singer, but loading each phrase
With history's overtones, love, joy

And grief learned by his dark tribe
In other orchards and passed on
Instinsctively as they are now,
But fresh always with new tears.

FARM WIFE

Hers is the clean apron, good for fire
Or lamp to embroider, as we talk slowly
In the long kitchen, while the white dough
Turns to pastry in the great oven,
Sweetly and surely as hay making
In a June meadow; hers are the hands,
Humble with milking, but still now
In her wide lap as though they heard
A quiet music, hers being the voice
That coaxes time back to the shadows
In the room's corners. O, hers is all
This strong body, the safe island
Where men may come, sons and lovers,
Daring the cold seas of her eyes.

THOSE OTHERS

A gofid gwerin gyfan
Yn fy nghri fel taerni tân.
Dewi Emrys

I have looked long at this land,
Trying to understand
My place in it – why,
With each fertile country

143

So free of its room,
This was the cramped womb
At last took me in
From the void of unbeing.

Hate takes a long time
To grow in, and mine
Has increased from birth;
Not for the brute earth
That is strong here and clean
And plain in its meaning
As none of the books are
That tell but of the war

Of heart with head, leaving
The wild birds to sing
The best songs; I find
This hate's for my own kind,
For men of the Welsh race
Who brood with dark face
Over their thin navel
To learn what to sell;

Yet not for them all either,
There are still those other
Castaways on a sea
Of grass, who call to me,
Clinging to their doomed farms;
Their hearts though rough are warm
And firm, and their slow wake
Through time bleeds for our sake.

LOOKING AT SHEEP

Yes, I know. They are like primroses;
Their ears are the colour of the stems
Of primroses; and their eyes –
Two halves of a nut.

                    But images
Like this are for sheer fancy
To play with. Seeing how Wales fares
Now, I will attend rather
To things as they are: to green grass
That is not ours; to visitors
Buying us up. Thousands of mouths
Are emptying their waste speech
About us, and an Elsan culture
Threatens us.

                What would they say
Who bled here, warriors
Of a free people? Savagely
On castles they were the sole cause
Of the sun still goes down red.

THE MOOR

It was like a church to me.
I entered it on soft foot,
Breath held like a cap in the hand.
It was quiet.
What God was there made himself felt,
Not listened to, in clean colours
That brought a moistening of the eye,
In movement of the wind over grass.

145

There were no prayers said. But stillness
Of the heart's passions – that was praise
Enough; and the mind's cession
Of its kingdom. I walked on,
Simple and poor, while the air crumbled
And broke on me generously as bread.

IN CHURCH

Often I try
To analyse the quality
Of its silences. Is this where God hides
From my searching? I have stopped to listen,
After the few people have gone,
To the air recomposing itself
For vigil. It has waited like this
Since the stones grouped themselves about it.
These are the hard ribs
Of a body that our prayers have failed
To animate. Shadows advance
From their corners to take possession
Of places the light held
For an hour. The bats resume
Their business. The uneasiness of the pews
Ceases. There is no other sound
In the darkness but the sound of a man
Breathing, testing his faith
On emptiness, nailing his questions
One by one to an untenanted cross.

RESERVOIRS

There are places in Wales I don't go:
Reservoirs that are the subconscious
Of a people, troubled far down
With gravestones, chapels, villages even;
The serenity of their expression
Revolts me, it is a pose
For strangers, a watercolour's appeal
To the mass, instead of the poem's
Harsher conditions. There are the hills,
Too; gardens gone under the scum
Of the forests; and the smashed faces
Of the farms with the stone trickle
Of their tears down the hills' side.

Where can I go, then, from the smell
Of decay, from the putrefying of a dead
Nation? I have walked the shore
For an hour and seen the English
Scavenging among the remains
Of our culture, covering the sand
Like the tide and, with the roughness
Of the tide, elbowing our language
Into the grave we have dug for it.

KNEELING

Moments of great calm,
Kneeling before an altar
Of wood in a stone church

In summer, waiting for the God
To speak; the air a staircase
For silence; the sun's light
Ringing me, as though I acted
A great rôle. And the audiences
Still; all that close throng
Of spirits waiting, as I,
For the message.
                    Prompt me, God;
But not yet. When I speak,
Though it be you who speak
Through me, something is lost.
The meaning is in the waiting.

VIA NEGATIVA

Why no! I never thought other than
That God is that great absence
In our lives, the empty silence
Within, the place where we go
Seeking, not in hope to
Arrive or find. He keeps the interstices
In our knowledge, the darkness
Between stars. His are the echoes
We follow, the footprints he has just
Left. We put our hands in
His side hoping to find
It warm. We look at people
And places as though he had looked
At them, too; but miss the reflection.

THE BRIGHT FIELD

I have seen the sun break through
to illuminate a small field
for a while, and gone my way
and fogotten it. But that was the pearl
of great price, the one field that had
the treasure in it. I realize now
that I must give all that I have
to possess it. Life is not hurrying

on to a receding future, nor hankering after
an imagined past. It is the turning
aside like Moses to the miracle
of the lit bush, to a brightness
that seemed as transitory as your youth
once, but is the eternity that awaits you.

THE OTHER

There are nights that are so still
that I can hear the small owl calling
far off and a fox barking
miles away. It is then that I lie
in the lean hours awake listening
to the swell born somewhere in the Atlantic
rising and falling, rising and falling
wave on wave on the long shore
by the village, that is without light
and companionless. And the thought comes

of that other being who is awake, too,
letting our prayers break on him,
not like this for a few hours,
but for days, years, for eternity.

THE WHITE TIGER

It was beautiful as God
must be beautiful; glacial
eyes that had looked on
violence and come to terms

with it; a body too huge
and majestic for the cage in which
it had been put; up
and down in the shadow

of its own bulk it went,
lifting, as it turned,
the crumpled flower of its face
to look into my own

face without seeing me. It
was the colour of the moonlight
on snow and as quiet
as moonlight, but breathing

as you can imagine that
God breathes within the confines
of our definition of him, agonising
over immensities that will not return.

A MARRIAGE

We met
      under a shower
of bird-notes.
      Fifty years passed,
love's moment
      in a world in
servitude to time.
      She was young;
I kissed with my eyes
      closed and opened
them on her wrinkles.
      'Come,' said death,
choosing her as his
      partner for
the last dance. And she,
      who in life
had done everything
      with a bird's grace,
opened her bill now
      for the shedding
of one sigh no
      heavier than a feather.

DYLAN THOMAS

Dylan Thomas was born in Swansea on 27 October 1914 to parents whose roots were in rural, Welsh-speaking Carmarthenshire and Cardiganshire, counties the poet often visited as a boy; the farm Fernhill, near Llangain, where his aunt Ann Jones and her husband lived, was a favourite place of his. The poet's father was Senior English Master at Swansea Grammar School, where his son was a pupil between 1925 and 1931 but where he excelled in nothing except English. He had no other formal education and the fifteen months he spent as a junior reporter with the *South Wales Daily Post* were to be his only term of full-time employment. The four notebooks he kept between 1930 and 1934, by which time he was living in London, became the major source of his poetry until the end of the 1930s. In July 1937 he married Caitlin Macnamara and, in the following year, they went to live in Laugharne, Carmarthenshire. During the Second World War, having been found physically unfit for military service, he wrote radio and film scripts and took part in radio programmes broadcast by the BBC. In 1944 the Thomases went to live in New Quay, Cardiganshire, then in or near Oxford, and finally, in 1949, with their three children, made their home in the Boat House, Laugharne. Heavy drinking, a rumbustious lifestyle and the writer's fecklessness in financial matters brought their problems.

He nevertheless continued to write both verse and prose: his autobiographical short stories *Portrait of the Artist as a*

Young Dog appeared in 1940 and *Quite Early One Morning*, a selection of his broadcast work, posthumously in 1954. He had already published *18 Poems* (1934), *Twenty-five Poems* (1936) and *The Map of Love* (1939), and a fourth collection, *Deaths and Entrances*, appeared in 1946; he had also managed to complete his 'play for voices', *Under Milk Wood*. The writer visited the USA four times between 1950 and 1953, to great acclaim and primarily because he needed the large fees he could command there. His *Collected Poems 1934-1952* were published on 10 November 1952. It was during the last of his American tours that he collapsed in his hotel after a bout of drinking and he died at St Vincent's Hospital in New York on 10 November 1953. His body was brought back for burial in the churchyard at Laugharne, where his grave and the Boat House have become places of pilgrimage for his admirers in many parts of the world.

The poetry of Dylan Thomas is meticulously crafted and relies for its emotional power on the musical resources of the English language and a wide field of reference, not least imagery from the Bible and sometimes the oratory of the Welsh pulpit. In specifically Welsh terms, much of his work derives from unresolved tensions which arise from living imaginatively between two cultures, that of English-speaking Swansea and that of Welsh-speaking west Wales. As he matured as a poet, he moved away from a modish Surrealism and his early fascination with bodily functions, including the sexual, and attained a new lyricism in less obscure poems inspired by other people, the natural scene and his own boyhood.

The number of books about his life and work grows with every year that passes, for public and critical interest in him shows no sign of abating. It is regrettable, however, that the excesses of his bohemian way of life and the bally-hoo surrounding his premature death have tended to mask the high seriousness of his art and his influence on modern poetry in the latter half of the twentieth century.

THE FORCE THAT THROUGH THE
GREEN FUSE DRIVES THE FLOWER

The force that through the green fuse drives the flower
Drives my green age; that blasts the roots of trees
Is my destroyer.
And I am dumb to tell the crooked rose
My youth is bent by the same wintry fever.

The force that drives the water through the rocks
Drives my red blood; that dries the mouthing streams
Turns mine to wax.
And I am dumb to mouth unto my veins
How at the mountain spring the same mouth sucks.

The hand that whirls the water in the pool
Stirs the quicksand; that ropes the blowing wind
Hauls my shroud sail.
And I am dumb to tell the hanging man
How of my clay is made the hangman's lime.

The lips of time leech to the fountain head;
Love drips and gathers, but the fallen blood
Shall calm her sores.
And I am dumb to tell a weather's wind
How time has ticked a heaven round the stars.

And I am dumb to tell the lover's tomb
How at my sheet goes the same crooked worm.

ESPECIALLY WHEN THE OCTOBER WIND

Especially when the October wind
With frosty fingers punishes my hair,
Caught by the crabbing sun I walk on fire
And cast a shadow crab upon the land,
By the sea's side, hearing the noise of birds,
Hearing the raven cough in winter sticks,
My busy heart who shudders as she talks
Sheds the syllabic blood and drains her words.

Shut, too, in a tower of words, I mark
On the horizon walking like the trees
The wordy shapes of women, and the rows
Of the star-gestured children in the park.
Some let me make you of the vowelled beeches,
Some of the oaken voices, from the roots
Of many a thorny shire tell you notes,
Some let me make you of the water's speeches.

Behind a pot of ferns the wagging clock
Tells me the hour's word, the neural meaning
Flies on the shafted disk, declaims the morning
And tells the windy weather in the cock.
Some let me make you of the meadow's signs;
The signal grass that tells me all I know
Breaks with the wormy winter through the eye.
Some let me tell you of the raven's sins.

Especially when the October wind
(Some let me make you of autumnal spells,
The spider-tongued, and the loud hill of Wales)
With fists of turnips punishes the land,
Some let me make you of the heartless words.
The heart is drained that, spelling in the scurry
Of chemic blood, warned of the coming fury.
By the sea's side hear the dark-vowelled birds.

THIS BREAD I BREAK

This bread I break was once the oat,
This wine upon a foreign tree
Plunged in its fruit;
Man in the day or wind at night
Laid the crops low, broke the grape's joy.

Once in this wine the summer blood
Knocked in the flesh that decked the vine,
Once in this bread
The oat was merry in the wind;
Man broke the sun, pulled the wind down.

This flesh you break, this blood you let
Make desolation in the vein,
Were oat and grape
Born of the sensual root and sap;
My wine you drink, my bread you snap.

AND DEATH SHALL HAVE NO DOMINION

And death shall have no dominion.
Dead men naked they shall be one
With the man in the wind and the west moon;
When their bones are picked clean and the clean bones
                                                    gone,
They shall have stars at elbow and foot;
Though they go mad they shall be sane,
Though they sink through the sea they shall rise again;
Though lovers be lost love shall not;
And death shall have no dominion.

And death shall have no dominion.
Under the windings of the sea
They lying long shall not die windily;
Twisting on racks when sinews give way,
Strapped to a wheel, yet they shall not break;
Faith in their hands shall snap in two,
And the unicorn evils run them through;
Split all ends up they shan't crack;
And death shall have no dominion.

And death shall have no dominion.
No more may gulls cry at their ears
Or waves break loud on the seashores;
Where blew a flower may a flower no more
Lift its head to the blows of the rain;
Though they be mad and dead as nails,
Heads of the characters hammer through daisies;
Break in the sun till the sun breaks down,
And death shall have no dominion.

AFTER THE FUNERAL
(In memory of Ann Jones)

After the funeral, mule praises, brays,
Windshake of sailshaped ears, muffle-toed tap
Tap happily of one peg in the thick
Grave's foot, blinds down the lids, the teeth in black,
The spittled eyes, the salt ponds in the sleeves,
Morning smack of the spade that wakes up sleep,
Shakes a desolate boy who slits his throat
In the dark of the coffin and sheds dry leaves,
That breaks one bone to light with a judgment clout,
After the feast of tear-stuffed time and thistles
In a room with a stuffed fox and a stale fern,
I stand, for this memorial's sake, alone
In the snivelling hours with dead, humped Ann
Whose hooded, fountain heart once fell in puddles
Round the parched worlds of Wales and drowned each sun
(Though this for her is a monstrous image blindly
Magnified out of praise; her death was a still drop;

158

She would not have me sinking in the holy
Flood of her heart's fame; she would lie dumb and deep
And need no druid of her broken body).
But I, Ann's bard on a raised hearth, call all
The seas to service that her wood-tongued virtue
Babble like a bellbuoy over the hymning heads,
Bow down the walls of the ferned and foxy woods
That her love sing and swing through a brown chapel,
Bless her bent spirit with four, crossing birds.
Her flesh was meek as milk, but this skyward statue
With the wild breast and blessed and giant skull
Is carved from her in a room with a wet window
In a fiercely mourning house in a crooked year.
I know her scrubbed and sour humble hands
Lie with religion in their cramp, her threadbare
Whisper in a damp word, her wits drilled hollow,
Her fist of a face died clenched on a round pain;
And sculptured Ann is seventy years of stone.
These cloud-sopped, marble hands, this monumental
Argument of the hewn voice, gesture and psalm,
Storm me forever over her grave until
The stuffed lung of the fox twitch and cry Love
And the strutting fern lay seeds on the black sill.

A REFUSAL TO MOURN THE DEATH, BY FIRE, OF A CHILD IN LONDON

Never until the mankind making
Bird beast and flower
Fathering and all humbling darkness

Tells with silence the last light breaking
And the still hour
Is come of the sea tumbling in harness

And I must enter again the round
Zion of the water bead
And the synagogue of the ear of corn
Shall I let pray the shadow of a sound
Or sow my salt seed
In the least valley of sackcloth to mourn

The majesty and burning of the child's death.
I shall not murder
The mankind of her going with a grave truth
Nor blaspheme down the stations of the breath
With any further
Elegy of innocence and youth.

Deep with the first dead lies London's daughter,
Robed in the long friends,
The grains beyond age, the dark veins of her mother,
Secret by the unmourning water
Of the riding Thames.
After the first death, there is no other.

POEM IN OCTOBER

It was my thirtieth year to heaven
Woke to my hearing from harbour and neighbour wood
And the mussel pooled and the heron

160

Priested shore
The morning beckon
With water praying and call of seagull and rook
And the knock of sailing boats on the net webbed wall
Myself to set foot
That second
In the still sleeping town and set forth.

My birthday began with the water-
Birds and the birds of the winged trees flying my name
Above the farms and the white horses
And I rose
In rainy autumn
And walked abroad in a shower of all my days.
High tide and the heron dived when I took the road
Over the border
And the gates
Of the town closed as the town awoke.

A springful of larks in a rolling
Cloud and the roadside bushes brimming with whistling
Blackbirds and the sun of October
Summery
On the hill's shoulder,
Here were fond climates and sweet singers suddenly
Come in the morning where I wandered and listened
To the rain wringing
Wind blow cold
In the wood faraway under me.

Pale rain over the dwindling harbour
And over the sea wet church the size of a snail
With its horns through mist and the castle
Brown as owls
But all the gardens
Of spring and summer were blooming in the tall tales
Beyond the border and under the lark full cloud.
There could I marvel
My birthday
Away but the weather turned around.

It turned away from the blithe country
And down the other air and the blue altered sky
Streamed again a wonder of summer
With apples
Pears and red currants
And I saw in the turning so clearly a child's
Forgotten mornings when he walked with his mother
Through the parables
Of sun light
And the legends of the green chapels

And the twice told fields of infancy
That his tears burned my cheeks and his heart moved in
mine.
These were the woods the river and sea
Where a boy
In the listening
Summertime of the dead whispered the truth of his joy
To the trees and the stones and the fish in the tide.

And the mystery
Sang alive
Still in the water and singingbirds.

And there could I marvel my birthday
Away but the weather turned around.   And the true
Joy of the long dead child sang burning
In the sun.
It was my thirtieth
Year to heaven stood there then in the summer noon
Though the town below lay leaved with October blood.
O may my heart's truth
Still be sung
On this high hill in a year's turning.

THE HUNCHBACK IN THE PARK

The hunchback in the park
A solitary mister
Propped between trees and water
From the opening of the garden lock
That lets the trees and water enter
Until the Sunday sombre bell at dark

Eating bread from a newspaper
Drinking water from the chained cup
That the children filled with gravel
In the fountain basin where I sailed my ship
Slept at night in a dog kennel
But nobody chained him up.

Like the park birds he came early
Like the water he sat down
And Mister they called Hey mister
The truant boys from the town
Running when he had heard them clearly
On out of sound

Past lake and rockery
Laughing when he shook his paper
Hunchbacked in mockery
Through the loud zoo of the willow groves
Dodging the park keeper
With his stick that picked up leaves.

And the old dog sleeper
Alone between nurses and swans
While the boys among willows
Made the tigers jump out of their eyes
To roar on the rockery stones
And the groves were blue with sailors

Made all day until bell time
A woman figure without fault
Straight as a young elm
Straight and tall from his crooked bones
That she might stand in the night
After the locks and chains

All night in the unmade park
After the railings and shrubberies

The birds the grass the trees the lake
And the wild boys innocent as strawberries
Had followed the hunchback
To his kennel in the dark.

DO NOT GO GENTLE INTO THAT GOOD NIGHT

Do not go gentle into that good night,
Old age should burn and rave at close of day;
Rage, rage against the dying of the light.

Though wise men at their end know dark is right,
Because their words had forked no lightning they
Do not go gentle into that good night.

Good men, the last wave by, crying how bright
Their frail deeds might have danced in a green bay,
Rage, rage against the dying of the light.

Wild men who caught and sang the sun in flight,
And learn, too late, they grieved it on its way,
Do not go gentle into that good night.

Grave men, near death, who see with blinding sight
Blind eyes could blaze like meteors and be gay,
Rage, rage against the dying of the light.

And you, my father, there on the sad height,
Curse, bless, me now with your fierce tears, I pray.
Do not go gentle into that good night.
Rage, rage against the dying of the light.

IN MY CRAFT OR SULLEN ART

In my craft or sullen art
Exercised in the still night
When only the moon rages
And the lovers lie abed
With all their griefs in their arms,
I labour by singing light
Not for ambition or bread
Or the strut and trade of charms
On the ivory stages
But for the common wages
Of their most secret heart.

Not for the proud man apart
From the raging moon I write
On these spindrift pages
Nor for the towering dead
With their nightingales and psalms
But for the lovers, their arms
Round the griefs of the ages,
Who pay no praise or wages
Nor heed my craft or art.

CEREMONY AFTER A FIRE RAID

I

Myselves
The grievers
Grieve

Among the street burned to tireless death
A child of a few hours
With its kneading mouth
Charred on the black breast of the grave
The mother dug, and its arms full of fires.

Begin
With singing
Sing
Darkness kindled back into beginning
When the caught tongue nodded blind,
A star was broken
Into the centuries of the child
Myselves grieve now, and miracles cannot atone.

Forgive
Us forgive
Us your death that myselves the believers
May hold it in a great flood
Till the blood shall spurt,
And the dust shall sing like a bird
As the grains blow, as your death grows, through our heart.

Crying
Your dying
Cry,
Child beyond cockcrow, by the fire-dwarfed
Street we chant the flying sea

In the body bereft.
Love is the last light spoken.   Oh
Seed of sons in the loin of the black husk left.

II

I know not whether
Adam or Eve, the adorned holy bullock
Or the white ewe lamb
Or the chosen virgin
Laid in her snow
On the altar of London,
Was the first to die
In the cinder of the little skull,
O bride and bride groom
O Adam and Eve together
Lying in the lull
Under the sad breast of the head stone
White as the skeleton
Of the garden of Eden.

I know the legend
Of Adam and Eve is never for a second
Silent in my service
Over the dead infants
Over the one
Child who was priest and servants,

Word, singers, and tongue
In the cinder of the little skull,
Who was the serpent's
Night fall and the fruit like a sun,
Man and woman undone,
Beginning crumbled back to darkness
Bare as the nurseries
Of the garden of wilderness.

III

Into the organpipes and steeples
Of the luminous cathedrals,
Into the weathercocks' molten mouths
Rippling in twelve-winded circles,
Into the dead clock burning the hour
Over the urn of sabbaths
Over the whirling ditch of daybreak
Over the sun's hovel and the slum of fire
And the golden pavements laid in requiems,
Into the bread in a wheatfield of flames,
Into the wine burning like brandy,
The masses of the sea
The masses of the sea under
The masses of the infant-bearing sea
Erupt, fountain, and enter to utter for ever
Glory glory glory
The sundering ultimate kingdom of genesis' thunder.

FERN HILL

Now as I was young and easy under the apple boughs
About the lilting house and happy as the grass was green,
    The night above the dingle starry,
        Time let me hail and climb
    Golden in the heydays of his eyes,
And honoured among wagons I was prince of the apple
                          towns
And once below a time I lordly had the trees and leaves
        Trail with daisies and barley
    Down the rivers of the windfall light.

And as I was green and carefree, famous among the barns
About the happy yard and singing as the farm was home,
    In the sun that is young once only,
        Time let me play and be
    Golden in the mercy of his means,
And green and golden I was huntsman and herdsman, the
                          calves
Sang to my horn, the foxes on the hills barked clear and
                          cold,
        And the sabbath rang slowly
    In the pebbles of the holy streams.

All the sun long it was running, it was lovely, the hay
Fields high as the house, the tunes from the chimneys, it
                          was air
    And playing, lovely and watery
        And fire green as grass.

And nightly under the simple stars
As I rode to sleep the owls were bearing the farm away,
All the moon long I heard, blessed among stables, the
                                                    night-jars
        Flying with the ricks, and the horses
        Flashing into the dark.

And then to awake, and the farm, like a wanderer white
With the dew, come back, the cock on his shoulder: it
                                                    was all
        Shining, it was Adam and maiden,
            The sky gathered again
And the sun grew round that very day.
So it must have been after the birth of the simple light
In the first, spinning place, the spellbound horses walking
                                                    warm
        Out of the whinnying green stable
            On to the fields of praise.

And honoured among foxes and pheasants by the gay
                                                    house
Under the new made clouds and happy as the heart was
                                                    long,
        In the sun born over and over,
            I ran my heedless ways,
        My wishes raced through the house high hay
And nothing I cared, at my sky blue trades, that time
                                                    allows
In all his tuneful turning so few and such morning songs
        Before the children green and golden
            Follow him out of grace,

Nothing I cared, in the lamb white days, that time would
　　　　　　　　　　　　　　　　　　　　　take me
Up to the swallow thronged loft by the shadow of my
　　　　　　　　　　　　　　　　　　　　　　hand,
　　　In the moon that is always rising,
　　　　　　Nor that riding to sleep
　　　I should hear him fly with the high fields
And wake to the farm forever fled from the childless land.
Oh as I was young and easy in the mercy of his means,
　　　　　Time held me green and dying
　　　Though I sang in my chains like the sea.

ALUN LEWIS

Alun Lewis was born on 1 July 1915 at Cwmaman, a mining village near Aberdare; both his parents were schoolteachers and his father later became the town's Director of Education. The family took summer holidays at Penbryn in Cardiganshire, one of the poet's favourite places. He was educated at Cowbridge Grammar School, the University College of Wales, Aberystwyth, where he read History, and at Manchester University. In 1938 he joined the staff of the Lewis Boys' School, Pengam, enjoying a reputation as a gifted teacher, but in 1940, despite his pacifist convictions, resigned from the post and joined the Army as a commissioned officer. He found the life of the officers' mess uncongenial, preferring the company of his men, most of whom were from the valleys of South Wales, but had time to resume the writing of poems and stories which he had begun while at school. In July 1941 he married Gweno Ellis, a teacher of German at Mountain Ash Grammar School. In the autumn of the following year his battalion of the South Wales Borderers was sent to India, where another period of intense literary activity began. The poverty and nihilism of India affected him deeply and he began to suffer bouts of the depression that had dogged him for several years. In January 1944 he went with his regiment to Chittagong in Burma. There, although an Intelligence Officer, he was given permission to move into a forward position facing the Japanese. On 5 March 1944 he was found shot in the head near the officers' latrines; he died of his wounds six hours later. An Army court of inquiry concluded that his death was an accident, though the belief has persisted that he had taken his own life. Despite his comparatively small output – he published only ninety-four poems and twenty-five stories – Alun Lewis was recognized as an accomplished writer during his own short lifetime. Serious, idealistic, devoted to those he loved, particularly his wife, and intent on serving humanity as a writer, he was primarily concerned with what he called 'the twin themes of life and death', exploring them in verse and prose of a high order. His stories appeared in *The Last Inspection* (1943) and the posthumous volume *In the Green Tree*; his *Collected Stories* (ed. Cary Archard) were published in 1994. His two collections of poems are *Raiders' Dawn* (1942) and *Ha! Ha! Among the Trumpets* (1945); his *Collected Poems* (ed. Cary Archard) appeared in 1994 and a selection in the Corgi series in 2003. In everything he wrote there is compassion for the underdog, whether British soldier or Indian peasant, and a fine delight in the natural world, even in the parched landscapes of the sub-continent. His was a tragic vision, forced to early maturity by his military experience, and his death at the age of 28 was undoubtedly the single greatest loss sustained by Welsh letters during the Second World War.

RAIDERS' DAWN

Softly the civilized
Centuries fall,
Paper on paper,
Peter on Paul.

And lovers waking
From the night –
Eternity's masters,
Slaves of Time –
Recognize only
The drifting white
Fall of small faces
In pits of lime.

Blue necklace left
On a charred chair
Tells that Beauty
Was startled there.

ALL DAY IT HAS RAINED

All day it has rained, and we on the edge of the moors
Have sprawled in our bell-tents, moody and dull as boors,
Groundsheets and blankets spread on the muddy ground
And from the first grey wakening we have found
No refuge from the skirmishing fine rain
And the wind that made the canvas heave and flap

175

And the taut wet guy-ropes ravel and snap.
All day the rain has glided, wave and mist and dream,
Drenching the gorse and heather, a gossamer stream
Too light to stir the acorns that suddenly
Snatched from their cups by the wild south-westerly
Pattered against the tent and our upturned dreaming faces.
And we stretched out, unbuttoning our braces,
Smoking a Woodbine, darning dirty socks,
Reading the Sunday papers – I saw a fox
And mentioned it in the note I scribbled home; –
And we talked of girls, and dropping bombs on Rome,
And thought of the quiet dead and the loud celebrities
Exhorting us to slaughter, and the herded refugees;
– Yet thought softly, morosely of them, and as indifferently
As of ourselves or those whom we
For years have loved, and will again
Tomorrow maybe love; but now it is the rain
Possesses us entirely, the twilight and the rain.

And I can remember nothing dearer or more to my heart
Than the children I watched in the woods on Saturday
Shaking down burning chestnuts for the schoolyard's
                                                 merry play,
Or the shaggy patient dog who followed me
By Sheet and Steep and up the wooded scree
To the Shoulder o' Mutton where Edward Thomas brooded
                                                      long
On death and beauty – till a bullet stopped his song.

THE SENTRY

I have begun to die.
For now at last I know
That there is no escape
From Night. Not any dream
Nor breathless images of sleep
Touch my bat's-eyes. I hang
Leathery-arid from the hidden roof
Of Night, and sleeplessly
I watch within Sleep's province.
I have left
The lovely bodies of the boy and girl
Deep in each other's placid arms;
And I have left
The beautiful lanes of sleep
That barefoot lovers follow to this last
Cold shore of thought I guard.
I have begun to die
And the guns' implacable silence
Is my black interim, my youth and age,
In the flower of fury, the folded poppy,
Night.

THE MOUNTAIN OVER ABERDARE

From this high quarried ledge I see
The place for which the Quakers once
Collected clothes, my fathers' home,
Our stubborn bankrupt village sprawled
In jaded dusk beneath its nameless hills;

177

The drab streets strung across the cwm,
Derelict workings, tips of slag
The gospellers and gamblers use
And children scrutting for coal
That winter dole cannot purvey;
Allotments where the collier digs
While engines hack the coal within his brain;
Grey Hebron in a rigid cramp,
White cheap-jack cinema, the church
Stretched like a sow beside the stream;
And mourners in their Sunday best
Holding a tiny funeral, singing hymns
That drift insidious as the rain
Which rises from the steaming fields
And swathes about the skyline crags
Till all the upland gorse is drenched
And all the creaking mountain gates
Drip brittle tears of crystal peace;
And in a curtained parlour women hug
Huge grief, and anger against God.

But now the dusk, more charitable than Quakers,
Veils the cracked cottages with drifting may
And rubs the hard day off the slate.
The colliers squatting on the ashtip
Listen to one who holds them still with tales,
While that white frock that floats down the dark alley
Looks just like Christ; and in the lane
The clink of coins among the gamblers
Suggests the thirty pieces of silver.

I watch the clouded years
Rune the rough foreheads of these moody hills,
This wet evening, in a lost age.

GOODBYE

So we must say Goodbye, my darling,
And go, as lovers go, for ever;
Tonight remains, to pack and fix on labels
And make an end of lying down together.

I put a final shilling in the gas,
And watch you slip your dress below your knees
And lie so still I hear your rustling comb
Modulate the autumn in the trees.

And all the countless things I shall remember
Lay mummy-cloths of silence round my head;
I fill the carafe with a drink of water;
You say, 'We paid a guinea for this bed,'

And then, 'We'll leave some gas, a little warmth
For the next resident, and these dried flowers,'
And turn your face away, afraid to speak
The big word, that Eternity is ours.

Your kisses close my eyes and yet you stare
As though God struck a child with nameless fears;
Perhaps the water glitters and discloses
Time's chalice and its limpid useless tears.

Everything we renounce except our selves;
Selfishness is the last of all to go;
Our sighs are exhalations of the earth,
Our footprints leave a track across the snow.

We made the universe to be our home,
Our nostrils took the wind to be our breath,
Our hearts are massive towers of delight,
We stride across the seven seas of death.

Yet when all's done you'll keep the emerald
I placed upon your finger in the street;
And I will keep the patches that you sewed
On my old battledress tonight, my sweet.

ON EMBARKATION II

Before he sails a man may go on leave
To any place he likes, where he's unknown
Or where he's mentioned with a warm inflection
And hands are shaken up and down the street.
Some men avoid this act of recognition
And make the world a dartboard for their fling;
Oblivion is the colour of brown ale;
Peace is the backseat in the cinema.
But most men seek the place where they were born.

For me it was a long slow day by train.

Just here you leave this Cardiganshire lane,
Here by these milk churns and this telegraph pole,
Latch up the gate and cut across the fields.
Some things you see in detail, those you need;
The raindrops spurting from the trodden stubble
Squirting your face across the reaping meadow,
The strange machine-shaped scarab beetle
His scalloped legs clung bandy to a stalk,
The Jew's-harp bee with saddlebags of gold,
The wheat as thin as hair on flinty slopes,
The harsh hewn faces of the farming folks,
Opinion humming like a nest of wasps,
The dark-clothed brethren at the chapel gates;
And farther on the mortgaged crumbling farm
Where Shonni Rhys, that rough backsliding man
Has found the sheep again within the corn
And fills the evening with his sour oaths;
The curse of failure's in his shambling gait.
At last the long wet sands, the shelving beach,
The green Atlantic, far as eye can reach.
And what is here but what was always here
These twenty years, elusive as a dream
Flowing between the grinding-stones of fact –
A girl's affections or a new job lost,
A lie that burns the soft stuff in the brain,
Lust unconfessed, a scholarship let go
Or gained too easily, without much point –
Each hurt a search for those old country gods
A man takes with him in his native tongue
Finding a friendly word for all things strange,

The firm authentic truth of roof and rain.
And on the cliff's green brink where nothing stirs,
Unless the wind should stir it, I perceive
A child grow shapely in the loins I love.

SONG
(On seeing dead bodies floating off the Cape)

The first month of his absence
I was numb and sick
And where he'd left his promise
Life did not turn or kick.
The seed, the seed of love was sick.

The second month my eyes were sunk
In the darkness of despair,
And my bed was like a grave
And his ghost was lying there.
And my heart was sick with care.

The third month of his going
I thought I heard him say
'Our course deflected slightly
On the thirty-second day – '
The tempest blew his words away.

And he was lost among the waves,
His ship rolled helpless in the sea,
The fourth month of his voyage
He shouted grievously
'Beloved, do not think of me.'

182

The flying fish like kingfishers
Skim the sea's bewildered crests,
The whales blow steaming fountains,
The seagulls have no nests
Where my lover sways and rests.

We never thought to buy and sell
This life that blooms or withers in the leaf,
And I'll not stir, so he sleeps well,
Though cell by cell the coral reef
Builds an eternity of grief.

But oh! the drag and dullness of my Self;
The turning seasons wither in my head;
All this slowness, all this hardness,
The nearness that is waiting in my bed,
The gradual self-effacement of the dead.

THE MAHRATTA GHATS

The valleys crack and burn, the exhausted plains
Sink their black teeth into the horny veins
Straggling the hills' red thighs, the bleating goats –
– Dry bents and bitter thistles in their throats –
Thread the loose rocks by immemorial tracks.
Dark peasants drag the sun upon their backs.

High on the ghat the new turned soil is red,
The sun has ground it to the finest red,

It lies like gold within each horny hand.
Siva has spilt his seed upon this land.

Will she who burns and withers on the plain
Leave, ere too late, her scraggy herds of pain,
The cow-dung fire and the trembling beasts,
The little wicked gods, the grinning priests,
And climb, before a thousand years have fled,
High as the eagle to her mountain bed
Whose soil is fine as flour and blood-red?

But no! She cannot move. Each arid patch
Owns the lean folk who plough and scythe and thatch
Its grudging yield and scratch its stubborn stones.
The small gods suck the marrow from their bones.

Who is it climbs the summit of the road?
Only the beggar bumming his dark load.
Who was it cried to see the falling star?
Only the landless soldier lost in war.

And did a thousand years go by in vain?
And does another thousand start again?

IN HOSPITAL: POONA (I)

Last night I did not fight for sleep
But lay awake from midnight while the world
Turned its slow features to the moving deep
Of darkness, till I knew that you were furled,

Beloved, in the same dark watch as I.
And sixty degrees of longitude beside
Vanished as though a swan in ecstasy
Had spanned the distance from your sleeping side.

And like to swan or moon the whole of Wales
Glided within the parish of my care:
I saw the green tide leap on Cardigan,
Your red yacht riding like a legend there,

And the great mountains, Dafydd and Llewelyn,
Plynlimmon, Cader Idris and Eryri
Threshing the darkness back from head and fin,
And also the small nameless mining valley

Whose slopes are scratched with streets and sprawling graves
Dark in the lap of firwoods and great boulders
Where you lay waiting, listening to the waves –
My hot hands touched your white despondent shoulders

– And then ten thousand miles of daylight grew
Between us, and I heard the wild daws crake
In India's starving throat; whereat I knew
That Time upon the heart can break
But love survives the venom of the snake.

KEIDRYCH RHYS

Keidrych Rhys was born William Ronald Rees Jones at a farm near Bethlehem, in Carmarthenshire, on 26 December 1915. The name by which he was known in literary and journalistic circles was taken from a small river, the Ceidrych, which ran near his home. Educated at Llandovery Grammar School, he found his first job in a bank but was dismissed, and shortly afterwards, at the age of 21, left Wales to seek a career in journalism in London. He launched the influential magazine *Wales* in 1937 and, two years later, married Lynette Roberts, settling at Llan-y-bri in Carmarthenshire. The marriage was put under strain by his prolonged absences from home while serving in the Army and ended in an unhappy divorce in 1949; he then resumed his career as a journalist in London, notably as a Welsh columnist with *The People*, and remarried in 1954. He had an ebullient, quicksilver personality which delighted in gossip and controversy, especially if it involved members of the Welsh Establishment. A fluent Welsh-speaker, he was a lifelong supporter of Plaid Cymru. He was also an indefatigable impresario on behalf of Welsh writers and a gifted editor who did much to promote their work. Among the poets whom he published in *Wales* were Dylan Thomas, Idris Davies and R. S. Thomas. In his last years he dealt in antiquarian books from his home in Hampstead; he died in London on 22 May 1987. He edited, besides two selections of verse by poets serving in the armed forces, the anthology *Modern Welsh Poetry* (1944), which contains work by thirty-seven poets. Most of the poems in his only book, *The Van Pool* (1942), refer to the farming community of his youth and separation from his wife during war service.

THE PRODIGAL SPEAKS

Yes born on Boxing Day among childlike virgin hills
Too isolated for foxhounds even explaining much more than
                                    horoscope hours
Far north of a fox-earth county never seen through rose-
                                    tinted glasses
Middle of war; hamlet called Bethlehem; one shop; chapel.

Almost a second Christ! say; only son of a tenant-
Farmer of hundred odd acres growing corn for red soldiers
Merrily with a daft boy from an industrial school who
Spoke in strange tongue across our great Silurian arc of sky.

Cloudroll over flying brontesque heights; this early photo
Fiery enough this rusty pocket-knife recall now
A two-mile walk to school alone along a Roman road
Geese-fright on common the little sempstress staying a
                                    fortnight.

Wheels scotched below the varnished meadowlands
A jack-in-the-box handed down from a badly-
Loaded trap back from market town steaming pony
Gentle to touch mad dual-purpose bull in lane near thing

Lost to parents for days every summer on black mountain
With endless views once faint after first experience moral
Deadly nightshade plovers eggs wind cool as air
Under dairy slabs the tallest tree in whole Carmarthenshire

187

Where hedging match meant more than holiday by sea
Stitches at sports then poaching salmon Ben Christmas
Dan Joshua the bastards how hold gun snipe otter – bobs
Are symbols to a returning self like mushroom-in-dew oh
                                                    balm!

Country folk all goggle-eyed outside wedding inn
Damp dusks scarecrows whirring in a flickering light
Those secret see-saw spots that were our very own young
                                                    hearts
Before deep crises and Eirlys dead puritans gipsies of
                                        yesterday good-bye!

INTERLUDE

Simply I would sing for the time being
Of the wayward hills I must make my feeling
The rickety bicycle, the language of birds
Caught fishing up the church street for preaching words,
The deacon hawking swedes, the gyppos clapping on
Their way to vans over common's crushed sandstone
And the milk stands so handy to sit upon!
The roadmen laying pipes of local cement
The Italian's chip shop and the village comment
'No reserve; all they know on the tip of their tongue.'
That educated tramp from the lodging-house league.

The lady, the lake, both sleeping, the cattle
Called back through stories, bells silent, a deep down
                                                    rattle,

Comics, rivers well-named, dense gorse floodlights the
                        valley's
Gurgling. Grief in a mailbag; drama on trolleys.
Less and less shoeing for smith and farming's polite dying
'Messiah' in the chapel – but a warning, gulls crying
Up at Easter miners off the race's soothing colour.
Oh simply I sing down the masterly contour.

TRAGIC GUILT

No. I'm not an Englishman with a partisan religion.
My roots lie in another region,
Though ranged alongside yours.

But I can sense your stubbornness and your cohesion
And can even feel pride in your recent decisions
That anger reassures.

I know no love for disembodied principles, improbable tales.
The strength of the common man was always the strength
                        of Wales,
Unashamed of her race.

May this be also England's role to bring to birth.
May she draw opposite new powers from the earth.
Huge Shakespeare has his place.

I have felt in my bones comradeship and pity,
I have seen wonders in an open door blitz city.

Amid tremendous history, new pity.

189

YOUTH

I try to remember the things
At home that mean Wales but typical
Isn't translated across
The Channel: I try to create,
Doors grow into masts, love losses
In the village wood, but boyhood's
Fear fled into the pale skeleton
Of the dark mountain, into
The bilingual valley filled
Through a sail-hole of my drying
Feelings. But I try. Lightning
Is different in Wales.

ROLAND MATHIAS

Roland Mathias was born on 4 September 1915 at Ffynnon Fawr, a farmhouse in Glyn Collwn above Talybont-on-Usk in Breconshire. His father, an Army chaplain, served in Germany after the First World War and the boy was educated at British military schools in that country and at Caterham School and Jesus College, Oxford, where he read Modern History. Both his parents were Welsh but only his father was Welsh-speaking and the language of the home was English. During the Second World War he refused military conscription on Christian pacifist grounds and was jailed twice for his stand. After teaching for some years in England, he returned to Wales in 1948 as headmaster of Pembroke Dock Grammar School, a post he held until 1958 when he was appointed headmaster of The Herbert Strutt School at Belper in Derbyshire. In 1969, in order to return to Wales and devote his time fully to writing, he resigned from the headmastership of King Edward's Five Ways School in Birmingham and settled in Brecon. He died there on 16 August 2007. His contribution to the study of Welsh writing in English, as editor, critic, anthologist, historian, poet and short-story writer was very substantial. It began in 1949 when he was among the founders of *Dock Leaves*, which later became *The Anglo-Welsh Review*; he was the magazine's editor from 1961 to 1976. Among his most important works of criticism are *A Ride through the Wood* (1985) and *Anglo-Welsh Literature: an Illustrated History* (1987). With

Raymond Garlick he edited the anthology *Anglo-Welsh Poetry 1480-1990* (1990). He has published nine volumes of poetry: *Days Enduring* (1942), *Break in Harvest* (1946), *The Roses of Tretower* (1952), *The Flooded Valley* (1960), *Absalom in the Tree* (1971), *Snipe's Castle* (1979), and *A Field at Vallorcines* (1996); his selected poems, entitled *Burning Brambles*, appeared in 1983 and his *Collected Poems* under the editorship of Sam Adams in 2002. Almost all his writing, but particularly his poetry, has to do with the history, people and topography of Wales, especially the Border areas. Although it shows no major change over the years, his poetry is highly personal and, in the later books, increasingly religious in tone, for he was always a Christian poet who was not afraid to let his moral conscience speak. Its occasional complexities, usually a matter of allusion or erudition, are lightened by its vivid language, robust rhythms and meticulous craftsmanship.

CRASWALL

With a long stirrup under fern
From a small blast of oaks and thorn
The shepherd scours the circling hill
And the sharp dingle creeping to the well.

A trickle from the canting neck
A pony coughing in the track
Are all the stranger hears, and steep
Among the fern the threading of the sheep.

This is the boundary: different burs
Stick, stones make darker scars
On the road down: nightingales
Struggle with thorn-trees for the gate of Wales.

THE FLOODED VALLEY

My house is empty but for a pair of boots:
The reservoir slaps at the privet hedge and uncovers the roots
And afterwards pats them up with a slack good will:
The sheep that I market once are not again to sell.
I am no waterman, and who of the others will live
Here, feeling the ripple spreading, hearing the timbers grieve?
The house I was born in has not long to stand:
My pounds are slipping away and will not wait for the end.

I will pick up my boots and run round the shire
To raise an echo louder than my fear.
Listen, Caerfanell, who gave me a fish for my stone,
Listen, I am alone, alone.
And Grwyney, both your rivers are one in the end
And are loved. If I command
You to remember me, will you, will you,
Because I was once at noon by your painted church of Patricio?
You did not despise me once, Senni, or run so fast
From your lovers. And O I jumped over your waist
Before sunrise or the flower was warm on the gorse.
You would do well to listen, Senni. There is money in my purse.

So you are quiet. All of you, and your current set away
Cautiously from the chapel ground in which my people lie...
Am I not Kedward, Prosser, Morgan, whose long stones
Name me despairingly and set me chains?
If I must quarrel and scuff in the weeds of another shire
When my pounds are gone, swear to me now in my
                                                    weakness, swear
To me poor you will plant a stone more in this tightening field
And name there your latest dead, alas your unweaned
                                                    feeblest child.

                        A LAST RESPECT

The sun, disinterested, summer on either side
Of the watershed, glanced along every road
In the county. It was a weather just
For a last progress, a proportion of death
In the hazels' cardust and the early yellowing
Of the lake trees, of life too, tetchy and pale
In the blown colts that the cold cliff of winter
Would rear into stallions. The processional cars
Had sound, yes, but a small sound like dust
Dropping on dust and the rush of hedgerows
Touched and not touched, a sound like a sigh
Caught in the tunnel of hazels and falling
Back, wheel by wheel, bowing and hollowing
Towards the minor hierarchies of grief.
It was July: there was no want of leaf.
Flowers the shire over were not hard to come by.

The lane was south. Above Cantref hazed green
Shoulders held up the farther points, the pinnacles
Of Sion, and their shimmer was an eye
Over the dying world, a blood that the dead
Plead by and pilgrims when they wake.
The settled dust on the hazels looked less grey
Than the new dust raised as the wheeling drift held on
Slowly towards those mountains, no move
Of mouth or limb. Sure as the heart empties
The last thick syllables dissuade the tongue.

In this hiatus when no stolid ghost respires
All that was left of breath suddenly ruffed the flowers
On the bier ahead. The hearse, its guttural base,
Ground into some declivity of gear and all
But the elm and brass handles had air
About it and petals flying, impassioned as
Wings, an arc of will prescribed, mounting
And Sion crying, quick in the eyelash second.

Who are you to say that my father, wily
And old in the faith, had not in that windflash abandoned
His fallen minister's face?

DEPARTURE IN MIDDLE AGE

The hedges are dazed as cock-crow, heaps of leaves
Brushed back to them like a child's hair
After a sweat, and clouds as recently bundled
Out of the hollows whimper a little in the conifers higher up.
I am the one without tears, cold

195

And strange to myself as a stepfather encountered
For the first time in the passage from the front door.

But I cannot go back, plump up the pillow and shape
My sickness like courage. I have spent the night in a shiver:
Usk water passing now was a chatter under the Fan
When the first cold came on. They are all dead, all,
Or scattered, father, mother, my pinafore friends,
And the playground's echoes have not waited for my return.
Exile is the parcel I carry, and you know this,
Clouds, when you drop your pretences and the hills clear.

ABSALOM IN THE TREE

Hey, friend, I have been here a long time
Even if by my youth you would not think it.
The blood's half-purple stammers in my head,
My hands and feet are marrowfat, heavy
As feathers, unfit for the delicacies of undoing.
In the past hour impenitently this crown
Of shouldered gold, capillaried from the heart
Upwards, has agreed to let me down a bare
Inch, but understandably I have grown
Too little, even with brain at stretch, for
Ground to reach toe or anklewards to take
The strain. You seem a fellow unlikely to miss much.
Cut me down.

You must have got wind of the battle, man.
I take it you are my age, so bound to know

What the issues are. And now I look
At your sword-hilt and jerkin I can see
You were one of mine when the sun was higher
And the day in doubt. No, don't groan
Or deny the cause. There was a kind of glory,
Wasn't there, in breaking up their axioms
About their prurient heads and one by one
Bawling out the freedoms not to be kept from us
In this age we make? The kingdom, ah the kingdom
Of moods, of our celebratory rage! For its sake
Cut me down.

You are considering what? Your prior duty?
But that's a word to keep for those with rules
To break. Are we not opportunists, you
And I, life-tasters for a consummate generation?
But you slip away, the calculating pieties
Abroad in your face. Go, go. David my father, alone
And agonising, will gladden to know of the gold
Alive in this tree, will weep off the sudden lift
Of his eye from the worm and the ranging bone.
But what shall I do with forgiveness? the wry
Face of morality when it is sick? If I'm to be free
For his stock embraces, at least they will have to
Cut me down.

The wood is greener now than at my first hanging.
Ridiculous this freak unjading, happily
Clapping my pudding hands up to the dull
Crawl of the scalp I can barely recollect.

Dismembered, I am still companionable, the avid king
Of a part, coarse lord of pottage and the brown
Sweat-saddle jogging the distances. O I command
Something, yes, the darkness falling across my face
As I swing. Mephibosheth, if you like, grown
Heady, out of place, an arrant mover of trees
By his hair's temper? Yes, that is it. I shake
My kingdom already. Ah, behind me the sticks crack!
Cut me down.

Joab, it wasn't you I expected, with my gold
Tarnished and this arboreal gibe topping
My usual oratory. Old beetle-brow, shudder
Of gall, you showed me how suddenly a blade
Slides under the fifth rib. But tutorially you
Dared not improve on my father, for all your frown.
Didn't I cross your politics too, hear all men
Myself, subject each cause to my cold opinion?
Convention I killed, protocol rather. The crown
Must grasp how much more power by half political
Assassination has than your snickering knifework.
But you look fulfilled, as though you'd picked your hour.
... Cut me ... down ...

INDICTMENT

> Did you, John Arnallt,
> Sitting at table
> In your house at Llanthony,
> Say to your mother Walcot,

Thomas Poore the Irishman
And Harry Prosser, servant
In livery to the treasoned Earl,
That Her Majesty's kitchen
Was poisonous full of Cooks,
Naming Sir Robart Cicill
A Cook by his mother, my Lord
Bacon a Cook by the same
Error, Mr Attorney-
General Cook another,
And Master William Cook of Highnam
Beyond the Dean Forest
No more than a kitchen porter ·
Running hither and back
For the better provision
Of a supper of purges?

Did you, John Arnallt,
Coming out of your cups,
Clap this Prosser, murderer
Of one Stumpe of Walterstone
At Sir Gelly's command,
Cheerly on the shoulder, swearing
There should be no more *cawl*
In Wales till the Earl
Your Master should choke
Those Cooks with their own herbs?

You are a debtor three
Times over, a turbulent

Fellow whose affrays have given cause
For the Judges of Assize
Long to take bond of you.
And your cousins, Morgans
Of Penllwyn Sarff, no better.
A danger to all good
Governaunce you are, John Arnallt.
I name you to my Lord President
Of the Council at Ludlow
But go not from my house
By day because of your clamour
And much shouting.

THEY HAVE NOT SURVIVED

They have not survived,
That swarthy *cenedl*, struggling out
Of the candled tallut, cousins to
Generations of sour hay, evil-looking
Apples and oatmeal porringers.
A quick incontinence of seed
Cried in the barn, a mind to spit
And squat harried the gorse
Into burning, and the melancholy
Rhos burst into plots, as circumscribed
Only as the lean muscle yearning
Carefully for love could lay
Around each house. But of that
Merely a life or two, enough to multiply
Cousins like bloodspots in the wasted
Grass. Then a new swarming, under

An aged queen, before they walked
Their milgis over the ragged hill
They ghosted every shift, farming
A memory of that last-seen
Country that was never theirs.
It was not will was lacking then
So much as instinct, a gift
Of seed for their backyard culture,
A grip on the girl who bears.

They have not survived.
Coughing in terraces above
The coal, their doorsteps whitened
And the suds of pride draining
Away down the numbered
Steps to the dole, they denied
Both past and future, willing
No further movement than the rattle
Of phlegm, a last composure
Of limb and attitude.
For this dark cousinhood only I
Can speak. Why am I unlike
Them, alive and Jack in office,
Shrewd among the plunderers?

PORTH CWYFAN

June, but the morning's cold, the wind
Bluffing occasional rain. I am clear
What brings me here across the stone
Spit to the island, but not what I shall find

When the dried fribbles of seaweed
Are passed, the black worked into the sandgrains
By the tide's mouthing. I can call nothing my own.

A closed-in, comfortless bay, the branchy
Shifts of voyage everywhere. On a slope
Of sand reaching up to the hidden
Field or stretch of marram a tipwhite, paunchy
Terrier sits pat on his marker, yapping me
Bodily out of range. What in God's name is he
Guarding that he thinks I want of a sudden?

To the left is the island, granite-hulled
Against froth, the chapel's roof acute
As Cwyfan put it when the finer
Passions ruled, convergent answers belled
Wetherlike towards God. Ahead is the cliff
Eaten by sand. On the quaking field beyond
Low huts, ordered and menacing. Porth China.

Once on the island those last shingle
Feet I came by seem in threat.
Can you, like Beuno, knit me back severed
Heads, Cwyfan, bond men to single
Living? Your nave has a few wild settles
And phantasmagoric dust. And Roger Parry,
Agent to Owen Bold, has a stone skew-whiff in the yard.

Doubling back again is a small
Inevitable tragedy, the umpteenth

In a sinuous month. Now I avoid
The violent pitch of the dog, with all
And nothing to guard, remark his croup,
The hysteric note in the bark. Two dunlin,
Huffing on long legs, pick in and out of the tide.

A man on the beach, a woman
And child with a red woollen cap
Hummock and stop within earshot,
Eyeing my blundering walk. 'Can
We get to the island?' he asks, Lancastrian
Accent humble, dark curls broad. And I
Am suddenly angry. But how is my tripright sounder,
Save that I know Roger Parry and he does not?

BURNING BRAMBLES

The sea at a distance glints now and again, as though
This upland corner, puzzled with smoke, had a new heart
                                                    to show.

But the land is unhealthy, smelling of green-cut bramble
And rotting sticks; bumps in it, bare of all grass, resemble

Boils that the bold rooting whips had crossed, lanced once
                                                    of their pus
And left, foetid and out of sight. It is an old covert, the fuss

Of discovery long muted: in the back ditch the tins are so
                                                    many

Rust-flakes that part in the fingers, dusting on black bottles
rainy

Yet stoppered, a heap of old sins without consequence, save
Deep in the land's heart where the sods of the field wall gave

Them summons for turbulence. And now there is burning,
sullen
Bramble whips dragged a while since to their pyramid,
crestfallen

But free to strike and trip as they can. The one fire catching,
Out of the gusts from the north-west, needs that quick
watching

That one cannot give who forks and carries recalcitrant
Loops from the pyre lower down, full in the wind, only intent

On freeing himself and not falling, with the burdened fork
Wide of the body. It is a slow excoriation: the whips work

Back on the hand, mindless as snakes but bitter. And the
smoke
Is bitter, making the nose run and the freer arm for its soak

Keep a shirt-cuff handy. Even the flames bite back, leaving
The near scalp smoked and the green rotten smell of the
stalks waving

Threats overhead. The clog of leaves and sticks must be left
Momentarily on the ground. It is enough to unpile and shift

The endless loops of this waste, hearing the crackle behind
And knowing the smell of a life ill lived as it passes down
                                                    wind.

BRECHFA CHAPEL

Not a shank of the long lane upwards
Prepared our wits for the myth, the slimed
Substantiation of the elements. And the coot
With his off-white blaze and queasy paddle
Was an old alarm, the timid in flight
From the ignorant. The lowered shoulder
Of mountain it is, dabbled within the collar,
That shallows and darkens the eye, the first
Slack argent losing the light as bitterly
As the blackened water treads and nibbles
The reeds and bushes afloat in the new
Pool's centre. Beyond, a surviving ray
Points and fondles a reed-knot, the swan
That dreams on it taking no note of stumps
Or visitations. Nearer, however, and shifting
Like pillagers from weed to shore, settling
And starting raucously, hundreds of testy
Black-backs utter their true society, bankrupt
Hatred of strangers and bully unrest whichever
Marge they think themselves forced to. It
Is a militant brabble, staked out by wind
To the cropped-down pasture. Mud and the tricky
Green of the edge contrivingly clap it round
What's left of this latish day that began with love.

Opposite, to the west of the harsh lagoon,
Stands a chapel, shut in its kindred wall
With a score of graves. Legend on one
Cries a minister, dead of the heats in Newport
Before he came twenty-eight, his wife
Rambling on to her eighties. On another a woman
Loosens at thirty, her man afield on the mission
Ploughing till dark. O these stones trouble
The spirit, give look for look! A light from this
Tiny cell brisked in far corners once, the hand held
Steady. But now the black half-world comes at it,
Bleaks by its very doors. Is the old witness done?
The farmers, separate in their lands, hedge,
Ditch, no doubt, and keep tight pasture. Uphill
They trudge on seventh days, singly, putting
Their heads to the pews as habit bids them to,
And keep counsel. The books, in pyramid, sit tidy
On the pulpit. The back gallery looks
Swept. But the old iron gate to the common,
Rusted a little, affords not a glimpse
Of the swan in her dream on the reed-knot
Nor of the anxious coot enquiring of the grasses.
The hellish noise it is appals, the intolerable shilly-
Shally of birds quitting the nearer mud
For the farther, harrying the conversation
Of faith. Each on his own must stand and conjure
The strong remembered words, the unanswerable
Texts against chaos.

EMYR HUMPHREYS

Emyr Humphreys was born in 1919 in Prestatyn, Flint-shire, and brought up English-speaking in a Church-going family at Trelawnyd in the same county. He was educated at the University College of Wales, Aberystwyth, where he read History, learned Welsh and joined Plaid Cymru largely in response to the act of arson carried out by three of the party's leading members at Penyberth in 1936. During the Second World War, as a conscientious objector, he worked on the land and then went as a relief worker to the Middle East, and later to Italy where he was an official of the Save the Children Fund. On his return to Wales in 1946 he married the daughter of a Congregationalist minister, thus discovering the tradition of Welsh Nonconformity which he was to make a central theme of his writing. He has been a teacher in Wimbledon and Pwllheli, a drama producer with the BBC and a lecturer at the University College of North Wales, Bangor, but since 1972 he has lived as a full-time writer, latterly in Anglesey. In 1973 he served a short prison sentence as part of the campaign for a Welsh-language television service, the language being at the core of his politics. Generally regarded as the most distin-guished prose-writer in Wales today, he has published some two dozen novels. The finest single novel is *Outside the House of Baal* (1965), a portrait of a Calvinistic Methodist minister, but his major achievement is the septet of novels known under the collective title *Land of the Living*, which begins with *Flesh and Blood* (1974) and ends with *Bonds of Attachment* (1991). He has also published four books of poems: *Ancestor Worship* (1970), *Landscapes* (1976), *The Kingdom of Brân* (1979), and *Pwyll a Riannon* (1980); a selection of his verse appeared in the *Penguin Modern Poets* series in 1979 and in the Corgi series in 2005, and his *Collected Poems* were published in 1999. Like his novels, his poems seek a valid continuity with the Wales of the past, especially since the advent of Nonconformity, and he has made this quest the subject of all his writing. For a full understanding of his work and his particular view of Wales his book *The Taliesin Tradition* (1983) is essential reading.

ANCESTOR WORSHIP

I

The dead are horizontal and motionless
They take less room
Than the stones which mark the tomb

But the words they spoke
Grow like flowers in the cracked rock

Their ghosts move easily between words
As people move between trees
Gathering days and sunlight
Like fuel for an invisible fire.

II

Grandparents whose portraits hang
Like icons in our hearts
Carved out acres drew up codicils
To brace out lives
But the new estates cover the fields
All the names are changed and their will
Is broken up by sewers and pylons.

III

Our remote ancestors knew better.
They were all poets
They all wove
Syllabic love into their wooden homes

They saw the first invaders come
Pushing their boats through the water meadows
Their teeth and their swords glittering in the stealthy light
And they carved metrical systems out of their own flesh.

IV

The air is still committed to their speech
Their voices live in the air
Like leaves like clouds like rain
Their words call out to be spoken
Until the language dies
Until the ocean changes.

A ROMAN DREAM

The dust of the chariot race is in my hair.
I hide under the laurel bush like a piece of silver.
The guards use ferrets and before dawn they will find me.

Last night the Emperor painted his face green,
We all agreed this was the correct colour.
I was a little drunk. I agreed too much.

His god-like gaze discovered me,
An academic working on his uncle's prose.

I have long admired your style, he said,
But recently I find it makes the content suspect.
Come with me.

With green lips he kissed the short sword
And put it in my hands
With green hands, he exposed the prisoner's ribs,
An unknown prisoner whose face he said
For my sake had been covered.

Here, he said smiling. Here. Between the third and fourth
                                                        ribs.

                                                    Push.

Push.

Whose face was beneath the napkin?

Push.

I wish to be loved by all men
I have spent fifteen hours a day
On Odes to be admired
In addition to my academic work
My research
My teaching duties.

Push.

My contributions to enlightened journals
On the balance of ambition and duty to the state
On the rational content of the Imperial dream
On human dignity

Push

On precision in syntax
On language truth and logic

Push

His royal hand, soft and perfumed, closed over mine
With childlike suddenness pushing

The warm blood hit my face

Sounds came from my throat like vomit

The faces of gods are green, he said, not red.
Would you agree?
I nodded and I nodded.
Will you die for me?

I don't care what you choose but make your choice your own.
Fall on this sword like a Roman
Or swallow poison like a talkative Greek.

The air was cold as marble.

The green god was bored.

Or run to hiding like a rabbit and my guards will hunt you...

If I could get to the hills
Somewehere in Tuscolo beneath my teacher's ruined villa
There is a hiding place and a secret spring.
If I could find the strength to make the journey
There is dry blood on my lips
The dust of the chariot race is in my hair.

GŴR Y RHOS

There is no such thing as the image of a country
For this reason put up this flag for approval:
It is made of skin and stained with sunlight and tobacco
It speaks in pickled phrases the language of apples
And it is wide enough for a shroud.

It remembers the road as a track, pigs
In every sty, a railway running, a harbour
With ships, a quarry working, fresh fish, young people
And planting trees in holes big enough
To bury a horse.

This man is a king except
He makes his living emptying caravan bins
And uses English in the shop to avoid giving offence
To visitors who do not know
Where they are or who he is.

A DEMOCRATIC VISTA

Strange sanctuary this, perched on the rising cornstack
Like a desert saint on a broken pillar
Staring, eyes unstirring until hill field sea are one
The procession of thought blurred
Into the regular rising and falling of a sinewy arm
And the dry rustle of sheaves.
Tom Williams, Guto, Dick Williams, Wil bach, Dafydd Dew
                                                    and me,
We are the people; our conversation is smooth and
                                                    superficial
Like a veneer of grained wood, curves leading nowhere
Which was where they started.
We are the people for whom politicians shout and soldiers
                                                    fight
We sow and reap, eat and sleep, copulate in secret, think

In circumference of one dimension.
We are the sacred people, the secular mystery, the host,
Whitman's elastic deity, Marx's material, Rousseau's noble
                                                        savage
Mayakovsky's beloved –
Tom, Guto, Dic, Wil, Dafie and me –
Reasonably efficient between dawn and sunset
God chewing tobacco, God drinking tea, digesting rice.
We are the people.
God is not mocked.

FROM FATHER TO SON

There is no limit to the number of times
Your father can come to life, and he is as tender as ever he
                                                        was
And as poor, his overcoat buttoned to the throat,
His face blue from the wind that always blows in the outer
                                                        darkness
He comes towards you, hesitant,
Unwilling to intrude and yet driven at the point of love
To this encounter.

You may think
That love is all that is left of him, but when he comes
He comes with all his winters and all his wounds.
He stands shivering in the empty street,
Cold and worn like a tramp at the end of a journey
And yet a shape of unquestioning love that you
Uneasy and hesitant of the cold touch of death
Must embrace.

Then, before you can touch him
He is gone, leaving on your fingers
A little more of his weariness
A little more of his love.

TWENTY-FOUR PAIRS OF SOCKS

In the chest of drawers there are two dozen pairs of warm
                                                    socks.
The man who wore them had the secret of living.
He was prepared at any time to say what it was
so that as far as he was concerned
it was no secret.

When he lived I could not think
that what he believed brought him peace and happiness,
was the true source of content.
If he said FAITH I remembered his ulcer.
Whether installed by heredity or induced by anxiety
an ulcer is surely something that nags,
coaxed to grow in a greenhouse of despair.

If he modestly implied GOOD WORKS by his concern for
                                                    others
and his unswerving devotion to political idealism of the
                                            most naïve kind
I would like to point out that he never cleaned his own
                                                    boots
until his wife died
and as far as I know

no party he voted for or supported ever stood in danger
of being obliged to exercise power.

Sometimes his calm was unnerving
At others, one sock of a pair missing, or some such trifle
he would tremble and erupt –
the burst of red-faced fury
of an angry peasant cheated at a fair.

But mostly he was calm. Nearly always.
(Not counting a certain tremolo when he was swept with
righteous indignation.)
It was generally accepted that he was a good man,
and it pleased him deeply to know that his visits were
welcomed.
In the wards his presence, his nod and bow especially,
did everyone a lot of good.

Everything about him suggested that the secret was not his
own
but something given, something to share that came from a
source outside –
available to all like the warmth of the sun and words.

He was a preacher of course.
The drawers of his desk are packed so tight with sermons
they refuse to open.
His three suits of clerical grey hang in the little wardrobe.
In the chest of drawers there are twenty-four pairs of warm
socks.

HARRI WEBB

Harri Webb was born in Sketty, Swansea, on 7 September 1920, and brought up in Sandfields (St. Helen's), a working-class district of the town. He won a scholarship to Magdalen College, Oxford, where he graduated in the School of Medieval and Modern Languages. In 1941, having volunteered to serve in the Royal Navy, he saw action in the Mediterranean. On his return to Wales he learned Welsh, joined Plaid Cymru and worked briefly for Keidrych Rhys, editor of the magazine *Wales*, but soon left Plaid Cymru, which he found too cautious and pacifist, to join the Welsh Republican Movement. Moving to Cheltenham, he worked in the public library and joined the Labour Party, but returned to Wales in 1954 to take up an appointment as librarian in charge of the Dowlais branch of the Merthyr Tydfil Public Library. The Republican Movement was wound up in 1957 and so, disillusioned with the Labour Party's lukewarm attitude to the question of self-government for Wales, he rejoined Plaid Cymru; he was to edit the party's newspaper for two years and stand as its candidate in Pontypool at the General Election of 1970. Appointed Librarian at Mountain Ash, he moved to Cwmbach in the Cynon Valley in 1972 and, two years later, retired from the library service. He then wrote scripts for radio and television and became a popular reader of his poems, notably on the programme *Poems and Pints*. Having suffered a stroke, he was moved from hospital in Merthyr Tydfil to a nursing home in Swansea. There, on the

217

morning of 31 December 1994, he died in his sleep and, a few days later, was buried in the churchyard at Pennard, in Gower, from where his family had come. He had once described himself as 'a poet with only one theme, one preoccupation' whose work was 'unrepentantly nationalistic'. Most of his poems were written out of a passionate commitment to the cause of Welsh independence. Having studied the poetry of France and Spain, he saw little distinction between politics and poetry and took his role as People's Poet seriously, deliberately writing verse that was accessible and memorable. His poems have not only a historical perspective but also an awareness of contemporary realities; the scarred landscape and democratic traditions of South Wales were a special source of inspiration for him. His early poems appeared, together with those of Meic Stephens and Peter Gruffydd, in *Triad* (1963), but his first full collection was *The Green Desert* (1969) and his second *A Crown for Branwen* (1974); his ballads and squibs are to be found in *Rampage and Revel* (1977) and *Poems and Points* (1983). Perhaps his most famous poem is 'Colli Iaith', a threnody about the fate of the Welsh language. His *Collected Poems* (1995) were edited by Meic Stephens, who has also made selections of his political and literary journalism under the titles *No Half-Way House* (1995) and *A Militant Muse* (1998). A small selection of his poems is to be found in *The Stone Face* (2004).

LOCAL BOY MAKES GOOD

When Christ was born on Dowlais Top
The ironworks were all on stop,
The money wasn't coming in,
But there was no room at the Half Moon Inn.

The shepherds came from Twyn y Waun
And three kings by the Merthyr and Brecon line,
The Star shone over the Beacons' ridge
And the angels sang by Rhymney Bridge.

When Christ turned water into stout
A lot of people were most put out
And wrote cross letters to the paper
Protesting at such a wicked caper.

When Christ fed the unemployed
The authorities were most annoyed;
He hasn't gone through the proper channels,
Said the public men on the boards and panels.

When Christ walked upon Swansea Bay
The people looked the other way
And murmured, This is not at all
The sort of thing that suits Porthcawl.

When Christ preached the sermon on Kilvey Hill
He'd have dropped dead if looks could kill
And as they listened to the Beatitudes
They sniffed with scorn and muttered, Platitudes!

219

When Christ was hanged in Cardiff Jail
Good riddance, said the *Western Mail*,
But, daro, weren't all their faces red
When he came to judge the quick and the dead.

VALLEY WINTER

Under the gas-lamps the wet brown fallen leaves
Glitter like glass of broken beer bottles;
The feast is finished, the hangover remains.
This is the time to walk the Welsh valleys
Under the rain that has been falling for ever
And the days that never dawn hiding the hills.
The mountains have vanished into another world,
The rivers boil black from hell under concrete bridges
And from the lost mountains ponies and sheep come down,
Ghostly refugees in the streets that alone stand.
All the encompassing glory, the heroic crests
And soft voices of an older Wales are abolished
That we saw from every street-corner of our brief summer,
And the black axemen have felled the singing forests.
One day we will climb again the cliffs of clear air,
Walk by the carolling water, redeem our strength
On the high places of the old gods and battles.
But, for now, only the streets are real
Where wet crowds shuffle shopping
And nobody sings or fights, not even the drunks,
Where we wait for buses that are never on time
And drag our feet through fallen, long-fallen leaves.

ROMANTIC PEEPS AT REMOTE PEOPLES

I

We know the Etruscans only from their tombs,
They were a kindly people given to feasting,
To sport, conversation and the pleasures of love.
They excelled in some aspects of the minor arts
But were not very good at organization
And over-preoccupied, it seems, with death.
Their language lingered till historic times
But is now beyond reconstruction, quite extinct.
Their leading families, however, married
Into the Caesars, who could thus make claim
To be sort of Etruscan. They ruled the world
While the grass grew over their ancestral towns.

II

The paschal moon summons them from oblivion,
To its white face they lift the slaughtered lamb,
Old men in robes and turbans, Samaritans
Chanting a liturgy on Mount Gerizim
While keen photographers from *Paris-Match*
Capture the atmosphere of the scene.
But even in the Bible these were heretics
And have been stagnating for two thousand years
In their dead end. Their ceremonial tabernacles
Are English Army surplus bell-tents,
Their scriptures are a mediaeval fake,

They are degenerate from inbreeding,
Are maintained by charity and will soon die out.

III

Acknowledging the undoubted place of God,
It is more prudent to conciliate
His Adversary, say the Yezidi Kurds,
An interesting tribe of Manichees
Who claim, with every show of commonsense,
The Devil rules the world, whoever made it.
But nobody could call them diabolic,
Pathetic would be nearer the truth.
They are poor, ignorant and quite confused,
Not at all sure which obscure sheikh it is
Whose simple shrine serves as their meeting place
To venerate the serpent and the peacock.

IV

Of these a Roman writer has recorded
They fought well among their native forests
But fighting retail were beaten wholesale.
A thousand years later, one of their own sort
Told them, if they would be inseparable
Then they would be insuperable. But
They seem to have been incurably perverse,
Not uniquely so, but certainly fatally.
They have left few traces and these unremarkable,
Which is strange, considering they were said to be,
In their day, a vivid people.

THE BOOMERANG IN THE PARLOUR

Will Webb, a farmer's son from the cliffs of Gower,
Went as a young man to Australia, exchanging
The cramped peninsula for the outback, the frugal
Patchwork of fields for the prodigal spaces he rode
Along the rabbit-fence or under the soaring jarra.
When he came back he brought with him a boomerang
For the front-room mantelpiece, a spearhead chipped by an
                                                      abo
From the green glass of a beer-bottle, an emu-skin rug
And the poems of Banjo Paterson. To me, his son,
He looked for the completion of a journey
Stopped at Gallipoli, that in my turn I'd see
The river of black swans. The map of Australia
Was tattooed on his right arm.
                          And so I have
Another hypothetical Australian self,
The might-have-been man of a clean new empty country
Where nearly all the songs have yet to be sung.
It is this shadow that perhaps has led me
Past islands of enchantment, capes that could have been
Called deception, disappointment and farewell,
To the strange and silent shore where now I stand,
Terra Incognita: a land whose memory
Has not begun, whose past has been forgotten
But for a clutter of nightmares and legends and lies.
This land, too, has a desert at its heart.

THANKS IN WINTER

The day that Eliot died I stood
By Dafydd's grave in Ystrad Fflur,
It was the depth of winter,
A day for an old man to die.
The dark memorial stone,
Chiselled in marble of Latin
And the soft intricate gold
Of the old language
Echoed the weather's colour,
A slate vault over Ffair Rhos,
Pontrhydfendigaid, Pumlumon,
The sheep-runs, the rough pasture
And the lonely whitewashed houses
Scattered like frost, the dwellings
Of country poets, last inheritors
To the prince of song who lies
Among princes, among ruins.
A pilgrim under the yew at Ystrad Fflur
I kept my vow, prayed for my country,
Cursed England, came away

And home to the gas fire and television
News. Caught between two languages,
Both dying, I thanked the long-dead
Minstrel of May and the newly silent
Voice of the bad weather, the precise
Accent of our own time, taught
To the disinherited, offering
Iron for gold.

THE STONE FACE
discovered at Deganwy, Spring 1966

It may of course be John his father-in-law,
Their worst, our best, not easily discernible
After so many buried centuries. The experts
Cannot be sure, that is why they are experts.
But this stone face under a broken crown
Is not an impersonal mask of sovereignty;
This is the portrait of a living man,
And when his grandson burnt Deganwy down
So that no foreign army should hold its strength,
I think they buried the head of Llywelyn Fawr
As primitive magic and for reasons of state.

No fortress was ever destroyed so utterly
As was Deganwy by Llywelyn the Last,
The thoroughness of despair, foreknown defeat
Was in the burning and breaking of its walls.
But at some door or window a hand paused,
A raised crowbar halted by the stare
Of a stone face. The Prince is summoned
And the order given: Bury it in the earth,
There will be other battles, we'll be back –
Spoken in the special Welsh tone of voice
Half banter, half blind fervour, the last look
Exchanged between the hunted living eyes
And dead majesty for whom there are no problems.

The burning of Deganwy, the throne and fortress
Of Llywelyn Fawr shattered, his principality

Gone in the black smoke drifting over Menai
And his last heir forced into endless retreat
To the banks of Irfon and the final lance-thrust.
There was no return, no reverent unearthing.

A stone face sleeps beneath the earth
With open eyes. All history is its dream.
The Great Orme shepherds the changing weather,
On Menai's shores the tides and generations
Ebb, grumble and flow; harps and hymns
Sound and fall silent; briefly the dream flares out of the eyes
Then darkness comes again.

Seven hundred and fifty years of darkness.
Now in a cold and stormy Spring we stand
At the unearthing of the sovereign head,
The human face under the chipped crown.
Belatedly, but not too late, the rendez-vous is made.
The dream and the inheritors of the dream,
The founder and father, and those who must rebuild
The broken fortress, re-establish the throne
Of eagles, here exchange the gaze of eagles
In the time of the cleansing of the eyes.

ISRAEL

Listen, Wales. Here was a people
Whom even you could afford to despise,
Growing nothing, making nothing,
Belonging nowhere, a people
Whose sweat-glands had atrophied,

Who lived by their wits,
Who lived by playing the violin
(A lot better, incidentally,
Than you ever played the harp).
And because they were such a people
They went like lambs to the slaughter.

But some survived (yes, listen closer now),
And these are a different people,
They have switched off Mendelssohn
And tuned in to Maccabeus.
The mountains are red with their blood,
The deserts are green with their seed.
Listen, Wales.

SYNOPSIS OF THE GREAT WELSH NOVEL

Dai K lives at the end of a valley. One is not quite sure
Whether it has been drowned or not. His Mam
Loves him too much and his Dada drinks.
As for his girlfriend Blodwen, she's pregnant. So
Are all the other girls in the village – there's been a Revival.
After a performance of Elijah, the mad preacher
Davies the Doom has burnt the chapel down.
One Saturday night after the dance at the Con Club,
With the Free Wales Army up to no good in the back lanes,
A stranger comes to the village; he is, of course,
God, the well-known television personality. He succeeds
In confusing the issue, whatever it is, and departs
On the last train before the line is closed.
The colliery blows up, there is a financial scandal

Involving all the most respected citizens; the Choir
Wins at the National. It is all seen, naturally,
Through the eyes of a sensitive boy who never grows up.
The men emigrate to America, Cardiff and the moon. The girls
Find rich and foolish English husbands. Only daft Ianto
Is left to recite the Complete Works of Sir Lewis Morris
To puzzled sheep, before throwing himself over
The edge of the abandoned quarry. One is not quite sure
Whether it is fiction or not.

A CROWN FOR BRANWEN

I pluck now an image out of a far
Past and a far place, counties away
On the wrong side of Severn, acres
Of alien flint and chalk, the smooth hills
Subtly, unmistakeably English, different.
I remember, as if they were China, Sinodun,
Heaven's Gate and Angel Down, the White Horse
Hidden from the eye of war, Alfred at Wantage,
His bodyguard of four Victorian lamp-posts
And his country waiting for another enemy
Who did not come that summer. Everything
Shone in the sun, the burnished mail of wheat
And hot white rock, but mostly I recall
The long trench.

A thousand years from now
They'll find the line of it, they'll tentatively
Make scholarly conjectures relating it

To Wansdyke, the Icknield Way, Silbury.
They'll never have known a summer
Of tense expectancy that drove
A desperate gash across England
To stop the tanks.

　　　　　　Most clearly I see
The tumbled ramparts of frantic earth
Hastily thrown up, left to the drifting
Seeds of the waste, and the poppies,
Those poppies, that long slash of red
Across the shining corn, a wound, a wonder.

Lady, your land's invaded, we have thrown
Hurried defences up, our soil is raw,
New, shallow, the old crops do not grow
Here where we man the trench. I bring
No golden-armoured wheat, the delicate dance
Of oats to the harvest is not for me nor
The magic spears of barley, on this rough stretch
Only the poppies thrive. I wreathe for you
A crown of wasteland flowers, let them blaze
A moment in the midnight of your hair
And be forgotten when the coulter drives
A fertile furrow over our old wars
For the strong corn, our children's bread.
Only, Princess, I ask that when you bring
Those bright sheaves to the altar, and you see
Some random poppies tangled there, you'll smile,
As women do, remembering dead love.

JOHN STUART WILLIAMS

John Stuart Williams was born on 13 August 1920 at Mountain Ash, in the Cynon Valley. From the harsh conditions prevailing in that mining village during his boyhood he learned the Socialism to which he remained true for the rest of his life. Educated at University College, Cardiff, he began his career as an English teacher at Whitchurch Grammar School before his appointment in 1956 as Head of the Department of English and Drama at the City of Cardiff College of Education. He died in Cardiff on 26 January 2001. He made a significant contribution to Welsh writing in English as teacher, critic, editor and poet: he taught it to his students, wrote extensively about Alun Lewis and, with Meic Stephens, edited *The Lilting House* (1969), the first authoritative attempt to present selections from the work of twentieth-century Welsh poets in English. His four collections of poems are *Last Fall* (1962), *Green Rain* (1967), *Dic Penderyn* (1970) and *Banna Strand* (1975); the penultimate book includes a long poem for radio about the Merthyr Rising of 1831.

GWYNT TRAED Y MEIRW

The dead-foot wind creeps from the east
its razor open wide.
It shaves the people from the streets
and wipes them off inside.

The sign-board of the Butcher's Arms
clicks sadly in the air.
The bar shines like a coffin-lid,
you'll find no comfort there.

An empty bus runs like a hearse
upon the blackened road.
Though no one sits upon its seats
it carries an icy load.

So put your sheepskin jacket on,
your cosy fur-lined boots;
muffle up your winter fears,
the sap's shrunk to the roots.

However warm your secret thoughts,
whatever you've been told
by fat psychiatrist or priest,
the feet of the dead are cold.

OVERKILL

Now gooth sunne under woode:
Me reweth, Marye, thy faire rode.
Now gooth sunne under tree:
Me reweth, Marye, thy sone and thee.

A funnelled rage of fire and dust;
Me reweth, Marye, thy lost trust.
A whirlpool coiled in flesh and bone:
Me reweth, Marye, thee and thy sone.

The ravelled fibres of the cross:
Me reweth, Marye, thee and thy loss.
The signet fish burnt from the sand;
Me reweth, Marye, the broken bond.

The tree is split and fused in flame:
Me reweth, Marye, thy fair name.
The sun drags a barren stone:
Me reweth, Marye, thee and thy sone.

232

LAST WORDS

Oak-tree and ash
death in the morning,
fine words awash.

Cypress and yew;
garland of flowers,
footsteps in dew.

Laurel and bay;
I'd give them both
for the sweet smell of hay.

Rowan and birch;
summer in autumn,
nothing in church.

Acacia and plane;
we move from the dead
to the living again.

Tamarisk and pine;
you bow to your gods,
I'll stick to mine.

T. H. JONES

Thomas Henry Jones, known to family and friends as Harri, was born on 21 December 1921 at Cwm Crogau, a smallholding near Llanafan Fawr in northern Breconshire, and went to school in Builth. His people were Welsh-speaking but his mother spoke only English and he was brought up without the language. His studies in the English Department at the University College of Wales, Aberystwyth, were interrupted by war service with the Royal Navy, during which he saw action in the Mediterranean, but he completed them in 1947 and, two years later, took a master's degree for a thesis on the English metaphysical poets. His first job was teaching English at the Dockyard School for naval apprentices in Portsmouth; he also lectured for the Workers' Educational Association. In 1959, having failed to find a university post in Wales or England, he took up an appointment at the University of New South Wales in Australia, where he settled with his wife Madeleine and three small daughters. A handsome man and a fine reader of his own work, he was popular in literary and academic circles, but nevertheless prone to depression and given to bouts of heavy drinking. On the night of 29 January 1965 he failed to return home and, early next morning, was found drowned in an old rock bathing pool near his home. His ashes were returned to Wales and scattered in the churchyard of Llanfihangel Brynpabuan, not far from Cwm Crogau. His first collection, *The Enemy in the Heart* (1957), explored the tensions between a cultivated sensibility and the constraints of Puritanism, and showed the influence of Dylan Thomas, on whom he wrote a monograph in the *Writers and Critics* series. With his second, *Songs of a Mad Prince* (1960), he found his own voice, and in his third, *The Beast at the Door* (1963), which reflects his response to Australia and is much concerned with an expatriate's view of Wales, he wrote some of his finest poems. By the time of his death the dramatic complexity of his poems, and the vivid imagery and colloquial language he habitually used, had come to maturity. A passionate man who yearned for an ideal state of love which normal human intercourse could not provide, he used his gifts to record the despair and joy through which his search led him. In his synthesis of Eden, Wales, love and deracination, and able neither to escape nor draw sustenance from the religious faith of his childhood, he failed to find the contentment he craved but left us poems which, in their anguish, seem essentially modern. A posthumous volume, *The Colour of Cockcrowing*, was published in 1966 and his *Collected Poems* (ed. Julian Croft and Don Dale-Jones) in 1977. A selection of his poems appeared in the Corgi series in 2004.

POEM FOR MADELEINE

An ocean or embrace away
The weeping of my love fulfils
The sensual vision and the prayer.
Lost in the clarity of day,
Bewildered in the hurt of air,
My words are rain her sorrow spills.

A century or kiss ago
The generations in her eyes
Answered my urgency of prayer.
Now with the words I do not know
The vision in the random air
Of absence casually dies.

O love upon the distant shore,
O love so absent from my nights,
O image of my ecstasies,
O love, grant pardon to me for
Estranging time, estranging seas,
And all refusal of delights.

And grant me pardon, love, for pride
Expert in disobedience.
Forgive me that I could not reach
You when your longing cried.
And grant me pardon, love, for each
Failure of will, deceit of sense.

DIFFERENCE

Under God's violent unsleeping eye
My fathers laboured for three hundred years
On the same farm, in the expected legend.
Their hymns were anodynes against defeat,
But sin, the original and withering worm,
Was always with them, whether they excelled

In prayers, made songs on winter nights,
Or slobbered in temptation, women, drink.

I inherit their long arms and mountain face,
The withering worm sleeps too within my blood
But I know loneliness, unwatched by God.

GORSE IDYLL

Her hair was like the sunlit gorse,
　　Her body like the gorse on fire,
And what we knew of souls we'd take
　　To any fair for hire.

I took her to the golden gorse,
　　We made a gold to-do.
No deacon sighed with such content
　　As we, when we were through.

Deacons and gorse in any land
　　Would be so far apart –
And all the lands I walk through now
　　I have a double heart.

RHIANNON

My daughter of the Mabinogion name
Tells me Ayer's Rock is ten times higher than
A house, and she, being seven today,
Would like to see it, especially

To ride there on a camel from Alice Springs.
She also says she wants to be a poet –
Would the vision of that monolith
Stay in her mind and dominate her dreams
As in my mind and dreams these thirty years
There stays the small hill, Allt-y-clych,
The hill of bells, bedraggled with wet fern
And stained with sheep, and holding like a threat
The wild religion and the ancient tongue,
All the defeated centuries of Wales?

LAND OF MY FATHERS

Some frosty farmers fathered me to fare
Where their dreams never led, the sunned and blue
Salt acres where Menelaus once made ado
Because Paris also thought Helen was fair;
And now this ancient sunburnt country where
Everything's impossibly bright and new
Except what happens between me and you
When I ransack your bright and ravished hair.

Always I feel the cold and cutting blast
Of winds that blow about my native hills,
And know that I can never be content
In this or any other continent
Until with my frosty fathers I am at last
Back in the old country that sings and kills.

A CONFUSION OF BRIGHT WOMEN

It was a confusion of bright women troubled
Me this morning between sleeping and waking,
The jargon of their names making a twittering
In my head and their too well remembered bodies
Making in mine the usual disturbance.

Olwen, and Blodwen, Mary, Jane, and Anne,
Megan and Deborah and Marguerite,
Came back like ghosts to stir my ghostly blood.
All honest housewives now, or maybe dead,
Though still for me causing this bright confusion.

And some indeed were daughters of the swan,
And others, though not beautiful, were merry girls.
Their hair of different colours, and their eyes.
Go from me now, trilling your tender names,
Forgotten girls I once was glad to know.

One had a mole like Imogen, and one
Was witty even in the morning, and one
Would sulk for hours, rejecting kisses.
How am I tangled still in those endearments
Murmured to your sweet and bygone names.

Comfort myself against this bright confusion
In this uncertain time between sleeping and waking.
If I should call you by some other name,
What matter so that I hold you rightly
And make this poem for you, only for you?

BACK?

(to R. S. Thomas)

Back is the question
Carried to me on the curlew's wing,
And the strong sides of the salmon.

Should I go back then
To the narrow path, the sheep turds,
And the birded language?

Back to an old, thin bitch
Fawning on my spit, writhing
Her lank belly with memories:

Back to the chapel, and a charade
Of the word of God made by a preacher
Without a tongue:

Back to the ingrowing quarrels,
The family where you have to remember
Who is not speaking to whom:

Back to the shamed memories of Glyn Dŵr
And Saunders Lewis's aerodrome
And a match at Swansea?

Of course I'd go back if somebody'd pay me
To live in my own country
Like a bloody Englishman.

But for now, lacking the money,
I must be content with the curlew's cry
And the salmon's taut belly

And the waves, of water and of fern
And words, that beat unendingly
On the rocks of my mind's country.

GIRL READING JOHN DONNE

Her arms bare, and her eyes naked,
She tells her borrowed book, *I am in love*,
And the fierce poem jumps about under her skin.

Mr, the almost anonymous lecturer
Who prescribed this text for her undoing,
When he said *Goodmorrow* to his shaving self,
Remembered how she crossed her legs in class,
Thought vaguely of writing a poem, a declaration,
But after breakfast went on marking assignments.

The girl sits blazing in the Library,
Alight over the poem to which she says
I am in love, I am in love. And the poem's
Words flame up to her unseeing eyes.
She does not need to read, only remember
The poem says *I love* to her exposed
And wanted flesh.
                    She reads naked in the Library.

Mr every now and again is deflected
From his marking, boredom, marking time,
To wonder momentarily if he was right
To ask of vulnerable innocence
What it thinks about the imprisonment
Of a great Prince.
                           His automatic pencil,
Cancelling an ampersand, dismisses
The futile question. He feels morally secure
Because he didn't interrogate them,
Her, about her, his favourite Elegie.
At that minding of bed's America
He resolutely goes on marking.

                                        It's marking time.

And the naked girl in the Library
Reads a naked poem to herself, and says
I am in love, I am in love, over and over
Until the poem's canicule and sear
Become unbearable, when she burns out
To dissertate over a coke or coffee
On anything, anything except this poem,
This love, bare longing, that bed, this poem.

And elsewhere a great Prince in prison lies.

BUILTH WELLS

A picture of a town beside a river:
Schoolcaps, girls' knickers, French letters,
And French teachers, beside the sylvan Wye:
How beautifully my memories lie.

Builth, Buallt, spa of no renown,
But sprawled about the grassy Groe,
Along the brawling reaches of the Wye,
Where I'll go home to die.

Small town, home of a great footballer
And of a greater choir, O Builth.
Stay small beside my memoried Wye
Where all my poems lie.

ROBERT MORGAN

Robert Morgan was born on 17 April 1921 in Bargoed, Glamorgan, but his family moved to Penrhiw-ceibr in the Cynon Valley when he was an infant and it was there he grew up. He left school at the age of fourteen to work with his father in the local colliery. In 1947, having written a short story for the South Wales Miners' Eisteddfod which was critical of the conditions existing underground after nationalization of the mines, he was offered a place at Fircroft College in Birmingham and in 1953 qualified as a teacher at Bognor Regis College of Education. For many years he taught boys with special needs at a school in Portsmouth. He died at his home in Denmead on 6 August 1994. Besides short stories, novels, an autobiography and verse-plays, he published about a dozen booklets of verse, almost all of which is about mines and miners, as were his paintings. The principal ones are *The Night's Prison* (1967), *On the Banks of Cynon* (1975) and *Voices in the Dark* (1976); his *Selected Poems* appeared in three volumes in 1993. Although his experiences as a collier left an indelible mark on him, he made no political points in his writing and was content simply to describe the hardship, dangers and comradeship of the miner's life.

VILLAGE

The village clings to the hill breast.
The stubborn grey streets, drenched
Under cloud tears, know patience,
Toil and grief. A Wesley chapel,
Rich with musical silence, sags
Under the slow tide of the hill slag.
Below, a pit, bunched with metal
And dust, smokes and trembles above earth
Holes lamplit with men and boys
At work in rocky danger and darkness.

The village clings to the hill breast
And women wait meekly in this bleak
Place, as women have waited for a century,
For the shift's end and the safe return
Of the last man and boy to a warmth hearth.

BLOOD DONOR

The searching was easy and memory ripens
On the grey earth picture of Rees
In his grimy vest soaked in blood.
Forty-eight years under tense rock
Had stripped him like a tree with roots
In slag and marked him with texture of strain
And accident. But it was slow legs
And dust-worn eyes that were to blame.

245

The iron rock-bar was still in his hands
Held like a spear of a fallen warrior.
The rocks had dyed his silver hair red
And the heavy bar was warm and worn.
Blind flies swarmed in the blood-sweat
Air and the tough men with bruised
Senses were gentle, using distorted
Hands like women arranging flowers.

On the way out through roads of rocky
Silence you could sense images of confusion
In the slack chain of shadows. Muscles
Were nerve-tight and thoughts infested
With wrath and sharp edges of fear.
Towards the sun's lamp we moved, taking
Home the dark prisoner in his shroud of coats.

PETER HELLINGS

Peter Hellings was born in Swansea on 1 August 1921. During the Second World War he was employed in the Harbour Office of the Great Western Railway, and was working in the town's docklands in February 1941 when they were bombed by the Luftwaffe. He then joined the RAF, serving in Africa and the Middle East, and afterwards took a degree in English at University College, Swansea, but left Wales in 1952 to become a teacher in the Birmingham area. On his retirement in 1985 he returned to live at Coed-y-bryn, near Llandysul in Cardiganshire. He died on 24 September 1994. His first book of poems, *Firework Music*, appeared in 1950. A number of privately printed booklets, including *A Swansea Sketchbook* (1983), all written after his return to Wales, were collected under the title *A Form of Words: an autobiography in verse* and published posthumously in 1995; this book consists, for the most part, of a long sonnet sequence reflecting the places in Wales, England and France which meant most to him. His *Selected Poems* appeared in 1998. With his French wife Madeleine, he translated a selection of ballades, *Versions of Villon* (1999).

ACADEMIC FESTIVAL

*On the occasion of the Swansea University College
Graduation Ceremony at the Brangwyn Hall*

I Congregation of the Waters

The crowds flow in, dull floods along dry channels
In midsummer.
                Splashes of recognition
Flatter, and humour and chatter without intermission
Raise a herd rumour under symbolic panels
Pinker than life, an empire scoured of fleas,
Indecently riotous for daylight.
                      Still they stream
Dazing the ushers to a fish-dark dream
With furious little rivers and big tributaries
Assembling into a lake of ruffled conjecture:
When are the prizes, when will we see our son
Rewarded, slaving and labour done, and the lecture
Be read, and the praises,
                when will we see our daughter
Ascend the dais,
           not as of old for the slaughter,
But flowerless, and clad in black, and with all her clothes
                           on...

II Entry of the Pedagogues

This is a silent splendour. The crowd stands.
Here are no drums and trumpets, paraphernalia
Of power, attendant sandwich-men and bands,

248

Strumpets and bums – that would indeed be a failure
Of tact, to those whom we owe respect.
                                    They come
Heralded by the thunder of their feet
On carpet, twisted heads and curious hum
Of those standing and waiting in awe to greet
The black gowns bellowing silently, the blare
Of scarlet hoods, green facings trimmed with fur
Mounting the stage as furtively as they dare
Wearing disguise:
                        for well they know the stir
These soundless trumpetings arouse, and therefore
Uneasily wear them like the trumpery of a whore.

III Honoured in Welsh

The court and senate seated, and each new graduate
Honoured in Welsh.
                        But here's no dragon fire
Of eloquence, though the Welsh tongue's a great
Conjuror, and can set a flag on fire
As at Llyn, Carmarthenshire, and still carries great weight
And is even lovelier sung.
                        But there's no choir,
The Chairs are harder and more forbidding of late
Lamented professors, and each new bard is a liar
Boasting two tongues which always can be blended
But never completely divided. There lies our weakness.
The young man lifts his head:
                        there is a sickness

Asleep in the soil, where tongues, like roots are tended.
Our birth with the world's blood was tainted,
so
Pure Welsh is a dark flower we failed to grow.

IV Invocation to the Mastersinger

Polite applause flies up, a flight of pigeons
Scattered by handclaps' rapid rifle fire
That sends this tame praise sweeping round a spire
To settle again, like faiths and dead religions,
And sunlit dust.
For whom is this applause
But that mediaeval image on the stage,
A burning, stooping, gaunt dark man, who draws
Over his sober coat the heritage
And air of timelessness,
as if he walked
Clear out of context, and had at his bed's head
Twenty volumes of Aristotle bound in red
And handsome black,
yet softly swore, and talked
Despite degree, to any man, and wore
The smiling irony of the learned poor.

V Dance of the Apprentices

There is a sound of revelry, and bright
Eyes mirror lights, and at last trumpets sound;
Intelligent conversations, and the trite

War records worn with repetition, drowned
In clattering glasses, swiftly degenerate
To a ghost's memory shot with lust and beer
And lashed with laughter, in which we celebrate
Forgotten triumphs and unconquered fear,
A different fellowship.
                    In the past we were
Apprentices to another war, yet here
With all illusions lost, we would prolong
Victories time has reversed:
                              the old
Are scrupulously romantic, while the young
Though cynical, are tremulously bold.

MOTLEY

Two years elapsed; we were sent overseas;
at Wilmslow waiting was not new: routine
inspections of kits, nits and dormitories
and paperpicking squads to keep grass clean.

Behind the library blockhouse where we hid,
a uniformly average motley rout,
none was more motley than the drooping Yid
quoting more poetry than I'd heard about.

Looking up at a girl corporal on a course,
with hands in pockets, drooping fag, he said:
'Excuse me, miss, d'you want to buy a horse?'

From then on that man had to be my friend
on the long voyage that too soon might end:

damned East-End Atheist Russian Jewish Red.

RALPH'S
(by the station)

At seventeen I discovered Dostoyevsky
and Dylan's Twenty-Five; when I was able
in the Arcade I bought Igor Stravinsky
and Beethoven (six shillings a red label).

I dipped into the pool of Everyman,
tasted the sounds of Wagner back to Balfe;
the library kept Diaghilev, Myth and Man,
and French surrealists.
                    Always there was Ralph,

with old and new secondhand unread poets,
theology, Wales, who-dunnits, how-to-do-its.
I spent whole half days reading on my feet.

Because he's gone, there's nowhere much to meet
or wait for trains.
                    In winter wet and cold
his casual words were bound in red and gold.

LESLIE NORRIS

Leslie Norris was born on 21 May 1921 in Merthyr Tydfil. His first job was that of rates clerk in the town hall. Called up for military service with the RAF, he contracted severe blood poisoning within a few weeks, and had to be invalided out. In 1948, anxious to leave post-war Merthyr, he enrolled at the Teacher Training College in Coventry. From 1952 to 1958 he taught at schools in Yeovil and Bath, and was headmaster of Westergate School in Chichester, then lectured at Bognor Regis College of Education. In 1973 he was invited to become Visiting Professor at the University of Washington in Seattle, and so began a long association with American universities. On his return to England, he found himself so unsettled by the experience of America that he resigned his principal lectureship at Bognor Regis and resolved to earn his living by his pen. He made further visits to the United States, spending several months on a small island off the coast of Maine, then in 1983 went to Brigham Young University in Utah. He was soon made Christiansen Professor of Poetry in the English Department there and, in 1989, was appointed Humanities Professor of Creative Writing. In the same year he cut his last physical ties with Wales by selling the cottage at Saron in Carmarthenshire which he had owned since the 1950s. He lived in Orem, not far from Provo, where the Mormon university has its main campus and where he died on 6 April 2006. The town of his birth figures prominently in his writing, though, as with Glyn

Jones, it is to the Merthyr of his boyhood, economically depressed but socially vibrant, that he looked back. The countryside beyond Cefn-coed, especially the Brecon Beacons and the natural world of hill, stream and meadow, often appears in his work. His later poems reflect the looser styles of modern American poetry and the harsher landscapes to which he was drawn. He published a dozen books of poems, some of which are *Finding Gold* (1967), *Ransoms* (1970), *Mountains Polecats Pheasants* (1974), *Islands off Maine* (1977), *Water Voices* (1980), *Sequences* (1988), and *A Sea in the Desert* (1989). His *Selected Poems* appeared in 1986, his *Collected Poems* and *Collected Stories* in 1996, and a small selection of his poems entitled *Water* in the Corgi series in 2004.

AUTUMN ELEGY

September. The small summer hangs its suns
On the chestnuts, and the world bends slowly
Out of the year. On tiles of the low barns
The lingering swallows rest in this timely

Warmth, collecting it. Standing in the garden,
I too feel its generosity; but would not leave.
Time, time to lock the heart. Nothing is sudden
In Autumn, yet the long, ceremonial passion of

The year's death comes quickly enough
As firm veins shut on the sluggish blood
And the numberless protestations of the leaf
Are mapped on the air. Live wood

Was scarce and bony where I lived as a boy.
I am not accustomed to such opulent
Panoply of dying. Yet, if I stare
Unmoved at the flaunting, silent

Agony in the country before a resonant
Wind anneals it, I am not diminished, it is not
That I do not see well, do not exult,
But that I remember again what

Young men of my own time died
In the Spring of their living and could not turn
To this. They died in their flames, hard
War destroyed them. Now as the trees burn

In the beginning glory of Autumn
I sing for all green deaths as I remember
In their broken Mays, and turn
The years back for them, every red September.

EARLY FROST

We were warned about frost, yet all day the summer
Has wavered its heat above the empty stubble. Late
Bees hung their blunt weight,
Plump drops between those simplest wings, their leisure
An ignorance of frost.
My mind is full of the images of summer
And a liquid curlew calls from alps of air;

But the frost has come. Already under trees
Pockets of summer are dying, wide paths
Of the cold glow clean through the stricken thickets
And again I feel on my cheek the cut of winters
Dead. Once I awoke in a dark beyond moths
To a world still with freezing,
Hearing my father go to the yard for his ponies,

His hands full of frostnails to point their sliding
To a safe haul. I went to school,
Socks pulled over shoes for the streets' clear glass,
The early shops cautious, the tall
Classroom windows engraved by winter's chisel,
Fern, feather and flower that would not let the pale
Day through. We wrote in a cold fever for the morning

Play. Then boys in the exulting yard, ringing
Boots hard on winter, slapped with their polishing
Caps the arrows of their gliding, in steaming lines
Ran till they launched one by one
On the skills of ice their frail balance,
Sliding through time with not a fall in mind,
Their voices crying freely through such shouting

As the cold divided. I slid in the depth
Of the season till the swung bell sang us in.
Now insidious frost, its parched grains rubbing
At crannies, moved on our skin.
Our fingers died. Not the warmth
Of all my eight wide summers could keep me smiling.
The circle of the popping stove fell still

And we were early sped through the hurrying dark.
I ran through the bitterness on legs
That might have been brittle, my breath
Solid, grasping at stabs of bleak
Pain to gasp on. Winter branched in me, ice cracked
In my bleeding. When I fell through the teeth
Of the cold at my haven door I could not see

For locked tears, I could not feel the spent
Plenty of flames banked at the range,
Nor my father's hands as they roughed the blue
Of my knees. But I knew what he meant
With the love of his rueful laugh, and my true
World unfroze in a flood of happy crying,
As hot on my cheek as the sting of this present

Frost. I have stood too long in the orderly
Cold of the garden, I would not have again the death
Of that day come unasked as the comfortless dusk
Past the stakes of my fences. Yet these are my
Ghosts, they do not need to ask
For housing when the early frost comes down.
I take them all in, all, to the settled warmth.

THE BALLAD OF BILLY ROSE

Outside Bristol Rovers Football Ground –
The date has gone from me, but not the day,
Nor how the dissenting flags in stiff array
Struck bravely out against the sky's grey round –

Near the Car Park then, past Austin and Ford,
Lagonda, Bentley, and a colourful patch
Of country coaches come in for the match
Was where I walked, having travelled the road

From Fishponds to watch Portsmouth in the Cup.
The Third Round, I believe. And I was filled
With the old excitement which had thrilled
Me so completely when, while growing up,

I went on Saturdays to match or fight.
Not only me; for thousands of us there
Strode forward eagerly, each man aware
Of tingling memory, anticipating delight.

We all marched forward, all except one man.
I saw him because he was paradoxically still,
A stone against the flood, face upright against us all,
Head bare, hoarse voice aloft, blind as a stone.

I knew him at once, despite his pathetic clothes;
Something in his stance, or his sturdy frame
Perhaps, I could even remember his name
Before I saw it on his blind man's tray. Billy Rose.

And twenty forgetful years fell away at the sight.
Bare-kneed, dismayed, memory fled to the hub
Of Saturday violence, with friends to the Labour Club,
Watching the boxing on a sawdust summer night.

The boys' enclosure close to the shabby ring
Was where we stood, clenched in a resin world,
Spoke in cool voices, lounged, were artificially bored
During minor bouts. We paid threepence to go in.

Billy Rose fought there. He was top of the bill.
So brisk a fighter, so gallant, so precise!
Trim as a tree he stood for the ceremonies,
Then turned to meet George Morgan from Tirphil.

He had no chance. Courage was not enough,
Nor tight defence. Donald Davies was sick
And we threatened his cowardice with an embarrassed kick.
Ripped across both his eyes was Rose, but we were tough

And clapped him as they wrapped his blindness up
In busy towels, applauded the wave
He gave his executioners, cheered the brave
Blind man as he cleared with a jaunty hop

The top rope. I had forgotten that day
As if it were dead for ever, yet now I saw
The flowers of punched blood on the ring floor,
As bright as his name. I do not know

How long I stood with ghosts of the wild fists
And the cries of shaken boys long dead around me,
For struck to act at last, in terror and pity
I threw some frantic money, three treacherous pence –

And I cry at the memory – into his tray, and ran,
Entering the waves of the stadium like a drowning man.
Poor Billy Rose. God, he could fight
Before my three sharp coins knocked out his sight.

WATER

On hot summer evenings my aunt set glasses
On a low wall outside the farmhouse,
With some jugs of cold water.
I would sit in the dark hall, or
       Behind the dairy window,
Waiting for children to come from the town.

They came in small groups, serious, steady,
And I could see them, black in the heat,
Long before they turned in at our gate
To march up the soft, dirt road.
       They would stand by the wall,
Drinking water with an engrossed thirst. The dog

Did not bother them, knowing them responsible
Travellers. They held in quiet hands their bags
Of jam sandwiches, and bottles of yellow fizz.
Sometimes they waved a gratitude to the house,
       But they never looked at us.
Their eyes were full of the mountain, lifting

Their measuring faces above our long hedge.
When they had gone I would climb the wall,
Looking for them among the thin sheep runs.
Their heads were a resolute darkness among ferns,
          They climbed with unsteady certainty.
I wondered what it was they knew the mountain had.

They would pass the last house, Lambert's, where
A violent gander, too old by many a Christmas,
Blared evil warning from his bitten moor,
Then it was open world, too high and clear
          For clouds even, where over heather
The free hare cleanly ran and the summer sheep.

I knew this and I knew all summer long
Those visionary gangs passed through our lanes,
Coming down at evening, their arms full
Of cowslips, moon daisies, whinberries, nuts,
          All fruits of the sliding seasons,
And the enormous experience of the mountain

That I who loved it did not understand.
In the summer, dust filled our winter ruts
With a level softness, and children walked
At evening through golden curtains scuffed
          From the road by their trailing feet.
They would drink tiredly at our wall, talking

Softly, leaning, their sleepy faces warm for home.
We would see them murmur slowly through our stiff

Gate, their shy heads gilded by the last sun.
One by one we would gather up the used jugs,
     The glasses. We would pour away
A little water. It would lie on the thick dust, gleaming.

ELEGY FOR DAVID BEYNON

David, we must have looked comic, sitting
there at next desks; your legs stretched
half-way down the classroom, while
my feet hung a free inch above

the floor. I remember, too, down
at The Gwynne's Field, at the side
of the little Taff, dancing with
laughing fury as you caught

effortlessly at the line-out, sliding
the ball over my head direct to
the outside-half. That was Cyril
Theophilus, who died in his quiet

so long ago that only I, perhaps,
remember he'd hold the ball one-handed
on his thin stomach as he turned
to run. Even there you were careful

to miss us with your scattering
knees as you bumped through
for yet another try. Buffeted
we were, but cheered too by our

unhurt presumption in believing
we could ever have pulled you down.
I think those children, those who died
under your arms in the crushed school,

would understand that I make this
your elegy. I know the face you had,
have walked with you enough mornings
under the fallen leaves. Theirs is

the great anonymous tragedy one word
will summarise. Aberfan, I write it
for them here, knowing we've paid to it
our shabby pence, and now it can be stored

with whatever names there are where
children end their briefest pilgrimage.
I cannot find the words for you, David. These
are too long, too many; and not enough.

HUDSON'S GEESE

Hudson tells us of them,
the two migrating geese,
she hurt in the wing
indomitably walking
the length of a continent,
and he wheeling above,
calling his distress.

They could not have lived.
Already I see her wing
scraped past the bone
as she drags it through rubble.
A fox, maybe, took her
in his snap jaws. And what
would he do, the point
of his circling gone?
The wilderness of his cry
falling through an air
turned instantly to winter
would warn the guns of him.
If a fowler dropped him,
let it have been quick,
pellets hitting brain
and heart so his weight
came down senseless,
and nothing but his body
to enter the dog's mouth.

A SEA IN THE DESERT

1

A little sea
        in the night
    ran its inch of tide
about the bole of the peach tree,

hesitated,

came fawning to my door,
     cringed,
          fell away.

Its small crests,
    its ebb,
        broke my sleep.

2

A little sea
       was running in the desert.
   It came in
       under the edges of the breeze,
a true sea,
    sharpening the air with salt,
        filling hourly through the night.

It remembered white ships,
    clippers out of China
        freighted with tea and roses,
           sea-swans
   holding gales in their wings,
storms off the coast of fragrant Spain, snarling.

     It hurled
  against my walls
      its gathering whips and drums,
        dropped away,
its throat rattling with pebbles.

3

I got up,
    opened my door
        to this unbelievable sea.

       My yard was lit by silent moonlight.
Parched grasshoppers chirruped in the ditches.

4

But still the sea broke
    on the beaches of my ears.

       My skull was a shell
    holding the noisy tides
pouring unseen over the desert.

5

A man is moon to his own sea –
he draws it after him,
like a dog it follows him
the days of his life.

All that night I heard the sea make
and ebb, a sea formed
of grains of remembered oceans,
fed by rains and rivers

of days I had finished with.
It carried old sticks in its mouth.
In the morning a tide's detritus,
twigs, small round stones, a can,

lay in uneven lines
on the charred grass.

6

A hermit thrush sings for me
in dry arroyos its liquid note.
I have heard in the desert
unrecognised birds, charmers,

lift up their single whistles,
long separated, distant,
purified by distance, among
the grassless dunes.

I have thought them calling me.
I have heard the voices
of an invisible sea
whispering with boys'

voices, heard in its dry waves
the pattering of boys' feet
through the built canyons
of the past, I have heard

such singing. The mocking-bird
has sung for me. Each day
the waters of that sea
are rising blindly to the full.

BORDERS
(i.m. John Ormond, died May 4th 1990)

The border I knew best was halfway over
the bridge between the town and Breconshire.
Beneath,
  the river's neutral water
moved on
   to other boundaries.

I walked the bridge each Saturday, stopped
at a guessed measure,
lived a moment in adventurous limbo.
Did I stand on air then, invisibly
taken to some unknown world, some nowhere?
Where was I then? I was whole
but felt an unseen line
divide me, send my strong half forward,
keep my other timidly at home.

I have always lived that way,
crossed borders resolutely
while looking over my shoulder.

Not long ago
driving in America
in high cold desert country below the Rockies,
I saw at the roadside
parked on an acre open as the moon,
a ring of shabby cars
old Chevies and Caddies,
some prosperous trucks.
The Indians were showing on folding tables
their ceremonial silver, heavy necklaces, rich
with turquoise and hammered squash-blossom, oval
silver bangles.
                    Navajo and Zuni,
old tribes, hardy and skilled.
They stood behind their work in the flat wind,
not smiling.
I love the things they make,
haggled for a buckle for my belt,
silver, a design
rayed like the cold sun,
and, walking away, saw
cut into the concrete
the meeting place of four states.
Crouched there, I placed a foot in Utah,
a foot in Arizona, my palms flat
in the dust of Colorado and New Mexico.

Restless as dust, scattered.

A man I knew, my old friend,
moved out as I did, but returned,
followed his eyes and crossed the borders
into his own country. When he left,
it was to see his place from a distance
and peacefully go home. The world grew small
for him, to one country, a city, a house.

His mother, calmly and nobly dying,
asked on her last day for champagne
which she had never tasted. She wet her lips,
and in the evening called into her room
someone unseen. 'Who would have thought it,'
she said, very clearly, and crossed the border
for which all others are a preparation.

And Sally Taylor, her mother dying in the next room,
heard women's voices, young and laughing,
come in to fetch the old lady.

Border, boundary, threshold, door –
Orpheus moved either way, the living and the dead
were parted by a thin reflection
he simply walked through. But who can follow?

For all the boundaries I have crossed, flown over,
knowingly, unknowingly, I have no answers;
but sit in the afternoon sun, under mountains
where stale snow clings in shadowy patches,
remember my friend, how he had sung,
hope he is still singing.

PEACHES

In his life he has made seven gardens, two
from the untilled meadow, some in good heart
after the spades of other men. One, unkempt
inside its formal Georgian walls, he brought
to perfect order out of wilderness, its geometric
beds to flower, renewed its lawn, cut back
its gnarled espaliers and clipped their trimmed limbs
to the limestone. He remembers the rough bark
of those old varieties, pears mostly, and how
he hit the supporting nails into the mortar.

This is the first time he has grown a peach tree.
It is the third year of the small tree's bearing,
and already his black dog has cleared the lowest
bough of its green fruit, nibbled the flesh,
left a scatter of kernels about the grass. No matter,
there's plenty. He has posted a stout cross
beneath the branches, else a heavy harvest of peaches
pulls the whole bush down. Watching the early blossom
has been his pleasure, the frail brevity of blossom
blown in cold weather, then the incipient fruit.

He does not walk in the garden until evening,
the days too hot for his uncovered head. When shadows
spread from under the trees, he stands there,
near a dusty lilac, surprised by hot gusts
out of the desert. His roses are abundant now.
He has let them grow and mingle, throwing their trails

271

over and through the massed green of other shrubs.
Alba and gallica roses, damask roses, centifolia roses,
an old moss rose, a bed of hardy rugosa. Refreshed
by roses, he cherishes the garden air, his head filled

with generations of perfume. Far in his life,
he nods to the spent iris, remembering how in water
his yellow flags stood high, how as a child he took
in his father's garden bright vegetables from the soil,
and how in the autumn hedge blackberries glowed.
It is his way of life to desert his gardens.
The neighbour's evening lamps light up the peaches.
Fruit is ripening, orchards everywhere ripen.
He throws a fallen peach to his black dog.
The animals were not expelled from Eden.

HIS FATHER, SINGING

My father sang for himself,
out of sadness and poverty;
perhaps from happiness,
but I'm not sure of that.

He sang in the garden,
quietly, a quiet voice
near his wallflowers
which of all plants

he loved most, calling them
gillyflowers, a name

learned from his mother.
His songs came from a time

before my time, his boy's
life among musical brothers,
keeping pigeons, red and blue
checkers, had a racing cycle

with bamboo wheels. More often
he sang the songs he'd learned,
still a boy, up to his knees
in French mud, those dying songs.

He sang for us once only,
our mother away from the house,
the lamp lit, and I reading,
seven years old, already bookish,

at the scrubbed table.
My brother cried from his crib
in the small bedroom, teething,
a peremptory squall, then a long

wail. My father lifted from
the sheets his peevish child,
red-faced, feverish, carried
him down in a wool shawl

and in the kitchen, holding
the child close, began to sing.

273

Quietly, of course, and swaying
rhythmically from foot to foot,

he rocked the sobbing boy.
I saw my brother's head,
his puckered face, fall
on my father's chest. His crying

died away, and I
read on. It was my father's
singing brought my head up.
His little wordless lullabies

had gone, and what he sang
above his baby's sleep
was never meant
for any infant's comfort.

He stood in the bleak kitchen,
the stern, young man, my father.
For the first time raised
his voice, in pain and anger

sang. I did not know his song
nor why he sang it. But stood
in fright, knowing it important,
and someone should be listening.

RUTH BIDGOOD

Ruth Bidgood was born in 1922 at Seven Sisters, near Neath, and went to school in Port Talbot, where her Welsh father was an Anglican vicar. After reading English at St. Hugh's College, Oxford, she served as a coder with the Women's Royal Navy Service in Alexandria; she later worked for *Chambers Encyclopaedia* in London. She began writing after her return to Wales during the 1960s when she settled in Abergwesyn, near Llanwrtyd in Breconshire, an upland, sparsely populated area which became the focus for much of her work as both poet and historian; she has recently moved to Beulah, a few miles away. Besides numerous articles on the history of Breconshire and Radnorshire, and a history of Abergwesyn, *Parishes of the Buzzard* (2000), she has published eight books of poems: *The Given Time* (1972), *Not Without Homage* (1975), *The Print of Miracle* (1978), *Lighting Candles* (1982), *Kindred* (1986), *The Fluent Moment* (1996), *Singing to Wolves* (2000) and *Symbols of Plenty* (2006). Her *Selected Poems* appeared in 1992 and her *New and Selected Poems* in 2004. She is pre-eminently the poet of mid-Wales, a remembrancer of its people and landscapes; what attracts her are its bare hills, standing stones, abandoned mines, ruined farmsteads and the traces of former lives which she makes articulate without a note of nostalgia or false sentiment.

LITTLE OF DISTINCTION

Little of distinction, guide-books had said –
A marshy common and a windy hill;
A renovated church, a few old graves
With curly stones and cherubs with blind eyes;
Yews with split trunks straining at rusty bands:
And past the church, a house or two, a farm,
Not picturesque, not even very old.
And yet, the day I went there, life that breaks
So many promises, gave me a present
It had not promised – I found this place
Had beauty after all. How could I have seen
How a verandah's fantastic curlicues
Would throw a patterned shadow on the grass?
Or thought how delicate ash-leaves would stir
Against a sky of that young blue? Or know
Trees and grey walls would have such truthful beauty
Like an exact statement? And least of all
Could I have foreseen the miles on hazy miles
Of Radnorshire and Breconshire below,
Uncertain in the heat – the mystery
That complements precision. So much sweeter
Was the day than the expectation of it.

BURIAL PATH

When we carried you, Siân, that winter day,
over four rivers and four mountains
to the burial place of your people,
it was not the dark rocks of Cwm-y-Benglog

dragged down my spirit,
it was not the steepness of Rhiw'r Ych
that cracked my heart.

Four by four, Siân, we carried you
over the mountain wilderness of Dewi,
fording Pysgotwr and Doithe,
crossing Camddwr by Soar-y-Mynydd,
Tywi at Nant-y-Neuadd; every river passed
brought us the challenge of another hill beyond.

Again and again from his rough pony's back, our leader
signalled with his hazel-staff of office
four, breathless, to lay down your coffin,
four, fresh in strength, to bear you
up the old sledge-ways, the sinew-straining tracks,
the steeps of Rhiw Gelynen and Rhiw'r Ych.

I with the rest, Siân, carried you.
The burial-path is long – forty times and more
I put my shoulder to the coffin
before the weary journey was accomplished
and down at last through leafless oaks
singing we carried you to the crumbling church,
the ancient yews, at the burial-place of your people.

It was not then my heart cracked, Siân,
nor my soul went into darkness.
Carrying you, there was great weariness,
and pride in an old ritual well performed –
our friend's firm leadership, smooth changes

from four to four, the coffin riding
effortlessly the surge of effort.
And at the grave, pride too in showing
churchmen how we of Soar knew well
ways of devotion, fit solemnity.

But with your grave whitened – the last ceremony –
and my neighbours, as I had urged them, gone ahead,
then it was I felt the weight of death
for the first time, Siân, and I knew
it would be always with me now
on the bitter journey that was not yet accomplished.

Now as I went down Rhiw'r Ych alone
and turned west over the ford of Nant-y-Neuadd,
I knew there was only darkness waiting
for me, beyond the crags of Cwm-y-Benglog.
It was then my heart cracked, Siân, my spirit
went into that darkness and was lost.

ALL SOULS'

Shutting my gate, I walk away
from the small glow of my banked fire
into a black All Souls'. Presently
the sky slides back across the void
like a grey film. Then the hedges
are present, and the trees, which my mind
already knows, are no longer
strangers to my eyes.
The road curves. Further along,

a conversation of lights begins
from a few houses, invisible except as light,
calling to farms that higher in darkness
answer still, though each now speaks
for others that lie dumb.
Light at Tŷmawr above me, muted by trees,
is all the light Brongwesyn has,
that once called clearly enough
into the upper valley's night.
From the hill Clyn ahead
Glangwesyn's lively shout of light
celebrates old Nant Henfron, will not let
Cenfaes and Blaennant be voiceless.
I am a latecomer, but offer
speech to the nameless, those
who are hardly a memory, those
whose words were always faint
against the deafening darkness
of remotest hills.
For them tonight when I go home
I will draw back my curtains, for them
my house shall sing with light.

CHURCH IN THE RAIN

Wrapped in rain the small church
stands high. There are no graves
on the north, the devil's side,
where blown soaking trees
transmit his cajoling cry
Let me in in in

To the south the sober congregation
of stones endures in grey uprightness.
The land slopes down into mist.

Inside the church I switch on lights,
shut the door on that crying in the trees.
Now there is the sweetness
of being dry when it rains,
having light after dreariness.
A soft confusion of voices
laps against this refuge.
Hide me, they say, comfort me
I want that which is no dream
That which is no dream
I want   I want

Thomas Powell died;
Catherine his mournful wife
cries and wants. Wine stands
in a vessel near the altar.
All ye who travail come
They are coming in from the rain
Crying Save me, love me
and always that other wails
Let me in

As I leave, rain slacks. From the porch
I see the world in negative,
land eerily pale, sky black. Tonight
in my lighted room I feel the power
of that beleagured place, miles away,

lightless in a night of rain and voices.
I want that which is no dream
That which I want is no dream
I want   I want
Let me in

Heavily falls, on and on, the rain

HAWTHORN AT DIGIFF

When I was a child, hawthorn
was never brought into our house.
It was godless to throw a pinch
of spilled salt, or dodge ladders,
yet no-one ever carried in
the doomy sweetness of red may or white.

Down there by the river,
shivering with heat, is Digiff,
a house full of hawthorn. The tree
grows in the midst of it, glowing
with pale pink blossom, thrusting
through gaps that were windows,
reaching up where no roof
intervenes between hearth and sky.

On the hill, sun has hardened
old soggy fields below the bluebell woods.
Rusty wire sags from rotten posts.
Outcrops, couchant dinosaurs, share
rough comfort with a few unshorn sheep.
Below, gardens have left their mark.

I bring a thought into this day's light
of Esther and Gwen, paupers:
Rhys and Thomas, shepherds: John Jones,
miner of copper and lead:
who lived here and are not remembered,
whose valley is re-translated
by holiday bathers across the river,
lying sun-punched: by me:
by men who keep a scatter of sheep
on the old by-takes.

At Digiff is hawthorn on hearth and bed-place.
Seen close, the tree is flushed
with decay. Sick lichened branches
put out in desperate profusion
blossom that hardly knows
an hour of whiteness before slow dying
darkens it. This is that glowing tree
of doom and celebration,
whose cankered flowers I touch
gently, and go down to the ford.

OLCHON VALLEY

June has lit such a summer fire,
such a fire in the hedges! Sober hazel-leaves,
tipped orange-pink, flare out of green,
burn translucent against the sun.

Once there was lit such a towering fire,
such a fire in the valley! Those who sat,
sober hearers, by hidden hearths, flared
out of homespun and leather, out of curbed flesh,
to spirit, to power, climbing and spreading –
flame the Word lit, words fanned.

Not a flame from that conflagration
breaks out here today, not a drift of its ashes
blurs the black slopes over the valley. But a fire
that was always here at the heart of quiet
gathers us into its congregation.

MERTHYR CLYDAWG

Clodock; it sounds rustic, and English.
Clydawg; the lost Welsh is back. He seems
an off-beat martyr. Killed for love,
out hunting, by a jealous rival; yet,
a prince who led in battle and prayer,
his story has a spice of miracle. Oxen
(helped by a broken yoke) refused
to drag his body over the ford, insisted
that here should be his burial-place.

In the church, the gallery's music-table
might be straight from Hardy. But Latin
on a dug-up stone remembers
'that faithful woman the dear wife
of Guinnda', who centuries back
lived in this place of shifting boundaries,

strife, loss, perpetual haunting, garbled names,
Welshness in the soil's depth,
unacknowledged riches,
uncomprehended power.

QUESTION

Bronfelen, tawny hill –
was there a house here?
None now. Nothing known.
Only the blaze of the hill –
red-brown bracken in autumn,
red speckling thin white of December,
residual red under new green fronds
in the growing year.
A boundary zone
between known and unknown;
a place of blurred identity;
an acreage that's lost
the filaments tying it once
to something recognisable,
unique, to things lived
and for a time remembered. Still,
now and again, people ask
'Was there a house here?'
as if something scattered might
cohere, some force be acknowledged,
some elusive meaning might find
its irrefutable words.

JOHN ORMOND

John Ormond Thomas was born in Dunvant, Swansea, on 3 April 1923, the son of the village shoemaker, and brought up in an English-speaking home. Educated at the University College of Swansea, where he read Philosophy and English, he joined the staff of *Picture Post* in 1945 – largely on the strength of a sheaf of poems he had sent to the editor. Four years later he returned to his hometown to work as a sub-editor with the *Swansea Evening Post*. In 1957 there began what was to become a long career with BBC Wales as director and producer of documentary films, which included studies of Welsh painters and writers such as Ceri Richards, Kyffin Williams, Dylan Thomas, Alun Lewis and R. S. Thomas. He died in Cardiff on 4 May 1990. As a young man, having brought out a book of verse in collaboration with two English poets, he had been advised by Vernon Watkins to publish no more verse until he was thirty, and this advice he accepted, destroying most of his early work. It was not until 1966, when he was 43, that he began publishing again, his poem 'Cathedral Builders' heralding a new phase of creativity. His first book, *Requiem and Celebration* (1969), which shows him endeavouring to find his own mature voice, includes a number of what he called village poems, as well as the long poem 'City in Fire and Snow', written in memory of the old Swansea destroyed by German bombs in the winter of 1941. Local and elegiac these poems may be but they also tackle universal themes such as personal identity, communal loyalty and love between men and women, confronting the numinous with honesty and fortitude. His second book,

Definition of a Waterfall (1973), includes many of his best-known poems. Besides a concern for family and locality, especially the Dunvant of his boyhood, he found most of his themes in the natural world, bringing to his appreciation of it a metaphysical wit which he had cultivated as an under-graduate at Swansea. His poems about people are infallibly precise, their gentle humour underscoring the compassion with which he viewed the quiddities of human nature. There is nothing angry or vicious in them; they seek, rather, to appreciate the joys of life and come to terms with its sorrows, without sentimentality. His last work appeared in *Selected Poems* (1987), written in Cortona in Italy where, towards the end of his life, he found an inner peace and contentment. A good selection of his work appeared, with that of Emyr Humphreys and John Tripp, in the *Penguin Modern Poets* series (27, 1979); another was made for *Cathedral Builders*, published in a fine edition by Gwasg Gregynog in 1991, and another for the Corgi series entitled *Boundaries* (2004).

AT HIS FATHER'S GRAVE

Here lies a shoemaker whose knife and hammer
Fell idle at the height of summer,
Who was not missed so much as when the rain
Of winter brought him back to mind again.

He was no preacher but his working text
Was *See all dry this winter and the next.*
Stand still. Remember his two hands, his laugh,
His craftsmanship. They are his epitaph.

MY GRANDFATHER AND HIS APPLE-TREE

Life sometimes held such sweetness for him
As to engender guilt. From the night vein he'd come,
From working in water wrestling the coal,
Up the pit slant. Every morning hit him
Like a journey of trams between the eyes;
A wild and drinking farmboy sobered by love
Of a miller's daughter and a whitewashed cottage
Suddenly to pay rent for. So he'd left the farm
For dark under the fields six days a week
With mandrel and shovel and different stalls.
All light was beckoning. Soon his hands
Untangled a brown garden into neat greens.

There was an apple-tree he limed, made sturdy;
The fruit was sweet and crisp upon the tongue
Until it budded temptation in his mouth.
Now he had given up whistling on Sundays,
Attended prayer-meetings, added a concordance
To his wedding Bible and ten children
To the village population. He nudged the line,
Clean-pinafored and collared, glazed with soap,
Every seventh day of rest in Ebenezer;
Shaved on Saturday night to escape the devil.

The sweetness of the apples worried him.
He took a branch of cooker from a neighbour
When he became a deacon, wanting
The best of both his worlds. Clay from the colliery

He thumbed about the bole one afternoon
Grafting the sour to sweetness, bound up
The bleeding white of junction with broad strips
Of working flannel-shirt and belly-bands
To join the two in union. For a time
After the wound healed the sweetness held,
The balance tilted towards an old delight.

But in the time that I remember him
(His wife had long since died, I never saw her)
The sour half took over. Every single apple
Grew – across twenty Augusts – bitter as wormwood.
He'd sit under the box-tree, his pink gums
(Between the white moustache and goatee beard)
Grinding thin slices that his jack-knife cut,
Sucking for sweetness vainly. It had gone,
Gone. I heard him mutter
Quiet Welsh oaths as he spat the gall-juice
Into the seeding onion-bed, watched him toss
The big core into the spreading nettles.

CATHEDRAL BUILDERS

They climbed on sketchy ladders towards God,
With winch and pulley hoisted hewn rock into heaven,
Inhabited sky with hammers, defied gravity,
Deified stone, took up God's house to meet Him,

And came down to their suppers and small beer;
Every night slept, lay with their smelly wives,

Quarrelled and cuffed the children, lied,
Spat, sang, were happy or unhappy,

And every day took to the ladders again;
Impeded the rights of way of another summer's
Swallows, grew greyer, shakier, became less inclined
To fix a neighbour's roof of a fine evening,

Saw naves sprout arches, clerestories soar,
Cursed the loud fancy glaziers for their luck,
Somehow escaped the plague, got rheumatism,
Decided it was time to give it up,

To leave the spire to others; stood in the crowd
Well back from the vestments at the consecration,
Envied the fat bishop his warm boots,
Cocked up a squint eye and said, 'I bloody did that.'

DEFINITION OF A WATERFALL

Not stitched to air or water but to both
A veil hangs broken in concealing truth

And flies in vague exactitude, a dove
Born diving between rivers out of love

In drums' crescendo beat its waters grow
Conceding thunder's pianissimo

Transfixing ancient time and legend where
A future ghost streams in the present air:

289

From ledge to pool breakneck across the rocks
Wild calm, calm chaos skein their paradox

So that excited poise is fiercely dressed
In a long instant's constant flow of rest,

So that this bridegroom and his bride in white
Parting together headlong reunite

Among her trailing braids. The inconstancy
Is reconciled to fall, falls and falls free

IN SEPTEMBER

Again the golden month, still
Favourite, is renewed;
Once more I'd wind it in a ring
About your finger, pledge myself
Again, my love, my shelter,
My good roof over me,
My strong wall against winter.

Be bread upon my table still
And red wine in my glass; be fire
Upon my hearth. Continue,
My true storm door, continue
To be sweet lock to my key;
Be wife to me, remain
The soft silk on my bed.

Be morning to my pillow,
Multiply my joy. Be my rare coin
For counting, my luck, my
Granary, my promising fair
Sky, my star, the meaning
Of my journey. Be, this year too,
My twelve months long desire.

ANCIENT MONUMENTS
for Alexander Thom

They bide their time off serpentine
Green lanes, in fields, with railings
Round them and black cows; tall, pocked
And pitted stones, grey, ochre-patched
With moss, lodgings for lost spirits.

Sometimes you have to ask their
Whereabouts. A bent figure, in a hamlet
Of three houses and a barn, will point
Towards the moor. You find them there,
Aloof lean markers, erect in mud.

Long Meg, Five Kings, Nine Maidens,
Twelve Apostles: with such familiar names
We make them part of ordinary lives.
On callow pasture-land
The Shearers and The Hurlers stand.

Sometimes they keep their privacy
In public places: nameless, slender slabs
Disguised as gate-posts in a hedge; and some,
For centuries on duty as scratching-posts,
Are screened by ponies in blank uplands.

Search out the farthest ones, slog on
Through bog, bracken, bramble: arrive
At short granite footings in a plan
Vaguely elliptical, alignments sunk
In turf strewn with sheep's droppings;

And wonder whether it was this shrunk place
The guide-book meant, or whether
Over the next ridge the real chamber,
Accurately by the stars, begins its secret
At once to those who find it.

Turn and look back. You'll see horizons
Much like the ones that they saw,
The tomb-builders, milleniums ago;
The channel scutched by rain, the same old
Sediment of dusk, winter returning.

Dolerite, porphyry, gabbro fired
At the earth's young heart: how those men
Handled them. Set on back-breaking
Geometry, the symmetries of solstice,
What they awaited we, too, still await.

Looking for something else, I came once
To a cromlech in a field of barley.
Whoever farmed that field had true
Priorities. He sowed good grain
To the tomb's doorstep. No path

Led to the ancient death. The capstone,
Set like a cauldron on three legs,
Was marooned by the swimming crop.
A gust and the cromlech floated,
Motionless at time's moorings.

Hissing dry sibilance, chafing
Loquacious thrust of seed
This way and that, in time and out
Of it, would have capsized
The tomb. It stayed becalmed.

The bearded foam, rummaged
By wind from the westerly sea-track,
Broke short not over it. Skirted
By squalls of that year's harvest,
That tomb belonged in that field.

The racing barley, erratically-bleached
Bronze, cross-hatched with gold
And yellow, did not stop short its tide
In deference. It was the barley's
World. Some monuments move.

SALMON

first for, and now in memory of, Ceri Richards

The river sucks them home.
The lost past claims them.
    Beyond the headland
It gropes into the channel
Of the nameless sea.
    Off-shore they submit
To the cast, to the taste of it.
It releases them from salt,
Their thousand miles in odyssey
For spawning. It rehearsed their return
    From the beginning; now
    It clenches them like a fist.

The echo of once being here
Possesses and inclines them.
    Caught in the embrace
Of nothing that is not now,
Riding in with the tide-race,
    Not by their care,
Not by any will they know,
They turn fast to the caress
Of their only course. Sea-hazards done,
They ache towards the one world
    From which their secret
    Sprang, perpetuate

More than themselves, the ritual
Claim of the river, pointed
    Towards rut, tracing
Their passion out. Weeping philosopher,
They reaffirm the world,
    The stars by which they ran,
Now this precise place holds them
Again. They reach the churning wall
Of the brute waterfall which shed
Them young from its cauldron pool.
    A hundred times
    They lunge and strike

Against the hurdles of the rock;
Though hammering water
    Beats them back
Still their desire will not break.
They flourish, whip and kick,
    Tensile for their truth's
Sake, give to the miracle
Of their treadmill leaping
The illusion of the natural.
The present in torrential flow
    Nurtures its own
    Long undertow:

They work it, strike and streak again,
Filaments in suspense.
    The lost past shoots them

Into flight, out of their element,
In bright transilient sickle-blades
    Of light; until upon
The instant's height of their inheritance
They chance in descant over the loud
Diapasons of flood, jack out of reach
And snatch of clawing water,
    Stretch and soar
    Into easy rapids

Beyond, into half-haven, jounce over
Shelves upstream; and know no question
    But, pressed by their cold blood,
Glance through the known maze.
They unravel the thread to source
    To die at their ancestry's
Last knot, knowing no question.
They meet under hazel trees,
Are chosen, and so mate. In shallows as
The stream slides clear yet shirred
    With broken surface where
    Stones trap the creamy stars

Of air, she scoops at gravel with fine
Thrust of her exact blind tail;
    At last her lust
Gapes in a gush on her stone nest
And his held, squanderous peak
    Shudders his final hunger

On her milk; seed laid on seed
In spunk of liquid silk.
So in exhausted saraband their slack
Convulsions wind and wend galactic
 Seed in seed, a found
 World without end.

The circle's set, proportion
Stands complete, and,
 Ready for death,
Haggard they hang in aftermath
Abundance, ripe for the world's
 Rich night, the spear.
Why does this fasting fish
So haunt me? Gautama, was it this
You saw from river-bank
At Uruvela? Was this
 Your glimpse
 Of holy law?

THE GIFT

From where, from whom? Why ask, in torment
All life long when, while we live, we live in it?
As pointless to ask for truth in epiphanies
That throb in the fire, rustle, then fall into ash;
Or why stars are not black in a white firmament.
Enough that it was given, green, as of right, when,
Equally possible, nothing might ever have been.

TUSCAN CYPRESSES

Black-green, green-black, unbending intervals
On far farm boundaries; all years are one to them.
Their noon stillness is beyond decipherment.
They are at the beginning and end of the heart's quandaries.

On the darkest night roadside they judge the earth's turning,
On hills the brightness of stars is the brightness of day.
Each like a young bride is awake at too-soon dawn and
                                    hurrying midnight,
Yet each, like every death, is uncaring, each unknown.

They stand like heretics over long-decayed churches.
Some single as lepers are doomed to keep watch alone.
For those single ones, blast out their roots and detonate
Your only certainty; the curse upon you is whole.

They are the silences between the notes Scarletti left
                                    unwritten,
The silence after the last of Cimarosa's fall.
They are all seasons, they are every second of time.
They do not improvise, all is in strict measure.

Though they reach to the impossible they never outgrow
Or deceive themselves, being nothing but what they are;
They know nothing of angels only of the enticement of hills.
They look down on lakes, the persuasive sea's vainglory.

They have seen the waters divide for divinities
But that was long ago so now peace possesses them;

Their only restlessness is the need for great annexations;
They would come into their inheritance by black growth
                                        and stealth.

They march over the border into Umbria;
Their uniform gives no glint of the sunlight back.
As the gun-carriages threaten by they are the darkness
Of future suicides and firing-squads ahead.

Their solemnity is of Umbria, of burnt earth.
Even they do not know the bottom of it all, the last
Throw of the dice, the black rejoicing, the dying,
The vegetable lie, the audacity of bright flowers.

They barely respond to the stark invention of storms.
Enemies of the living light, they are Dido's lament.
They grow in the mind, haunting, the straight flames
Of fever, black fire possessing the blood.

They have stood at the edges of all events, rehearsed
Vergil's poems before he was born, awaited his death
In another country. Only the oldest of oaks can converse
                                        with them
In the tentative syllables of their patient language.

Lorenzo stood among them as the black-scarved women
Buried a child under cold, motionless candlelight,
The red banners of death and the white surplices.
Lorenzo would die soon, wasted, his wife gripping his ankle.

Are they the world's memorial, its endless throng
Of tombstones? Are they the existence of light before it was
										born?
That aloofness, that uncaring of what is and what is not;
Are they all spent grief at knowing no knowing?

They do not recognise this given world from another,
Having watched Adam and Eve limp from the garden,
The serpent ingratiate itself into the world's only apple tree,
The silver rivers of Eden begin their grey tarnish.

They are the trustees and overseers of absentee landlords,
Keeping a black account of the generations of thin, uneasy
										labourers.
They withhold judgements and watch traditions die,
Are unrejoicing over the wedding party dances.

They have watched man and woman lie down in their
										vows, and wake
Into happiness made new by morning,
And observed the *contadini* setting out for the yellow fields,
Not caring whether they should return or not return.

They watched the Great Death blacken the land,
Agnola di Tura del Grasso, sometimes called The Fat,
Bury his five children with his own two hands,
And many another likewise, the grave-diggers dying

Or running, knowing of more than death, into the hills.
There death stood waiting between the cypresses.

The terraces of vine and olive retched with the weight of
                                                     their dying.
The terraces crumbled and the new famine began.

The cypresses stood over it all in the putrefaction
Of silence; silence of chantings dead in the priests' throats;
Silence of merchant and beggar, physician and banker,
Of silversmith and wet-nurse, mason and town-crier.

The cypresses stood over it all and watched and watched;
You could not call this enmity, it is the world's way.
Their stance seems set as though by ordinance and yet it is
                                                               not.
It is merely the circumstance of the mystery, the reason for
                                                         churches.

They are not everything, but they are trees.
They watch the pulse in heaven of cold stars
And the common smoke gone up from the body's burning,
They know the sourness of vinegar,

The sweetness and smiling of holy wine,
But they partake of neither in spirit;
Cannot be bribed into turning away, not even briefly.
There is no buying off their vigilance.

They are the melancholy beyond explaining,
Beyond belief. Accepting this, they are not tempted
To put on more than their little green.
Theirs is the dark of the unbelieving, the unknowing, the
                                                 darkness of pits.

Some few are deformed, though fewer
That in their multitudes and assembling legions
Their particles might have been heir to.
From birth their spines are erect, their outlines the essence
of given symmetry.

Departure from this is brief aberration;
They must look down from their own escarpments of air,
the wild lilies beneath them,
The wild mignonette, the dog-rose unheeded.
If they could smile a gale would storm south over Africa.

Each one is the containment of every one there was,
A compounding of all cypresses, of all their stillness,
They are the elegant dancers who never dance,
Preferring to watch the musicians, the bustling ones.

They are trees, but they are more than trees,
They go deeper than that. They are at the heart
Of the ultimate music, the poor loam and Roman melody of
Keats's body
Sings silently beneath them.

What will there be of them when all men are gone?
No one to witness the seed of their secret cones,
The deep black seed, the seed beginning in Eden, coming
from nothing,
From the beginning falling in Eden.

Only they can tell of that old story and they are silent
For all the long wisdoms have passed into them;
So silence, since it all comes to nothing.
See how it all burns, all, in the black flames of their silence,
their silence, untelling.

DANNIE ABSE

Dannie Abse was born in Cardiff in 1923 and grew up in the city. After studying at the Welsh National School of Medicine, he moved in 1943 to London where he continued his medical studies at King's College and Westminster Hospital; his military service was done in the RAF. Qualifying as a doctor in 1950, he worked as a specialist in a chest clinic on the fringes of Soho; he lives in Golders Green. He has kept in touch with Wales through his support for Cardiff Football Club and his presidency of the Welsh Academy, the national association of writers, and for many years he had a home at Ogmore-by-sea; he also edited the anthology *Twentieth Century Anglo-Welsh Poetry* (1997). He has published some sixteen books of verse; they include *After Every Green Thing* (1948), *Walking under Water* (1952), *Tenants of the House* (1957), *A Small Desperation* (1968), *Funland* (1973), *Way Out in the Centre* (1981), *Ask the Bloody Horse* (1986), *On the Evening Road* (1994) *Arcadia: One Mile* (1998) and *Running Late* (2007); many of his poems on Welsh themes are to be found in *Welsh Retrospective* (1997). He has also written a number of prose works, mainly autobiographical, which include *Ash on a Young Man's Sleeve* (1954) and *A Poet in the Family* (1974). His *Collected Poems 1948-88*, entitled *White Coat Purple Coat*, appeared in 1989 and his *New and Collected Poems*, nearly three hundred in all, in 2003; a small selection was published in the Corgi series as *Touch Wood* in 2002. At the heart of his work lies a fascination with the foibles of human nature and he reserves his warmest admiration for those who have refused to conform and have suffered as a consequence. As a Jew, albeit secular, he is particularly sensitive to political pressures; a stronger awareness of his Jewish identity has come to the fore in his mature work and some of his later poems deal specifically with the Holocaust. In all his verse there is, in about equal measure, a deep melancholy and a sheer delight in everyday experiences, some of which is based on his experiences as a doctor. His poems have a haunting power, in which there is a place for nostalgia, humour, irony, optimism and a delicious sense of the incongruous and mysterious.

EPITHALAMION

Singing, today I married my white girl
beautiful in a barley field.
Green on thy finger a grass blade curled,
so with this ring I thee wed, I thee wed,
and send our love to the loveless world
of all the living and all the dead.

Now, no more than vulnerable human,
we, more than one, less than two,
are nearly ourselves in a barley field –
and only love is the rent that's due
though the bailiffs of time return anew
to all the living but not the dead.

Shipwrecked, the sun sinks down harbours
of a sky, unloads its liquid cargoes
of marigolds, and I and my white girl
lie still in the barley – who else wishes
to speak, what more can be said
by all the living against all the dead?

Come then all of you wedding guests:
green ghost of trees, gold of barley,
you blackbird priests in the field,
you wind that shakes the pansy head
fluttering on a stalk like a butterfly;
come the living and and come the dead.

Listen flowers, birds, winds, worlds,
tell all today that I married
more than a white girl in the barley –
for today I took to my human bed
flower and bird and wind and world,
and all the living and all the dead.

LETTER TO ALEX COMFORT

Alex, perhaps a colour of which neither of us had dreamt
may appear in the test-tube with God knows what admonition.
Ehrlich, certainly was one who broke down the mental doors,
yet only after his six hundred and sixth attempt.

Koch also, painfully, and with true German thoroughness,
eliminated the impossible to prove that too many of us

are dying from the same disease. Visible, on the slide
at last – Death – and the thin bacilli of an ancient distress.

Still I, myself, don't like Germans, but prefer the unkempt
voyagers who, like butterflies drunk with suns,
can only totter crookedly in the dazed air
to reach, charmingly, their destination as if by accident.

That Greek one, then, is my hero who watched the bath water
rise above his navel, and rushed out naked, 'I found it,
I found it,' into the street in all his shining and forgot
that others would only stare at his genitals. What laughter!

Or Newton, leaning in Woolsthorpe against the garden wall,
forgot his indigestion and all such trivialities,
but gaped up at heaven in just surprise, and, with
true gravity, witnessed the vertical apple fall.

O what a marvellous observation! Who could have reckoned
that such a pedestrian miracle could alter history,
that, henceforwrd, everyone must fall, whatever
their rank, at thirty-two feet per second, per second?

You too, I know, have waited for doors to fly open, played
with your cold chemicals, written long letters
to the Press; listened to the truth afraid, and dug deep
into the wriggling earth for a rainbow with an honest spade.

But nothing rises. Neither spectres nor oil, nor love.
And the old professor must think you mad, Alex, as you
rehearse

poems in the laboratory like vows, and curse those clever
scientists
who dissect away the wings and haggard heart from the dove.

THE GAME

Follow the crowds to where the turnstiles click.
The terraces fill. *Hoompa*, blares the brassy band.
Saturday afternoon has come to Ninian Park
and, beyond the goal posts, in the Canton Stand
between black spaces, a hundred matches spark.

Waiting, we recall records, legendary scores:
Fred Keenor, Hardy, in a royal blue shirt.
The very names, sad as the old songs, open doors
before our time where someone else was hurt.
Now, like an injured beast, the great crowd roars.

The coin is spun. Here all is simplified,
and we are partisan who cheer the Good,
hiss at passing Evil. Was Lucifer offside?
A wing falls down when cherubs howl for blood.
Demons have agents: the Referee is bribed.

The white ball smacked the crossbar. Satan rose
higher than the others in the smoked brown gloom
to sink on grass in a ballet dancer's pose.
Again it seems we hear a familiar tune
not quite identifiable. A distant whistle blows.

Memory of faded games, the discarded years;
talk of Aston Villa, Orient, and the Swans.
Half-time, the band played the same military airs
as when the Bluebirds once were champions.
Round touchlines the same cripples in their chairs.

Mephistopheles had his joke. The honest team
dribbles ineffectively, no one can be blamed.
Infernal backs tackle, inside forwards scheme,
and if they foul us need we be ashamed?
Heads up! Oh for a Ted Drake, a Dixie Dean.

'Saved' or else, discontents, we are transferred
long decades back, like Faust must pay that fee.
The night is early. Great phantoms in us stir
as coloured jerseys hover, move diagonally
on the damp turf, and our eidetic visions blur.

God sign our souls! Because the obscure staff
of Hell rule this world, jugular fans guessed
the result halfway through the second half,
and those who know the score just seemed depressed.
Small boys swarm the field for an autograph.

Silent the stadium. The crowds have all filed out.
Only the pigeons beneath the roofs remain.
The clean programmes are trampled underfoot,
and natural the dark, appropriate the rain,
whilst, under lamp-posts, threatening newsboys shout.

RETURN TO CARDIFF

'Hometown'; well, most admit an affection for a city:
grey tangled streets I cycled on to school, my first cigarette
in the black lane, and, fool, my first botched love affair.
First everything. Faded torments; self-indulgent pity.

The journey to Cardiff seemed less a return than a raid
on mislaid identities. Of course the whole locus smaller:
the mile-wide Taff now a stream, the castle not as in some
black,
gothic dream, but a decent sprawl, a joker's toy façade.

Unfocused voices in the wind, associations, clues,
odds and ends, fringes caught, as when, after the doctor quit,
a door opened and I glimpsed the white, enormous face
of my grandfather, suddenly aghast with certain news.

Unable to define anything I can hardly speak,
and still I love the place for what I wanted it to be
as much as for what it unashamedly is
now for me, a city of strangers, alien and bleak.

Unable to communicate I'm easily betrayed,
uneasily diverted by mere sense reflections
like those anchored waterscapes that wander, alter, in the
Taff,
hour by hour, as light slants down a different shade.

Illusory, too, that lost dark playground after rain,
the noise of trams, gunshots in what they once called Tiger
                                                          Bay.
Only real this smell of ripe, damp earth when the sun
                                                  comes out,
a mixture of pungencies, half exquisite and half plain.

No sooner than I'd arrived the other Cardiff had gone,
smoke in the memory, these but tinned resemblances,
where the boy I was not and the man I am not
met, hesitated, left double footsteps, then walked on.

THE FRENCH MASTER

Everyone in Class II at the Grammar School
had heard of Walter Bird, known as Wazo.
They said he'd behead each dullard and fool
or, instead, carve off a tail for the fun.

Wazo's cane buzzed like a bee in the air.
Quietly, quietly, in the desks of Form III
sneaky Wazo tweaked our ears and our hair.
Walter Wazo, public enemy No.1.

Five feet tall, he married Doreen Wall,
and combmarks furrowed his vaselined hair;
his hands still fluttered ridiculously small,
his eyes the colour of a poison bottle.

311

Who'd think he'd falter, poor love-sick Walter
as bored he read out *Lettres de mon Moulin*;
his mouth had begun to soften and alter,
and Class IV ribbed him as only boys can.

Perhaps through kissing his wife to a moan
had alone changed the shape of his lips,
till the habit of her mouth became his own:
no more Walter Wazo, enemy No. 1.

'Boy,' he'd whine, 'yes, please decline the verb to have,'
in tones dulcet and mild as a girl.
'Sorry sir, can't sir, must go to the lav,'
whilst Wazo stared out of this world.

Till one day in May Wazo buzzed like a bee
and stung, twice, many a warm, inky hand;
he stormed through the form, a catastrophe,
returned to this world, No.1.

Alas, alas, to the Vth Form's disgrace
nobody could quote Villon to that villain.
Again the nasty old mouth zipped on his face,
and not a weak-bladdered boy in the class.

Was Doreen being kissed by a Mr Anon?
Years later, I purred, 'Your dear wife, Mr Bird?'
Teeth bared, how he *glared* before stamping on;
and suddenly I felt sorry for the bastard.

A NIGHT OUT

Friends recommended the new Polish film
at the Academy in Oxford Street.
So we joined the ever melancholy queue
of cinemas. A wind blew faint suggestions
of rain towards us, and an accordion.
Later, uneasy, in the velvet dark
we peered through the cut-out oblong window
at the spotlit drama of our nightmares:
images of Auschwitz almost authentic,
the human obscenity in close-up.
Certainly we could imagine the stench.

Resenting it, we forgot the barbed wire
was but a prop and could not scratch an eye;
those striped victims merely actors like us.
We saw the Camp orchestra assembled,
we heard the solemn gaiety of Bach,
scored by the loud arrival of an engine,
its impotent cry and its guttural trucks.
We watched, as we munched milk chocolate,
trustful children, no older than our own,
strolling into the chambers without fuss,
while smoke, black and curly, oozed from chimneys.

Afterwards, at a loss, we sipped coffee
in a bored espresso bar nearby
saying very little. You took off one glove.
Then to the comfortable suburb swiftly

where, arriving home, we garaged the car.
We asked the au pair girl from Germany
if anyone had phoned at all, or called,
and, of course, if the children had woken.
Reassured, together we climbed the stairs,
undressed together, and naked together,
in the dark, in the marital bed, made love.

NOT ADLESTROP

Not Adlestrop, no – besides, the name
hardly matters. Nor did I languish in June heat.
Simply, I stood, too early, on the empty platform,
and the wrong train came in slowly, surprised, stopped.
Directly facing me, from a window,
a very, *very* pretty girl leaned out.

When I, all instinct,
stared at her, she, all instinct, inclined her head away
as if she'd divined the much married life in me,
or as if she might spot, up platform,
some unlikely familiar.

For my part, under the clock, I continued
my scrutiny with unmitigated pleasure.
And she knew it, she certainly knew it, and would not
glance at me in the silence of not Adlestrop.

Only when the train heaved noisily, only
when it jolted, when it slid away, only *then*,

daring and secure, she smiled back at my smile,
and I, daring and secure, waved back at her waving.
And so it was, all the way down the hurrying platform
as the train gathered atrocious speed
towards Oxfordshire or Gloucestershire.

IN LLANDOUGH HOSPITAL

'To hasten night would be humane,'
I, a doctor, beg a doctor,
for still the darkness will not come –
his sunset slow, his first star pain.

I plead: 'We know another law.
For one maimed bird we'd do as much,
and if a creature need not suffer
must he, for etiquette, endure?'

Earlier, 'Go now, son,' my father said,
for my sake commanding me.
Now, since death makes victims of us all,
he's thin as Auschwitz in that bed.

Still his courage startles me. The fears
I'd have, he has none. Who'd save
Socrates from the hemlock,
or Winkelried from the spears?

We quote or misquote in defeat,
in life, and at the camps of death.

Here comes the night with all its stars,
bright butchers' hooks for man and meat.

I grasp his hand so fine, so mild,
which still is warm surprisingly,
not a handshake either, father,
but as I used to when a child.

And as a child can't comprehend
what germinates philosophy,
so like a child I question why
night with stars, then night without end.

LAST WORDS

Splendidly, Shakespeare's heroes,
Shakespeare's heroines, once the spotlight's on,
enact every night, with such grace, their verbose deaths.
Then great plush curtains, then smiling resurrection
to applause – and never their good looks gone.

The last recorded words too
of real kings, real queens, all the famous dead,
are but pithy pretences, quotable fictions
composed by anonymous men decades later,
never with ready notebooks at the bed.

Most do not know who they are
when they die or where they are, country or town,
nor which hand on their brow. Some clapped-out actor may

imagine distant clapping, bow, but no real queen
    will sigh, 'Give me my robe, put on my crown.'

        Death scenes not life-enhancing,
    death scenes not beautiful nor with breeding;
yet bravo Sydney Carton, bravo Duc de Chavost
who, euphoric beside the guillotine, turned down
    the corner of the page he was reading.

        And how would I wish to go?
    Not as in opera – that would offend –
nor like a blue-eyed cowboy shot and short of words,
but finger-tapping still our private morse, '… love you,'
    before the last flowers and flies descend.

A LETTER FROM OGMORE-BY-SEA

        Goodbye, 20th Century.
        What should I mourn?
        Hiroshima? Auschwitz?
        Our friend, Carmi, said,
        'Thank forgetfulness
        else we could not live;
        thank memory
        else we'd have no life.'

        Goodbye, 20th Century.
        What shall I celebrate?
        Darling, I'm out of date:
        even my nostalgia

317

is becoming history.
Those garish, come-on posters
outside a cinema,
announce the Famous
I've never heard of.
So many other friends, too,
now like Carmi, have joined
a genealogy of ghosts.

But here, this mellow evening,
on these high cliffs, I look down
to read the unrolling
holy scrolls of the sea. They are
blank. The enigma is alive
and, for the Present, I boast,
thumbs in lapels, I survive.

ALISON BIELSKI

Alison Bielski was born in Newport, Monmouthshire, in 1925, into a family named Prosser whose roots were in the Chepstow area. Educated at Newport High School, she became secretary to the Press Officer of Bristol Aeroplane Company and later worked with the British Red Cross in Cardiff and in bookshops in Tenby. Since 1986 she has lived in Cardiff. From 1969 to 1974 she was, with Sally Roberts Jones, honorary joint secretary of the English-language section of Yr Academi Gymreig, the national association of writers now known as Academi. A prolific poet, she has published a number of booklets of her verse and four main collections: *Across the Burning Sand* (1970), *That Crimson Flame* (1996), *the green-eyed pool* (1997), and *Sacramental Sonnets* (2003). She has also written 'visual poetry', including typographical and 'concrete' poems.

TOKEN

walking this winter beach alone
over cold arcs of barren sand
I will give him a white stone

small universe to hold and own
rounded as time within his hand
walking this winter beach alone

caught between ebb-tide's sobbing moan
and cliff grass leaping on green land
I will give him a white stone

harder than truth, colder than bone
or flesh, then he shall understand
walking this winter beach alone

that destiny's salt wind has thrown
this token down dark pebbled strand
I will give him a white stone

there is no heart in monotone
grey sea, sky, rock make no demand
walking this winter beach alone
I will give him a white stone

BORDER COUNTRY
(in memory of my mother)

I have come to take you
to border country
where land is white
and long contours
stretch unmarked
into winter light

this field we cross
is emerald green

you will leave colour
I cannot keep you
from walking on
into that pallor

snow covers grass
we wait knowing
the road is barred
you hold one pass
in that brittle hand
to show the guard

flesh of your flesh
I am left behind
quite separate
with your hair and eyes
my identity
shatters at this gate

EAGLES

we are summoned to Illtud's bed
two abbots placed at foot and head
so small he lies
with dying eyes
watching me Isanus tall and still
'on wings of gold' he struggles to say
'an eagle will carry my soul away'

so soon so soon on a sunlit day
an eagle will carry his soul away

now bold Atoclius at his feet
gazes through window to midnight street
yet Illtud's face
shimmers with grace
for one who loves that world of the town
so he whispers gently 'on wings of lead
an eagle will carry your soul to God'

so late so late on a rainy day
an eagle will carry his soul away

rushlight flickers on Illtud's brow
his hollow face is fallen snow
frail as a flake
on winter lake
he waits for thunder of heavy wings
at foot and head we struggle to pray
then an eagle carries his soul away

322

RAYMOND GARLICK

Raymond Garlick was born in the London suburb of Harlesden in 1926 and brought up in North Harrow. At the age of four he contracted a mysterious disease, thought to be septicaemia but never diagnosed, and left hospital with a severely damaged foot. Sent to convalesce with his grandparents at Degannwy on the North Wales coast, he discovered a rugged landscape with which he felt an immediate affinity. He finished his schooling at the John Bright School in Llandudno. Having read English and History at the University College of North Wales, Bangor, he became a teacher of English at Pembroke Dock and later in Blaenau Ffestiniog by which time he had converted to Roman Catholicism. He was one of a small group who launched *Dock Leaves* (later *The Anglo-Welsh Review*) and was the magazine's editor from 1949 to 1961, when he joined the staff of an International School at Eerde in the Netherlands. Returning to Wales in 1967, he took a post at Trinity College, Carmarthen, where he was Principal Lecturer in the English Department and Director of the Welsh Studies course; he still lives in Carmarthen but is no longer a Catholic. During the campaigns of civil disobedience organized by *Cymdeithas yr Iaith Gymraeg* (The Welsh Language Society) in the 1960s and 1970s, members of his family were among those who, by non-violent methods, challenged the law in a bid to win a greater degree of official status for Welsh. His major contribution to our appreciation of the English-language literature of Wales was made in his monograph, *An Introduction to Anglo-Welsh Literature* (1970). With Roland Mathias he edited *Anglo-Welsh Poetry 1480-1990* (1990). The unity of his first three volumes of poetry, namely *A Sense of Europe* (1968), *A Sense of Time* (1972) and *Incense* (1976), is apparent in their common themes, which include a Nationalist view of Wales as an integral part of European civilization, a celebration of people in the praise-tradition of Welsh-language poetry, a passionate concern for justice and non-violence, and a preoccupation with language, especially English as one of the languages of a fully bilingual Wales. When the poet fell silent in the 1980s after the publication of his *Collected Poems 1946-86* (1987), it was feared he would write no more poems. Then, in 1992, there appeared *Travel Notes*, which showed him to have attained a new serenity. Many of these poems are about places in the Mediterranean, while others reflect his staunch Republicanism and his horror at the violence perpetrated in the name of the British State. A small selection of his poems is to be found in *The Delphic Voyage* in the Corgi series (2003).

CONSIDER KYFFIN

Consider Kyffin now – as Welsh
a word-spinner as you could wish,
who wove in both tongues, using yours
before you some four hundred years;
John Davies out of Hereford,
Holland of Denbigh – men who fired
their flintlocks through the border wall
loaded with English words as well.
Remember Lloyds and Llwyds, Vaughans,
who opened with their quills both veins
of language, giving life to myth –
the forked tongue in the dragon's mouth.
The others, too, who went astray
down some bypath of history –
their Welsh but not their Welshness lost:
in all, upon the muse's list
a hundred names – your pedigree,
you greener branches of the tree.

In silted bays of old bookshops –
shelved and becalmed like ancient ships
in saffron havens, I have rocked
their boats, long run aground and wrecked;
eased dusty covers open, looked,
clambered inside entranced, unlocked
each bulkhead page from stern to beak
and in the cabin of his book
come on the poet at his ease.

Some – seamen, scribbling in the haze
of voyages to where Wales joins
the world's end: Samwell, Poet Jones.

Others – upcountry parsons, squires,
hotblood students in Oxford squares,
curates penning in the Poems of Hughes –
by candlelight in a creaking house
under the wheeling universe
cutting and polishing a verse.

They are the root from which you stem –
and you have never heard of them.

ANCESTORS

William Oliver maker
Of winnowing machines, John Wood
Labourer in the fields of
The eighteenth century. You are good
Forefathers for a man to have.
You might have understood

My making with words, my zest
For earth and spade. William Beere
Tea merchant, savouring the joke.
And William Garlick, pioneer
Of that name in Wales, who long
Ago committed me here.

But of them all, the humble names
In the registers, I think of you
Nicholas Garlick, martyr,
And Derby Bridge your rendezvous,
In the armada year, with light.
You were an extremist too.

SAUNDERS LEWIS AT NEWTOWN

Ironically enough
It was an English chapel. Bluff
As a sandwich-board
The wall proclaimed 'Worship the Lord',
But the beauty was heard
Not seen, the holiness was word –
Fresh as an evening thrush
In that mahogany and plush.

Spare, nimble, sparrow-like,
He climbed behind the pulpit's dyke
Above the sea of us
Rippling below. Calm, without fuss
He took his stance, began
His panegyric, preaching Ann,
Ann and her wheeling words
Brushing Wales like a spring of birds.

Farmer, professor, knight,
Dominican and Carmelite,
You, the predestinate,
I, the stranger within the gate,

327

All made one by the word,
The voice, the song, the singer, heard
Ann's sacred nightingales
Chant in the cupola of Wales.

CAPITALS

Moscow,
like a Christmas tree,
glisters on the linen snow.
Fabergé red stars filigree
the mast-high spires, glitter and flow
over the square's starched sea
below.

Madrid,
a fortress on a height.
chessboard of stone, a granite grid
lifted and spread to the lancing light
staring down from the sun's arched lid:
of Europe's cities knight
and Cid.

Dublin,
in a Yeatsian haze,
Liffey waters strong as gin,
back-streets like a Chinese maze,
and Trinity, a palanquin –
the Book of Kells ablaze
within.

And Rome,
the white and marble rose
of Europe, rising from the foam
of all the fountains art unfroze
from conduits in time's catacomb:
which in their spray disclose
the dome.

Paris,
and the Seine's long psalm
holding in parenthesis
hundred-tapered Notre Dame –
pavilion of the genesis
of joy, and heaven's calm
chrysalis.

And Bonn,
empalaced on the Rhine,
where Beethoven looked out upon
symphonic counties-palatine.
Over river, bridge and swan
that fierce gaze, leonine,
once shone.

Cardiff
swirls about the numb
and calm cube of its castle cliff:
rune of departed power for some
to others towers a hieroglyph
of sovereign power to come
if if.

And last,
sun-ambered Amsterdam –
the churning hurdy-gurdy's blast
chiming with carillon and tram:
canal and concrete here contrast
their tenses, and enjamb
the past.

Europe:
young ap Iwan's yard,
Gruffydd Robert's vision scope,
Morgan Llwyd's hoist petard:
source to which our ballads grope –
context, compass-card
and hope.

AGINCOURT

Seven of the Welsh archers
Whose arrows eclipsed the sun
In icy susurrations
When Agincourt was done
Had gone there from Llansteffan.
When that day's death was won

If any of them lived
I wonder what they thought.
I lived in Llansteffan

And I know Agincourt –
The bonemeal verdant meadows
Over which they fought:

Green places, both of them now,
But then, in 1415,
At Agincourt the blood
Clotted the buttercups' sheen,
And the earth was disembowelled
Where stakes and hooves had been.

And far off, in Llansteffan,
Castle, village and shore
Flowered in the marigold sun.
Did those seven men explore
The contrast of this peace
With another English war?

MATTERS ARISING

No doubt what you say is right.
In Wales we shall never see
A terrible beauty born.
No rose of tragedy,
Petalled in crimson and black,
Will sway on this post office roof.
Swansea gaol will receive
No heroes, unshaven, aloof,
For the cells' chill liturgy

And the rites of the firing-squad.
Whatever beauty's in blood
Will not bloom here, thank God.

I met an Easter man
In Dublin long ago –
Senator, Minister now –
Who told me: 'You will know
When you find yourself picking off,
Like roses whose day is done,
From behind a garden wall
The soldiers of Albion –
You'll know as you see them fall,
And you feel the frost of fear
Icing your ambushed spine,
That what you hope for is near.'

I have lived where blood
Had flooded down men's hands.
Though I look for a Wales
Free as the Netherlands,
A freedom hacked out here
Is a freedom without worth,
A terror without beauty.
Here it must come to birth
Not as a pterodactyl
Flailing archaic wings,
But the dove that broods on chaos –
Wise as a thousand springs.

ANTHEM FOR DOOMED YOUTH
Swansea, 27 November 1971

My hope is on what is to come.
I turn in anguish from the servile, dumb

Present – from an indifferent people, shut
To justice, crouching in the heart's dark hut.

I turn to the future, to a Wales hung
With the names, like garlands, of today's young.

Outside the court the three stood in the sun,
Poised, at ease, in the soft chrysanthemum

Light of Swansea, the bitter city. They
Alone knew freedom on that icy day.

Policemen, advocates, recognized in those
The radiance of the uncorrupted rose

Glowing above their court well's mantled scum.
Even the judge, that perched geranium,

Saw it: and traded on it – to retail,
After the verdict, his unheard-of bail,

Honouring their integrity's claim,
Which he would deny when the sentence came.

O unjust judge, mere expert in the sleight
Of hand of law, do you sleep at night?

Be sure your victims sleep sounder than you
In the bitter place you condemned them to.

And you, Mr Secretary of State,
Setter-up of committees, what fate

Have the history books in store for you,
Who can watch while the young are spitted through?

Who can wait on a touring troupe's report
While conscience is crucified in court?

My rhyme tolls for you all, beats its slow drum.
My hope is on what is to come.

from NOTES FOR AN AUTOBIOGRAPHY

4

Looking at life's untidy plan
As lived so far, an Englishman
(Ever more English by the year
It seems), must ask himself: Why here,
Why Wales, for half a lifetime,
For a whole life in verse and rhyme?

Just here and in the Netherlands
I've paid the taxman's thrusting hands;
Here only scratched my cross, always
For Wales, upon election days;
Here only, other words have clung
Like honey to my clumsy tongue –

The language of my children's life.
Here I have earned a living rife
With satisfactions. Here I've changed
The earth's face slightly, rearranged
Its features in new gardens which
May last beyond my own last ditch.

In Wales, because long years ago
My grandfather proposed to mow
The lawns of his retirement here
Beside the Conwy. Year on year
Of holidays brought us. The war
Finally opened me the door

Of Wales for a lifetime. So,
Non-patrial, a mestizo
Of cultures, see this worker-ant
Unmasked now as an immigrant
Since '39. Another world,
Unimagined, now unfurled

Like an imago from its shell
Flexing its wings on asphodel:

A landscape and two languages
And literatures; green ages
Of history, another nation,
Another world. Civilization.

Except for the genes' cryptogram,
Everything I have and am
Has come from Wales, as life's windfall.
What can it mean to own it all,
Belong to it and be at home
In Wales by right of chromosome?

One could wish to have been born
To this, but it's useless to mourn
Biology. The imperial genes
That use us as their go-betweens
Hand down the ciphered ukase.
The English form will not erase.

To want to deny one's history
Must always be a mystery
To the English mind. Ask it
Whether it thinks itself fit
For a little self-rule, it grins
At your joke, or kicks your shins.

Can you imagine them voting
Against themselves? Demoting
Their language, mounting an attack
Upon it? Try it, and stand back

To take the consequences.
The English man their own defences

Manfully. Can you conceive
What they must think of you, who heave
Brickbats at your best, disgrace
The landscape's strong, unyielding face
With weakness worthy of a serf?
Wales's battle was lost on the turf

Of playing-fields of county schools
Where boys were made the system's fools:
What we in Wales call education
Marx defined as alienation.
Chapel too has played its part
In neutering Fluellyn's heart.

Chapel produced a Welsh mind curled
Round soul, sin, and another world;
And Rugby's a more recent name
For turning life into a game;
Strolling off from reality
To players' bar or chapel tea.

But Britishness is the villain,
The bacillus in the brain,
The bully word with the barmy
Associations – army,
Empire, jingoism, crown,
A long history of doing down

Other people, far and near.
Buy British. Be British. Shakespeare
Wasn't, nor Chaucer, Milton,
Dafydd ap Gwilym. It's gone
Now, of course, the pseudo-nation,
The grandiose old railway station

On one of history's branch lines –
Except for bits preserved as shrines
By elderly collectors
And certain Welsh electors
Who (the empire dead) chose to become
Colonials by referendum.

My theme's the need to go and meet
Your fate upon your own two feet,
Learning to walk without a crutch,
Teaching the heart to leave its hutch:
Survival and identity,
And the primacy of pity.

These were people who didn't think
Such things important; who could sink
Identity as though of not much
Value, choose the British crutch.
These verses stumble out to try
To stir you into asking why.

MERCER SIMPSON

Mercer Simpson was born in Fulham, London, on 27 January 1926. Educated at Magdalene College, Cambridge, he came to Wales in 1950 to take up a post as Senior English Master at Monkton School in Cardiff. From 1967 to 1984 he lectured at the Polytechnic of Wales. He died in Cardiff on 11 June 2007. As a critic he wrote extensively about Welsh writing in English and published four books of poems, *East Anglian Wordscapes* (1993), *Rain from a Clear Blue Sky* (1994), *Early Departures, Late Arrivals* (2007) and, postumously, *Enclosures and Disclosures* (2007).

EXODUS FROM BLAENAVON

A mined-out community. No miracles
could call it back to life. Abandoned seams
have settled their dust on the work ethic.
Big Pit's now a museum. Its winding-gear squeals
in the wheelhouse while you gently descend
in a canary-green cage. It's a mere three hundred feet
to shaft bottom, and then over slippery rails
to the five-foot face. Across the valley
scaffolding masks rebuilding at the ironworks.
Between them the compact trading estate
pretends there's a future, down a dead end.
In Blaenavon's heyday, happiness meant staying alive,
raising children under a passably dry roof,
keeping a fire in the grate, food in the larder,

and the front doorstep scrubbed spotless.
Cleanliness rubbed shoulders with Godliness
in a tin bath on the kitchen floor. The one hope,
faith in the World to Come: crossing Jordan,
taking the Minister's Word for it
in the full-throated chapel, even beside
slanting headstones in the shallow graveyard.
At a funeral, any faint rumble would make
the hand tremble holding the hymn-book.
After firedamp, hellfire flickered. But inside,
the singing stayed upright. Subsidence,
clawing upwards, resurrection's paradox,
splintered the road like a mirror in the rain.
Crazed too as old china the sepia photographs
recording the hardlined, bluescarred lives
screwed down inside pit darkness,
the rows of stalls like terraced houses.
After day-shift they'd climb to starlight
sprinkling the wintry smokehaze in a narrow bed
of sky like mourning crêpe. The coffin-lid
was being hammered down. Its nails were shining.

HENRY VAUGHAN VISITS HIS GRANDFATHER
AT TRETOWER

I sense your presence in your visionary country:
Tretower's round keep, concentric strength
holding dark secrets, blood on its ruined walls,
old feuding's shadow where the sun breaks in

like a wary thief, where what would be illumined
is out of reach of history, thankfully buried:
then peace, civilisation, culture, a more settled order
for your ancestors' move across the water-meadows
into the great house growing up around its courtyard
with only a fortified gatehouse for defence.
These are the shifts of history, territorial disputes,
the alluvial land for grazing cattle,
the river banks for fishing, the woods across the Usk
for hunting deer, for felling timber. But for meditation
the mediaeval garden of the white rose on the south wall,
the sun reflecting from its stones the warmth for vines.
Below it, the brisk river with its waters' chatter
bubbled over the stones; and a cleansing wind
scoured the old enmities from the valley floor.
You lifted up your eyes to the Black Mountains
whose secretive valleys run in from further east
where distant Gwent holds out green skirts to dry.
Back here's your territory of universal love
looking through nature at the face of God.
Later in the clear starlight of a visionary night
you apprehended the Universe, God at the still centre
of the calm, slow-moving prayer-wheel of the stars
displaying eternity as a ring of infinite light.

JOHN TRIPP

John Tripp was born in Bargoed, Glamorgan, on 22 July 1927, and brought up from the age of six in the north Cardiff suburbs of Birchgrove and Whitchurch; his father was a farrier in Taff's Well. After leaving school at the age of sixteen, and serving three years as a conscript in the Army, he had various jobs before becoming a journalist in London, latterly as a press officer at the Indonesian Embassy and the Central Office of Information. In the early 1960s he was one of a group of expatriates who formed the Guild of Welsh Writers in London, which was later to merge with the Welsh Academy. In 1969 he returned to Cardiff and thereafter lived precariously as a freelance writer. From 1973 to 1979, when it suspended publication, he was literary editor of the magazine *Planet*, and he took an active part in the affairs of the Welsh Union of Writers at whose convivial gatherings his rumbustious nature was given full rein. He died at the home he shared with his elderly father in Whitchurch on 16 February 1986. A booklet of his poems, *Diesel to Yesterday*, appeared in 1966 as part of the Triskel Poets series. He went on to publish six more volumes of verse: *The Loss of Ancestry* (1969), *The Province of Belief* (1971), *Bute Park* (1971), *The Inheritance File* (1973), *For King and Country* (1980) and *Passing Through* (1984). A selection of his work appeared in the *Penguin Modern Poets* series in 1979 and his *Collected Poems 1958-78* in 1978; John Ormond edited his *Selected Poems* (1989). The main themes of his verse are the history of

Wales and the present condition of its people. An English-speaking Welshman, with left-wing and pacifist convictions, he was concerned not only with his own roots but also with what he vehemently denounced as the materialism of contemporary society. He used a journalistic style to record what fascinated him most: the spectacle of the once great now fallen on hard times. An accomplished and popular reader of his own work, he sometimes turned a laconic eye on himself as poet-observer, grizzled by suburban living but still capable of humour, anger and compassion.

DIESEL TO YESTERDAY

There is downpour, always,
    as the carriages inch into Newport:
perhaps six times in ten years
    of a hundred visits to custom,
the entry to my country is uncurtained
    by rain or mist. I look
at the shambles of sidings and streets,
    the rust of progress and freight wagons,
the cracked façades of bingo cinemas.
    Sometimes I expect to see
the callous peaked caps and buttons
    of visa-checkers, cold sentries
on a foreign border, keeping out the bacillus
    in hammering rain and swirling fog.
Often I wish it were so, this frontier sealed
    at Chepstow, against frivolous incursion
from the tainting eastern zones.

Patience vanishes with frayed goodwill
    at the sight of the plump bundles
tumbling into Wales.
    They bring only their banknotes
and a petrol-stenched lust for scenery
    to shut in their kodaks,
packing out the albums of Jersey
    and the anthill beaches of the south.
They stand in line for pre-heated grease
    in the slums of the crumbled resorts,
nose their long cars into pastureland
    and the hearts of ancient townships
that now are buried under chromium plate.

I catch myself out in error, feel
    ignoble in disdain.
The bad smell at my nostril
    is some odour from myself –
a modern who reeks of the museum,
    not wanting his own closed yesterday
but the day before that,
    the lost day before dignity went,
when all our borders were sealed.

SOLILOQUY FOR COMPATRIOTS

We even have our own word for God
in a language nourished on hymn and psalm
as we clinched to our customs and habitats.

All those decades ago
in the chapels of the scarred zones,
lean clergymen made it quite clear
He had singled us out as his chosen.
He would care for the beaten Welsh people.
But now the strangers come to bang more nails
in the battered coffin of Wales.
                              Their sleek cars
slam up the passes and through the green vales,
the bramble shudders from the screaming exhausts.

A tangled image of pits and poverty,
Eisteddfodau and love on slag heaps
invades their haphazard minds.
Four hundred years of the King's writ
have not shaken their concept of our role: foxy, feckless,
articulate, mercurial, lyrical and wild,
we are clogged with feeling,
ranting preachers on the rebellious fronde.

All our princes gone, betrayal and sack
ended in a seal on parchment.
Our follies have all been almanacked, and our bards
are piping on reeds where once the trumpets sounded.
Death is the ancient popular topic we nibble.

Inept, they say, like the Irish
we have fought too long for the crumbs
from rich men's tables.
                              How could they know

for one moment of the steely wonder
of pride in legend in a sunken past,
the stiff stubborn strap to our backbone
that makes others still seek us out?

SEPARATION

But this night is the same
as any other night. The clocks bang.
It will pass like other nights,
while the squirrel twitches in his sleep,
the farmer sags bone-weary to his cot.

I will watch another sunset, clear and tangerine,
as cattle trail to their barns,
another dawn breaks through the west.
Somewhere the fox will stir in his loneliness,
a fieldmouse camp in an ancient boot.

If only we had been a simpler pair,
engaged in piecemeal tasks
on some outlying croft,
instead of the busy unimportant ones
everyone told us were correct.

Days will melt into days
when not even the shape of your hands
will be remembered,
not even the curve of the mouth
or the quiet sentences of disgust.

The lady in the shop still has her gout,
the neighbour hoses and hoses his car,
the tits land on the milk-tops,
the baker delivers one hovis and sliced.
Calamity on the radio does not touch us.

So I shall wait for more trains,
move from this point to that,
write you a last line about property.
I will observe it all as before
and wish we'd been simpler as the nights close in.

ON MY FORTIETH BIRTHDAY

When I was forty the stocktaker came
to take stock. He was dressed in black
like that old advertisement for Sandeman's port.
Let me see your books, he said.
I blew the dust off my ledgers
and showed him the blank pages.
These are nothing but blank pages, he said.
Are you trying to be whimsical?
He had the flat voice that BBC announcers use
when they describe calamity.
My plans are still maturing, I said,
I am on the point of doing something important.
An old lady in Port Talbot likes two of my poems
and she's ordered two copies for the library.
I am piling my rubbish against oblivion,

stacking it against the dark.
If you go up to Aberystwyth
you'll find my name misspelt in the dust.

He looked at me in contempt
right through to the lack of backbone.
Yes, he said, but what have you done?
What have you actually done with your lovely life?
Well, I said, it's like this ...
I groped for the cudgelled album
Where the corpses were kept.

Outside was the switchyard, with the expresses
coming at one another from all directions.
I hadn't heard a bird around here for years.
Loneliness came down like a lid.

I'll be back, old Sandeman said,
you'd better get those pages filled...

TOMCAT

While others were curled on their evening rugs
or purring on laps to a loving stroke,
this one was loosening dustbin-lids
to get at the fish-heads. With a rattle and crash
he'd dive in to select the garbage.

We say we like cats for their coldness,
seeing in their chill the slow dignity

we wish we possessed – no messy affection there,
nothing of slop to bring a rift
between Tom and his lessons in reality.

We had a blackbird family in a laurel hedge.
He waited on the wall for treacherous dusk,
squeezed through the branches and murdered the mother
and chicks. We saw the red feathered remnant, scattered
in a raging minute from life to gobbling death.

Those like him that lope in predatory dark
are men's men, criminals looting on the run.
If they see a hot cat on a roof, sex is the second choice
to a guzzling kill. His ancestors lived on farms,
the equal of anything vicious on four fast legs.

His history was probably short, a panther thrown out
from a series of heaving litters
stinking in a barnyard of cat orgy –
his mother and brothers drowned in a shuttered barrel.
Flung in a ditch, he began with grass-high vision.

He stared at the battlefield, grew bigger on mouse and
                                                    sparrow,
checked the competition and liked what he saw.
No pamper of milk came to soften him,
human hands were to spit and bite at.
When he arrived in our garden, his pessimism was quite
                                                    complete.

349

No one ever called him pussy, except old ladies
fuddled in sentiment. A black scavenging scrag,
for a month he shocked birds from the lanes,
rummaging wherever a stench was pleasing
and lodging on a sack in the shed.

There they found him, asleep, and clubbed him to a pulp.
He wouldn't taste full cream now, or caviare from tins.
Lean aloof prowler, he deserved no catafalque.
But after they threw him in a pit, I put him on a spade
and buried him under a scarecrow hanging in the wind.

WALNUT TREE FORGE

My father shod horses in the sun
while I threw old shoes at an iron pin.
From the bank of the canal I saw
a kingfisher dive like a blue-green streak
clean through the water and out again
with lunch in its beak, then glide
to its fish-boned hole in the bank.

My father would look up from his work
and lean against the door to rest
from the bending, the weight on his back
of a shire, big and restless in the heat,
that tested all his muscles and skill.
He would wipe his brow with a rag.
'Did you see a kingfisher, then?' I nodded.

He never welcomed the big horses
made for show, all rump and heavy
with the spoilt pride of their runners,
shone to a tantrum and cockade gloss
for anything but work. These gave him
a rough hour of shifting and fret,
too pampered by the hands of others.

It was labour to him, one more task
for a pound, the ponies coming in a string
on a good day. To me it was freedom
from arithmetic, as golden time used up
so easily. There were just the two of us,
the ring of the shoes hitting the pin,
and a kingfisher, and a shire, in the long-ago sun.

CONNECTION IN BRIDGEND

In the bus café, drinking tea, I watch
nothing happening in Bridgend.
I mean, there is rain, some shoppers
under canopies, tyres sloshing them
from the gutters. Otherwise not much.

(Do those Pakistanis feel the cold?
What are they doing in Bridgend?
How did they land here, and those lost
Sikhs and Chinamen?
I am sorry for them, they look bereft.)

In the café a young mother is being given
stick by her two boys. They want Coke
and her baby cries for no reason
unless he's seen enough of Bridgend.
I feel an odd kinship with him.

At last my bacon sandwich is done;
it was something to look forward to,
slicing a minute's delight into the murk.
Balancing the plate, I hold the sad babe
while his mother fetches the Coke.

Then a one-armed paperseller comes in
with a strip of frayed ribbons on his coat.
He wants to tell me his story,
so I listen while the baby sobs
and his brothers suck straws.

An hour ago, I was alone; now
there are six. Even the café-owner
squeezes out a smile. We are in it
together, until the last buses go out.
One by one they leave the bays.

JOSEPH P. CLANCY

Joseph Patrick Clancy was born in New York in 1928, of Irish and French extraction. He joined the staff of Marymount Manhattan College in the city in 1948 and was, for many years, Professor of English Literature and Theatre Arts there. He and his wife, both Roman Catholics, have lived permanently in Aberystwyth since 1990. He spent several long periods in Wales, learning to read Welsh, while preparing his first books: *Medieval Welsh Lyrics* (1965) and *The Earliest Welsh Poetry* (1970); they were reprinted in 2003 as *Medieval Welsh Poems*. His reputation as the most accomplished of all translators from the Welsh was confirmed by a third volume, *Twentieth Century Welsh Poems* (1982). Since then he has translated the poems of Gwyn Thomas, Bobi Jones, Saunders Lewis and Alun Llywelyn-Williams, as well as prose by Kate Roberts. He has also published three collections of his own verse: *The Significance of Flesh* (1984), *Here and There 1984-1993* (1994) and *Ordinary Time* (2000). The poems by which he is represented here show the influence of the *cywydd* form, especially the seven-syllable line ending with a stressed syllable followed by a line ending with an unstressed. He has also published a volume of essays on poetry and translation, *Other Words* (1999).

LOVE'S LANGUAGE

Teach me a tongue for lovers,
A language of his and hers.
Not the diction of doctors,
Frigid words for a warm bed,
Their antiseptic Latin
Translating persons to things.

Shall I weave for us a web
Of metaphors to mantle,
A soft chanting for her ear,
Our night's delightful doing?
Shall I speak of cwm and peak,
Of firm stem and fine flower,
Of apples and of berries
And the groves of tree and fern?
Shall I talk of key and lock,
Of splendid mount and rider,
Of shaft planted in target,
Or keen sword at ease in sheath?
I could whisper the wedding
Of the fish leaping upstream;
I could spell out the story
Of tender gates, secret shrine,
Of the priest's life-giving knife,
The victim her own altar.

But no: I will not smother
Bare facts with blanketing words.

I need a speech as simple
And stripped as our lively selves,
A liturgy of naked
Letters for our act of love.
There are words I have not said:
I use them, and I stutter.
Sound roots, but rotten branches.
Can the language of the tribe
Be purified of the filth
From centuries of dirty
Mouths and sniggering scribbles
Upon lavatory walls?

No lover in Lawrence, I,
No prelapsarian linguist
Naming his Eve's shameless parts,
And yet, no Manichean:
Dumfounded by her body,
Reduced to the use of braille,
I praise with reverent hands,
With a fine art of fingers,
The smooth skin of her belly
And the dear heft of her breasts,
And I woo and wed her flesh,
Mouth upon mouth, in silence,
A husband, a clumsy man,
A lover lacking language.

ANNIVERSARY

Lost, and I cannot recall
What he was like, that boy who,
Nineteen long summers ago,
Stood with you at the altar,
Vowing for life, not lightly,
Knowing little what was meant.

Richer, poorer; sickness, health;
Better and worse; the nineteen
Years converted the abstract
Words into body and blood.
Our flesh-sharing, your bearing
Eight children and my neglect,
The easy quiet evenings
Together, the nights you turned
Away with dreadful stillness
Unable to tell me why,
My harsh words and your weeping
(Language is my world and yours
Is silence, in grief and joy),
Daily delights in common,
Pride and pain, children changing,
My illnesses, your fatigue –
Enough of this foolish list!
We have outlived the couple
So confident as they vowed.
We are these years of marriage.

I know, now, what the words mean.
I know too I shall never
Know you wholly, however
Many our years, I know best
(After three separations
In nineteen years) I am not
A single self without you.
This first anniversary
Apart, in separate beds,
One long night and two hundred
Miles between us till we meet
For a late celebration,
A long-delayed conjunction
Of bodies and hearts and minds,
A sharing once more of words
And silence, a new wedding,
This night, alone, once again
I make these vows, now meaning
All that our marriage has meant
And will mean, all surprises
And trials of love between us.
The brash boy to whom you gave
Yourself is a flawed man who
Blesses your gift, and vows love.

A CYWYDD FOR KATE
married June 20, 1970

Twenty years since I waited,
A first-time father, afraid
For you, climbing the winding

Stair to the lintel of life,
Afraid of those fragile steps,
Fearful of your exposure
To light and air, the wearing
Years to come, fearing that I
Would fail you in performing
A father's role, unrehearsed,
No script to follow, no cues.
Then from those pangs of waiting
The birth of wonder and joy,
The moment of your entry,
Wrinkled and pink and bawling
And utterly beautiful.

Reduced, now, to my proper
Bit player's role, quite content
To speak a prelude and yield
Center stage to you, linger
In the wings, I wait once more,
Feeling no father's envy
Of your leading man, finding
The wonder and joy reborn
As you, serene and lovely,
No girl, but a woman grown
Pledge yourself to a new life.
Yours, now, is the unwritten
Play, the improvisation,
But mine again the first fears
For you, knowing that marriage

Is an art that none can teach,
How false it would be for me
To offer you direction.

No paternal platitudes
From me, then – but permit me
Merely a benediction.
A happy marriage? For you,
That wish would be unworthy.
May you live your marriage vow
To the full, its joy, its grief,
Unregretful, forgetting
Not one word you speak today,
But learning more each moment
What the words mean by making
The word flesh as you embrace
The man, the world you marry.
May you celebrate each day
Creation, crucifixion,
And each day's blessing of birth.

Dear daughter, may Love in you
Learn a new incarnation.

A CYWYDD FOR CHRISTMAS

Each year a bit more weary
As we complete our home-made
Liturgy: the last-minute
Cleaning up, the candle lit,

The tree (defiantly real)
Trimmed, and the tiny figures
Set carefully in the crèche,
The final Advent service
Interrupting the hurried
Wrapping of gifts in each room
(Glorious waste of gay paper),
And the children's presents fetched
From closets in their absence –
Whether in bed or at church –
And strewn through the living room
For morning's still exciting
Entry and flurried finding,
Though boy and girl to become
Man and women must challenge
Our rite, and we watch it change
Slowly, inexorably.

Accept, dear, alteration
In them and in us, affirm
The bond of love unbroken
In spite of all departures
From childhood, custom, and home,
As we celebrate once more
Our ritual's consummation.
This has not changed: the quiet
Exchange of gifts, and the kiss,
Without passion, confirming
Each year the new birth of Love.

DOUGLAS PHILLIPS

Douglas Phillips was born on 11 February 1929 in Carmarthen, where his parents were shop-keepers. Educated at Queen Elizabeth Grammar School in the town, and at Wadham College, Oxford, he served in the Royal Navy for two years and then became a journalist, working as a sub-editor with the *Western Mail* in Cardiff. In 1962 he left journalism for teaching and, four years later, was appointed to a lectureship in English at Derby College of Art and Technology. He died in 2002. He published two books of poems, *Merlin's Town* (1965) and *Beyond the Frontier* (1972), as well as a monograph in the *Writers of Wales* series (1981) on the life and work of another Carmarthen poet, Sir Lewis Morris (1833-1907), highly popular in his day but now largely unread.

TO SIR LEWIS MORRIS

Excuse me, Sir Lewis, I hope you won't mind my addressing
you
Directly, even though you almost became Poet Laureate, for I
Was born in the same town, looked at the same view
Over the Towy, but of course, unlike you, have yet to die.

Yes, we even went to the same school, though not on the
same day;
Reading Tennyson's Idylls in a draughty classroom, how
was I to guess

361

That he had many times walked with you along this way,
A guest, a fellow-poet, at your home address?

Unknowingly, we rub shoulders with the dead, their ghosts
Pass, invisible pedestrians on the pavement, we
Walk on, never realising how close their muted behests.
We encounter our pasts daily; they nod unobtrusively.

Years later, reading a guide-book or local history, we awake
To the truth we denied when we slept; too late to retrace
Our steps in those years when with dull opaque
Eyes all we saw was what the sense of sight showed to our
face.

I must have passed you many times running down to the
river,
A boy, to watch the dark coracles, or later arm-in-arm
With my first girl-friend. How could I ever
Have seen you, immune as I was to any imaginary muse's
charm?

I apologise if I have invaded your privacy.
Impossible not to acknowledge you now I have grown
Up with some inexplicable interest in poetry, even though
your residuary
Reputation is perhaps one you would not willingly own.

Even a Laureate is not necessarily a resident statue
In poetry's marathon, so I should not grieve at being
passed over:

You have your grave here on this hill; at least with a view
Like this beauty needs no shrine built by a purely verbal
lover.

Even those umpteen editions of yours – twentieth or was it
twenty-first? –
Best-selling Epics of Hades, now consigned to second-hand
shelves,
Gather dust as quietly as this evening veils with its mist
The bright sun setting on your unscanned second selves.

A knighthood, fame, an applauding audience, such were
the fruits
Of the golden apples of your Pre-Raphaelite Hesperides.
Accept my salutations, though scorn the implied roots
Of my pity. How could I condescend in face of such
heydays as these?

BRIAN MORRIS

Brian Morris was born in Cardiff on 4 December 1930. Educated at Worcester College, Oxford, he taught at the Universities of Birmingham, Reading and York before his appointment as Professor of English at Sheffield University in 1971. From 1980 to 1991 he was Principal of St. David's University College, Lampeter, resigning in order to take his seat in the House of Lords as Baron Morris of Castle Morris, a title he took, with typically impish humour, from the tiny hamlet in Pembrokeshire where his family had its roots. In the House of Lords he was the Labour Party's Deputy Chief Whip from 1992 to 1997; he also served as Vice-Chairman of the Trustees of the National Portrait Gallery and as a member of several committees in Wales. He was a prominent lay-member of the Anglican Church and edited a volume of essays on liturgical reform, *Ritual Murder* (1980). He died in Derby on 30 April 2001. Besides his academic work – he edited the *New Mermaid Dramatists* series and the *New Arden Shakespeare* – he published five books of verse: *Tide Race* (1976), *Stones of the Brook* (1978), *Dear Tokens* (1987) and *The Waters of Comfort* (1998); his *Collected Poems* appeared a few days before his death. He also wrote a monograph on Harri Webb in the *Writers of Wales* series (1993). Many of his poems are about places and people in Wales, a country he explored during his years at Lampeter; the mountains of Snowdonia and the rivers of west Wales were among his favourite subjects.

UPON THE PRIORIE GROVE,
HIS USUALL RETYREMENT

'Vivi tu, vivi, o Santa Natura?' (Leopardi)

Leaving Brecon's old foursquare red sandstone cathedral
On the left, and crossing the little iron bridge
Over the Honddu, the traveller discovers
A rural paradise. So all the guide books say.

Less true if you go in March: then in the high elms
Baroque rooks tower, wheel, or hang squatting on the wind,
Building like God's masons their black twig roof bosses
In this green nave. Each rasping voice a sceptic's wheeze.

Yet rooks cheer us; high nests are prophets of summer.
That scratching song calls up memories of canons
Long dead, shades of Caroline divines, grave prelates
In lawn sleeves. But this grove has older memories,

Less distinct, but imaged in this green furniture.
Gothic extravagances drip from every tree.
Look where the poisonous ivy scores his false twists
On the oak, like crazy veins outside the body,

Veins variocele, public, strangling the stiff stock,
Binding and winding, carrying a deadly sap
And visiting tenderly each hair root and branch.
The invisible made visible appals us.

Underfoot the drifts of soft gold honey-fungus
Glow in the damp shade, trailing their deceptive fire
Over the rotting bark; the parasitic crop
Reminds us of the golden druidic sickle.

Daphne, whose throbbing heart once pulsed inside each tree,
Died long ago, if indeed she ever came here.
The goodly train, Celtic and Roman, is exiled,
And not a hint of Nymph trips, traps, or hunts here now.

And, gentle traveller, do not expect when Windes
And Teares of Heav'n shall these green curles bring to decay
Elysian apotheosis of this grove:
Such solutions are strictly unattainable.

You and I have to go on living with these trees.
We are unlikely to survive them. Stand, noting
The significant point made by ivy-veined oaks;
For in this grove there are no other spectators.

AT NON'S WELL

Look down, holy lady, on this fountain
Marking the place close to the cliff's edge where
One harsh night, fourteen hundred years ago,
You felt your time come. You dropped a saint here,
In thunder, lightning, and in teeming rain.

It was labour in vain, lady, it was

Labour in vain. Aneirin, Cadwal, all
Court bards who sang such songs about your boy
Forgot to write them down. Chronicles fail
To provide details. Hagiographers

Came too late. Too few manuscripts survived.
At the Synod of Brefi all agree
He spoke like a god, but apart from that
No facts remain. No, my girl, in one way
He might as well not have been born. Or lived.

Historians are always truth's traitors.
Some miracle did happen here where, caught
Unprepared, you squatted down, heaved and strained.
We still come to this spring, to celebrate
Mystery: the breaking of the waters.

AT TRE'R CEIRI

There were giants in Llŷn in those days, and they lived on
                                                this mountain
Behind these drystone walls piled high to keep secrets and
                                                hutch holy
Things from the god-searching singing wind off the sea
                                                twelve fields below.

The peak of Yr Eifl towered over them, more psalmist than
                                                guardian,
For it lifted their eyes to the fierce sun drowning beyond
                                                Ireland

And gave them scale, while the rubble trickling slowly
                              down the scree slopes

Taught them comparative weight and the fragility of all
                                        flesh.
They were invincible in all other respects. So they stood
                                        gods
Among men, gods of power and hate, gods who looked
                              down on their people

In purest contempt for that they were weak and small and
                                        subservient,
And for that they worshipped, and lifted up their mute eyes
                                   in their turn,
And for that they drew their water from deep in St
                        Aelhaearn's well.

Up on Tre'r Ceiri water came from a spring which sang
                              below ground
And emerged blinking. They never enclosed it, or put
                              stones round it,
Or (*O fons Bandusiae*) cut any kid's throat on an altar.

There was no need, the stones were sufficient protection.
                                   The walls now
Are ruinously splayed, but the stream still flows, and the
                              well is full.

And at the mountain's foot still swings the eternal eroding
                                        sea.

TRYFAN

The pale horse and his high rider climb it easily,
While the pack horse drops his great head as he plods on
Tasting his cold iron bit in the valley track;

The black goat rides confident and prime, and the hare
Trusting in the thrust of his sure and trembling thigh
Mounts after. Dead and quick serve this age-old goddess.

Plotinus told of rare moments of perfection
Which are incapable of further process. She,
Never proceeding, poised, petrified, and staring

In pharaonic calm, stands pyramidal – dry
Hieroglyph of passive purity of being,
Female, serene. I do not mock Plotinus' thought.

Daughter of chaos, the blinding paradisal
Light that shone at her gestation delivered her
After great age. Ten thousand years of driving rain

Weathered the live stone child into a woman's shape.
And now no lover dares take her, no man goes up
On her immutable perfection for the sheer

Fear of her cliffs, and falling off her, slowly through
This clear light and exemplary airy brightness
In a straight line to death. This involved equation

Is solved, secretly, by every man when he learns
That love is no more but a certain coveting
To enjoy woman's beauty – and is dashed for it.

Adam and Eve sit imparadised on that height,
Perfect sentinels, guarding their goddess mother.
Far below in the darkness, in the tight chapel

Light burns, and aged, dashed, imperfect, fallen men
Sing penitential psalms. Young men, in that warmed air,
Stare, flooded with relief, at fine women grown old.

IN CARDIGAN MARKET

Auntie Jane fish, they call her. She is rough,
Rawboned, fat, toothless, fifteen stone of grin
And grumble. Her voice cuts the market din
Like a saw on a nail. She stinks enough
Of fish to change the colour of the light.
Her phosphoresent flesh's steaming glow
Drips female sweat and friendship. Traders know
Men come for miles and buy from morn till night.
Daily she sells the princely salmon, trout,
The vulgar herring and the vicious eel
With ancient eyes, lobsters black from the creel,
All fresh, all caught before the stars went out.
All day she squats here, nodding her big head,
Richly alive among the silvery dead.

TONY CONRAN

Tony Conran was born in 1931 in Khargpur, Bengal, India, where his father was a railway engineer. Brought back to Wales suffering from cerebral palsy, he was raised by his grandparents in Colwyn Bay on the North Wales coast. He was educated at the University College of North Wales, Bangor, where he read English and Philosophy, and in 1957 was appointed Research Fellow and Tutor in the English Department there, a post from which he retired in 1982; he lives in Bangor. He is a convert to Roman Catholicism. He came to prominence with the publication of *Formal Poems* (1960) but it was as translator of *The Penguin Book of Welsh Verse* (1967) that he won a wider reputation; this masterly book was reissued as *Welsh Verse* in 1986. He has also published two influential books of essays which deal, *inter alia*, with aspects of Welsh writing in English and the technicalities of translating verse: *The Cost of Strangeness* (1982) and *Frontiers in Anglo-Welsh Poetry* (1997). His own poems have been published in numerous pamphlets, booklets and books, the most important of which are *Spirit Level* (1974), *Life Fund* (1979), *Blodeuwedd* (1988), *Castles* (1993), *All Hallows* (1995), *A Gwynedd Symphony* (1996), *Visions & Praying Mantids* (1997), *Eros Proposes a Toast* (1998) and *The Red Sap of Love* (2006); his Collected Poems appeared as *Poems 1951-67* in 1974 and his selected poems as *Theatre of Flowers* in 1998. Tony Conran's work as a translator is an integral part of his own creative work as a poet and critic. In medieval

Welsh poetry he found a culture in which the poet was not an alienated, marginal figure, but one at the community's centre, giving voice to its values, trying to speak on its behalf and creating cultural coherence; he is critical of poetry which is merely the expression of a poet's private thoughts or feelings. Many of his poems are typically addressed to a named person or written for a particular occasion, while others are staunchly anti-capitalist and anti-imperialist.

AN INVOCATION OF ANGELS
1958

In the secret, inflexible walls of our need
That moment when the womb
First leaps to the beloved – O hostile and
Illimitable grace! Gabriel,
– You of green wings –
                  hear our prayer...

Consider the youth. A Welshman at twenty
Is either an awkward edition of fifty
Or else he's gone English. Two varieties
Persist – roughly, the sheep and the goats.
The sheep go bleating after some pipes of Pan,
The Blaid or the Chapel. Belief's not scarce
In Wales, and a dark, indestructible belief
It usually is: slogans come out, time
After time, like a nestling cuckoo
That's after a finch. Seven hundred years
Of obstinate repetition against all odds

Have done their work: to relax from faith,
To allow the intellect play,
Meant treason.

And the goats? Rebels, leaders of thought,
But so conscious of standing on quicksand,
That to believe in anything is cruelty,
It so saps their lifeblood to the mire
Sucking beneath them. What informed faith
Can ever again feed charity in Wales?
Love that is clear as a mountain stream,
Intellectual charity, that is not puffed up,
That goes straight-eyed to the pit,
That wipes a child's nose with the same concern
As it builds sanatoria, that is not put off with words
And induces a sly disregard for uplift
And the indulgence of the *hwyl*: Love, great Love
Wherein the scattered leaves of all the world
Ingather like a volume, make one people,
One faith. one charity, thy servants who dwell in Wales,
A haystack's needle in continuing legion.

O Micha-el, rebuker of discord,
Thrust into hell Satan and all his angels
Wandering the world for the ruin of souls.

Consider my people. Seven hundred years
(But an old splendour dies hard)
Of generosity, courage, quicksilver
Dispositions geared to a mainly

Genealogical salvation. A man's root
Going down to the rich loam – that was the crux
That fixed him like a dye, giving him
Covenant and right to be lamented
In formal *marwnadau*. That's all gone.
The great lords, father to son,
Changed pretty quickly to English.
And as Siôn Cent might say,
'Where are they now?' *Mae'r siwrnai i Loegr?*
Mae'r swyddau mawr, os haeddir?
An obsolete conception, practice for
An adolescent writer of odes.
Gone to the wall.

Consider my people. Saints from an arrogant stock.
Even today the Welsh male is arrogant,
Secretly arrogant, under his subservience.
Saints of prodigious sermons,
Revivals, Pantycelyn, and the mysticism
Like a mist lifting below Snowdon. And the arrogance,
The pride not to be English,
Not to be this or that, dividing
Bethesda from Seion at opposite ends
Of the one village...

Lordship is gone. Sanctity a failing investment,
Its credentials suspect. Consider my people,
Twice bereft of their leaders. In the mines
Of the South, Nye Bevan takes fire,
Prometheus of a Red Olympus

374

Like a ghost town – fireworks
Terrible in an English garden, splendid
As an army with banners. The Arts Council mentality
Minces in teashops, talks glibly of
Striking a blow for Wales – five more minutes
In Welsh on the Welsh BBC.

But the Welsh lord's like a phoenix, a chick
Impossible to eradicate. And yes,
The aristocracy of intellect could come,
Has come already, in a few, displaced souls,
Of the third or fourth generation.
Like all aristocracies, that of the intellect
Is a matter of breeding. God spare us our lords,
This time, that the English temptation,
The wolf with privy paw, take not away
The sweetness when the fire should rest,
As I have seen them go – young people,
The third or fourth generation of the mind,
Stolen from Wales.

                    O Raphael,
Sociable spirit, guard with your prayerful ministry
The lordship and the governors of coming Wales,
That their blood be not tempted,
And the star of an ancient purpose
Not be eclipsed in their lordly inclinations!

Rather may my right hand forget its cunning,
O Raphael, protector of pieties.

FOR THE MARRIAGE OF HEULWEN EVANS
1956

As wind, as trees in tumult, haphazard
    As rocks in Nant Ffrancon,
    As the sea dusted with dawn,
    I'll deal for you my blessing.

May love be gentle as a moth, stroking
    The moon upon rushes;
    Like a lark into sunlight
    May he go glad to your bed.

Generous may he be, and strong, like a lord
    Conniving no mischief;
    Honourable in the world,
    And to you, always splendid!

Tall in Llyn Ogwen reflected hills
Are by the ripples shut in black bars:
So I, no matter how I turn – always
    My hope is waived, and no true image.

But of your children may be made whole
All fragmentary generations,
And the calm lake of your Welsh truth body
    The ancient mountains, rock for hard rock.

THE BOMBING OF GUERNICA
a recitation to music for Bernard Rands

Dark labourers pondered this April day
the black enrobement of fat wives.

Still life of an early morning. Harsh shadow and hard light.
Tenderness and brutality in the gesture of laying a cup.

Barn life.Yard life. Devotional
chickens peck and squawk in the muck.

Old fury to old fury
Rumours with jeering malice
What their own Swastika shall do.

(Swastika, hope of the world,
Whose eyes bulge through thick spectacles
To a yawning sun ...)

Hag unto hag reports
This mourning that shall come to market
Like a farmer.

The black birds stand in the corners of the sky.
Their talons are bright,
Their eyes dull with the mechanical
Violence of street louts.

The black birds are ultimate cynics. Sunlight
Is pretext to be dead.

To be herded into death like cattle,
To kill with the brilliant gold of bullets.

They lift their talons to the sky, these black birds,
And delicately tilt their wings
To a precision of narrow prey;
They pockmark the cobbles with gold.

The sky is ripe and yellow like an apple.
The sea questions the horizon, the blue drum
Of the Atlantic is felt amid lemons.
The bloodshed of countless sunsets
Has come to roost in the town of yellow walls.

A bride in the churchdoor in her white veil
Has smiled to the golden suitor. Old women
At solemn vespers of their toothless gossip
Scutter profanely to shelter in screech and nudeness
Pain's undiscrimating phallus of gold.

The bloodshed of many an Atlantic sunset
Ricochets from children. Priest carries Calvary
And dies of a blind man's spear in the kidney
And is crossed as he dives to a nameless death
In the panic of a calling far beyond his.

And the proud birds that stand in the sky's corners
Look uncomplainingly down at the saffron city
With its public emptiness emphatic with corpses,

Its wailing masked by their engines, its mourning
Phlegmatic to their height as starving beggars.

The yellow walls still stand in the applelight
Of an afternoon immemorially transparent
And the gold blood on the cobbles
Is inviting as a widow. Swastika's drum
Must be Pied Piper, call rats from quaking holes.

The black birds gather, then with a scream
Target the saffron town. Façades crumble.
Swastika's great drum echoes along blue gorges
To drag the huddling mobs from privacy
Under the talons wailing for dead man.

Blossoming mornings of winter,
Put no face to the child that sleeps.

Put no feature, no eye or lip,
To the body that sleeps in frost.

Don't remember the sickness of touching
That smouldering charred face

Or the tomb we founded for God
On bones of vomiting gold.

Strict acid light of morning,
Put no face to the child that sleeps.

SILVER SPOON

for Cynan, my godson

Light in the half-inch bowl
Reflected
Is a star blazing in an argent field,
The shield trisected

Where it lies, by a corner of walls and ceiling
White and gold.
Filled with the radiant grain of metal
Myriadfold.

The slender stem reaches upward
Like a flower stalk
To the crest where a squat little dragon
Ungainly walks.

I'm a bit nonplussed about giving you
Such a trinket.
It won't keep you warm. It won't love you.
You can't eat or drink it.

But today, like one of the Kings,
I come from far.
Little World-Saviour, I fulfil your rites,
I follow your star.

They will pour the water over your face,
My holy one,

And yourself not sure yet whether birth was good
Or wisely done.

They will fold great hands about you. Waters
Will wet your eyes.
The cold rain darkens on the rocks of your exile,
Falls from blind skies.

Child, it is difficult. Having got used to the dry
Feel of world, yet
To be pressured again, and shocked into birth's
Strenuous wet.

Nor can gifts help. They hardly make sense:
How can I give
When the concept GIFT is not separable
From how you live?

How futile my timely present
Becomes in this Now
Where the christening waters of Bethlehem
Crown your brow!

Yet what I have brought, I must give.
I could not stand
In this spot where all is offered
With a void in my hand.

Gifts whose only point is the formal
Act of giving

Can arbitrarily be given meaning
Like charms for living.

All I can give are symbols
Of once and soon –
Heraldic things – gold, frankincense, myrrh –
A silver spoon.

When you are four or five, they will hand it to you,
Cynan, and say:
'Your godfather gave you this
On your christening day.'

And you will look at the little Welsh dragon
And see the shield
Where the light's trapped like a blazing star
In an argent field.

It will remind you where you were born,
And perhaps, you'll guess
How a wise man seeing your star in the east
Came to bless.

ELEGY FOR THE WELSH DEAD,
IN THE FALKLAND ISLANDS, 1982

Gŵyr a aeth Gatraeth oedd ffraeth eu llu.
Glasfedd eu hancwyn, a gwenwyn fu.
                              – Y Gododdin (6th century)
(Men went to Catraeth, keen was their company.
They were fed on fresh mead, and it proved poison.)

382

Men went to Catraeth. The luxury liner
For three weeks feasted them.
They remembered easy ovations,
Our boys, splendid in courage.
For three weeks the albatross roads,
Passwords of dolphin and petrel,
Practised their obedience.
Where the killer whales gathered,
Where the monotonous seas yelped.
Though they went to church with their standards
Raw death has them garnished.

Men went to Catraeth. The Malvinas
Of their destiny greeted them strangely.
Instead of affection there was coldness,
Splintering iron and the icy sea,
Mud and the wind's malevolent satire.
They stood nonplussed in the bomb's indictment.

Malcolm Wigley of Connah's Quay. Did his helm
Ride high in the war-line?
Did he drink enough mead for that journey?
The desolated shores of Tegeingl,
Did they pig this steel that destroyed him?
The Dee runs silent beside empty foundries.
The way of the wind and the rain is adamant.

Clifford Elley of Pontypridd. Doubtless he feasted.
He went to Catraeth with a bold heart.
He was used to valleys. The shadows held him.
The staff and the fasces of tribunes betrayed him.
With the oil of our virtue we have anointed
His head, in the presence of foes.

Phillip Sweet of Cwmbach. Was he shy before girls?
He exposes himself now to the hags, the glance
Of the loose-fleshed whores, the deaths
That congregate like gulls on garbage.
His sword flashed in the wastes of nightmare.

Russell Carlisle of Rhuthun. Men of the North
Mourn Rheged's son in the castellated vale.
His nodding charger neighed for the battle.
Uplifted hooves pawed at the lightning.
Now he lies down. Under the air he is dead.

Men went to Catraeth. Of the forty-three
Certainly Tony Jones of Carmarthen was brave.
What did it matter, steel in the heart?
Shrapnel is faithful now. His shroud is frost.

With the dawn men went. Those forty-three,
Gentlemen all, from the streets and byways of Wales,
Dragons of Aberdare, Denbigh and Neath –
Figment of empire, whore's honour, held them.
Forty-three at Catraeth died for our dregs.

A SQUARE OF GREY SLATE

*presented to Pedro Perez Sarduy, Cuban poet, at the Wales-
Cuba Resource Centre at the National Eisteddfod 1985 in Rhyl*

Days I have been wondering, Señor,
How I should speak:
The very language I use being wrong
For Eisteddfod week.

And yet I'm not satisfied
To mumble it glumly
As a mere *lingua franca*
Between Cuba and Cymru.

My tongue's my own, True Thomas says.
How then
Can I speak in the crowding name of all Welsh
Women and men

To offer you, Señor, the brotherhood
Of Welsh Wales?
How can I strike red fire from the very iron
Of our chains?

This morning early, I went to my rainy garden
Hoping to find
A messenger – perhaps a riddle
Of times out of mind –

A palimpsest of my people, a forgotten tryst
That I could keep

For them this Monday morning
Of Eisteddfod week.

There in the path was this square of grey slate.
Let that stone
Be my herald, I said, let its mute cry down the years
Atone

For my English. Let it speak
Where I cannot
Of the Welshness of Wales
Now, on this spot.

Men die here for stone. The ancient strata eroded
By rain, by frost,
Till the massif's a mere negative
Of what it was...

Señor, stone is the stuff of oppression
In this land.
Look, the conqueror's castles, Rhuddlan, Rhuthun, Denbigh
Still stand.

No one in Wales is untouched by rock.
Coal and slate
– Laid down before dinosaurs walked the world –
Dominate

Vast tracts of our industry, our past.
It was for stone

That the shanty-towns mushroomed
To chapel and home.

Rock was our vortex. Our working class
Was drilled from it.
Their dream and their discipline answered
The greed of the rich.

Strike. Lock-out. Depression.
Let this stone lip
Tell of those terrible years.
Now, slate-tip, coal-tip

Rear up like pyramids. Pharaoh and Israelite
Share
The memorial of the dump
Under wide air.

Welsh poets in love, Llywelyn Goch, Dafydd or Iolo,
Used to sing
Poems to thrush or tomtit, salmon or north wind
– Anything

Under the moon that moved, he'd make it
Ambassador,
Messenger, *llatai*, for him, to travel
Straight to his girl's door

And tell her how much he loved her
And how much

He died, died for the sight of her,
Died for her touch.

Now therefore I command this square of grey slate
To go *llatai* for me
Through the Westerlies and Trades
To the Carib Sea.

Go, little Fidelista of slate,
To the midmost
Of the Americas, where the plumes of royal palm
Mark Cuba's coast.

Go to the sugarcane fields, the rice paddies,
The orchards –
Go where the blacks once died like flies
As the cash flowed northwards.

And tell them, slateling, about our country,
This place of stone
At the edge of Capital's shadow
As the day comes on.

CASTLES LIKE SLANG

1

Castles are like slang. They savour first
As a weapon, a bright deployment –

And who hasn't been taken with the trick of a phrase,
The impudent fit of it, into the language?

It's the answer to need. Suddenly
We can say what we know. It chortles in our teeth.

2

To dark Donegal a rowboat beaches
To pulling hands. They uncrate sweet guns.

Their arms cradle them like food. Fingers
Smooth along butts, test sights for true.

Like weapons the world over, their beauty
Is passionate as birth. Shall they kill? Will I live?

The slang word weeds it in our acres
The cliché's hegemony oppresses us.

3

I have walked tunnels of the Wehrmacht
Where the big guns wheeled out from the fjell.

U-boats nestled like bees. Grey fjords
Were hard on the longings of men.

They still have the disconsolate smell
Of building sites where nothing can happen.

Rubbish won't be cleared. Suddenly
The warmth of soft fern opens to an insane granite.

4

It is terrible the revenge we take on castles,
Burn everything that burns, strip the lead roof.

Towers hang slipshod as we play King Kong,
Throw buttresses into the sea, tear curtain-walls like paper.

It is terrible. And the clichés die down
In vast rubbish heaps of language, poisoning wells.

5

But rock calls to rock. Phrases
Erode to dialect, glint from children's songs.

Spleenworts star dark crevices. Stonecrop
Wanders the old mortar. Lichens dye in rings.

Soon the trees will come. Primroses
And violets huddle by the stumpy wall.

And before this weapon becomes what it always was
– Geology and the processes of soil –

before this folly inches like a scree
and slips utterly to ground,

Alys, aged six, turns cartwheels in the court,
Enfys, aged four, sings out from two-foot walls.

HERBERT WILLIAMS

Herbert Williams was born in Aberystwyth in 1932. At the age of 16 he contracted tuberculosis and spent two years in a sanatorium at Talgarth, Breconshire. He later became a journalist in Aberystwyth and Cardiff, writing for the *South Wales Echo* and the *Western Mail*, and producing programmes for BBC Wales; he lives in Cardiff. He has written a great deal on Welsh historical topics, including battles and stage coaches, as well as biographies of the industrialist David Davies and John Cowper Powys, a collection of short stories, *The Stars in their Courses* (1992), and three novels, *The Woman in Back Row* (2000), *Punters* (2002), and *A Severe Case of Dandruff* (1999). His books of verse are: *Too Wet for the Devil* (1963), *The Dinosaurs*, which appeared in the Triskel Poets series in 1966, *The Trophy* (1967), *A Lethal Kind of Love* (1968), *Ghost Country* (1991) and *Looking through Time* (1998); his New and Selected Poems, *Wrestling in Mud*, appeared in 2007. He is particularly interested, as a writer, in personal relationships and the impact on people's lives of authority in all its manifestations. His poems use plain diction to reveal the pathos of even the most humdrum of lives.

NOTHING TO REPORT

Give me the insignificant times,
When circulation managers moan,
And no-one is looking for sacrifice,
And honour is safely left alone.

Give me the strictly anonymous hours
Unfit for heroes, the lightweight day
When girls get married, and old men snooze,
And history looks the other way.

The bones lie white on the path to glory,
The finest hour bleeds like rain,
And a thankful nation's victory hymn
Is drowned by the infant's cry of pain.

Give me the unexceptional time
When work is honest, and hands are clean,
And nothing happens, except that, *God!*
The boys grow tall, and the grass grows green.

THE OLD TONGUE

We have lost the old tongue, and with it
The old ways too. To my father's
Parents it was one
With the *gymanfa ganu*, the rough
Shouts of seafarers, and the slow
Dawn of the universal light.
It was one with the home-made bread, the smell
Of cakes at missionary teas,
And the shadows falling
Remotely on the unattempted hills.

It is all lost, the tongue and the trade
In optimism. We have seen

Gethsemane in Swansea, marked
The massacre of innocents. The dawn
Was false and we invoke
A brotherhood of universal fear.
And the harbour makes
A doldrum of the summer afternoon.

Even the hills are diminished.
They are a gallon of petrol,
There and back. The old salts
Rot. And the bread
Is tasteless as a balance sheet.

Oh yes, there have been gains.
I merely state
That the language, for us,
Is part of the old, abandoned ways.

And when I hear it, regret
Disturbs me like a requiem.

A CELEBRATION

You will know it, the ragwort,
Though not perhaps by name –
A yellow flower, full
Of mischief for the gardener.
A common weed, populous
As common people, and as apt
To make the best of an indifferent lot.
You will know its pertinacious ways,

Its bland possession of a tumbled soil,
And you will wonder why
I celebrate its impudence.

Well, I will tell you. There is a spot
In Cardiff where the Taff
Flows between grubby banks. The view
Is nonexistent. Concrete, bricks,
And traffic brash as pain.
Between the road and river runs
A row of rusty railings. And just here
The ragwort grows. A common weed.
But such a blaze of beauty that it blooms
Redemption on the urban blasphemy,
And justifies itself like Magdalene.

EPITAPH

He was in no sense an eminent man.
Nobody feted him at the Savoy,
Measured his profits, or even
Tossed him an O.B.E. He lived
Strictly in anonymity, save
For a certain local reputation
In the art of understanding Government documents,
And helping the bewildered
To claim a crumb from organised Mammon.

He was proud of this skill. He was not,
In the finest sense, modest. He would speak
Complacently of how he refused

A drink among drinkers, and was
Admired for it. You may condemn this
Parading of virtue, but why let it vex you?
He was, after all, unworthy of notice,
He was in no sense an eminent man.

And yet I remember his
Passion for knowledge, the way he
Pursued it in the earnest manner of the humble:
Penny readings, night classes,
University extension lectures – these
Were his curriculum. And he never
Rebelled against learning, although his bread
Was rarely more than formally buttered.
It was, for him,
Reward in itself, not a means
Of immediate grace and material glory.

And now the dust stops his mouth, and worms
Deride his dignity, I recall
His affection for children, the happy
Knack of his laughter, and the way
He would hoist his cap and shout 'Great Scotland Yard!'
I remember how he made failure
An honoured possession. And I feel
An indignation with death, although I expect
No-one to share it. For triumphantly I declare it –
Save for the mighty love he inspired,
He was in no sense an eminent man.

THE ALIENS

They brought a foreign warmth
To valleys bleak with strife
And Calvinism, brewing
A relaxation in the coffee cups.
And sunny voices learned
The mysteries of a tongue
Dark with the shadows of an ancient war.
They read the native ways
But kept, perhaps, an irony
Hidden behind their friendly, Latin eyes.
But they were too polite
To mock our self-denial,
And anyway, it wasn't good for business.

Their cafés, innocent
Of obvious sin, were yet
Viewed with disapproval by the folk
Who idolised a God
Who never smiled on Sunday,
And thunderously visited a curse
On all who stepped inside
To buy a box of matches for
A pipe of surreptitious Sabbath peace.
And yet the cafés spread.
And they became accepted.
And God, at last, was able to relax.

Times change. Some chapels now
Are turned to supermarkets,
The gospel is according to demand.
And hedonistic clubs
Have striptease on a Sunday,
Behind the seventh veil lies the promised land.
But still the Rabaiottis,
Bracchis and Antoniazzis
Keep their faith in God intact
And their attitude polite:
The customer, of course, is always right.

DEPOPULATION

They say this is no place for the ambitious.
The young men leave, trailing
A pity for the people left behind,
Nailing the coffin of the town they go,
Finding refreshment in familiar lies.

And far from the accustomed hills they build
The stucture of success which they were told
Would monument their paragon advance,
If only they were bold enough to leave
The moment they were old enough to go.

So now this is no place for the ambitious.
With every decade it is more
Conclusively a place that people leave
The moment they are bold enough to go.

And some have no regrets. But others find
A virtue in the ruins left behind,
And long to verify the truths
Their fathers read, and tread
The ways that scored their rooted enterprise,
And nurture a simplicity, until
A darkness comes to cover up their eyes.

But ambitious they are, ambitious to a man,
Made ambitious by their education,
Prisoners of their nourished talents.

So they display the customary
Pity for the people left behind.
But their bleak hearts speak
The bitter language of the dispossessed.

COUNTDOWN TO THE GULF

The more or less accomplices
were mildly stirred to gladness by it all.
The thrill of it, the sense
of drama in the air.

They read the papers eagerly, the rude
tabloids crying war. A new
tyrant was a marvellous invention.
Where else to focus hate, after the thaw?

The trim accountancy began.
X men on this side, Y on that. Z tanks,
and oh, the warplanes! Suddenly
our skies were clear. The jets
that skimmed Plynlimon now skimmed Araby.

Some raised the palm of peace and sent out doves.
The palm soon withered, and the doves
fluttered their tattered wings.
The air was poisoned and they could not breathe.

The careless children played their airy games,
their dark eyes gleaming and their hands
skittering like birds. How could they know
their simple virtue was of no account?

The threadbare politicians spoke,
saying important things. And over all
a silence lay. Complicity
hung like a shroud between the sun and man.

Like shrivelled leaves the spent days shivered down,
till none were left. The branches of the tree
of life were bare. The killing game began.

FUNERAL ORATION

It's kind of you to come. You're busy people,
and dead men have such shady habits, dragging
workers from their desks and factory benches.
The country really can't afford such gestures.

I shan't delay you long. I simply wish
to thank you for the honour you have done me,
the love you gave me when I was among you,
the trick of laughter and the gift of sorrow.

I loved my wife as rivers love their channels,
I flowed within the confines of her being
not simply out of matrimonial habit,
but in the truth that comes with years of sharing.

I loved my children too. My lovely children.
They grew like trees beside that flowing river,
their shapes and colours changing with the seasons,
their brave roots reaching out to one another.

I had my virtues and my imperfections,
and leave the world no better than I found it.
I'll go to earth as cunning as the foxes,
and let the hunters find another quarry.

DANIEL HUWS

Daniel Huws was born in London in 1932 and brought up Welsh-speaking. Educated at Peterhouse, Cambridge, where he read Celtic Languages, Old Norse and Icelandic, he taught in London before his appointment to the staff of the Department of Manuscripts at the National Library of Wales. He retired in 1992, having worked at the Library for more than thirty years, latterly as Keeper of Manuscripts. He has published two books of verse, *Noth* (1972) and *The Quarry* (1999).

FROM AN OLD SONGBOOK

The girl was sensational, he was a creep,
His eyes were like pebbles while hers were so deep
That at night the thought of them left me no sleep
They so plainly knew something was lacking.

As I leaned on this tree I could only advise
That touch it or eat it sure nobody dies
Of a bite of the fruit that will open your eyes
Till like gods you gaze out on the garden.

But somehow we managed to cock up the show
By upsetting the gaffer, old who-do-you-know,
Your one with the voice who's accustomed to go
For his walk in the cool of the evening.

And she whom I love goes eating her bread
In the sweat of a bloke who'd be happier dead
While the horny heels come bruising my head
As I choke on the dust of the desert.

So you beasts of the field take warning by me
However so subtle you think you may be
Keep your tongues to yourselves or the Old Man will see
That you drag out your days on your bellies.

INDELICATE

Served by the quiet woman with the brown eyes
In the delicatessen indelicate even to think
That the sound when she turns aside and movingly
Slices salami evokes the jingle of bedsprings.

THE ORNITHOLOGIST'S FRIEND

The ornithologist, like a doctor
Pronouncing my dissolution, said they were gone.
Lapwings which years ago had abandoned the lowlands
Could no longer be found in the hills, not in these parts.

But he was wrong, for two peewits cry
As they stumble and slide in air like men in snowdrifts
Above the field by the mountain road where I walked
With a headful of sounds which came from no creature on
                                                    earth.

402

No, my darlings, I've too many secrets already.
What would I give to know that you had kept yours,
To find you in twelve months' time drunkenly wheeling,
Summoning me away from your airy domain
Where the gelding stands alone in the field full of rushes.

GOODBYE TO TUDOR

In forgiving mood, this sultry July afternoon,
The last lingering child will be gone
From the gates of Tudor Secondary Modern School,
A school most teachers gratefully shun.

The intimate daily struggle so calmly ends,
Without victory to either side.
Goodbye to the staff and to the boys more sadly
And the girls most sadly I have replied.

And a friend offers congratulations, echoing
Complaints I should have kept unsaid:
'My God, you must be glad to leave.' My children,
For his ignorance I could strike him dead.

THE HOUSE OF SELF-DESTRUCTION

Ominously did the planets foregather
In the twelfth house so full of danger
To the crab in his massive shell who would rather
Sidle a mile than meet a stranger.

BRYAN ASPDEN

Bryan Aspden was born in Blackburn, Lancashire, on 2 May 1933 and educated at the University of Durham, where he read English. He moved to Wales in 1965, making his home at Conwy on the North Wales coast, and working as a local government officer in Llandudno. A Quaker, he learned Welsh and wrote a little in it. He died on 23 March 1999. His two books of poems are *News of the Changes* (1984) and *Blind Man's Meal* (1988).

NANT HONDDU
(for David Jones)

A grail of gorse; basketwork hedges
Threaded with birds. It's the end of March;
Spring still an outline map. These windflowers
And a purse of woodsorrel all that's filled in –

Two memories merging from the same month
Ten years apart, and at different ends of the path
That crosses your land and marks an eastern border.
When you were here you painted two black ponies

Grazing in a cup of the hills; a wattle fence;
Lopped ash and oak; a coverlet of fields;
Forestry rising to the shaved head of the moor –
A land man had neighboured long enough

To turn its grudge to giving – though the gifts
Weren't even-handed, nor was the taking.
You hankered for its comfort, grown up away.
After the first war came here to paint, to study, to recover.

You painted the river coming from Penny Beacon
Or Hay Bluff, past Capel-y-ffin, Pont-y-Wyrlod
To Garn Farm, Dôl Alice, Crucorney
Where three centuries of change have got their tongues

Round the place names, and Englished but not misplaced
                                                    them.
Ten years ago I drove the Austin Cambridge
By the side of Nant Honddu, parked where the sign
Pointed a peglegged walker over Hatterall Hill
Away from Wales, to Hereford cattle and apples.

Today in the wind's gap above Bodfari I watch
Sheep, a sheepdog, two ponies; try to learn
Like you 'the creatureliness of things'; find
Some kindly forms, words that would heal the hurt
Of this land with its boundary in its heart.

WHICH WE ARE

Charnwood, standing with its tin hat on
Among a Home Guard of gooseberry prickles
And blackcurrants loaded with the dud grenades
Of big bud, remembered its war service
On Kinmel Camp and squinted as it spied

Two strangers from its uncurtained windows.
When we moved in, the garden followed us
Through the door – not that we knew one from the other
Where the honeysuckle wangled its way
Under the wallpaper, and bats whittled at the evening
Inside the walls, till their fur cooled
And they poured themselves into the dusk.
Through the windows, in spring, we heard
A raven getting stuck on its first verb.

Gwynt-y-Mynydd creaks like its own footsteps
On the stairs. Rain taps the roof.
We live inside a drum and we are part
Of the music that we're listening to.
Under the clouded pewter of the winter skies
The mountain comes closer, pushing
Humped fields with their boulder scree of sheep.
When it's almost dark Trefor has a choice
Of Mad Dan Dado with his matchstick spaceship
Or Un Llygoden Fach waving his cutlass
Over a translated Armada. Five more minutes
One for each year, then it's 'amser'. He concentrates
On wasting nothing. 'Tell me a story,' he asks.
'Tell it in Welsh or English, which we are.'

ERW FAWR

Candied fruit is served
on the gateposts this morning.
Candyfloss ravels from a drain

and cars skitter on the road
while I walk Mot past Erw Fawr
that we've watched grow
from a sowing of breezeblocks
to streetlamps on concrete stalks;

what's left of a field,
plasterboard crumbs, cement on ivy,
a hedge in ribbons;
ragwort and yellow rattle
where voles ring their bells: 'Blind, blind!'
as the day owl kerbcrawls by.

You know the spot I mean:
its culture of small dogs, half coconuts,
the nurseryman's favourite escallonia,
'Apple Blossom'; lawns with cypress bollards
and merrygorounds of washing? A nice place
to build a greenhouse after Manchester;
where Stan and Connie, Con and Stanley
petition for the planting of trees?

We live across the way. The corner site,
with the bent aerial, the sales-model Citroen Visa;
rhododendrons cringing in the wind,
sick of their diet of limestone chips;
our two children; our two tongues; our two
remaining hens, and their rare eggs.

VIN AUDENAIRE

It would be nice to sit and drink again
in some Berliner Bahnhof Bistro
Vin Audenaire and wisherwater.

New Year's Eve at Olga's. Tomorrow, Paris –
Mr Norris changes toupées at the border.
'Drop in for Himbeergeist or a Prairie Oyster.'

Yes I remember the thirsties:
streetfights, brownshirts, Blue Riders and the Threepenny
                                                    Opera
while the Reichsmark dips and sinks.

Bogeyed from dosshouse, soup kitchen,
with a false passport and a new name,
blond herrenvolkporn in his pocket

on a park bench where lindens drip
an arts dropout dole addict
does up his duffel and dreams of Sturm und Drang.

'Back Britain, bugger blacks,
restore Biggles, birch, Roast beef
and Rupert Brooke.'

Twilight of the Gods? Walhalla?
Open the cabinet. Pour a doctored stiffener.
Wolf it down and Tebbit on.

BRYN GRIFFITHS

Bryn Griffiths was born in Swansea in 1933. Leaving school at the age of 14, he served seven years in the Merchant Navy and, after the seamen's strike of 1960, spent a year at Coleg Harlech. In London during the early 1960s he was a prominent member of the Guild of Welsh Writers, the group which later merged with Yr Academi Gymreig. He edited *Welsh Voices* (1967), an anthology of verse by contemporary poets. Since then he has lived mainly in Australia, where he has worked as an arts officer, journalist and script-writer. He has published a dozen books of verse, which include *The Mask of Pity* (1966), *The Stones Remember* (1967), *Scars* (1969), *The Survivors* (1971), and *The Landsker: Poems of Pembrokeshire* (1994); the last-named remembers the three years he spent at Eglwyswrw as an evacuee during the Second World War. Many of his later poems, collected in *Sea Poems* (1988), reflect his life as a sailor.

TALLEY ABBEY

Here above the scattered stones of Talley Abbey, a bird bullets
Down the sky, drops down to die and stuns the clear air,
To where the lake lies dreaming in the still winter's day.

The eye, caught in the dark valley's timeless clutch,
Sees the twin worlds of air and water work once more –
A finned and diving bird below the water's floor!

Talley, one great rising arch of forgotten faith,
Remains in mind, cross-nailed by time, in the years
That wheel from childhood to the final darkness of our fears.

Five centuries away from sainthood, God's one boxed room
Of blind prayer stands, stone on stone, under the blasphemy
of birds,
By the waiting water where no faith will ever burn again!

A sadness slumbers here in lake and dumb gray wall –
All signs of sanctity gone in the work of weather, man and
bird –
Challenged only by the cry of creatures feathered, finned and
furred.

The lake remains, stones winter crack and fall, and Wales
Lives on in the stunted men who walk her lanes and lonely
hills...
The memoried nets sieve still and only the dogma kills.

The old land creaks on in heave of mountain, crack of furrow,
Where this race and their speech stubborn the tide of history
As the nightwind cries along the lakeside and stirs the water's
face.

And now, here above lake and abbey, another soaring bird
Spins in the trawled sky over Talley; and only a dog's distant
bark
Disturbs the valley's silence and the slow dusk of Mabinogion
dark.

THE MASTER

You worked me well, Mr Thomas,
Duw, mun, all that writing
About an old nobody like me...
Exposing me, Prytherch, like that.
Jawl! Who would have believed it, mun –
Asking all those old questions all the time,
Ordering me about, just about,
And never believing anything I said...

That day when you came down
From Moel y Llyn and asked me
(In Welsh, of course)
If I ever realised the drabness
Of my stark environment –
Whatever that meant –
And the meaning of my life...
And you a vicar, too.

Well, now, Mr Thomas, I've never
Really given it much thought, you see –
I mean there's the farm to look after,
The milking, and the sheep to tend,
And one doesn't get much time
For other things. But I've fine company,
You know: Siân's a good dog,
A good friend.
You did push me a bit hard at times,
Mr Thomas, and tired me with talk,
But I don't really gob much, you know,

411

And I didn't care much for you saying
Of my 'half-witted grin'.
I'm not dull. I go to the eisteddfodau
And I know all about englynion –
And what more do I need than that?

You're in your world and I'm in mine.
I don't go to church, you see –
Chapel's good enough for me!
(And you making the village
Work to your words...)
I mean, who are you to talk?
Up there, high and mighty in your vicarage,
Playing the lord in Eglwys Fach.

DYING AT PALLAU

I remember him now as he was then,
Lying near death in the creaking house,
On that wild night in Wales
When the wind stole breath and the bombing rain
Beat against the farmhouse windows –
Beat through the surf of rushing trees
Where the tides of darkness spilled and ran
Over the drowned fields...
And his children, come again to his side,
Praying away the waters of his death.

Tom Davies of Pallau: farmer and man;
Eighty-seven years in this cage of toil;
Deacon and teacher of the green and country crafts

To the changing children, growing into peace ...
He lay, willow-thin under the heavy quilts,
With all his death apparent
In a hand's thin bone; breathing harshly
With the pressure of his farming years.

Aye, I remember him that night –
His whispered Welsh greeting as I came in –
Barely heard above the vast echo
Of the wind, and the rain exploding
On the room-reflecting window-panes –
And all the kindness living in his eyes
As he slowly died towards the attic of his days.

The old house lives on in the warring winds,
Creaking still in all the weathers of Wales,
Imbued with the memory of his life and gentle ways.

STARLINGS

Starlings at dusk pour across
the dull beacon of the distant sun.

A high crying, cold as winter
in the day's dark metal, they spin,

eddy and spill down towards
the horizon's walking throng of trees.

This fist of birds, flashing black
against the sky's red warning,

batters through the wooden veins
and tells the buds of coming summer.

The slow sap, thick with a season's sleep,
quickens with the clashing song

of the driven starlings, stirs
the sluggish branches to tell

the buried roots of Spring ...
And yet time hangs like a dead fruit.

Who knows this cycled secret
of spinning birds and sensing trees?

Who hears the signals sounding there?
Only blind eyes see the breaking year!

The soundless voice that tells the trees,
the wheeling arm that swings

this black fist of starlings, is rooted
in the ten million years that hover here.

HOLY JOE

Holier than you or I, or so he thought,
He stood, summer and winter,
On the seafront and the Guildhall Green,

Haranguing the Sunday promenaders
Making their way towards the sea.

A small battered lighthouse of faith
In the gray sea of the grimy town,
Holy Joe clamoured and cried
Of our lost souls, the empty chapels,
The dead ends of all our days.

Few gave him any serious thought,
Or listened to his spinning lightfall of words,
But he lent a colour to colourless lives
And sometimes moved us to tears
With the pain of his peculiar grace.

And when at last he died he left
A lasting space that still jars the Green,
Accusing the very air with empty presence,
Lingering long after in the minds
Of Sunday promenaders making for home and tea.

And years later, when passing the Green,
I still see a shadowy figure standing there,
Hands waving like wheeling seabirds,
Words falling in silent thunder
Through the volumes of the misted air.

STUART EVANS

Stuart Evans was born in Swansea on 20 October 1934 and brought up at Ystalyfera in Glamorgan. He read English at Jesus College, Oxford. After service in the Royal Navy, he taught at Brunel College of Advanced Technology and, from the mid-1960s, worked for BBC Radio in London as a producer in the Schools Broadcasting Department. He died in 1994. It was as a novelist that he established his reputation, with eight long, technically complex novels which are more inclined to the philosophical than is usual in English fiction. They include *Meritocrats* (1974), *The Caves of Alienation* (1977), *The Gardens of the Casino* (1976), and a quintet known as *The Windmill Hill Sequence*. He also published two volumes of verse, *Imaginary Gardens with Real Toads* (1972) and *The Function of the Fool* (1977).

JARDIN MUNICIPAL

This ritual sailing of paper boats, sensible
Use of dusty paths, sampling of women, pleasure
In well kept grass, seems to be invested
With some ulterior meaning, an academic idea
Which has nothing to do with grey cadavers
Or the feasible theory of a Third Force.

This is reality. It is what we sometimes fight
For and about: trampled dust on which children

Habitually meet disappointment, affording
Parents rich luxuries of sentiment and worry.
Not difficult to imagine death over there:
Obedient, experienced, quite without malice.

Louts who battle near the artificial pools
Smell and putrefy before the eyes of ladies
Walking poodles called Platon and Achille.
Lovers touch and old clergymen hear far off
Music, dreaming of sin in Saigon and Cairo.
Only heroic statues are cold, solid, unlikely.

But every city has them somewhere: noble riders
Gazing beyond the plunging heads of noiseless
Horses, resolute, stern and deaf. Infantrymen
In war learn to ignore the slight ripping
Noise of a bayonet. Perhaps democracies have to
Withstand every form of gorgeous nonsense.

In all this well meaning order among grocers
With toothache, rheumatic dustmen, playing
Children on a Sunday afternoon, I am more
Than usually exasperated at feeling nothing.
Instead of these gardens, I want a Sahara
Of a place where rocks, corpses, willows, whores

Eagles, fountains, philosophers, dancers have
Their place, and birdlime is good for stonework,
Where scorpions flicker on the broken courts.

That is what such monumentally noble egoism
Deserves; or else to be blackly frozen, naked
Above a crowd striking matches on the noble arse.

BLUE CARNATIONS

Oh no, it is *I* who have the sense of direction,
And it is *you* who are good with maps. And yet,
Much more patient than you think you are, much
More generous than you claim I can be, you put
Up with my loud assertions, laugh when you are right.

And it occurs to me that since our early days
Together, I have always been following the maps
You have sketched and that my sense of direction
Tells me only how to find you and it is always you
Who really know where we are and how not to be lost.

I shall go on blustering, making you laugh;
And teasing you when you pretend to be careless.
But your maps make sense and meaning of our world:
And I am happy to go on walking until I find
Blue carnations or any other token of loving you.

JON DRESSEL

Jon Dressel (his first name is an abbreviation of Jones) was born in Saint Louis, Missouri, in 1934 but grew up across the Mississippi in the steel town of Granite City, Illinois. His mother's parents had emigrated to the United States from Llanelli in 1895. Educated at Northwestern University in Chicago and Washington University in Saint Louis, he was an officer in the U.S. Navy between 1956 and 1969, president of his family's dairy company and assistant city editor for the Saint Louis newspaper, the *Globe-Democrat*. From 1969 to 1976 he was Assistant Professor of English at Webster University in St Louis. He first came to Wales in 1961 and made regular visits thereafter until 1973 when he was given sabbatical leave to lecture at Trinity College, Carmarthen. In 1976, in co-operation with Central University of Iowa, he established the Wales Study Centre for American Students at Trinity College; he retired in 1998 but still visits Wales regularly. He has published four books of poems: *Hard Love and a Country* (1977), *Ianws Poems* (1979), *Out of Wales: Fifty Poems 1973-1983* (1984) and *The Road to Shiloh* (1994). Many of Jon Dressel's poems explore his Welsh ancestry and reflect his life in the village of Llansteffan in Carmarthenshire.

YOU, BENJAMIN JONES

You, Benjamin Jones, dead seventeen
years of a weak chest and mill-dust
before I was born, known by me

through the passionate prisms of your
wife and daughter, my 'mamgu' and
mother; I could never pronounce the

Welsh, she became 'Mimi' ... imagine, a
Puccini heroine from Llanelli, and her,
from middle years on, always close

to fifteen stone, though in the small gilt
wedding picture on my wall she is
lovely as Olwen resurrected

Victorian ... and you, dashing as all
get-out in that wing-collar and brave
moustache; why in God's name did you

come to America, why did you come
to Pennsylvania to discover greed, get
mad, join the union, grub through strikes,

get scabbed, hymn your way west, losing
jobs, leading choirs, fathering eisteddfodau?
why? I found your trunk in Illinois, in a

cellar, the ivory baton, the warped books, the
Welsh words, strange beneath floodstains;
what drove you there, to the prairie, the

Mississippi, to die in 1918, forty-seven,
your cariad, your mortgage, five children at
your side? You sang The Star-Spangled Banner

as your eyes glazed, they said: God, no, Duw,
Arglwydd Dduw, I say, at dusk in this house
in Llansteffan's green October, what do I

know of you, of ash-blown grief, Benjamin Jones?

HARD LOVE AND A COUNTRY

Elizabeth Jones, Mamgu Fawr; you were
fifty-nine when I saw light; my mother
married late, but with promise, as you'd

have it; even so, you locked them out
when they came home from the Caribbean;
to hell with you, said Lucian Dressel, his

German dander up, and wheeled for a hotel
before you could unlatch the screen; after that
you got along; he became your advocate.

Widowed at forty-two you were, end of
the first war, left in the steel town
on the Mississippi with four daughters and a son

and a hollow frame house in the long dingy
shadow of the stack-spired mill; you half-
possessed me, as you had my older cousins,

I was forever overnight, forever in late
sun in your four o'clock kitchen, smelling your
bread, imbibing your tea, wondering at your

gossip, on the telephone in Welsh; Sioni Bach
I was, the all-American Welsh boy, protected
to his gonads by the cozy hulk of you. Later,

I cut your grass, took out your ashes, stopped
for snacks on the way home from junior high,
even when you weren't there; you'd have been hurt,

someone else played first base till I'd had my
solitary welshcakes and coca-cola; it was absurd.
You coughed and coughed all night in the early

stages of your cancer, and I listened, alone,
fourteen, in another room; I was on my way
to a poker game with high school cronies

when I saw the final ambulance; I rode with
you, held your hand, watched the tubed and wasting
weeks in hospital, heard your comatose prayers

in Welsh; years later, awake in Llanelli,
I understood the both of us, at last;
hard love you gave me, Mamgu Fawr,

hard love and a country; hard, this hour.

DAI, LIVE

Prytherch is dead. We have no right
to doubt it, let alone dispute. We must
contend with men we have in sight,

like Dai here, who is clean
as dirt. The rumor in the pub
is that he hasn't been seen

out of that ripening outfit
since the investiture. It may
be a form of protest, though it

seems more likely, ten pints down,
he's just too whipped to shuck that
wind-grey coat, every button gone,

peel those frazzling sweaters, rife with him
and earth, let those grime-stiff trousers
fall, or try to fall, before things dim.

Too whipped, perhaps, to kick those mud-
brindled boots to a corner, or toss
that crust of a cap to a bed-

post, if he has one. No farmer, Dai,
he digs around the village, roads,
sewers, God knows what, digs all day,

digs everywhere, turns up pints,
grubs of coin for the slot, studies men
who commute to Carmarthen, nods, squints,

grunts a little rugby, weathers at his end
of the bar like a cromlech, drones
like the surf when those with more voice bend

the last elbow in hymn, leaves alone
with a guttural wave, boulders into night,
a man-shape hulking like an age of stone,

that knows no women, but lives with what it knows,
hard as breath, or a December rose.

THE SHOP GIRL

My name is Annette. I am fat,
or will be when the potato
finally has its way. I was born
to the council house. My father
is a road man and my mother

waits at Wimpy's. In another Wales, before
the broadcast image and the tabloid slang
from London, I might have gone to chapel,
felt stifled, spoken differently, thought
of other things. As it is I hang
around bus shelters, grease my eyelids,
go to Plug's Disco and buy platform shoes.
I was glad to leave school, conditioned
as I was to look on sixteen
as my age of liberation.
It was true. There are worse places
than Littlewoods. I have my paycheque
and a boyfriend, a taste for babycham,
and a vague vision of prams. Having
no larger needs or illusions, I will
be happy enough, and die, if I am lucky,
at my ease with Sunday telly at the age
of eighty-two. What is the dream
of Wales to me? Even the poet who
toys with me on this page understands
that in my kept inertial dullness I am
utterly invincible, and make his hand go slack.

SAM ADAMS

Sam Adams was born in 1934 at Gilfach Goch, Glamorgan. Educated at the University College of Wales, Aberystwyth, he taught at Lockley School in Bristol before becoming a lecturer in English at Caerleon College of Education in 1968. He joined Her Majesty's Inspectorate of Schools in 1974 and has lived for many years in Caerleon. He has contributed to the study of Welsh writing in English as editor and critic. From 1973 to 1975 he was editor of *Poetry Wales*. Among the anthologies he has edited is *Ten Anglo-Welsh Poets* (1974) and he has contributed three monographs to the *Writers of Wales* series; he has also edited the *Collected Stories* and *Collected Poems* of Roland Mathias. For the last eleven years he has written a 'Letter from Wales', dealing with literary matters, in *PN Review*. His own poems have been published in *The Boy Inside* (1973) in the Triskel Poets series, *Journeying* (1994) and *Missed Chances* (2007).

MARTINS' NEST

In the old shed, high up, much magnified
And lit by sunlight gay with dust,
A martins' nest, like half an acorn cup

Or a clay blister plastered to the rafter.
And the parent birds gleaming in stippled
Rays like blue-black flames, then swallowed

Without trace in the scaled and roughcast cyst.
Despite the ladder's awkward stance, I climbed
Among rods of sun impelled through rusty pores

Rotted in the thin roof's corrugations,
Slanting pencil-thick to the oily floor,
Solid enough to my light-fingered touch.

A crusted chalice growing from the beam
Descended slowly to my upraised eyes;
Though my young feet fumbled rungless spaces

My giant head rose by the lip.
In spontaneous combustion of feathers
The fledglings fled, their wingbeats scattering

Through the falling shed; I remember
The ladder reeling and my father's shout
Slicing the sunbeams before the light went out.

SLIDING

Do you remember the ritual of candle wax,
The lanes of rubbed grass pale-gold like flax?
Do you remember how we used to slide,
Sharing the cardboard, down the mountainside,
You with your slim girl's thighs spread wide
Accommodating my narrow loins? Your hands
Held fast my summer shirt,

And when the ride began
You pressed your head against my back
And bit my shoulder till it hurt.

Do you recall the gasping flight
As the cardboard swished down the narrow track?
There were jarring bumps when your legs clung tight,
And I thrilled
At your light cries
Though I couldn't see for the dust in my eyes.
Too soon, too soon the final thump
Left us sprawled and stilled
At the foot of the tump.

ONION SELLERS

These our Green Men from a fruitful land,
The stuff of myth, legends in their own time,
(They traded Celtic tongues with Mam and Dats),
Claude, Yves or François, Johnny to us all,
From wide sky and salt-smacked air of Léon

Descend an underworld of basement flats
Condemned houses and unwanted cellars
In Cardiff, Sheffield, London, Aberdeen;
Bearded persephones, self-sacrificed
For six months each year to our sullen towns.

In rooms redolent of sacred garlic
They plait heavy rosaries of brown beads

To bring to our bland doors, industrious
Apostles of a vegetable world
Live-green and golden and richly flavoured.

HILL FORT, CAERLEON

From this tree-finned hill
Breasting the breeze –
Leaf shadows like water shifting,
Sounds of water always moving
In the preening of so many leaves –
I can look down over old Caerllion.

In the aqueous rush of bracken fronds
Breaking round, and in a sound
Clearer now, once heard,
An unbroken hum
Like some instrument endlessly strummed
On one low note, or the tone

Of wires looped from pole
To pole vibrating through wood
Where we pressed our ears,
There is a sense of something living,
Breathing, watching here
As I push towards the rampart mound.

The path is blocked. A swarthy
Sentry bars my way, his spear-
Tip sparks with sunlight.

He challenges in accents I know well;
The words I recognise but the sense eludes.
I am ashamed and silent. He runs me through.

MISSED CHANCES

My father, a proto-biker,
Had leathers made for flyers,
Greatcoat, helmet, jodhpurs,
Of the First World War. His machine was olive drab,
A dinosaur. 'The old Arley' he called it,
A kick-start, air-cooled, 45-degree V-twin
With a twelve-horse roar that on still days
Foretold his coming by a mile or more.

His last bike he never rode,
But single-handed charmed the snarl from it again
After thirty years of silence.

We could talk that over now,
Explore the subtleties of carburettor, crankcase,
Cylinder and bore, and how the left hand
Slowly gains the right's departed lore.

Too late of course. That moment passed
Before I learned to ask and listen,
Ask again, lest conversation perish
On the sudden, final closing of the door.

AT THE SPANISH STEPS

February again, late afternoon:
Black fingers tilt
The fountain's silver, quick
In its marble spoon.
Sun stripes spilt
From a shadowed alley
Across the cobbled square
Will not linger there.
Darkness follows soon.

Severn, sentry in the march
Of life, saw the fountain,
Like a foundered boat, lurch
At its mooring. Light ebbing,
Descended the steep stair, ran
One thirty steps across the square, sobbing,
To the trattoria,
Bought supper for a dying man.

Six sentry paces past the narrow cot,
Two at the blank wall,
Six paces back, turn,
Three at the tall,
Shuttered windows. Look down:
There in the marbled hull,
Like blood, the waters for a moment burn.

After the death mask,
The scissored curl of auburn hair,
After the bonfire, the sickbed burned to ash,
After the vengeful smash
Of unflawed pots, the room waits,
Still at last, stripped bare.

And troupes of lovers pass
To climb the steps and meet
With others going down, or pause
To sit and lean together, close.
Water in the wallowing boat
Catches a gleam, holds it afloat.

Like Severn, I see the sun's snail track
Recede across the water's black,
Walk six paces back.

SALLY ROBERTS JONES

Sally Roberts was born in London in 1935. Her parents brought her to live in Llanrwst and then Llangefni when she was sixteen. Educated at the University College of North Wales, Bangor, where she read History, she worked as a reference librarian in the London borough of Havering from 1965 to 1967. While living in London she was a leading member of the Guild of Welsh Writers, the expatriate group which later merged with the English-language section of Yr Academi Gymreig, of which she later served as honorary joint Secretary and as Chair from 1993 to 1997. She returned to Wales in 1967 on her appointment as Reference Librarian with Port Talbot Public Libraries; she still lives in the town. With her late husband, Alwyn Jones, she established a publishing business known as Alun Books in 1977. Sally Roberts Jones has published a history of Port Talbot and a study of Dic Penderyn. She has also written a monograph on Allen Raine in the *Writers of Wales* series (1979) and a novel, *Pendarvis* (1992); she is one of the editors of the poetry magazine *Roundyhouse*. Her four books of verse are *Turning Away* (1969), *Sons and Brothers* (1977), *The Forgotten Country* (1977) and *Relative Values* (1985). Much of her poetry is set in and around Port Talbot, past and present; it is informed by a steely sense of irony, an awareness of the historical perspective and an ability to reveal the dark side of the most mundane circumstances and events.

A SMALL TRAGEDY

They came up in the evening
And said to him, 'Fly!
All is discovered!'
And he fled.

A quiet little man,
Of no importance.
In fifty years he had acquired
Only flat feet and spectacles
And a distressing cough.

After a month or more,
(He having gone so quickly)
An inspector called
And they began to find the bodies.

A large number of them,
Stuffed into cupboards and other corners.
(At work he was tidy,
But files and paper-clips
Are matters of some importance).

In the end, of course,
He was hanged,
Very neatly,
Though pleading insanity.

A quiet little man,
Who knew what to do with files and paper-clips,
But had no ideas about people
Except to destroy them.

REMEMBRANCE DAY: ABERYSTWYTH

Spray by the castle hurls across the rail.
The mermaid stares forever across the sea,
Dry-eyed; they lay their poppies at her feet,
But she looks away, to the movement of a sail
Far over breakers; knows not their fallen dead,
Hears not their Autumn hymn or the signal guns.

Spray by the castle, spray in November air,
Yearn for the land as she for the empty wave,
(As the dead, perhaps, for their lost and silent home).
Everything empty; castle and crowd and wreaths
Separate beings; and over them, kissing the rain,
The shape of a fish in bronze, without speech, without soul.

On Sundays remember the dead – but not here.
This is another country, another lord
Rules in its acres, who has no respect for love.
Always the sea sucks at the stones of the wall,
Always the mermaid leans to the distant sail;
Already the wreaths are limp and the children wail.

COMMUNITY
(Mr Rogers, buried April 26, 1972)

There has been a death in the street.
Drawn curtains, collections for wreaths –
The historians call it Cymortha,
Assume that it is vanished
In the steam of industrial birth.

We're the size of a village: forty houses,
A shop. Over fences the women gossip,
Watch weddings and growings – observe
The proper and ritual tact
Of those who must live with their kin.

No blood ties, it's true; our bonds
Are accent and place – and desire
For much the same ends. We are not
Political animals; held
An Investiture feast for the children,

And praised all that pomp. On Sundays
Expediency pegs out the washing:
If God is not mocked – well, He knows us –
I suppose it was like this before
When Piety lay in the clouds, an oncoming thunder.

There has been a death in the street;
We are less by that much. Statistics
Cannot say what we lose, what we give:

436

Questionnaires for the Welfare Department
Tell industrious lies.

We adapt. To the chimneys, the concrete,
The furnace, the smoke, the dead trees.
Our fields are the names of roadways,
Our flocks and our language are gone:
But we hold our diminished city in face of the sun.

PALM SUNDAY / SUL Y BLODAU

You might call it the dead run.
A slow, country bus, trundling along the high road,
Disembarking at each chapel gate
Its cargo of flowers – flowers and women,
Each in her second-best jacket,
Prepared for the weather.

I too. In my bag are the trowel,
Daffodils, paper, two jam jars;
I ride among beauty, these delicate trumpets of April.
It is almost a pastoral: sunlight, white clouds on blue oceans,
New buds on the branches, lambs leaping –
The wind's knife at their throat in the sunshine.

And I too will descend,
Open the gate, find that corner
Where people unknown lie remembered;
Will harvest the weeds, wash the mud stains
Away from the stone, place new holders
In leaking memorial urns.

Earth under my nails, feet half frozen,
I wedge fallen jars with the chippings
Against the wind's malice; feel pity
For beauty that dies – that I slaughter
By offering here its frail gold.

Later, on the bus, I ride homeward
Past clumps of cold fire;
Note a patchwork of meetings, conversations
Of annual strangers. It seems
A curious, silent beginning
Beneath the sharp rain.

ANN GRIFFITHS

In little time I stake my claim
To all the panoply of fame.
My words are air, their manuscript
Forgetful flesh, a bony crypt
To lay these stillborn creatures in.

This foolishness of light intent
I turn to praise, my patterns meant,
Poor gift, for Him by whose free gift
My life is bought; the seasons sift
Away my youth, my fear, my sin.

The fire upon my hearth is tame,
God's gentle creature; now my name

Is signed in polished oak and brass,
My soul is singing, clear as glass,
Pure as this babe I bear within.

My songs as light as ash are spent;
My hope's elsewhere, a long descent
In flesh and land – and yet the air
Stirs with fresh music, calls me where
Intricate webs of words begin.

Lord, let me not be silent till
All earth is grinding in Your mill!

TURNING AWAY

I turn away and say 'You do not love me';
Cry bitterly; remember, at this tune,
How all the clichés seemed as sound as apples,
How all the days were stopped at one high noon.

Not quite believing, now I rack each sentence
For meanings that no words could ever hold;
Drag out distinctions, hesitations, use them
On either side according to the mood.

So long without you, that the summer garden
Is overgrown with weeds, a hectic crop
Whose woody stems and vast flamboyant flowers
Blot out the seedling beds they overtop.

Until at last I take them as the pattern,
Expect the skies will suddenly explode
With all the dreams at once, in technicolour,
No effort now, no diffidence allowed.

And when that does not happen, and the poppies
Wither in sudden dryness, overlook
The slow, established colour of the garden,
Rose tree, forget-me-not and seedling oak:

But turn away and say 'You do not love me';
Of all the clichés note but only this,
Most lovers die, incur their final glory
Only through pain; that love's translated loss.

PETER GRUFFYDD

Peter Gruffydd was born in Liverpool in 1935. Evacuated to North Wales early in 1941, he learned Welsh before going to the University College of North Wales, Bangor, where he read English. He has spent most of his life in England, teaching and writing, and lives now in Bristol. As Peter M. Griffith he published his early poems, with those of Harri Webb and Meic Stephens, in *Triad* (1963). Since then he has contributed to many magazines but has published only one collection of verse, *The Shivering Seed* (1972).

MACSEN WLEDIG TO THE WELSH

Well, I knew they were foolish.
After all, did I not warn them
That my tiny chair held two
Not a whole gaggle of swish
Scholars and a failed people
Whose din breaks my heart in the moo
And baa of their weeping?

Ah my people, in your keeping –
What? A fingerhold on Dafydd,
A conviction of the past, a whorish
Twilight of dreams that, with
Your lack of courage, is seeping
Up your marrow-bones; clownish
How you wail and weep!

Ah my people, can you not keep
Your inheritance amongst you?
The scars, you say, lie deep
And how diligently you reopen the blue
Old wounds, living on your ancient wrongs.
Man, go wail in Annwn and beat gongs
To muddle yourselves more.

I cannot be ashamed again.
That is past now and the ore
(As your scholars say to gain
Understanding with their eyes shut)
Of your loded history is mined away.
Fact that you listen to me shows the hut
Where you hid, the past; turn and face day.

SHEPHERD

Time had spaced the air with infrequent
Jags of rock and the ground was quick
With boulders and ideas of years past.
A capped and mufflered shepherd and two dogs
Were granite over the wambling sheep.
The peace of eagles brooded on the crags.

Sharply, to the sudden shrill peep
Of the man's tongue, one of the furred blocks
Snaked over the wizened grass and, free
From the weight of time which dog and man felt

442

In their stiffening bones, harried the leisurely
Sheep, cropping the brown and bents of the hill.

Here the trio were master, but in the lorried
Town they slipped and dodged on the roads, like
Their sheep, chivvied by the oil and noise
Of traffic: what caught them into our time?
Nothing, except the pressure of mortality.

The wind withers, years drown on rain rocks
As the sheep mortgage the dwindling grass.
Over them hoods the blankness of a wasted,
Even though fair and sunset, sky;
And that still vigilance of man and dog.

WOMAN WITH CHILD

Swift she caught my finger up
To her side, like the handle of a cup.
Small but heavy with child
She seems to me now gone wild
With secrets chanted by a lost tribe
Round fires, lost in time's bribe
Of history and the lovely curse of breath.

What sure, delving hands have done
And senses have locked from the slum
Of mind rests, rocks, fulcrum'd
Near the lusting world: drummed
From flesh, hot and weary, the child

Sits, spinning the past with mild
Hands, ready to slip like a bright
Wet fish into our dark daylight.

from THE SOLDIER'S FLUTE

When you wake a cornet drags a snagging path
across your mind; dark still hoods in, pressed
to ice-crazed glass; the coke-stove's cold and dead.

Sleep's muggy exhalation, groans, someone's wrath
at finding pissed-in boots and the knowing, depressed
certainty of where you are clings round heart and head.

Moisture beds on guttering's underside like pale slugs
along its rusty length; each small breath condenses
on window-glass; fingers draw squeaking hearts and names.

Soon the brown speaker nailed up on a ceiling lath
belches, burrs and brass-music coughs out distorted,
makes Jock tuck his flute away, soft sound mute and bled.

The wooden barrack-hut is dense with sleep, drugs
your lungs, your dream-slit eyes, presupposes
order but cannot conceal dawn's greater frames.

We jostle round chill basins certain that verucca spores
drill our sore feet from damp and rotten duck-boards:
there are three spotted mirrors per thirty anxious men.

Old blades scrape lathered chins, styptic-pencil pores
stain brownish red, haste fills the ablutions as hordes
clatter, run in, out that block's heaving, swearing den.

What day will bring know and do not know
but now the light's congealed in night, cold water
gushing, splattering into cracked wash-basins.

Turn out, you bloody men! Guttural shouts from doors,
hob-nailed boots batter, skid, hit the flinty, broad
paths between patch-lit huts – Fall in! I'll count to ten!

Beyond snuffling, coughing lines, dim trees a bow
of light spills from ablutions. The last arrive and later,
Shun! Lines snap up, waver – SHUN, you monkey's cousins!

Behind the leery, peering NCO's ancient mounds, a rath,
loom up in rising dawn, wobbling shapes compressed
into broken ramparts by morning mist's dense spread.

I'm looking at you, you bleeding pig! Stare ahead,
glaze over, do not allow your fear to be expressed
in eye or stance for the delight of Sergeant McGrath.

Over his snaky, poking head those mounds float, a low
pale trail of mist leaving, like smoke from a shell-crater,
and in Jock's mind rigid ranks are bars of a mute tune.

Ahh-bou-URN! We wheel, march off, men from Glasgow,
boys from the fields, old cairns falling behind; traitor
reality kills illusions with day's stiletto bloom.

445

Our boots strike sparks from the paths, too close behind
other heels, stumble, kick – Pickmeup, you sodding clown!
In the canteen morning's half-light dies on bacon-rind,

on gelatinous tea and hoary bread and down
the tables nervy faces lean to eat in day's purblind
touch; night's aborted dreams fall to routine's frown.

SOME FATHERS

They borrowed ten bob, sloped off
to the pub or club, grew potatoes,
caulis, leeks in dead-straight lines,
remembered, I mean, were in, the Second
World War, cracked jokes about Hitler,
Goebbels, Stalin, even Churchill,
did odd things like look after
old ladies in their rich incontinence
or drew cartoons, sketched for small mags.

They seemed to have lots of patience,
except when opening times loomed
over some petty duty, like work.
Mine had a second childhood, a red
scooter which he regularly came off,
half-pissed back from a country pub,
mistook a bush for a turning home.
He carried on until Mother nagged
him into giving up his latecome
burn-ups, so went sketching no more.

446

I'm a father now, think my sons could
sometime achieve this state, make tea
like tar, maybe keep allotments, worry
about their kids, trudge to some bloody
boring job to feed the family's faces,
swear with cronies, be hurt when kids
call them old fart, stupid sod or worse,
wonder where they too went wrong.

Pray there's no war to haunt their nights,
make them keep graveyard horrors at bay
with favourite ales, quips and long tales.
Nuclear families, bowed with labels, stagger
on, the sperm-count falling day by day.
Still I remember those fathers, leaning on
sticks, pint in hand, know they had a sense
of what it's all about, a cod-code to keep
and a smile for outrageous stupidity
because it was to be expected.

ANNE CLUYSENAAR

Anne Cluysenaar was born in Brussels in 1936 and taken to England just before the outbreak of the Second World War. She read English and French Literature at Trinity College, Dublin, and in 1961 became an Irish citizen. In 1987, having taught at Trinity College, King's College, Aberdeen, and the Universities of Lancaster and Birmingham, she withdrew from academic life to concentrate on writing and painting. Since 1987 she has run a self-catering smallholding at Llantrisant, near Usk; she also taught Creative Writing at the University of Wales, Cardiff. She is a co-founder of the Usk Valley Vaughan Association which publishes the magazine *Scintilla*. Among her books of poems are *A Fan of Shadows* (1967), *Nodes* (1971), and *Double Helix* (1982); *Timeslips: New and Selected Poems* appeared in 1997.

from VAUGHAN VARIATIONS
'*Dead I was, and deep in trouble.*'
– 'The Holy Communion'

5

The hillside's a fall of water –
loud, late-spring shower
dropping warm light
from leaf to leaf.
Bright sprays of beech
drop shadow, dots of it,

448

onto the dry grit road.
At the edge, there's a shine of ivy,
its pale downy new tips
feeling out for firm ground.

Why do they draw me so?
After months in the this and that,
hardly trying to live as joy
can let you, I'm grit dry.
Through love, was his way. To a sense
of God. Attention becoming prayer.
Only his mind's movement,
flung beyond circumstance, traced
in changed words, is left me.
The gesture's wordless message.

After the rain, the path's a shade
less dry, and my mare's neck
and my jersey and the path itself
steam, a grey warmth rising
on all sides, like breath.
On the trochees of her walking hoof-beats
vowels and consonants of the forest
improvise their almost-sentences.

What I don't know how to make words of
seems to be said all around me.
I copy what I can. Images.
Taking advantage. The rest
works on untainted. Still distant.

16

On the sudden death of a friend's wife

'But life is, what none can express.'
                              – 'Quickness'

After the first shock, days
of (despite myself) thinking
'it could not have happened'
then raising my eyes and
being astonished instead that
the world was still there
and myself still seeing it.

In one of those first days
we saw her, the white doe,
slowly stepping between
the pine-dark edge
and a bright bulge of pasture
along our furthest fence.
One, two, three steps
only, as she passed
moving only her long legs
behind the tiers of may-blossom.

By the time I got over there
to see if I could catch
sight of her still standing,

maybe, among the tree-trunks –
dark uprights of them floating
among bluebells, thickening
one behind the other until
no more spaces could be imagined
there wasn't a sign of her:
no tuft on the barbed wire
and the grass wasn't silver
where her hooves might have brushed it.

Was this the place? Or further
along the fence – perspectives
being what they are and we
too excited to count fence-posts?
And then against the light,
there were soft holes
in the grass, no more than that.
Her step had been so high,
so certain, as she passed.

I stood between the near scent
of the may and the vast wafting
dimness of so many bluebells.
My husband gone back in the house,
there was nothing to see but
the edge of an empty field and
a woman standing at the edge.

I found it hard to imagine
the weight of the doe, so flat
and white she looked, stepping

in profile behind the may,
her neck vertical as a periscope.
Any warmth she had breathed
into this air, invisible now,
must be drifting with the pale seeds
of the sallow in a great bank
of slow-moving forest breath.

In spite of myself, I strained
after a hint of hesitating white.
There was just a blueness there,
a rise and fall of distance
among closing trees. Dim
but, when focussed on, intense.

23

Thinking of Denize Morgan carrying the Vaughan twins

> And make hills blossom like the vales...
> Till from them, like a laden bee,
> I may fly home, and hive with thee.
>   – 'The Bee'

Her heart-beat flows round them, in them, like a footfall.
Not yet time to breathe. There are no choices.
There is no guilt. The world is making them.

On the sill of her window, by a guttering candle,
the Book's left open. On its linen pages,
thoughts in English, which they'll learn to read by.

Already translated, twice over. In the starlight,
a cock's lizard eye suddenly blazes.
His blood is warm now, but still remembers.

Likewise, twin foetuses are shape-changers.
Two becoming one. One becoming two again.
Amoeba. Fish-curl. Mammalian limb-buds.

The cock's cry pulses out into the darkness,
calls up the bouncing brilliance of daybreak.
Westward, tree-tops shimmer in the window.

She turns, stretches. Where she left it, Genesis
heaps open against the dawn. She thinks of Tyndale.
No-one can choose their time. What changes!

Orphaned, widowed, remarried by twenty,
at least she has round her the things of childhood –
the walls of Newton, the sounds of her farm yard.

When her parents were living, I guess she scrambled
from this very house (in the years of Elizabeth)
to pick, on the Allt, little bunches of flowers.

She'd still see the magic in the clear bright honey
her bees make of them. Would love to gather
herself, from the hive – the brittle lattice.

I lend her my memories: the cool sweetness,
the crumbled chewy cells, and that ancient
right, and sin – humankind's plunder.

Who else would have passed to their linked spirits
such a sense of matter? Its crumbling and containing?
Or voiced, from print-strokes, a beat of life-blood?

'*Nec erubuit silvas habitare Thalia*':
two boys in Wales receiving that message,
time and space between. Elegant. Primitive.

'Honey in woods'. Wild bees of inspiration.
Maybe they tracked them, found out the roof-nook
in old St. Bridget's, where the bees nested?

Sixteen seventy-six, its bell was founded.
For a 'bee-hive' bell-tower of 'no known architecture'.
(Image from childhood. Image in a poem.)

On a model suggested by the local doctor?
Or to honour him? Or by grateful readers,
recalling the dark years, a shut up building?

It's gone, the church where their mother worshipped,
where Thomas was rector. Henry's traces lie now
in the shade of a new, inaccessible spire.

These days, in the valley, the steady bell,
when it steps our way, brings few of us back.
Some literalists. Some hearers of metaphor.

By his tomb, eyes closed, I listen to its beat.
Brood on how births bring change. How a life
may transform other lives by the choices it makes.

There's the road you took on your war-horse, and later
on your doctor's nag. And here you worshipped,
in a space whose walls were bowed by the bell-tower.

I open my eyes on a wild-flower knot,
made of common species, with a twisted stalk
to hold them together, laid on your tomb.

What a walker might damage. Someone who reads
both you and nature. And would honour both.
A bee is giving its blessing, they're so fresh!

JOHN POWELL WARD

John Powell Ward was born in Felixstowe in Suffolk in 1937. Educated at the Universities of Toronto, Cambridge and Wales, he was a lecturer in Education at University College, Swansea, from 1963 to 1989, but has now retired; he spends part of the year in Reynoldston in Gower. From 1975 to 1980 he was editor of *Poetry Wales* and now edits the *Border Lines* series. Besides critical works on Wordsworth, Raymond Williams and R. S. Thomas, he has published nine books of poems: *The Other Man* (1968), *The Line of Knowledge* (1972), *From Alphabet to Logos* (1972), *To Get Clear* (1981), *The Clearing* (1984), *A Certain Marvellous Thing* (1993), *Genesis* (1996), and *Late Thoughts in March* (1999); his *Selected and New Poems* appeared in 2004. At once philosophical and tender, and rich in their allusions and technical skill, many of his poems are concerned with the natural world, especially environmental issues, and with contemporary events.

THE BURGLAR

I lock all the doors each night, I lock
Off separate rooms, I seal the house
As tight as glue about me, force
Myself to try and sleep; still in the dark
The whole thing isn't mine; I think,

I hear the clock, next to that a chink
Of noise below from one who's in, who knows

456

His way like I do; stops and stands and goes
Like I do; link by link
Dismantling treasure till each shelf is bare

Then straight back to the night, where the black air
Shuts like a gate behind him into place.
I think of day, the sun's beat on my face.
I toss and turn till morning. Don't ask me where
He's from, or why I've never loved
The things he steals, or why I don't compare
Him with myself. I know one thing:
At night he comes, I hear him working there.

ON THE LAKE

And he sat, silent as water,
in the stern, a bare rug on his
knees, and a dead perch on the
thwart, dark hills a circling
audience for the fish's eye,
staring up, at the night's expanse
above, and at the hills, and a tiny
village and Post Office black on
the shore, and he drew his oars
from the water with no sound, the
blades' flat surface themselves
wet pools, and the lake's
tremendous tilt, to the naked
hills, and he eased another fish,
from the rod's barb, and it

glimmered, and at that moment,
he flicked his rod, from behind him,
and it went up, and the apex of
its cast, touched the North Star,
then fell, past Sirius, past the
meeting of black sky and hills,
sliced into two a farmhouse and
its milking-sheds, sliced down
through clumps of deciduous trees
and oaks, and a stone well, into
the lake, and the rod's needle-
point, pricked the water's surface,
and he waited, and rowed a
silent stroke, and three drops fell
from the oars' arms, and lay like
tiny lakes on the gunwales, and the
rollocks' joints squelched, and he
waited, and he and the hills and
the level lake, passed the night,
while on those hills' further side,
another one lay, a smaller silver
tree-lined lake, staring up from
the hills' timber, like a fish's eye.

THE GUARDS

Thou hast made us for Thyself... – St Augustine

We get a stock of bees for food.
I concentrate, yet am afraid
Of options gone, there's always been

Distraction. What is that thing,
The dark thing certainly not wrong
That holds the centre and from which
All our attentions always switch?

The swarm drops on the laid-out cloth.
A few crawl to the wooden fort
We left; the hive. We watch. Untaught
Then like a moving heap of earth
They take possession of that tang
And waxy place. Then ten weeks from
Their slit the mindless workers come

For pollen masticated crude
For young in each sealed loaded cell.
Then swarm. Invaders are destroyed.
Drones die purged on the landing-sill.
On time in gauntlets and a veil
I sugar where ten thousand live
And take the lid up from the hive.

A detail of the bees swings up
And peels off left to get me. Dip,
Savage the gloves, sting leather in
Their suicidal ire and die.
In suit and net and warily
I thieve their honey-frames by hand,
Vats of brown liquid churned like sand.

What do they guard, with this fierce work,
Vibrating so hard those weak wings

Directing scent? We puff more smoke.
The brood chamber is black as hell.
But who and what you are, wee queen,
Eludes still, like my childhood, clean
As me decked out in this white shell.

WINTER

I see across the fields a whole
Flock of sheep being rounded up
By a dog. It looks from
Here like a black slug, it lies so
Flat on the snow. Then darts
Through the hedge, a shiny but skilled
Black streak across the white. Then I see
A five-barred gate in front of
Those fields, angular against
Those fields. And there's
The agricultural man, making
Little I dare say from this
Well-fed but tiny flock, yellow-grey
Across the white, the sheet white
Of that field. And if I walk to my cottage
Curving the corner of the hilly
Lane still white with unridden snow, and I
A scholar get back to my room, then I'll
Look out at the snow and then back at
The cool white pages on my
Desk, pages of snow and the
Mysterious black streaks upon them.

AT THE POOL

We stood there on a winter's day.
The rootless horn-wort often seen
In shallow moorland pools was there.
This pond a spring or watering-hole
For Gower horses. Picked, this weed
Had dangling a tube of slime
Meniscus on its emerald green.
Immersed again it spreads its full
Feathers about in loose relief,
Back in wild, icy water. If

We looked at it, we stared at it
In fact, just like the 'nature class'
That we in some ways have become,
Living out here. Bogweed, starwort,
A long-haired not a spongy moss
We'd never known, its thrilling stems
The legs of centipedes. And this
Was all so tiny. Aren't we so?
Our own three faces loomed above
The oasis in the gorse and thorn.

Sun's cold December face looked down
By ours and found the beetles there.
A thousand of them under ice.
An exhibition under glass.
Tom picked a handful of the mud;
A leggy water-louse was pulled

461

From weeks of sleep, and came to air
Knowing its moment suddenly.
It nudged and nosed the ooze till Tom
Lowered it gently back, like I

Would settle himself down into bed
At night again, when woken up.
Every jump that insect made
Had human feeling, human verb.
You pressed a hand down on the ice.
A bubble slid beneath across
Like mercury, sword-blades of grass
Sent shadows to the greasy floor
In globules; several beetles moved.
Whirligigs, Tom's brother said.

Such winter and no sound at all,
Where have the creatures gone, their shells?
The tiny decomposing wings
Of damsel-flies? No trace or sign.
Above, a hunter jet alone,
Then two, one miles away, its sound
Pursuing like an open jaw
To swallow men up, like a pike.
What do these microscopic things,
These wee crustaceans know? How can

We say we aren't as them? Our whole
Galactic night a molecule
On some aquatic being's leg

Or hair. I cling to the belief
In something more than human life,
A trillion times ourselves or else
So small no microscope could see
Its skin. A bird clicks, rattles in
The thorn bush, scrapes the air, its throat
A castanet that zips away

Off from its island in this pool
Worn by the horses come to drink
And slice the clay away, each mound
An island. Lines of algae fill
Canadian pondweed's swollen buds.
Our careful faces leave the bugs
Their biosphere and stronger spring,
A bubble underneath each wing
For buoyancy. We walk, blow frost
And God knows what else round the sky.

THE IRISH SEA FROM ST.DAVIDS

How often you stare at its face
Half-asleep and knowing it makes you so.
Hypnotized by the quietist to and fro.
Helped by its drawing off restlessness.

Waves as primaeval endless re-writing.
Words slipped in, crossed out, crests toppling over
Without punctuation, a passaage of water
Weighing its content; waves quoting, citing.

Some the tentative movements of the blind.
Some sewing, weaving and unravelling.
Some come in tired from a day's travelling.
Some wave to you, are just the mind.

Some hit rock then are vertical spray.
Some are young dolphins dozing.
Some are envelopes opening, some closing.
Some launder, dry, and put themselves away.

Tired now and shivering I watch it all.
There's radioactive junk out there.
To think when we were young it was pure.
Tides don't change much. They rise and fall,

Destined in their sea-sway to continue working.
Dumping is the sea's capacity itself.
Divers scratching around the continental shelf,
Doing their pollution research, are just checking.

Beautiful how sea spreads out its hands and repents.
Botulism, chemicals and raw sewage. Then
By degrees next year another thing. Yet again,
Bent on exposing our newest innocence,

As we love to from time to time,
Almost we must go on challenging this place,
A spinning ball, just to survive us.
And so it will. Our children's home.

Children play on the cliff near the edge.
Could I save one, that fell by going too far?

Clamber the outcrop and haul it back from there?
Careful how you withdraw from the ledge

Of these fantasies and return to staring.
On the left, rocks sloshed by the sea's swell.
On the right, the path to the saint's well.
Out front our new-seen sea, weeping, still caring.

HURRY UP PLEASE, IT'S TIME

They saved the rain in butts; took pulp and jars
To the new recycling plant; they halved
Their electricity and bore the single bulb
Of a furtive lamp; they adapted the car
To clean-fuel specification. They grew carrots
And turned the Sunday papers into compost.
They walked or bicycled instead of drove;
They put on heavy sweaters and thick
Socks and thus cut down their central heating.
They considered the lilies, how they grew,
And read their secondhand books, still wondering
If even Solomon's wisdom could suffice
To save the human venture that began
In Eden; its art, its buildings and its law.

But I can't tell you how this all worked out;
Its hour had not yet come; only
The unaborted children who survive
Will know of that, staring at their hands
Like monkeys, asking what to do next.

ALUN REES

Alun Rees was born in Merthyr Tydfil in 1937. Educated at University College, Cardiff, where he read Zoology for one year, and Sheffield University where he read English for two, he became a journalist, first with the *Sunday Telegraph* and, from 1979 to 2001, as a sports writer with the *South Wales Echo* in Cardiff, where he still lives. He belongs to the group known as Red Poets, of which Mike Jenkins is also a member. He has published four books of poems: *My Name is Legend* (1962), *Release John Lucifer!* in the Triskel Poets series (1973), *Kicking Lou's Arse* (2004) and *Yesterday's Tomorrow* (2005). Many of his poems deal with aspects of the Radical history of Wales, especially that of his hometown, and with marginalised people who have no voice of their own.

RELEASE JOHN LUCIFER!

It's time they let the devil out of hell.
Remember how they threw him in a cell
and tossed away the key? And all because
he figured he could run the business well,
perhaps a little better than the boss.

This was the boy most likely to succeed.
'This is the kind of fellow that we need,'
imagine heavenly civil servants saying.
But not the sort they wanted in the lead.
Yet even Pilate granted Christ a hearing.

466

Take-over bids for heaven happen once.
Angelic cops allow no second chance.
The company directors called a squad
to clear the meeting. They were late for lunch,
and they were getting hungry. So was God.

MY MOTHER'S MOTHER

Mrs Williams the fish-shop, next door to Zion,
is the way she is remembered by the neighbours.
I can recall her as a small, thin woman
with kindness in her hands. No starving cat
called at her door in vain, and no sun shone
without the gift of her rare happiness.
Zion, the chapel, stood next door to her house,
and filled with singing on a Sunday night.
She could remember days when people meant it
to hail in song the power of Jesu's name,
when Zion was more than the name of a grey stone building.
Next door to Zion she lived most of her days,
and when the final illness came it seemed
the singing filled her house, and she was glad.
And it is fitting that this kindly woman,
filled with a love for this world and the next,
should be remembered by the neighbours so:
Mrs Williams the fish-shop, next door to Zion.

TAFFY IS A WELSHMAN

Taffy is a Welshman,
Taffy is no thief.
Someone came to Taffy's house
and stole a leg of beef.

Taffy made no protest,
for he doesn't like a row,
so the someone called on him again
and stole the bloody cow.

They stole his coal and iron,
they stole his pastures too.
They even stole his language
and flushed it down the loo.

Taffy is a Welshman,
Taffy is a fool.
Taffy voted no, no, no
when they offered him home rule.

Six days a week upon his knees
Taffy dug for coal.
On the seventh he was kneeling, too,
praying for his soul.

And now the mines are closing down
and chapel's had its day,
Taffy still lives upon his knees,
for he knows no other way.

Now sometimes Taffy's brother
will start a row or so,
but you can bank on Taffy:
he doesn't want to know.

For when they hanged Penderyn
he had nothing much to say,
and when Saunders Lewis went to jail
he looked the other way.

Taffy is a Welshman
who likes to be oppressed.
He was proud to tug his forelock
to a Crawshay or a Guest.

They give him tinsel royals,
so he has a pint of beer,
and sings God Bless the Prince of Wales
as he joins the mob to cheer.

Now Taffy is a fighter
when he hears the bugle call.
Name any war since Agincourt:
Taffy's seen them all.

He's fought in France and Germany
and many another land;
he's fought by sea and fought by air
and fought on desert sand.

469

He's fought for many a foreign flag
in many a foreign part,
for Taffy is a Welshman,
proud of his fighting heart.

He's fought the wide world over,
he's given blood and bone.
He's fought for every bloody cause
except his bloody own.

THE CABBAGES OF MAIDANEK

At Maidanek they killed the Jews
and turned them into soups and stews.

First they were stripped and showered. Then
into delousing rooms, and when

down through the vents came cyanide
like a blue snowfall the Jews died.

They sold the dentures off for cash
and burned the bones for fertile ash,

and laid that ash upon a field
and fed the camp upon its yield.

Enriched with Jewish remains and toil
cabbages rose from Jewish soil,

their leaves all green with growing's tones,
their veins as strong and white as bones.

But did the blue-eyed Aryan troops
know they were eating kosher soups?

Or realise that they, perforce,
grew steadily Jewish course by course?

It was so efficient, so well designed:
each death was stamped and sealed and signed.

Each Jew was killed in triplicate,
then resurrected on a plate.

A million and a half were killed:
oh, what a shame if the soup were spilled

to go to waste down some dark drain
and make their sacrifice in vain.

And how to understand? Don't try;
just eat your cabbage up, and cry.

KIPLING REVISITED

If you can vote yourself enormous pay-offs
    while shutting factories down and sacking staff;
if you can ignore the human cost of lay-offs
    and go skipping blithely backwards with a laugh;
if you can raid a pension fund for profit

and claim you're well entitled, being boss,
advising those objecting to come off it
for chaps like you must never take a loss;

if you can urge the jobless to rely on
market forces to get them back on track;
if while war's waged you keep a beady eye on
large profits to be stolen from Iraq;
if you can fix the game to boost your fortune
while those you've robbed are left to beg for bread
and tell them it's a temporary distortion
and better times are waiting up ahead;

if you can snatch a public service (via
a PFI, which means the public pay);
if you can hoist your income even higher
and when the service crashes walk away;
if you can count your gold without a flicker
of conscience or one moment of self-doubt,
and go on looting, looting even quicker
in case the stream of money should run out;

if you can shout that working folk are greedy,
expecting job security and such;
if you can blame the undeserving needy
for problems, for they're asking far too much;
if you can fall asleep inside a minute
after a day of thieving just for fun,
yours is the earth and everything's that in it,
and – more – you'll be a capitalist, my son.

TEN PARLOUR SOCIALISTS

Ten parlour socialists
sounding mighty fine
till one joined a think-tank
and then there were nine.

Nine parlour socialists
whose policies were great,
but one sniffed high office
and then there were eight.

Eight parlour socialists
preached an earthly heaven,
but one got a City job
and then there were seven.

Seven parlour socialists
dealt capital big kicks
till one was head-hunted
and then there were six

Six parlour socialists
kept our hopes alive,
but one became a chat-show star
and then there were five.

Five parlour socialists
knocking on the door;
one got an answer
and then there were four.

Four parlour socialists
as red as red could be,
but one took a peerage
and then there were three.

Three parlour socialists
knew exactly what to do;
one joined the Cabinet
and then there were two.

Two parlour socialists
said democracy'd be fun;
Eurojobs came up for grabs
and then there was one.

One parlour socialist
remained the workers' hero
till he became a Blairite
and then there was zero.

GILLIAN CLARKE

Gillian Clarke was born in Cardiff in 1937. She read English at University College, Cardiff, and worked with the BBC in London for two years before returning to her native city in 1960. From 1974 to 1984 she taught at Newport Art Collge and since then has worked as a freelance writer and Creative Writing tutor; she lives near Talgarreg in Ceredigion. From 1975 to 1984 she was editor of *The Anglo-Welsh Review*. In 1990, with Meic Stephens, she took the initiative in founding Tŷ Newydd, the writers' centre at Llanystumdwy, and is now its President. In 2005 she was appointed Capital Poet of the City of Cardiff. A prolific poet, she has published seven main collections of verse: *The Sundial* (1978), *Letter from a Far Country* (1982), *Letting in the Rumour* (1989), *The King of Britain's Daughter* (1993), *Five Fields* (1998), *The Animal Wall* (1999), and *Making the Beds for the Dead* (2004). Her *Selected Poems* appeared in 1985 and her *Collected Poems* in 1997. Country life is at the heart of her poetry, but she is also concerned with family history, ecology and her own sense of womanhood, though she avoids polemics. Since her first poems were published in *Poetry Wales* in the mid-1960s, her example, as both poet and teacher, has influenced a new generation of Welsh women poets.

THE SUNDIAL

Owain was ill today. In the night
He was delirious, shouting of lions
In the sleepless heat. Today, dry
And pale, he took a paper circle,
Laid it on the grass which held it
With curling fingers. In the still
Centre he pushed the broken bean
Stick, gathering twelve fragments
Of stone, placed them at measured
Distances. Then he crouched, slightly
Trembling with fever, calculating
The mathematics of sunshine.

He looked up, his eyes dark,
Intelligently adult as though
The wave of fever taught silence
And immobility for the first time.
Here, in his enforced rest, he found
Deliberation, and the slow finger
Of light, quieter than night lions,
More worthy of his concentration.
All day he told the time to me.
All day we felt and watched the sun
Caged in its white diurnal heat,
Pointing at us with its black stick.

LUNCHTIME LECTURE

And this from the second or third millenium
B.C., a female, aged about twenty-two.
A white, fine skull, full up with darkness
As a shell with sea, drowned in the centuries.
Small, perfect. The cranium would fit the palm
Of a man's hand. Some plague or violence
Destroyed her, and her whiteness lay safe in a shroud
Of silence, undisturbed, unrained on, dark
For four thousand years. Till a tractor in summer
Biting its way through the longcairn for supplies
Of stone, broke open the grave and let a crowd of light
Stare in at her, and she stared quietly back.

As I look at her I feel none of the shock
The farmer felt as, unprepared, he found her.
Here in the Museum, like death in hospital,
Reasons are given, labels, causes, catalogues.
The smell of death is done. Left, only her bone
Purity, the light and shade beauty that her man
Was denied sight of, the perfect edge of the place
Where the pieces join, with no mistakes, like boundaries.

She's a tree in winter, stripped white on a black sky,
Leafless formality, brow, bough in fine relief.
I, at some other season, illustrate the tree
Fleshed, with woman's hair and colours and the rustling
Blood, the troubled mind that she has overthrown.

477

We stare at each other, dark into sightless
Dark, seeing only ourselves in the black pools,
Gulping the risen sea that booms in the shell.

HARVEST AT MYNACHLOG

At last the women come with baskets,
The older one in flowered apron,
A daisied cloth covering the bread
And dappled china, sweet tea
In a vast can. The women stoop
Spreading their cups in the clover.

The engines stop. A buzzard watches
From the fence. We bury our wounds
In the deep grass: sunburnt shoulders,
Bodies scratched with straw, wrists bruised
From the weight of the bales, blood beating.

For hours the baler has been moulding
Golden bricks from the spread straw,
Spewing them at random in the stubble.
I followed the slow load, heaved each
Hot burden, feeling the sun contained.

And unseen over me a man leaned,
Taking the weight to make the toppling
Load. Then the women came, friendly
And cool as patches of flowers at the far
Field edge, mothy and blurred in the heat.

We are soon recovered and roll over
In the grass to take our tea. We talk
Of other harvests. They remember
How a boy, flying his plane so low
Over the cut fields that his father

Straightened from his work to wave his hat
At the boasting sky, died minutes later
On an English cliff, in such a year
As this, the barns brimming gold.

We are quiet again, holding our cups
In turn for the tilting milk, sad, hearing
The sun roar like a rush of grain
Engulfing all winged things that live
One moment in the eclipsing light.

MY BOX

My box is made of golden oak,
my lover's gift to me.
He fitted hinges and a lock
of brass and a bright key.
He made it out of winter nights,
sanded and oiled and planed,
engraved inside the heavy lid
in brass, a golden tree.

In my box are twelve black books
where I have written down
how we have sanded, oiled and planed,
planted a garden, built a wall,
seen jays and goldcrests, rare red kites,
found the wild heartsease, drilled a well,
harvested apples and words and days
and planted a golden tree.

On an open shelf I keep my box.
Its key is in the lock.
I leave it there for you to read,
or them, when we are dead,
how everything is slowly made,
how slowly things made me,
a tree, a lover, words, a box,
books and a golden tree.

SHEILA NA GIG AT KILPECK

Pain's a cup of honey in the pelvis.
She burns in the long, hot afternoon, stone
among the monstrous nursery faces
circling Kilpeck church. Those things we notice
as we labour distantly revolve
outside her perpetual calendar.
Men in the fields. Loads following the lanes,
strands of yellow hair caught in the hedges.

The afternoon turns round us.
The beat of the heart a great tongue in its bell,
a swell between stone cliffs; restlessness
that sets me walking; that second sight
of shadows crossing cornfields. We share
premonitions, are governed by moons
and novenas, sisters cooling our wrists
in the stump of a Celtic water stoop.

Not lust but long labouring
absorbs her, mother of the ripening
barley that swells and frets at its walls.
Somewhere far away the Severn presses,
alert at flood-tide. And everywhere rhythms
are turning their little gold cogs, caught
in her waterfalling energy.

THE HARE
i.m. Frances Horovitz 1938-1983

That March night I remember how we heard
a baby crying in a neighbouring room
but found him sleeping quietly in his cot.

The others went to bed and we sat late
talking of children and the men we loved.
You thought you'd like another child. 'Too late,'

you said. And we fell silent, thought a while
of yours with his copper hair and mine,
a grown daughter and sons.

481

Then, that joke we shared, our phases of the moon.
'Sisterly lunacy,' I said. You liked
the phrase. It became ours. Different

as earth and air, yet in one trace that week
we towed the calends like boats reining
the oceans of the world at the full moon.

Suddenly from the fields we heard again
a baby cry, and standing at the door
listened for minutes, eyes and ears soon used

to the night. It was cold. In the east
the river made a breath of shining sound.
The cattle in the field were shadow black.

A cow coughed. Some slept, and some pulled grass.
I could smell blossom from the blackthorn
and see their thorny crowns against the sky.

And then again, a sharp cry from the hill.
'A hare,' we said together, not speaking
of fox or trap that held it in a lock

of terrible darkness. Both admitted
next day to lying guilty hours awake
at the crying of the hare. You told me

of sleeping at last in the jaws of a bad dream.
'I saw all the suffering of the world
in a single moment. Then I heard

a voice say "But this is nothing, nothing
to the mental pain".' I couldn't speak of it.
I thought about your dream as you lay ill.

In the last heavy nights before the full moon,
when its face seems sorrowful and broken,
I look through binoculars. Its seas flower

like cloud over water, it wears its craters
like silver rings. Even in dying you
menstruated as a woman in health

considering to have a child or no.
When they hand me insults or little hurts
and I'm on fire with my arguments

at your great distance you can calm me still.
Your dream, my sleeplessness, the cattle
asleep under a full moon,

and out there
the dumb and stiffening body of the hare.

TRANSLATION

after translating from Welsh, particularly a novel by Kate Roberts

Your hand on her hand – you've never been
this close to a woman since your mother's beauty
at the school gate took your breath away,
since you held hot sticky hands with your best friend,
since you, schoolgirl guest in a miner's house,
two up, two down, too small for guest rooms
or guest beds, shared with two sisters,
giggling in the dark, hearts hot with boy-talk.

You spread the script. She hands you a fruit.
You break it, eat, know exactly how
to hold its velvet weight, to bite, to taste it
to the last gold shred. But you're lost for words,
can't think of the English for *eirin* – it's on the tip of your –
But the cat ate your tongue, licking peach juice
from your palm with its rough *langue de chat*,
tafod cath, the rasp of loss.

RS

for the poet R. S. Thomas, 1913-2000

His death
on the midnight news.
Suddenly colder.

Gold September's driven off
by something afoot
in the south-west approaches.

484

God's breathing in space out there
misting the heave of the seas
dark and empty tonight,

except for the one frail coracle
borne out to sea,
burning.

LAMENT

For the green turtle with her pulsing burden,
in search of the breeding-ground.
For her eggs laid in their nest of sickness.

For the cormorant in his funeral silk,
the veil of iridescence on the sand
the shadow on the sea.

For the ocean's lap with its mortal stain.
For Ahmed at the closed border.
For the soldier in his uniform of fire.

For the gunsmith and the armourer,
the boy fusilier who joined for the company,
the farmer's sons, in it for the music.

For the hook-beaked turtles,
the dugong and the dolphin,
the whale struck dumb by the missile's thunder.

For the tern, the gull and the restless wader,
the long migrations and the slow dying,
the veiled sun and the stink of anger.

For the burnt earth and the sun put out,
the scalded ocean and the blazing well.
For vengeance, and the ashes of language.

JOHN IDRIS JONES

John Idris Jones was born at Llanrhaiadr-ym-Mochnant, Denbighshire, in 1938, and brought up Welsh-speaking in Ruthin in the same county. Educated at the Universities of Keele and Cornell in the United States, he returned to Wales in 1967 to take up an appointment as a lecturer in English at the City of Cardiff College of Education. While living in Cardiff he launched his own publishing imprint, John Jones Cardiff Ltd, but returned to teaching in 1980 when he became a lecturer in English at Yale Sixth Form College; he lives in Ruthin. He has published four collections of his own verse: *Way Back to Ruthin* (1966), *Barry Island* (1970), *Football Match and Other Events* (1981) and *Renewals: Selected Poems 1958-1998* (1999).

GREEN COUNTRY, CLWYD

Place is important on this globe
of furrows with troughs of memory
following our plough. Everywhere
there are fragments.
A mound of earth will make a stone, or Caesar.

The snow lies thick, hands-deep, worlds
lie in layers in one place. Look!
look to the mountains anew.
In the snow the smallest creatures leave their prints.

Snow to water, dust to dust. But water
might be frost, or floods. Change ends in
change. Give everything a meaning, then
dirt is clay to the fist.

TO IOAN MADOG, POET, ANCESTOR

Grandmother spoke of you
(As she lay, arthritic, in her bed)
As a large man,
A blacksmith who shaped hoops for ships.
Portmadoc built them,
So many you could dance from deck to deck
The moil of labour in your ears mixed
With the rich note of the native tongue.

Nain died, and Grandfather
Had seen before his death
The house he had built,
Over the water near Port,
And the garden he made for his lineage –
Each stone he had carried
And the soil he had rubbed through his hands –
Signed away, and later sold for profit.
The family, fallen apart, accommodated him
As distant harbours do a broken ship.

I have, my only remnant of the past's wreck,
A book of your *barddoniaeth*,
With Nain's writing, beside the *in memoriams*,

Telling of the dead, for me, in English.
And in the shaped and stormy lines
A couplet, once famous, lies in state
Its echo in the chapels failing now.

Gwaed y groes a gwyd y graith
Na welir moni eilwaith.

Although I speak a bastard Welsh
These words of yours, ancestor,
With their raging sadness,
Might be a foreign tongue
Whose cadence I know
But cannot translate.

Beside the estuary on a cold slope
Close to their former home
My grandparents lie buried.
The cost of the gravestones was finally shared.
One day I looked for Taid's grave
But no stone then announced it.
Having failed, I stood on the long grass,
Looked through the trees and over the choppy water
To the town famous for sea-captains
And the legend of Madog
Who sailed, before Columbus, for the New World.

In Port, proud ships point no more
Their carved bows towards distant seas.
A boat steams in occasionally

With raw material for the explosives works.
The week-end sailings-boats are slim and haughty.
The wood has rotted, the mud has won,
And dogs roam the abandoned quays.
Port is bilingual, entertains tourists,
And on Sundays the young play tennis in the park.

The rich note fades:
The chapels loom;
The dirge seeps through the graven masonry.

Ni cheir diwedd
Byth ar swn y delyn aur.

So much is falling to ruin.
Let us hope, merely,
Ioan Madog,
Poet,
That time will leave us something of your song.

LLANDAFF CATHEDRAL

We were sitting having tea
Under those massive walls
In the afternoon sun
When a stream of lady visitors
Arrived in various shades of pastel.
They were lovely.
They all smiled and giggled,
Had their pictures taken

And had seams down the backs of their legs.

Then down the same path through the sun
Came two rows of choirboys
In long red frocks, with frills under their chins.
And one of them, a very small one,
Stared at Angela's long bare legs,
Nudged his companion,
And went with the side of his mouth
'Tch-Tch'.

MEIC STEPHENS

Meic Stephens was born in Trefforest, near Pontypridd, in 1938. He was educated at the University College of Wales, Aberystwyth, where he read French, and the University of Rennes. While living in Merthyr Tydfil in the 1960s, he taught at Ebbw Vale Grammar School but moved to Cardiff in 1966 as a reporter with the *Western Mail*. In 1965 he launched *Poetry Wales* and edited the magazine for eight years. From 1967 to 1990 he was Literature Director of the Welsh Arts Council. Appointed to a lecturer's post at the University of Glamorgan in 1994, he was given a personal Chair as Professor of Welsh Writing in English in 2000. Since its inception in 1971 he has been co-editor of the *Writers of Wales* series, and has edited, translated and written another hundred books, most of which deal with the culture of Wales; they include the verse anthologies *The Lilting House* (with John Stuart Williams, 1969), *Green Horse* (with Peter Finch, 1978) and *The Bright Field* (1991). His poems are to be found, with those of Harri Webb and Peter Gruffydd, in *Triad* (1963), and in *Exiles All* (1973) and *Ponies, Twynyrodyn* (1999); he also writes verse in Welsh, a language he learned as an adult. He is the Literary Editor of *Cambria* and contributes obituaries of eminent Welsh people to *The Independent*.

PONIES, TWYNYRODYN

Winter, the old drover, has brought
these beasts from the high moor's hafod
to bide the bitter spell among us,
here, in the valley streets.
Observe them, this chill morning, as
they stand, backsides against the wind,
in Trevithick Row. Hoofs, shod with ice,
shift and clatter on the stone kerb.
Steam is slavering from red nostrils,
manes are stiff with frost and dung.

Quiet now, last night
they gallivanted through the village,
fear's bit in teeth. Hedges were broken,
there was havoc to parked cars. Yet,
despite the borough council's by-laws,
these refugees are welcome here.
Fed from kitchen and tommybox, they
are free to roam the grit backlanes,
only kids and mongrels pester them.

We greet them as old acquaintances
not because they bring us local colour,
as the tourist guides might say, but
for the brute glamour that is with them.
Long before fences and tarmac, they
were the first tenants of these valleys,
their right to be here is freehold.

Now, in this turncoat weather, as
they lord it through the long terraces,
toppling bins from wet steps, ribs
rubbing against the bent railings,
our smooth blood is disturbed
by hiraeth for the lost cantrefi,
the green parishes that lie beyond
the borders of our town and hearts,
fit for nothing now but sad songs.

These beasts are our companions,
dark presences from the peasant past,
these grim valleys our common hendre,
exiles all, until the coming thaw.

HOOTERS

Night after night from my small bed
I heard the hooters blowing up and down the cwm:
Lewis Merthyr, Albion, Nantgarw, Tŷ-draw –
these were the familiar banshees of my boyhood.

For each shift they hooted, not a night
without the high moan that kept me from sleep;
often, as my father beyond the thin wall
rumbled like the turbine he drove at work, I

stood for hours by the box-room window,
listening. The dogs of Annwn barked for me then,
Trystan called without hope to Esyllt
across the black waters. Ai, it was their wail

I heard that night a Heinkel flew up
the Taff and its last bomb fell on our village;
we huddled under the cwtsh, making
beasts against the candle's light until the sky

was clear once more, and the hooters
sounded. I remember too how their special din
brought ambulances to the pit yard,
the masked men coming up the shaft with corpses

gutted by fire; then, as the big cars
moved down the blinded row on the way to Glyn-tâf
all the hooters for twenty miles about
began to swell, a great hymn grieving the heart.

Years ago that was. I had forgotten
the hooters: my disasters, these days, are less
spectacular. We live now in this city:
our house is large, detached and behind fences.

I sleep easily, but waking tonight
found the same desoilate clangour in my ears
that from an old and sunken level
used to chill me as a boy – the invisible hooter

that paralyses with its mute alarm.
How long I have been standing at this window,
a man in the grown dark, only my wife
knows as I make for her white side, shivering.

ELEGY FOR MRS MORDECAI

Yours was the poorest house in our street:
the windows were always broken, stopped with rags,
the porch and passage without a mat. When
waiting by the door for my butties, your strapping boys,
I had to hold my breath against the stench.

There were fifteen children, all told; but
never a man about the place who wasn't after what
you gave, our tidy neighbours used to say,
for a flagon or the next week's rent. You
were famous in the Rhydfelen pubs as Fag Ash Lil,

a painted bag whose charms were blown.
Yet, even among the particular wives, this much
was granted as your old trollop's due:
you commanded in your brood a loyalty
(some called it love) that was by no means common.

Clients, sickness, creditors, the police
or cronies, late and drunken, clamouring to be let in –
whatever commotion these visitors caused
your sons and daughters would be there, taking your side.
Back they would come to that rotten house,

the girls in their high heels, blonde as
Monroe and brazen too, the brothers all made good by now
not looking for trouble but nonetheless quick
to flash their knives or fivers for their mother's sake.
By such solidarity the world is moved

or so it seems to this small witness:
which may be why, with other harlots in the news
from Cyncoed to Mayfair and Los Angeles
whose kids will never have to demonstrate their love,
I choose to remember you, Mrs Mordecai.

GRAHAM ALLEN

Graham Allen was born in 1938 in Llandore, Swansea, where he still lives in the house in which he was brought up. Educated at the Universities of Wales and Cambridge, he taught for a few years in Northumberland and Nottingham before joining the staff of Coleg Harlech, where he was Senior Tutor in English and, before his retirement, Vice-Warden. He has written plays for the stage, a verse-play for radio, short stories and criticism. His two books of poems are *Out of the Dark* (1974) and *A Time, A Place* (1999).

OUT OF THE DARK

Old fellow, old one,
    sing me a song out of the dark,
    a scullery one, and I'll beat time still
    on the tin-bath.
    How clear you looked free of the work's dirt
    and bright with evening, your time for taking the air
    – you'd think breathing it was a work of art,
    my mother said.
    Sometimes before dressing, suds long at the elbow,
    you had me punch away at your bicep:
    always this strength; always the body,
    you tested everything on it,
    all life's fifty-year long shift.
    Suddenly, you must lie down with its strange stillness.

Older, I thought all you left of yourself
at home was a black ring round that bath,
water down the drain,
and me, cold leavings,
to remind my mother bitterly of you.

But do you remember sometimes on nights,
out of the street's noise never got used to,
you slept in my back-room, slipped carefully
into the rumpled shape of warmth I left you there,
each morning that ghostly crossing, you worn-out,
me head-full of Donne, Shakespeare and Keats?
– *Hyperion* to you was a beery windfall.
Now I get you into bed and out of it, ashamed.

My body was never my meal-ticket
in the burrow of street and foundry under
the rattling viaduct, the canal's dark bridges.
Do you think if I could give you this strength
I wouldn't?
With finger-tip touch I steady your shoulders
pretending you sit alone on the brand-new commode.

Old fellow, old one,
    sing me a song out of the dark,
    twenty years later,
    (must it be twenty years late?)
    let the morning find
    that shared shape in the bed,

499

-- no more cold crossings for us –
but the same flesh and warmth and need,
a father, a son.

A SCHOLARSHIP

I knew it possible that streets stamped into place
night and morning by workmen's stiff boots
could change with a bit of chalk, a few kids' games,
another world lift out of the pavement.
Perhaps I even thought we lived under some such game,
in burrows tunnelled under the hollow roll of the coal trucks
and the slow cattle waggons breathing through the dark slit
sides
with secret jerkstrained eyes if I climbed close enough,
near the sky latticed and turning through the slow wheels;
how different the night-express with its yellow clatter
across the roofs and still bedrooms – like a memory
that only a drunken Saturday song could reach.

But real enough the final visit to the fitting-shop,
meal-time, and the men underfoot,
just torsos haunched on the floor between still lathes,
the old fellow dumped before his work-tin,
his pint mug like a begging bowl waiting my rattle of news.
He wiped himself on a piece of waste, then congratulations
as we stood now, stiff-legged, stuck amid the grease-proof
bits,
shook hands as though he gave me leave to go
before I'd blurt out a new address,

as though I came to serve notice on him, and on home:
where we knew there was a table, set and neat,
where few called who didn't sit with us and eat.

THE SONG SHE BROUGHT

Lady, this is no snappy lingo.
No radio or teevee has sung me this.
For all the ad-man says, the whiteness
in my sheets is you naked there.
Outside a few foggy grunts on the river
– how those boats low in the night uneased.

But not my fate, no affinity there.
Lady, Lady, sing again the song you brought
through muffling fog and black water.
Let the foghorn stick in the river's throat
all night, like a bone.
We two move easier.

JOHN BARNIE

John Barnie was born in Abergavenny in 1941. Educated at Birmingham University, he taught English and American Literature at the University of Copenhagen from 1969 to 1982, when he returned to Wales; he lives at Comins Coch near Aberystwyth and has learned Welsh. He joined the editorial board of *Planet* in 1985 and became the magazine's editor in 1990, contributing essays on cultural, environmental and political topics; he retired in 2006. He also performs with the poetry and blues band The Salubrious Rhythm Company. His essays have been collected as *The King of Ashes* (1989) and *No Hiding Place* (1996), and his stories as *The Wine Bird* (1998). He has also published eight volumes of verse: *Borderland* (1984), *Lightning Country* (1987), *Clay* (1989), *Heroes* (1996), *Ice* (2001), *At the Salt Hotel* (2003), *Sea Lilies: Selected Poems 1984-2003* (2006) and *Trouble in Heaven* (2007).

NOTES FROM THE CARBONIFEROUS

Night. Lightning flickers without sound.
A breeze shivers through a forest of ferns.
Dawn. Blue sky washed clean. Fronds
shutter out light. Green shade. Insect hum.
Night. Clouds massed at dusk burst.
Ferns bend low, lower, under the weight of rain.
Dawn again. Two scorpions dart-stabbing
ride each other to death. Insect hum.

Night. Not a sound, stillness a being
that's come up close, there in the dark.
Dawn again. A lizard basks, utter attention
and inattention, head a bronze rock. Night.
the tick and tap of water after rain.

A HILL CHAPEL

I am Death; Fear me and honour the Lord,
merciful Redeemer, say the words scrolled out of the
skeleton's mouth; but on a summer's afternoon in the hush
with sparrows cheeping in hedgerow bushes, they're

easy to dismiss; sunlight and cloud-shadow chasing
up the slopes, and a kestrel feather-dusting the sky
with its wings; only the creaking of the floorboards
as you walk about, breathing air with a dustiness

of three hundred years ago, leaves a doubt; Death
eats with Mortality, and look what a meal they've
had, the remains scattered in the graveyard;
Death getting up and saying Amen, when the pewter plates
are

empty; the farmers knowing it would come to this
when they bent on large knees, if not to pray, to acquire
protective covering; the silence here is waiting, in a
way not found on the hills, for a sentence to be

finished, that might set things right; but whoever it
was has gone out into the sunlight and vanished;
what does Death think in the long interludes when
nobody comes and his words are unread; he is painted there

on the wall, a thing unholy, yet the most powerfully
present; and notice that he smiles, and has a tilt
to the head, as if deaf or partially blind, straining to
hear the curlew's cries; see the kestrel swoop to the kill.

ABOUT THE USK

If this were America, the river grumbles, I'd
be called Red and they'd make up a song
about me; I'm sure there are songs about the Usk
I say, poems too; fatuous begat fanciful, yes
the river says, I know; I mean real songs, *Which*

way, which way, does the Red River run, that
sort of thing; it turned its red back on me, a roil
of iron-blooded water; travelled fast by the
Blorenge out toward Newport and the sea; I'll
sing for you, I said; thanks, the river sneered,

I'll engage you for my hundred thousandth birthday
party; what's it like, it asked, not to be always
travelling on; what is sleep; I stir myself round in
pools from time to time, but the boredom is a cross
I throw off for the trout, those fat lozenges; I

don't know, I said, we're so different, how
to explain; I knew you when you were young, the
river says, didn't I; the one with the jam jar and
sticklebacks; a kingfisher watcher; and do you remember that
dipper walking under water right before you;

and the pair of sandpipers' light brown backs flying
away from you but never far from me, the river; yes,
I said, I can never forget; you people come and
go, looking into me, trying to discover me;
you always miss the trout jump, turning for the

splash; almost seeing, almost getting it right;
you must be tired of missing out, is that why you
invented second sight; ignoring this, I turned for home;
it's a kind of song, the river shouted, taking the big
bend at Llanvihangel; remember in future to call me Red.

AN UPTURN IN THE PRICE OF OIL

At night the churches are closed down,
and whether God is present in the absence of his children
is a question; but we, travelling, are safe in our cars;
are you there? yes; lights come up behind to inspect us,
float past, washing tarmac and hedges with yellow,

as everything which was future drifts by;
what is the present? that is where God lives, theologians say;
are you there? yes; and that must have been an owl
in the lights blundering between trees; I cannot help you,
God would say, it is not in my hands; since matter

505

found it could sustain itself alive; except for humans, a late
                                        flowering,
who first built churches to box in the spirit; then cars
for the body and computers for the mind; returning by
                                        these routes
to materiality; which is why churches have a smell
hinting at disappointment; Dominus vobiscum,

in Land Rovers and people carriers, pausing at midnight
                                        country crossings,
industrial fireflies' negatives of nature, before carrying on;
the few moths are flying ghosts, and owls the air and trees'
mythical spirits; where once all the lanes of Ceredigion
                                        teemed
with the whirl of a night's insects in a lazy burning;

then it was possible to believe; in what?
ask something else, the future is a night without stars,
the past only a picture book or story; it is best to deal in
                                        minutiae,
an unusual fly that lands on the sleeve, or migrating
                                        swallows
following the elegant lines of a bridge over blue water.

AT THE SALT HOTEL

One day I'll go to the sal-
t hotel in Mali (or Cha-
d) where thirst's on everyone'-
s mind/recline in a sal-

t chair on the salt veran-
da/shaded from a sky so blu-
e it's the hands of pray-
er/and call for the waterbo-
y who'll skip across the y-
ard's hexagonals of salt th-
e unacknowledged actio-
nplan of the face of god/I'l-
l whistle for life/then whi-
stle for death (softly/becau-
se he's a travellin' man li-
ke me)/and the boy bring-
s shrimp from the salt-shru-
nk lakes/veréé goot/you tr-
y/scooping up the grey wa-
ter crawlers salt resistor-
s oxygen exchangers/mmm-
m/with a zest for the blu-
e extremes/you buy/at the sal-
t hotel/thrusting dripping-
ng and wriggling god's ner-
ves for me to see in the pail.

FACTS

A bag of six inch nails; facts; a bag of brass
screws, the heads cut to hold the snug blade of a
screwdriver; facts; that's all there is at the iron-
monger's, angular, shining, penetrating, sharp

facts; and the men who come here are factual
men, putty under their nails; who know what to
order at the counter and rarely joke about facts;
they can measure up a job and give you a

price; they can walk past the felling axes straight
to the chain saw display, and pick one up with a hand
behind the guard, wielding it in a few quick strokes
testing for balance; the quiet samurai of facts; know

how the hand will be a brain for this industrial jaw
carried it out in the woods when it is spring; how
the hand will guide it through trees where
a green woodpecker flies off on an undulating path; where

a jay scratches its matchbox laughter, cut dead
by the powered-up saw, its groans and shivering, chained
to itself, showering bark, slipping through sapwood,
tearing out heartwood; until the tree tilts, wobbles

off its base followed by a rain of leaves, branches
popping, the trunk bouncing up once then still; beyond, now,
the scandal of life being here at all, beyond
the quick calculations that the man made, paying

money down, peeling notes from a back pocket
roll; jamming the roll again in the pocket; money
being a fact; banks being chapels of facts
that the people visit quietly in every town.

THE OTTERS

What's this with otters/ru
mmaging with snouts thr-
ough water/they seem all jum-
py with play/but the eye-
s feet teeth shiver with exci-
tement of fish/wince of ner-
ves when teeth strike to a ca-
ge of bone/slippery in a strea
m to emerge/the fish sla-
pping itself in jaws/to whipl-
ash away/(if it could)/fro-
m the nightmare bifurca-
tion of water and air/s-
ay again?/water and air/ah-
h/that the fish couldn't gue-
ss/shaken and eaten ali-
ve/life nipped out at the spi-
ne/so what's this with ott-
ers?/making a come-back/co-
me back/on the banks with we-
t fur-streaks and hazardou-
s eyes/saying life means death.

CHRIS TORRANCE

Chris Torrance was born in Edinburgh in 1941 and has been living on a smallholding in Glyn Neath since 1970. He dropped out of university, where he was studying Law, to concentrate on his writing; he has worked as a part-time tutor in Creative Writing at Cardiff University since 1976. Among his numerous publications are *Green Orange Purple Red* (1968), *Aries Under Saturn and Beyond* (1969), and his long poem-sequence *The Magic Door*, on which he has been working since the early 1970s. Parts have appeared as *The Magic Door* (1975), *Citrinas* (1977), *The Diary of Palug's Cat* (1980), *The Book of Brychan* (1982), *The Slim Book/Wet Pulp* (1986) and *Southerly Vector/The Book of Heat* (1996). His poems employ Open Field techniques learned from American poets and many are written for performance, often with the groups Cabaret 246 in the mid-1980s and latterly with Poetheat. He is concerned with landscape, particularly with the standing stones of the Neath Valley, and the natural life of the area in which he lives.

MAEN MADOC

the limestone pavement
partially submerged in grassy humps

a few red sandstone erratics
ponder the retreat of the ice

after climbing several
drystone walls &
'characteristically rubbly knolls'

there was the Stone
a sentinel on
the high & lonely moor
set into the matrix
of the Roman way, Sarn Helen

          The Court Jester
          By his artistry
          Influences affairs
          Of state in the
          Drenched lands
          Where an unbroken
          Dynasty of Kings
          Stretches back
          To a lone
          Standing
          Stone on
          A bald-
          Headed
          Conical
          Mountain
          primal inchoacy
          of pagan art
          the yin & yang
          firmly embossed
          within the wheel

sections variant
fooling the eye
a vertiginous spiral

sheepshearing solstice
dry Westerly brings
summer heat
all growth
sunstretched

noisome flyswarms rocket
from dung soup
ants eggs gathered
in galleries
just under
the surface of
the warm humus
circumnavigating
the mountain (Fan Llia)

the cycle
meanders
the perfect poem

fox's mask
expressionless
glares up at me
from the gutter
mangled remains
at Storey Arms

headwind baffling my strength
sit by Silurian erratic
crumbly conglomerate
menhir slab
laid
on the fair turf
of Mynydd Illtyd
megaphone echo
of a horseshow
in the mountains

silkiest maritime
summer high
swirling breezes the fields
the trees blurred washed out
cirrus tuffs moving up ahead in line

Boreas at my back
helps me up the cwm
at the head of Senni
to the Standing Stone, Maen Llia
rainspots dance in the
sunny cloudy wind.

THE FOX

I am
Brychan
the Red-haired,
of Garth Madryn

I am a fox
I retire
to a lair
Other foxes

live by me
in their burrows
their dens
their lairs

I like
my burrow
I like
to have cover

I
am Brychan, foxy,
light of foot,
maybe a little
short of stature

I am a knight
seeking folly
bearing a dictionary
not a lance
into the wilderness,
a place
of no boundaries,

of no law
of no MAAT
faster than light
slower than time

a love saxophone
peeling
a near-empty dancehall
a few shadowy couples
circling
or lounging at
corner tables

the fox
under linen
eyes bright
silver dowsing fork
glinting in jaw
trotting out over
shiny parquet flooring

pulling on the rope
over the wall

I am the fox
pulling you through changes.

THE HOUSE OF STONE

The house of stone
stuck
like a worn & stubborn thumb
in the Glen of Mercury
buffeted by endless rainstorms

etched fabric of cross-birch,
cross-thorn & cross-alder
mimicked by miniature frets
of lichen outgrowths
encrusted on
dead twigs

swinging amongst catkins in the fork of a hazel
is the wind-stripped corpse of a dead fox
hindquarters bared by weeks of galewash
the naked balls hanging pathetic between
thighs holed by death-blow or carrion creature

Large drops falling from the black branches
mud a & water thrown out from the welts
with every step taken

the floodgates of the loving season

February filldyke
February sproutkale
February pointbulb

Overgrown straggly hedgerow, through which
many holes & gaps have been worn by browsing stock

 the land drains slowly bogging up
  wormy mud for the woodcock
  & snipe up on the common; each quag
 releasing its abundance of soupy habitat for
 demoiselle, frog, pondskater, water beetle, rat-tailed
            maggot
 crowfoot, water plantain & forget-me-not;
 slippery green stones with caddises & tiny mussels
          underneath

a wealth, a plethora, a foodchain

peregrine, takes the woodcock
fox, takes the woodcock
gun, takes the woodcock

 his feathers & bones melt into the soil

JEREMY HOOKER

Jereme Hooker was born at Warsash, Hampshire, in 1941. Educated at Southampton University, he was a lecturer in English at the University College of Wales, Aberystwyth from 1965 to 1984. He then taught at the University of Bath, where he held a personal Chair, and returned to Wales in 2000 to take up a similar appointment at the University of Glamorgan; he lives now in Treharris, near Merthyr Tydfil. He has written extensively on the English-language literature of Wales, notably in these books: *David Jones: an Exploratory Study* (1975), *John Cowper Powys and David Jones* (1979), *The Poetry of Place* (1982), *The Presence of the Past* (1987), *Writers in a Landscape* (1996) and *Imagining Wales: a View of Modern Welsh Writing in English* (2001); he has also published a monograph on John Cowper Powys in the *Writers of Wales* series and a *Welsh Journal* (2001). He has published ten books of verse: *The Elements* (1972), *Soliloquies of a Chalk Giant* (1974), *Landscape of the Daylight Moon* (1978), *Solent Shore* (1978), *Englishman's Road* (1980), *Itchen Water* (1982), *Master of the Leaping Figures* (1987), *Our Lady of Europe* (1997) and *Adamah* (2002); his Selected Poems appeared as *A View from the Source* in 1982 and his Collected Poems as *The Cut of the Light* in 2006. His prose works, criticism and poems are concerned with the historical and mythic associations of landscape and with his own attachment to place, both in his native Wessex and in Wales.

BEIDOG

Sunlight and shallow water,
rocks, stones with red marks
like cuts of a rusty axe,
dark under hazel and alder,
broken white on blackened steps
and below the falls a cold pale green –
how shall I celebrate this,
        always present
under our sleep and thoughts,
where we do not see ourselves
        reflected
or know the language of memory
gathered from its fall?

Beidog running dark
        between us
and our neighbours, down
from Mynydd Bach –
this is the stream I wish to praise
        and the small mountain.

I am not of you, tongue
through whom Taliesin descends the ages
gifted with praise, who know
that praise turns dust to light.
        In my tongue
of all arts
this is the most difficult.

CURLEW

The curve of its cry –
A sculpture
Of the long beak:
A spiral carved from bone.

It is raised
    quickening
From the ground,
Is wound high, and again unwound,
    down
To the stalker nodding
In a marshy field.

It is the welling
Of a cold mineral spring,
Salt from the estuary
Dissolved, sharpening
The fresh vein bubbling on stone.

It is an echo
Repeating an echo
That calls you back.

It looses
Words from dust till the live tongue
Cry: this is mine
Not mine, this life
Welling from springs

Under ground, spiralling
Up the long flight of bone.

THE MASON'S LAW

Though the slate
where his hand slipped
could not stand
  worthy of a name,
at least it could lie
in his living room,
set in the floor.

Er Cof unfinished,
under our feet, recalls
the mason and his law:
  Honour the dead
with your craft;
waste nothing; leave
no botched memorial.

WIND BLEW ONCE

Wind blew once till it seemed
the earth would be skinned from the fields,
the hard roots bared.
    Then it was again
a quiet October,
red berries on grey rock
and blue sky, with a buzzard crying.

I scythed half-moons in long grass,
with nettle-burn stinging my arms,
bringing the blood's rhythm back.
        At night
in our room we lay in an angle
between two streams,
with sounds of water meeting,
                            and by day
the roads ran farther,
joined and formed a pattern
at the edge of vast, cloudy hills.

        The house was small
against the mountain; from above,
a stone on a steep broad step
of falling fields; but around us
the walls formed a deep channel,
with marks of other lives, holding
its way from worked moorland
to this Autumn with an open sky.

HILL COUNTRY RHYTHMS
for Robert Wells

Sometimes I glimpse a rhythm
I am not part of, and those who are
could never see.
        The hawk I disturb
at his kill, leaving bodiless,
bloody wings spread, curves
away and with a sharp turn

follows the fence; and the fence
lining a rounded bank flies
smoothly downhill, then rises
to wind-bowed trees whose shape
the clouds take on, and the ridge
running under them, where
the sky bears round in a curve.
On the mountainside stands
a square white farm, its roof
a cutting edge, but it too
moves with shadow and cloud.
            I glimpse this
with the hawk in view, lose it
to fenceposts and trees holding
a still day down, and wings
dismembered at my feet, while
down the road comes a neighbour
singing loudly, with his herd
big-uddered, slowly swaying.

PWYLL THE OLD GOD

'I would be glad to see a wonder,' said Pwyll
        'I will go and sit on the hill.'
                                    The Mabinogion

Pwyll the old god
may look through you,
when you look through eyes
of spiderwebs, through
tiny rainbows brilliant

as bluebottle shards, and see,
in a dance of gold flecks,
the mountain hang by a strand.

This may be his emblem:
a ram's skull with a thread
of silk between its horns,
but certainly you see
the everyday, the wonder:

Old windblown light
fresh as this morning;
rooks with black breasts
and silver backs; clear-cut
shadows brightening fields,
and over the ridge the sun,
curve of a dark body
in blinding white; everywhere
fragments of web shining,
that look like ends.

from VARIATIONS ON A THEME BY WALDO WILLIAMS
Imagining Wales
for Emyr Humphreys

A peal of thunder, a fall of mist.
Afterwards the sun glares, staring on emptiness.
It ignites an image of fire
on ashen hearths, paints
evacuated rooms with streaks of red,

stains the ruined stronghold
on the promontory.

The machines are shrouded.
The quarries sink deeper
under the shadows of their walls.
The mineshaft is a dwelling for bats.

The man sits on the mound
and stares at his hands.
He turns them over, reads the lines on his palms.

He sleeps and his dream is a coracle
in which he is tossed on a stormy sea
that has drowned the cantrefs.
He peers out, into the spray
that stings his eyes,
and gradually, out of the waters,
a mountain takes shape.
He bows his head over his hands.

He is walking alone on the shore
but is not alone.
He kicks over wrack, examines the guillemot
that flaps like an oiled rag in the wash,
the beached seal with a hole in its side.
He wanders alone thinking of the broken walls,
the silence leaking in,
the men and women who sit staring
at the backs of their hands.

What can he do that they will remember?

He knows that memory is a place
that can be lost, though it lose nothing;
a place where all things remain
to be imagined anew.

He sits on the mound alone
and looks at the lines on his palms.

He sleeps and his dream is a coracle
in which he listens, listens hard
against the crash of waters
storming round and past – listens
where there are no words,
no symbol, no metaphor
to bear him over the torrent,
nothing but courage, and his mind
that listens, listens hard
against the fall of silence
crashing round and past...

A peal of thunder, a fall of mist.
Afterwards the sun appears
travelling on its daily round.
The man sits on the mound
and looks at the lines on his palms.

JOHN POOK

John Pook was born in Neath, Glamorgan, in 1942, and educated at Queen's College, Cambridge, and the University College of North Wales, Bangor. Formerly a teacher of English at Ruthin, Denbighshire, since 1984 he has lived in Alpes Maritimes, where he has worked as an English teacher, technical editor and translator. He has published one collection of verse, *That Cornish-facing Door* (1975).

ENGLISH LESSON

I read the class the old legend
Of Bran, the son of Llyr,
And Branwen, Manawyddan,
Matholwch, king of Ireland
And the botched marriage with Wales.

Children believe in fables,
Magic cauldrons, a giant
Who wades across seas,
Starlings with the power of speech.
But that Cornish facing door

On the island of Gwales
Opening up an eighty years'
Grief, what can I tell them of that
Who are for ever slamming doors
Joyously shut for the sheer hell of it?

ANNIVERSARY

Ten years this week, my father
Officially described as a steelworker,
Was pressed between two gantry stanchions
Towards the end of his morning shift
And never came home.

Now my mother lives alone
Wears the memory of grief deep in the bone,
Weaves herself in the village fabric
Sings again in the evening chapel,
Always walks home.

And I, ten years on at twenty-five
Officially described as a lecturer,
Still a bit Welsh, the young poet,
Pray that I sing them with the right note
Rarely at home.

For now these twenty lines of song
Pressed between the stanchions of my thoughts
Are all my life to give them,
Twenty-five years in twenty short lines
Looking for home.

IN CHAPEL

I follow my mother in from the car
Under the side-arch, up the steps
And into the vestry schoolroom where
On Sunday afternoons we kept

The faith and flirted with the girls.
Though everything has changed, it all stays
Here exactly as it was; the smells
Of flowers, polished wood, the mops

Behind the piano in the corner,
The heavy Bible resting on the lectern.
Now, on Saturday night, my mother
Comes with dahlias, daffodils, her turn

On 'Flower Rota', ready for the morning.
Two decades and its faces flip
My mind while she spends some time arranging
Flowers, watering from the tap.

Predictably, like time, the jar fills up.
Tomorrow will see her worship here
As usual. Beer-dry, I think of the cup
She'll drink from. I shall be elsewhere.

WEEKEND AT HOME

Outside my window a lorry misses gear
Labouring towards Dyfnant Hill.
Potted plants rattle on the sill.
I have heard these sounds for twenty years

Cleave the air above this grey road.
The flower pot teeters on the ledge's
Lip, then settles back with age.
That lorry seems burdened with an old load.

Near the allotment children play,
Running into the patches we knew, their cries
Lilting away down the slope to the line.
Now their ghost train seems more real than I.

God, this is a calm place! The grass has been cut,
Even the wild dead sheep under tonsured green.
I sit at my typewriter looking serene,
Tapping like Catallus at my love and hate.

L'ART POÉTIQUE

In jars they sit, the ones
that didn't make it, foetus
of frog and rabbit, three-foot
embryo of calf slammed down
under the lid, imitation snout
nudging the glass, near
white membrane wrinkled
over the dead organs within.
Eyes that were never even blind
stare out under the foreskin.

The mother of Paul Verlaine
miscarried three times, put them
in jars in her bedroom;
Nicola, Stephanie and Elisa.
Paul smashed the glass to smithereens
but next day they were back
in identical jars, staring dully
out at their half-brother. His mother
said nothing, knowing how a poet
needs the experience.

ALAN PERRY

Alan Perry was born in Swansea in 1942, and still lives in the city. He studied painting at Swansea College of Art, taught Art at Penlan Comprehensive School, and has had several one-man exhibitions of his work. During his student days he worked in a variety of jobs, including that of navvy. His three main collections of verse are *Characters* (1969), *Live Wires* (1970) and *Fires on the Common* (1975); his New and Selected Poems appeared as *Dreaming from North to South* in 2006.

PROVERBS AND SAYINGS FROM THE ROADSIDE

It's a long long trench
that has no turning

Never take five
when you can take six

It takes two
to lift a shovel

Too many foremen
spoil the job

A foreman's work
is never done

Look up
before you light up

Holes have ears

It's an ill pick
that strikes a cable

Rolling stones
knock you silly

Drills should be seen
and not heard

Watch your toes
and your feet will look after themselves

Count your wages
before you get them

A pint in the Bird in Hand
is worth two in the Bush

Muck is cleaner
on the other side

People who live in mansions
should be stoned

Navvies might fly

As you dig your hole
so you must lie in it

A BRIEF ENCOUNTER

The other day Phil stopped me in the street –
he's hung up his overalls now, for good,
buried his shovel and pick –
'*Never neglect your books,*' he said,
'*I never had the chance.*'

I gave him half-a-crown to buy a drink,
hoping he might push it back;
instead, he took the coin and tipped his cap:
'*You can't go wrong,*'
he called after me down the street,
'*if you stick to your Latin and Greek!*'

LIVE WIRES

Albert, I saw today
the eight year old scar
we made together
in lone Dyfatty Street,
healed thoroughly now

above it thrive
twelve-storey flats

a children's park
swank tennis courts
sleek bowling green

and the town goes bustling by
while down below
the winding cable
runs silently and deep
humming in the dark

FIRES ON THE COMMON

I see in the flames
that far-off garden
where my father forked
the dry-wet grass.
                    Flames
lapped the apple trees; smoke
ran amok, billowing past
the greenhouse glass, then
yellowing up brute-black
bright sparks volcanoed.
                    Branch,
root and stem, pale petal, thorn,
dock, rhubarb leaf and fern:
everything burned; turf
choked and swam; the nettle blurred; the pod,
the soft white pith and tendril hissed; wood
cracked; ants sped; lice spat
and gushered stars.

                    We
drowned in the din. We urged it on.
My father, his great back glistening with sweat,
flung down the shaft and swore
brushing away the burning smoke of tears.

Back and fore all day
the pyre shrank and blew and grew
again.
          Behind tall rooftops red-hot buses rattled
to the sea.

Low to the ground at dusk it idled.
In the cool wake of its flowering smoke
grey hedgerows floundered.

We stood and stared.

Behind us the lawns were raked
the bushes pruned
                    the flames
were muffled under clods: a slow
thin trail weaved sideways
through the straw – faint wisps
that issued meekly in the dark
fanning the silence of the apple trees.

CHRISTINE EVANS

Christine Evans was born at Hardcastle Crags, near Halifax in West Yorkshire, in 1943 and educated at the University of Exeter. She settled in Pwllheli, her father's birthplace, in 1967, as a teacher of English, and still lives on the Llŷn peninsula, near Aberdaron. Her husband is a fisherman in the waters around Ynys Enlli (Bardsey) and she lives part of the year on the island. She has published seven books of poems: *Looking Inland* (1983), *Falling Back* (1986), *Cometary Phases* (1989), *Island of Dark Horses* (1995) *Growth Rings* (2006) and *Burning the Candle* (2006); her *Selected Poems* appeared in 2003.

CALLERS

It is always a shock when they take off their caps,
Those neighbouring farmers who call at our house.
They have to, of course, to have something to roll
Or to press or twist in their blunt, nervous hands;
But it makes them instantly vulnerable
With their soft bald spots or thinning forelocks.
They seem at once smaller, and much more vivid:
Leaping out of type to personality.

The smell of their beasts comes in with them,
Faint as the breath of growing things in summer,
Rich, as the days draw in, with cake and hay and dung.

537

They are ill at ease in the house:
One feels they would like to stamp and snort,
Looking sideways, but have been trained out of it –
As with leaving mucky boots beside the door.

Only small, swarthy men with the friendly smell on them;
Yet walls press close and the room seems cluttered.
I am glad to go and make obligatory tea
As their voices sway, slow with the seasons,
And, ponderously, come to the point.

SUMMER IN THE VILLAGE

Now, you can see
where the widows live:
nettles grow tall and thistles seed
round old machinery.
Hayfields smooth under the scythe
simmer with tussocks;
the hedges begin to go,
and the bracken floods in.

Where the young folk have stayed on
gaudy crops of caravans
and tents erupt in the roadside fields;
Shell Gifts, Crab Sandwiches, To Let,
the signs solicit by the gates, left open
where the milk churns used to stand;
and the cash trickles in.

'For Sale' goes up again
on farms the townies bought with good intentions
and a copy of The Whole Earth Guide;
Samantha, Dominic and Willow play
among the geese and goats while parents in the pub
complain about Welsh education and the dole.
And a new asperity creeps in.

Now, you will see
the tidy management of second homes:
slightly startled, old skin stretched,
the cottages are made convenient.
There are boats with seats;
dogs with the work bred out of them
sit listlessly by garden chairs on Kodakcolour lawns;
and all that was community seeps out.

UNSEEN ISLAND

From across the sleeping Sound
the unseen island
nudges at my consciousness –

wind-blown Enlli; nowhere
more steeped in calm,
more resonant of growing.

There, air trembles with associations
and I am played to a tune
I scarcely recognise

easy as water, but earthed.
Is it energy or faith
that breeds content in me?

Washed smooth, drawn out,
moulded to acceptance
like clay on a wheel,

so like a compass I am pointing
always where you lie –
elusive, shimmering –

but no mirage:
my unblurring.

THE FISHERMAN

Land speaks to him
Out beyond the islands:
You belong to me.

As he grows older, its beckoning
Becomes insistent. Walking the shore
For his nets, the wet sand blue
And scudding white with winter sky,
He leaves no prints. And yet
The gravestones at his back
Are the black wicks
Of his identity; the names on them

Outstare the tide. Hearing
The wind howl, its open mouth
Pressed against the window where he sits
To weld his lobster pots
Or coiling ropes, he's sure
His feet demand the firm horizons.
One more season; then the farm
Can home him and enfold him,
Warm with certainties.

Only, the sea longs
To lick
And lick him smooth.
His boat is turned
For harbour, but all day, inland,
He tastes the salt
That tightens on his mouth.

LLŶN

Skies tower here, and we are small.
Winters, we sleep on a flap of land
in a dark throat. We taste the salt
of its swallow. Huge cold breaths
hurtle over, cascade down
till we feel the house hunch.

When morning comes at last
houses sit up with pricked ears
on reefs of land the black tide

leaves, or sidle crab-wise
to the lane, their small squashed faces
giving nothing of their thoughts away.

In summer, flowers loosening with seed
reach out to fingerstroke
cars passing in the long sweet dusk.
Hay-meadows sigh. Pearl-pale
in the bracken on the headland
shorn ewes step delicate
and wary as young unicorns.

The sea we look out over is a navel
the wrinkled belly-button
of an older world: after dark
like busy star-systems, the lights
of Harlech, Aberystwyth, Abergwaun
wink and beckon. The sun's gone down
red as a wound behind Wicklow.
A creaking of sail away
Cernyw and Llydaw wait.

Once, here was where what mattered
happened. A small place
at the foot of cliifs of falling light;
horizons that look empty.
If we let ourselves believe it,
fringes.

ISLAND CHILDREN

Winter on the island now. No more
football in the field beside the bones
where Lleuddad's oratory stood;
only starlings muster and squabble
on the grass by the school,
child voices vanished, like the oats
shoulder-high in Carreg fields
like the tidy pride of lighthouse gardens
light leaping gold at dusk in every house.
Not even small ghosts hide in the bracken
hush whispers in the shadowy pews
or splash through pools on Pen Diban.
It's not memory but an electric pulse
that glances whitely from each window now.

Gwyndon, storm-started, 1929
then Mary Greta, his sister, in Nant –
followed by Mair, Nancy, Gwilym, Megan,
Guto and Brenda; big Wil Cristin
and tiny Jane at Tŷ Pella. Gwynfor,
last of the Dynogoch eight,
named for the Swnt too white to cross,
Bessie, Ifor and Wil from Carreg;
the children of the schoolmistress
Gwenda, Gwyn, and later, Sion Cadwaladr
and then the transitories in Plas –
little Billy Mark, boat-born, fearless
crawler between carthorse hooves,

and his sisters, Joanne and Pauline.
From blitzed London, soft-spoken Roger
faced daily battles in the gorse bushes
sticking up for Vivienne and Keith
while his dad, Jack Harris, dreamed up a windmill.
Gwenda, Ronald, Jean and Robin
the Cristin children Brenda painted,
their cheekbones folded high like wings;
Ernest, last name on the register,
last child on the island until 1960
and Iain christened in the Abbey ruins.
Then Kim and Angus made the beaches theirs
with Patrick, first baby in Carreg Bach
for a century, and in Dynogoch, Colin Siôn.
Now seventeen years on, a newer flowering:
the twins, fact-hungry Urien and Saiorse;
Poppy, fearless Lois, Bun and Dafydd Bach
with sea-green eyes and hair as bright
as rich red bracken under autumn sun.

May some of them,
their children or their children,
be back again next summer.

JOHN DAVIES

John Davies was born in Cymmer Afan, near Port Talbot, in 1944. Educated at the University College of Wales, Aberystwyth, he taught English at Prestatyn in Flintshire until his retirement in 1999. He has also worked in the United States – at the Universities of Michigan and Washington State – and spent a year as Visiting Professor at Brigham Young University in Provo, Utah. He still lives in Prestatyn where he has turned his hobby of wood-carving into a means of earning a living. He has published seven volumes of verse: *Strangers* (1974), *Spring in a Small Town* (1979), *At the Edge of Town* (1981), *The Silence in the Park* (1982), *The Visitor's Book* (1985), *Flight Patterns* (1991) and *Dirt Roads* (1997); *North by South: New and Selected Poems* appeared in 2002. His poems have been praised for their formal precision and for their blending of delicate lyricism with intellectual toughness, of witty observation of people and places with a deeply meditative response to life and death. Above all, he is concerned with the need for roots.

DANDELIONS

Now, they are fleeing downstream, those dandelions
my small daughter has not-quite-thrown:
she raised her arm and let them go, and
the bridge sent its long dark shadow after them.

545

They flutter around boulders, wriggle, risk
the trees' fingers trailing, as though to justify
not just her casual faith in them but, too,
momentum, what the casually hurrying river's for.

She stands, beckoning at water and dandelions
and the sunlit afternoon. And I cannot tell her why,
now that she wants them back, they are beyond us
both. Useless to explain the river runs one way.

THE BRIDGE

Gareth, this photograph you sent
records August when we met again –
in a city this time like a rocket base.
White clusters judder at the sky.
Our vantage point's a spur of rock
and ahead a bridge, the Golden Gate,
takes off through floes of mist.

I was your second-in-command.
Talking, we watched all afternoon
quick ferry boats pay out the distances
that would always haul them back.
Now that you're at ease in sunlight west
of everywhere, roads you took
return east to Colorado then freeze up.

And we talked of another place,
the bleak hometown ten months before.

Rain rinsed the streets. Our father dead,
we'd gathered in an emptied house
to mourn new space between us all.
Comings, goings, made less sense.
Distance ahead blurred out the focus.

A year from now, ten years, let this bridge
still be there still strung firm
across flotations and coldwater miles,
this connection our father tightened
in a town of steel to show us
the meeting-point survives
and wherever we rediscover it is home.

from THE VISITOR'S BOOK

I

Just where along the line did this voice start
chirping cheerio and chap, my language
hopping the frontier? Things fall apart,

the sentry cannot hold. Distant, he will keep
barking 'Where d'you think you are, boy? On stage?
Back of the gwt!' My cover, see, isn't deep.

My ear/year/here sound suspiciously the same.
Should I say 'I'll do it *now*' don't bank on it.
And, upstarts, some new words seem assumed names:

547

brouhaha sounds like the Tory Hunt tearing fox-
gloves. *Rugger* too. I can't say *Dammit*
or ride phrases trotting on strong fetlocks.

These days, language slouching through me lame
from the States is – well, a whole new ballgame.

II

Cymmer Afan: wet pensioned streets fagged-out
claim only drifting is possible here.
At journey's end, no surge but smoke, no sound
from the deep except some lorry's threshing.

I was towed dreaming on this stretch years back,
a boxed childhood bobbing between high walls.
Then steel's fist pulled the plug on coal
so I was flushed down to Port Talbot.

No, on the whole I don't think I'd go back –
though I do for the usual half-reasons
and took my daughter once. Like me, perhaps
she'd pick up the sonar blips. Nettle-stung,
she proved only the seer's point that one's
Lost Valley is just another's vale of tears.

VIII

To swerve from village chapel to a town's
high-stepping church is, in midfield caught,
to feel life-forces collide, one woodbrown

and squat, all Welsh (my father must have thought
I'd catch faith like the measles), that tall other
dazzling in a blonde-haired surge of incense
with etiquette's deft sidesteps my mother
introduced me to. Pity, I made no sense
of either. And announcements – usually
in Ostrich – from the pulpit's grandstand failed
to clear up the game's essential mystery.
Even now I am not sure what I've missed.
From bare boards, sudden, to brass altar rail:
it's partly the shock has kept me atheist.

IX

The tv set, stirring itself, confides
in my father in Welsh. Bored, I can see
outside the steelworks signal in the sky
to streets speaking pure industry.

His first language I did not inherit,
a stream my father casually diverted
to Cymmer clean past us all. Brisk shifts
of my mother's tongue worked in my head.

My wife and daughter speak it, strumming
on green places, a running water-beat
beyond me. But though I've picked up some
of the words, they do not sound like mine.
It is like hearing what might have been.
Pointless to mourn that far-off rippling shine.

STARTING POINT

Where you started from didn't stop because you left.
Well, no. Hard though to take unflinching
new kinds of doubt you were ever there.
Since the station slumped beyond rescue
way past rails, the river's hauled no hardware.
In clean water, rust keeps coming through.

Expecting patronage – the child you were
the place seemed too, elsewhere made you adult –
it covers tracks, blurs highlights, spreads.
Still, leaves in the playground jump. Sheds leaning
on back lanes forgot to change. Both parents dead,
what but those streets know who you've been?

Once left, the starting place goes soon,
arrives where the road that shrugged you off
chose what's now resolutely called home.
And called home is what you are when slopes pause
for slate roofs to slice a river. Or say honeycombed
workings sag – it's as if new accents echoed yours.

Anywhere, anyway, terraced houses glimpsed
bring in that hill you mean to cross before
it's too late. For difference haunts too, offering
another self to visit, at least a different slant.
But there's a tug. You keep on looking back. Nothing
almost. You were never meant to leave and can't.

from READING THE COUNTRY

VII THE WEATHERCOCK

After Glyndŵr struck, grass sprang in the streets
where deer grazed. Now all that's behind the town
whose quarries are shrouded in forestry.
Ignore the big hotel's recent breakdown,
shops for sale, demented peacocks shrieking
at Llanrwst. But does its castle (occupied)
belong to it or does ...? Which tongue to speak?

Difficult. All manoeuvres must be deft.
Hovering, even the bridge can't decide
which is the Conwy's right bank and which left.
No wonder the weathercock's in a twist.
These days it recalls, airing its tall tail,
a favourite son, the one Welsh nationalist
peer of the English realm in all of Wales.

VIII BARRENNESS
for Kyffin Williams

Best of all your paintings at Oriel Môn
I liked that figure in a rockscape. Sky's
going one way, the man another (down),
and mountains after him, heave black stone,
mad as thunder. He is elderly, spry.
He is about to leave the frame or drown.

Now a trained English eye might take this chap
for Everyman in a painted sermon
on barrenness, all you need ever know.
But names matter: in coat and damp, flat cap,
this is Dafydd Williams on the mountain.
It's one moment, place. One life. And for now –
rained on, grimly passing through his portrait
homeward-bound – Dafydd wants out of it.

XI THE OLD LANGUAGE

is yours if your word for home means 'here'.
Whatever it nudges from retirement,
sharp-eyed, beckons lost worlds words nearer.
It makes more connections than were meant.

Streams clear the throats of derelict caves
to deliver rivers that have outgrown
ruin fluently in slate villages,
in towns that are mills still dressing the flow.
Here is not home and doesn't sound (riches
pour past!) much like my country. But it is.

Echoes outlast sound. Listen, nudged awake,
they too murmur. Says earth's vocabulary
of names on scribbled surfaces, it takes
more than one tongue to speak a country.

GRAHAM THOMAS

Graham Thomas was born in Abertillery, Monmouthshire, in 1944, and educated at the University College of Wales, Aberystwyth. He was for many years a chemistry and physics teacher at Nantyglo in his native county. Most of the poems in his only collection of verse, *The One Place* (1983), take a sympathetic but unsentimental view of everyday scenes and events.

BREAKFASTS

Each morning she comes down
Dressed for winter, summer and winter.
A cup of tea, a cigarette, and then
She reads aloud the parts of the paper
That catch her eye: a favourite story
With animals perhaps, or the weather, children;
Tales you would not care to read
Given the choice, or the paper, first;
And then the ritual of births and deaths
And the chance to tell us all, again
How soon one comes after the other
In any, every house. We flinch
And scrape our feet under the table,
Crunch our cereal louder, make
Noises with the tea, but listen,
Unspeaking, till the end. Bad habits live
Long with us, and this one came
When she was a child – one of her tasks,

The first of the day, to read out loud
The morning paper to her father,
Blind at twenty-six, who never
Once saw his children but gave them all
A face, a name, choosing in her
His patient eye. And over the years,
Unable to spare the habit, she has
Kept alive the tie that grew
Between herself and him; passed on
To each new child who came to fill
His place around her table such
Moments of her joy, her fear,
They too, by listening, grew to see.

A FROG

Came into the school one day
Out of the long grass at the back,
Another on the trail that brought us
Sheep and ponies from the hill,
Mice from the hayfield, rabbits, cats,
And a long line of dogs from the houses above
Restless and shivering in the wind
Till end-of-lesson bells. This one
I wouldn't have known was there, except
For all the noise outside my room –
Choruses of shrieks and catcalls,
Sounds fierce enough to hurt, to kill,
Then only my sudden shout to save it
Quick death beneath a pair of clogs.

'How can you bear to touch that thing,
So cold, so slimey?' I cradled it
Gently between my hands, and noticed
The body gleaming like new oil,
The still, green head, black buds of eyes,
That moon-terrain of camouflage
Quilting its back. But not for these kids
A matter of such sentiment:
Rather a sudden end like this,
Spiked on a fence, or crushed by a wheel,
Than any word which might betray
Their mapping of the old estate –
Tough, unyielding, not soft at all.
I carried it outside, and as I trudged
Towards the wettest, muddiest part,
Thought how easy it was to feel,
For once, so certain; then left it there
Carefully where the rushes grow,
Beside the dipping trees, the quiet stream,
In its own territory.

AT YNYSDDU

There were two surprises for us
On the road that day. First
The mill, the one I should have known
Because of the name Cwmfelinfach;
And then, as the road arched upward
Over the mass of the hill, the bluebells
Studding the hedges all the way down

Past Islwyn's house. Unexpected
Finding them there, and commoner too
Than willow herbs on banks, in ditches,
Beside the sudden stream, the school –
Heads of a vivid, spiky blue
That held us with their beauty, yet
Seemed alien for it somehow,
Out of place. I went expecting
The Big Tip and the shadowed streets,
The crumbling chapels with their high
Inscriptions hammered out in Welsh
All but forgotten. I saw them too.
But, driving to work each day, it was
The bluebells that I noticed, those
That come back every spring, the old
Promise to be true made good
Again and again. Turning my head,
I hoped to raise my eyes. Instead I saw
Only our own the alien now.

THE ONE PLACE

You can stay too long
In the one place. Year
Follows year and the same
Patterns are repeated:
You come to be contented
With them as they are, to learn
To love them for the way
They always stay the same.

But, though they grow too close
For you to lose, you listen
Carefully as the land erupts
Outside their limits,
Half-hoping for a tremor
To reach as far as this, a door
Burst open and the shock
Of dissidence to welcome in.

PAUL EVANS

Paul Evans was born in Cardiff on 3 January 1945; his father was an Anglican vicar in the city and later in Mountain Ash. Educated at Llandovery and Sussex University, where he read English, while still an undergraduate he briefly edited a poetry magazine, *Eleventh Finger*, which published the work of the European avant-garde. He settled in Brighton, earning a living as a bookseller, lecturer and organiser of the American Resource Centre at the Polytechnic of Central London. His first wife's family owned a house known as Taldir on the slopes of Cader Idris where he began rock-climbing, not so much as a hobby as a passion. He fell to his death on 28 January 1991, while climbing on Crib-y-ddysgl in Snowdonia. Among his books of verse are *Current Affairs* (1970), *True Grit* (1971), *February* (1972), *Prokovief's Concerto* (1975), *Schneider's Skink* (1977), *The Manual for the Perfect Organisation of Tourneys* (1979) and *Sweet Lucy* (1983).

from THE MANUAL FOR THE PERFECT ORGANISATION OF TOURNEYS
for Peter Bailey

I

the mountain

translucent

in winter sun
shoulder of crystal

558

it is not, as Henry Miller says
of Capricornians
           that we are
'perpetually bidding goodbye
to all that is terrestrial'
rather
   that everything
– of earth, of sky –
needs us to name it

not that by naming
the nebula in Andromeda
we make it ours
but that
       we can create
(courtesy of George Crumb)
Music of the Starry Night
by covering the piano strings
with sheets of paper
'thereby producing a distortion
when the keys are struck'

the mountain is not
El Capitan
       as Ansel
Adams exactly captures it
nor that loved shape even
changing always, yet
never less than solid
raked by fingers of

evening sun
filtered by shadow
we've watched
                breathless
from the doorway of Taldir

I wrote it once:
'there is the mountain'
as if to say
              what are you going
to do about it?

irreducible things
now embedded in
                  my self
                  your self
the mountain is
inside us

    but not ours

not even that we want
a world to feel at home in
or a world whose natural forms
provide us with an alibi
or a cure for depression

after all
    I ran screaming
off the mountain once
pursued by no phantom

of my own creation
              rather
a co-creation: mine
and the mountain's

(it was a silent scream)

don't think I'm
turning Platonic

the mountain is there
              right now
with sharp stones,
grass gullies –

              one in particular where
(I curse myself still)
I could have made it
with a girl
    but didn't

and one where I did
with someone else
              in the warm sun –

but can a memory
be that real?

'is it not rather
that art
    rescues nature

from the weary and
sated regards
of our senses?'

(George MacDonald: Phantasies)

weary, yes –
                sated, no

SWEET LUCY

'Where does everybody go
after they die?'
is a clear-eyed question
in the voice of a child
six years old
in high-heeled shoes
and a teenage dress.

Bop on, sweet Lucy.
Never die.

TALKING WITH DEWI
(i.m. Dewi-Prys Thomas, architect, 1916-1985)

I wonder, did you read the book
By Adrian Stokes, called *Smooth and Rough*,
A title that could well describe
The course of our relationship,

Begun when I, intruding on
Your far seigneurial domain,
First came to Taldir and displayed
A charmless adolescent lust?
Your midnight footsteps in the hall
Should surely have forewarned me I
Was trespassing where I should not,
In dalliance upon the bed
(Well, sleeping-bag upon the floor)
With the dark step-daughter of the king,
Usurping his manorial rights,
Too much at home, too soon, within
His castle-wall. Or worse: just plain
Oblivious of his majesty.

Your edict – that unwanted guests
Should always do the decent thing –
Came to me through byzantine ways:
I left. Proleptic move! And you,
Distributing a wry largesse,
In your own car, right royally,
Processed me to the nearest train.

*

In later years, by marriage made
Familiar of your house, I took
Delight to pit my night visage
Against your own across the room,
Disturber of your solitude

When all the female company
That fluttered to your whim by day
Had been exhausted into bed.

Antagonist! And yet, I shared
With you the calm of summer night,
The lake-side garlanded with lights
All doubled in the watery glass,
And urban dark, insomniac
With distant cars and muffled quacks.

I see you now, beneath the lamp
That seems to hold within its shade
The smoke that rises from your fag,
A small domestic thunder-cloud,
Before which, shortly, I retreat.

Shirt-sleeved, you read into the dawn.

*

Then Taldir, too, became for me
A second home – the Magic Place,
Encircled with a mountain-ring
That seemed to hold at bay all harm –
Until my follies banished me
To exile that was permanent.

No more of that! The maudlin mode
Is not what I set out upon.

I asked you, did you read a book
By Adrian Stokes, called *Smooth and Rough*?
He quotes the words of Doctor Freud:
'A man who doubts his own love may,
Or must, doubt every lesser thing.'
Is that my guilt? Ah, yes. But then,
Don't all we humans live with doubt,
Not only in these squalid times
But ever since the first man-ape
Found fire would scorch and yet was good?
That love could warm and freeze his heart?
First architect, he raised a roof
For shelter, and because he knew
The earth he loved did not love him,
And from his abri on the cliff
Gazed out upon a wilderness
And swore one day it would be his.

*

Daily, you stared up at the hill
Called Gribin, where the folly stood
So perfect in your dreaming eye
It finally was never built.
The wind still combs the crest of pines
Above the clearing, where I watched
The antic gestures of a band
Of madmen dancing in a ring.

One summer, under your command,
We grubbed up bushes, chopped down trees,

565

Moved stumps and stones, as you stood by
Against a tumbled wall and puffed
Your smoke-wreathed visionary plan.
Result? Much sweat. Some blisters. And,
For me, a wasp-sting on the arm.

Next year, the rhododendron-tide
Swept back and drowned it all, but left
Your hortus siccus high and dry.

*

Each morning, in a reverent hush,
The household waited silently
Your distant bathroom-cough that warned:
The tyrant of the tea-cup stirs.
Perfectionist! You could be gruff,
Were petulant, then charmed, by turns.
Your fulsome rhetoric, Merlin-like,
Could magically empty rooms.

Close reader of the elegy
I wrote upon your neighbour's death,
You poète manqué (self-styled so)
I wonder what you'd make of this
Attempt at talking with the dead
In verse that, while it teases, weeps.
No doubt, we'd argue over words
You'd sat long hours beneath the lamp
Examining with minute care,
As I have done, constructing them.

The poet, like an architect,
Labours to make his poem stand
As firmly in the flux of time
As quarried slate and Cambrian stone.

Cunedda's son, you did not doubt
But kept your father's memory.
You fought the gauleiters of taste
And held the pulsing sinuous line.
Now you and he both occupy
The deep lacuna of the earth.
May rowan-torches blaze the air
Above Rehoboth and your tomb.

RICHARD POOLE

Richard Poole was born in Bradford, Yorkshire, in 1945. Educated at the University College of North Wales, Bangor, where he read English and completed an MA thesis on Anglo-Saxon and Old Norse poetry, he taught for thirty years at Coleg Harlech; he lives at nearby Llandanwg and is a fluent Welsh-speaker. He edited *Poetry Wales* between 1992 and 1996. His extensive work on Welsh writers includes a biography of Richard Hughes. A selection of his translations of poems by T. H. Parry-Williams appeared as *That Fool July* in 2003. He has published a trilogy of fantasy novels for teenagers, *The Book of Lowmoor*, and four books of verse: *Goings* (1978), *Words before Midnight* (1981), *Natural Histories* (1989) and *Autobiographies & Explorations* (1994).

FALLING BACK ON KANT

In order to annihilate the pain of your absence
I was driven to initiate
a programme derived from the Aesthetic.

I commenced by subtracting from my notion of you
all that appertains to understanding:
as, for example, my belief that you love me,
my acute apprehension that you cannot be wrong,
my conviction that your absence is my hurt.

Left then with empirical intuition alone,
I went on to subtract from my knowledge of you
all that sensation – the contingent – affords:
the glitter of your eyes in the twilight, disturbing me,
the yielding of your mouth against mine, each caress –
inexorably, one by one, our sensual delights.

At last, love, all that remained were space and time –
space infinitely filled with nothing for ever.

WORDS BEFORE MIDNIGHT

Our son lies drowned in deep seas of sleep.
It is impossible to tell what dream-things
inhabit him. His breathing is so light
I cannot think it inconvenient
to the evanescent business of the air.

He would be thus in death – but with the absence
of this faint rose-bloom from his cheeks.
That is what most of all I could not bear.
Even to imagine it quickens a sour
shudder along my heart. But what put death there?

Love, let's go to bed. At a time such as this
the desire I feel for you cannot be told
from my need. But I need not importune
what you will grant without giving me,
that which I shall seize surrendering.

And now, desiring spent, we lie back
in not unamicable darkness,
mimics of the makers of the child
in the next room, to whom, indiscriminate,
we gave uncertain life, certain death.

EVENING ON THE BEACH

1

Now that the imperatives of blue are softening –
how pale the mountains are in the pale evening!

Escarpments lose their sharpness,
their contours wavering,
crags assume the air's transparency:
      uncertainty
intensifies within these rock-masses
      till their quanta
melt and flow against the azure of the sky ...

2

Dune behind my back, sand under my feet,
these are solid things. My boots
kick into pebbles and broken shells,
the beach slanting slides
and disappears beneath a water-quilt,
white at the fringe.

A single gull over the boatyard
sails; in the harbour boats
recline at all angles, all colours,
sails furled. Rigging clacks
against a mast, wind compels it,
and a pair of swans, their cygnets obedient,
drift seaward on a river
not yet swollen by the tide.

3

The mountains have dissolved in evening light –
        less material
than thought, the merest gauze of memory.

The middle-sea is viscous milk,
white curdles on white.
At the horizon, sky
drowns itself in water,
sea breathes air.

At my feet, arrival turns
to withdrawal, withdrawal arrival:
water's perfect oxymoron whispers on.

EXTRAVAGANT LOVE

When I take you in my arms
                                    I take the world –
        its lands, islands,

each familiar cape
and undiscovered shore;
what to me are lakes, rivers,

sea and ocean when I plunge
into that liquid realm
which lies within your flesh?

What to me
are the sands of Mars,
Pluto's ice,

Mercury's fires?
You are my turning Venus:
in your contours, your seasons,

I glut myself with nature –
you are inexhaustible.
What are nebulae and novae,

galaxies, the void between them,
the polarities
of a coldly blazing sky?

Surrendering myself,
I shall sink into that darkness
where the protons dance like planets

round their solar nuclei:
            deeper still,
    in the gaps between quarks –

            those inner spaces
    which divide your trinities –
            lie the mysteries you are.

THE CRY

The rag and bone man's cry comes ripped and stark
out of the morning air. And yet the morning air is bright.
Whose bones and rags are ready for the dark?

Today we promenade about the park,
conversing wittily. We smile. Our smiling teeth are white.
The rag and bone man's cry comes ripped and stark

out of the afternoon. Clouds disembark
at the day's verge. We taste the light.
Whose bones and rags are ready for the dark,

whose brains and fingers? Every known landmark
dissolves under twilight.
The rag and bone man's cry comes ripped and stark

out of the evening air. And then the bark
of a black dog. The owls are poised for flight.
Whose bones and rags are ready for the dark?

Perhaps, through a distant country's air, a skylark
drops its song. Here abruptly, out of night,
the rag and bone man's cry comes. Ripped and stark,
whose bones and rags are ready for the dark?

AIR: AN ARIA

To be air, atmosphere
To be what substantial phenomena are not
                    but not insubstantial
To embrace, to enclose
To be a gaseous ocean on whose floor creatures walk
                    through whose depths creatures swim
To contain even a planet in one's blue envelope

To be subtle, to be intricate
To fill interstices
To abhor vacua
To treat democratically all geometries
To caress with indifference iron flesh water
To flow, to be liquid
                    but not as liquid is

To be everything's outside
To be inside also
To be sucked into lungs along with smoke and smells
To assume inner shapes, as of bagpipes, bellows, balloons,
                                    basketballs
To erupt from constriction in a belch or fart
To be the stuff of inflation

                    but amenable to government
To fuel filibusters, put the wind into windbags
To be needed
To be taken for granted also

To constitute a medium where things may go hang:
clouds hawks helicopters hang-gliders
                    and the dust-motes
that glitter in oblique shafts of light in silent rooms

To be compelled by the currents of one's own simple self
To be benign, to be enraged
To be a hurricane, a breeze
To whip seas into cream, to pluck funnels out of ships
To scatter leaves ash smoke
To fan a flame, to cool a cheek
on the island of Sark or by the lake in Harold Park

To be, underwater, a translucent globe
To adhere to the salt skin of weeds and sea-flowers
                    to the rubbery, the glaucous
To inhabit the complacent orifices of a sponge
or the latticed cells of a white medusa
Detached, to rise up with a bubble's jocularity
To burst through the cutis into this enormous self
                    which is oneself and, unhoused,
To be at home

To be the ripple of a piccolo, the sonority of a horn

To move through the cycle of photosynthesis
To be inhaled by a plant's stomata as CO2
                    when the sun is overhead
To be decomposed inside green arteries
To be exhaled by a vegetable mouth as O

To press in upon a man or a woman or a child
with the weight of three elephants
                    tusked and adult but
to trouble them less than the palp of a fly

DUNCAN BUSH

Duncan Bush was born in Cardiff in 1946. Educated at Warwick University and Wadham College, Oxford, he has taught at schools, colleges and universities in Wales, England and the USA, and is currently *Chargé de cours* at the Ecole Européenne in Luxembourg; he lives in Blaschette in Luxembourg but spends part of the year at Ynys-wen in the Swansea Valley. Besides a novel, *Glass Shot* (1991), he has published eight books of poems: *Nostos* (1980), *Aquarium* (1983), *Salt* (1985), *Black Faces, Red Mouths* (1986), *Masks* (1994), *The Hook* (1997), and *Midway* (1998); in *The Genre of Silence* (1988) are to be found the poems of Victor Bal, a fictitious Russian poet who is persecuted and 'disappears' during Stalin's time.

GWLAD, GWLAD

Far from the old landed
recusant genealogies behind
their diapered brickwork
and stagged-oak deerpark,

here even God's low-church,
the damp-ridden chapels
built on proletarian pence
and shopkeeper's shilling

where all stand equal
in their own sight and
preferred in His, refusal
bred like rickets in the bone:

a people so stiffnecked,
yea, verily unto sullenness,
they'll duck to advantage
but look up to no man.

SUMMER 1984

Summer of strike and drought,
of miners' pickets standing on blond verges,
of food parcels and

hosepipe bans ... And as (or so
the newspapers reported it) five rainless
months somewhere disclosed

an archaeology of long-evicted
dwellings on a valley-floor, the reservoir
which drowned them

having slowly shrunk towards
a pond between crazed banks, the silted
houses still erect,

even, apparently, a dusty
bridge of stone you might still walk
across revealed intact

in that dry air, a thing not seen
for years; just so (though this the papers
did not say)

the weeks and months of strike saw
slowly and concurrently emerge in shabby
river-valleys in South Wales

– in Yorkshire too, and Durham,
Kent and Ayrshire – villages no longer
aggregates of dwellings

privatised by television, but
communities again, the rented videos and tapes
back in the shop,

fridge-freezers going back
– so little to put in them, anyway – and
meetings, meetings in their place,

in workmen's clubs and miners' welfare
halls, just as it had been once, communities
beleaguered but the closer,

the intenser for it, with resources
now distributed to need, and organised to last,
the dancefloors stacked

with foodstuffs like a dockside, as if
an atavistic common memory, an inheritance
perhaps long thought romantic,

like the old men's proud and bitter
tales of 1926, was now being learnt again,
in grandchildren and

great-grandchildren of their bloodline:
a defiance and a unity which even sixty years
of almost being discounted never broke.

BRIGITTE BARDOT IN GRANGETOWN

Off Ferry Road, the toilet of a garage where
the mechanics come at lunch to cut the hands' grease
with green Swarfega jelly, glancing once

at themselves in the rust-foxed mirror, and then
go in to eat brought sandwiches and play
pontoon with the soft, soiled pack,

three walls of the cubicle sporting the odd grey
newsprint pin-up, some *Kay* or *Tracy*,
alike as playing cards,

and then a whole closed door facing you (if
ever you sat over the stained bowl)
or Bardot as she was at twenty,

and thirty-five, and is now, in her smiling
puppy-fat fifties, still corn-blonde,
and then more of her

again (with one of Ian Rush) out where they eat,
over the workbench's oil and
hacksaw-dust, the clenched vice.

The boy who put all hers up was a six-month
Government trainee. A bit simple, they all thought.
A headbanger, the fat one said.

He had a thing about her, the boy, grinning
foolishly, half-proudly, when they kidded him, told him
she was old enough to be

his mother. *That slag?* the fat one said once.
*Look at her. She's anybody's. Even saving baby seals
all she knows how to do*

is lie down with one. And laughed: soft, smirched face
looking at that photo, then at the one of her
naked, hands raised as if to pin or

loose her hair, the honey-hued still-teenage
body, milky Mediterranean behind her, evening.
He left the other week,

the trainee. He didn't finish, he never even came
back for his tools. So now they're
anybody's like the photos:

like, the fat one knows, the photos always are.

CROCUSES

In the seconds after
the knock he may have
tried to burn the poem
that would kill him. But
words are hard to
kill. Print turned
silvery as the page went black.

They put him in the big
house on the outskirts with
white bedsteads and no
windows. But word
went down the heating pipes,
leaked out through
even screamproofed walls.

In the end someone probably
shot him on a train
going east, or just off it,
and hid the body in the
ground. Here and there his
words came slowly up like
crocuses, in winter.

THE SONG IN OUR HEART

Uncle Cliff had seen Cologne's finest blocks
a gridmap of scorched rubble
above cellars floored with human fat –

'Precision Bombing'
about the Cathedral untouched.
Aunty May had Meissen figurines

he'd looted from hinterland villages
where rooms were intact
and Ed, tall, ginger, ten years my senior,

an S.S. Officer's dress dagger
and a motorcyle-rider's yellow-glassed
goggles, with one lens starred.

His father years later confided
to me heavily of other things he'd seen:
the half-buried dead;

the hanged prisoners; a girl – 'Thirteen?
Fourteen?' – who lived in a ruined
stairwell, and 'took on all

comers, a fag apiece. The going rate.
You had to pay the mother.'
More he'd witnessed,

and wouldn't speak of,
only shake his head and say,
as if there was thin comfort in the cliché,

'The ones who went into the camps,
they had the worst of it'.
Then Ed did his National Service over there,

and Germany became B.F.P.O.40
on 'Forces' Favourites' every Sunday,
With A Song In My Heart wafting across

the nation's kitchens
in the reek of swede and cabbage-water,
the spit of roasting potatoes

spooned brown with beef juices.
Aunty May wrote in and requested
Frankie Lane singing *Jezebel*

– we had the 78 – and we waited
to hear it played for him, the whole
network of uncles, aunts, cousins

listening, like all the families in the land,
the great mycelium,
while the roast darkened and we read

about playboy 'Baby' Pignatelli
or Princess Ira Furstenberg
losing glamorously at Wimbledon

584

in Teddy Tinling's oohlala knickers.
They too were part of our Sunday,
along with those other exotics

Queen Soraya, the Aga Khan
and Ascot tipster 'Prince' Monolulu
with his keyboard grin.

It was the early 'Fifties. Churchill was back
at Number Ten, rationing was over,
Suez was far away. From a People's War

we were in the victorious, vicarious
aftermath of sports pages, sex crimes and
'Society Gossip' – all those tiffs or shaggings

magnified below stairs:
scullions agog for Sunday scandal
from that eternal, footman's press.

'CAROLINE': A COUNTY LIFE

Even, I think, before she saw the house,
the wall to the gate he turned in at told her
this was the man she should marry.
An estate-wall – dentilated, buttressed

and stepped to the land's long downslope –
it was in that brick which is

the pale, crumbling red of old money.
She was a January bride, aflush

with her own good looks and
the reception's swank. The honeymoon
was on Mustique. When the marriage broke
she stayed near – as failed students do

in bed-sits in university towns, wistful
for status, a lost social rung. There was
a son. But he came home each term taller
in a badged blazer of flecked grey flannel,

and was a prig at twelve. Occasionally
she slept with an acquaintance of
her ex-husband's; one night his cousin;
and once with the Lord Lieutenant of the county.

Twice she fell off her bar-stool in The Flag.
Her voice became more hectoring, a bray,
while she grew stout, eccentric, sour –
milk dribbling away to rennet

through a sieve. The barman called her
'Margaret Rutherford' behind her back.
She started drinking in her room.
No biography can pinpoint where a life

first started to go wrong – where her naïve,
excited *arrivisme* was poisoned,

or how the rural gentry still close ranks.
All that's clear is that she reached

a menopause of misery one mild July night
with a fog of drizzle in the air. But once
she'd counted all fifty-odd white pills
into her mouth and gulped them down

with swigs of gin, what shocked
the coroner and press and public was how
she lay a full month in her dressing-gown
till someone shouldered down the door.

RHUBARB

So I dug it up – had to prise and chop
it out with the spade-edge, so deep it went –
from the gritty black loam of his garden

in Glamorgan: ancient like a badger
sett or yewtree, the buried crown of it
tubed and rooted like a great muddy heart,

arch of pulmonary artery, stump
of vena cava and aorta. I
stuffed it in a green Marks & Spencer bag

I'd carried home some singlets and a pair
of shirts in, packed it in the back of
the crammed car and next day took it (illicitly)

past Customs at Dover and Calais and
down through Belgium into Luxembourg via
border booths unmanned since the Schengen signings.

Dug it a hole in our new-cleared plot here,
soil so light, dry, each soft block of it lying
on the blade then sliding off and crumbling

to instant tilth, such easy digging you
expect salt water to seep up into
the trench, as at the beach: soil dust-fine, yet

wonderful appletrees it grows, and maize,
bigarreaux and *quetsches*, carrots and parsnips –
anything which sinks a long enough taproot.

Then I forked in strawy horse manure and
buried it to the papery scar-tissue
on the top, pink nodes showing, and three great

leaves already starting to uncrinkle.
We live here at 330 metres a.s.l. –
over a mountain's height – and face due west

where sunsets make it seem we're at an edge
of the world. Springs at Blaschette come slow, late
but bride-white with blossom, and we sit out

at nights as if on deck while our terrace
darkens, looking down along our neighbour's
cow-pasture, where in month-long-standing snow

one February night we heard thin screams of
mating foxes, saw paired eyes shine, re-shine
to opal in the Maglite's torchbeam. They'd scented

the new season at six below – a month before
the cranes, raucous for Scandinavia, and two
from my diary's first swallow. Fifty last April,

my senses sharpen too, and each Springtime's
more acute. Last night I read till late, then
went outside and saw Orion in clear sky

but already pivoting away below
the hill till Autumn next, and I overheard
the nightly silence of the high Gutland.

Deer moved in the beechwood, hares in the fields.
My sons slept in their bedrooms and my wife
in our bed. We're 'at the heart of Europe' here,

get a Babel of channels, use our French
every day. But if they bury my heart
they'll have to dig it a hole somewhere else:

in Kent, where I saw my first son born, or
in Brecknockshire or deep-laned Herefordshire;
on Devon's red coast, where I learnt to swim ...

Because the stones in the water get clearer
every day as the water gets deeper,
and the flow's faster the further you wade.

I'm no patriot, and I'm proud of it.
But it's into language we're born, it's there
we discover the world. I'll eat it raw,

the first stick: the rose-pale fleshy cusp,
the only part sweet of itself, then on
and on in mouthfuls, the crimson stalk paling

to green with its pulled threads of skin, dabbing
and dabbing it in gritty white sugar
the glands in my jawline watering and

making half-soured faces:how I ate it
as a child from my father's railway-line
allotment the day he told me its name.

TONY CURTIS

Tony Curtis was born in Carmarthen in 1946. Educated at the University College of Swansea, he was a teacher at schools in England for five years before returning to Wales to teach English at the Polytechnic of Wales, the forerunner of the University of Glamorgan, where he is now Professor of Poetry and Director of the post-graduate course in Creative Writing; he lives in Barry. He has published eight books of verse: *Album* (1974), *Preparations* (1980), *Letting Go* (1983), *The Last Candles* (1989), *Taken for Pearls* (1993), *War Voices* (1995), *The Arches* (1998), *Heaven's Gate* (2001), and *Crossing Over* (2007); his *Selected Poems 1970-1985* appeared in 1986. He has also edited books about the visual arts and four anthologies of verse: *The Poetry of Pembrokeshire* (1989), *The Poetry of Snowdonia* (1989), *Love from Wales* (with Siân James, 1991), and *Coal* (1997), and written a monograph on Dannie Abse in the *Writers of Wales* series (1985). He has a wide range of subjects, including the domestic, and an unsentimental tone, clear and persuasive, often casual but informed with wit and sympathy for human suffering and misfortune. A small selection of his poems is to be found in *Considering Cassandra* (2003) in the Corgi series.

TO MY FATHER

Bellringing was another
of the things you didn't teach me.

591

How many crooked ladders did we climb?
How many belfries did we crouch in?
The musty smell of the years in the wood beams,
the giant domes balanced to move
against a man's pull.
Stories of jammed trapdoors and madness
in the deafening that draws blood.
Once you rang for the Queen
and I watched
all that pomp ooze into the cold stone of the cathedral.

I wanted to take the smooth grip of a rope
and lean my weight into it.
I wanted timing.
I wanted you to teach me
to teach my son's son.

Turning your back on that
brings our line down. What
have you left me? What sense
of the past? I could have lost myself in the mosaic
of Grandsires, Trebles and Bobs,
moved to that clipped calling of the changes.

I know now the churchbells' coming over the folded
town's Sunday sleep carries me close to tears,
the noise of worship and weddings and death
rolling out
filling the hollow of my throat.

PREPARATIONS

In the valley there is an order to these things:
Chapel suits and the morning shift called off.
She takes the bus to Pontypridd to buy black,
But the men alone proceed to the grave,
Neighbours, his butties, and the funeral regulars.
The women are left in the house; they bustle
Around the widow with a hushed, furious
Energy that keeps grief out of the hour.

She holds to the kitchen, concerned with sandwiches.
It is a ham-bone big as a man's arm and the meat
Folds over richly from her knife. A daughter sits
Watching butter swim in its dish before the fire.
The best china laid precisely across the new tablecloth:
They wait. They count the places over and over like a rosary.

SOUP

One night our block leader set a competition:
two bowls of soup to the best teller of a tale.
That whole evening the hut filled with words –
tales from the old countries
of wolves and children
potions and love-sick herders
stupid woodsmen and crafty villagers.
Apple-blossom snowed from blue skies,
orphans discovered themselves royal.
Tales of greed and heroes and cunning survival,
soldiers of the Empires, the Church, the Reich.

593

And when they turned to me
I could not speak,
sunk in the horror of that place,
my throat a corridor of bones, my eyes
and nostrils clogged with self-pity.
'Speak,' they said, 'everyone has a story to tell.'
And so I closed my eyes and said:
I have no hunger for your bowls of soup, you see
I have just risen from the Shabbat meal –
my father has filled our glasses with wine,
bread has been broken, the maid has served fish.
Grandfather has sung, tears in his eyes, the old songs.
My mother holds her glass by the stem, lifts
it to her mouth, the red glow reflecting on her throat.
I go to her side and she kisses me for bed.
My grandfather's kiss is rough and soft like an apricot.
The sheets on my bed are crisp and flat
like the leaves of a book...

I carried my prizes back to my bunk: one bowl
I hid, the other I stirred
And smelt a long time, so long
That it filled the cauldron of my head,
Drowning a family of memories.

IVY

The choking ivy we lopped and sawed and tore
and one day – yes, in a blast of anger – burned
from the old pear still clings.

As we axed and ripped the tentacles
it slaked its biceps, unclenched its fist.
I climbed and hacked while you
dragged great clumps of ivy to your bonfire.

But high in the thirty-foot summits
clogging this season's hard, sour pears
the last clutch of parched, rootless stuff
worn like a wig still weighs on the tree.

By October winds should have scattered the dead leaves
and you'll watch me climb again to snap
the final twists of brittle tendril.

At full stretch I shall prise them loose
then feed them down through the bare branches.
And you, my boy, will look up to me with impatience
like a climber at the bottom waiting for ropes.

TAKEN FOR PEARLS

In muddied waters the eyes of fishes
are taken for pearls.

As those two trout, little bigger than my hand then,
taken by spinner at Cresselly on an early

summer's day in the quiet afternoon
before the season's traffic. Only

595

a tractor in an unseen field
stitching the air like a canopy over it all.

And the taste of them pan-fried nose to tail
by my mother. The sweet flesh prised from

cages of the most skilfully carved bone.
I closed my eyes and she smiled for me.

THE DEATH OF RICHARD BEATTIE-SEAMAN
IN THE BELGIAN GRAND PRIX, 1939

Trapped in the wreckage by his broken arm
he watched the flames flower from the front end.
So much pain – *Holy Jesus, let them get to me* –
so much pain he heard his screams like music
when he closed his eyes – the school organ at Rugby,
matins with light slanting down
hot and heady from the summer's high windows.
Pain – his trousers welded by flame to his legs.
His left hand tore off the clouded goggles –
rain falling like light into the heavy trees,
the track polished like a blade.
They would get to him, they were all coming
all running across the grass, he knew.

The fumes of a tuned Mercedes smelt like
boot polish and tear gas – coughing, his screams rising

high out of the cockpit – high
away back to '38 *Die Nurburgring.*
He flew in with Clara
banking and turning the Wessex through a slow circle
over the scene – sunlight flashing off the line of cars,
people waving, hoardings and loudspeakers, swastikas
and the flags of nations lifted in the wind he stirred.
She held his arm tightly, her eyes were closed.
He felt strong like the stretched wing of a bird,
the course mapped out below him.
That day Lang and Von Brauchitsch and Caracciola
all dropped out and he did it – won
in the fourth Mercedes before a crowd of half a million
– the champagne cup, the wreath around his neck,
An Englishman the toast of Germany
The camera caught him giving a Hitlergruss.

Waving arms, shouts and faces, a mosaic
laid up to this moment – La Source – tight – the hairpin
the trees – tight – La Source – keeping up the pace
Belgium – La Source hairpin too tight.

With the fire dying, the pain dying,
the voices blurred beneath the cool licks of rain.
To be laid under the cool sheets of rain.
A quiet with, just perceptible, engines roaring
as at the start of a great race.

INCIDENT ON A HOSPITAL TRAIN FROM
CALCUTTA, 1944

At a water-stop three hours out
the dry wail of brakes ground us down
from constant jolting pain to an oven
heat that filled with moans and shouts
from wards the length of six carriages.

We had pulled slowly up towards the summer
hills for coolness. They were hours distant,
hazy and vague. I opened the grimy
window to a rush of heat
and, wrapped in sacking, a baby

held up like some cooked offering from its mother –
Memsahib... meri buchee ko bachalo... Memsahib take –
pushed like an unlooked-for gift into my arms.
She turned into the smoke and steam.
I never saw her face.

As we lumbered off I unwrapped
a dirty, days-old girl, too weak for cries.
Her bird weight and fever-filled eyes
already put her out of our reach. By Murree Junction
that child would have emptied half our beds.

At the next water-stop my nurses left her.
The corporal whose arms had gone looked up at me

and said, *There was nothing else to do.*
Gangrenous, he died at Murree a week later.
His eyes, I remember, were clear, deep and blue.

PORTRAIT OF THE PAINTER HANS THEO RICHTER
AND HIS WIFE GISELA IN DRESDEN, 1933

This is the perfect moment of love –
Her arm around his neck,
Holding a rose.

Her wisps of yellow hair
The light turns gold.
Her face is the moon to his earth.

Otto's studio wall glows
With the warm wheat glow
Of the loving couple.

This is after the dark etchings,
The blown faces. This is after Bapaume –
The sickly greens, the fallen browns.

She is a tree, her neck a swan's curved to him.
His hands enclose her left hand
Like folded wings.

This is before the fire-storm,
Before the black wind,
The city turned to broken teeth.

It is she who holds the rose to him,
Theo's eyes which lower in contentment
To the surgeon's smock he wears for painting.

This is the perfect moment,
The painted moment
She will not survive.

This is before the hair that flames,
The face that chars. This is before
Her long arms blacken like winter boughs.

This is the harvest of their love,
It is summer in the soul,
The moment they have made together.

From Otto's window the sounds of the day –
The baker's boy calling, a neighbour's wireless
Playing marches and then a speech.

HEAVEN'S GATE
for Dannie and Joan Abse

Outside the Mughal Empereor in the sharp air
under a sky precise as a map
we point at Hale Bopp and its final, slow
splash out of our world into the depthless dark.
Full up with lamb pasanda, chicken jalfrezi

and puffed, sweet nan, we couldn't be
more earth-bound, more remote from flight.

There they go,
the thirty-three California crazies
who gave up on our century.
They're dead as dodos sailing through heaven's gate
in the gas stream of the comet
with their personal guides, the aliens.

While we, full of wind and spice, look
up from the jammed tight car park,
without envy or scorn,
but warm in friendship and food
and the pleasure of living this night
six million by six million miles below
the chaos of the gas and rock that now,
just now, completes this perfect sky
with a painter's smear of titanium white.

PENNYANNE WINDSOR

PennyAnne Windsor was born in the west of England in 1946 and moved to Swansea in 1968 but recently went to live in Cornwall. She has worked as a teacher and youth worker, and for the National Association of Citizens' Advice Bureaux, and has been involved with the women's movement for many years. She has also worked as a performance poet and has been part of a two-woman jazz and poetry group known as The Old Pros. Her six collections of verse are *Heroines* (1984), *Running Wild* (1986), *Dangerous Women* (1987), *Like Oranges* (1989), *Crashing the Moon* (1994), and *Curses and Dances* (1996). Almost all her poems have to do with her identity as a woman and women's issues.

DANCING WOMAN 1

by day
I go to work
and cook and shop and sew and mop
say the proper thing in the proper place
with a pretty smiling face
have three children and a spouse
a keep fit class, two library tickets and a mortgage on the
house

but late at night
and out of sight

I throw my clothes away
and dance

at night
I am a clever witch
a scheming bitch
a madonna sick of sainthood
a mother tired of being so good
a princess who will not go to sleep
a widow who declares she will not weep
a school girl who says she will not be a wife
an independent woman with her own exciting life

at night
I might be anyone
at night
and out of sight
I throw my clothes away
discard my children and my spouse
my keep fit class, my library tickets and the mortgage on
                                                    the house
and dance

quite by luck or chance
no one has guessed
the secret I confess to you
yet walking down the street
hair neat, make up discreet
I sometimes tap the paving stone

skip between the cracks
unwittingly betray the fact
at night
and out of sight
I throw my clothes away
and dance

LIKE ORANGES

i am a no-good
waster-of-a-woman
drinking wine in bed
hair unkempt
face crinkled up
with sleep and sex

i dream away the days
watching
the sun steal unswept rugs
catching
dots of dust

basking

the sun seduces me
my breasts are sweet and ripe
and i am full of juice
like oranges

oh –
i am a lovely
wanton
wicked
wayward
waster-of-a-woman

HEROINES

We are the terraced women
piled row on row on the sagging, slipping hillsides of our
                                                          lives.
We tug reluctant children up slanting streets
the push chair wheels wedging in the ruts
breathless and bad tempered we shift the Tesco carrier bags
                                          from hand to hand
and stop to watch the town

The hill tops creep away like children playing games

our other children shriek against the school yard rails
'there's Mandy's mum, John's mum, Dave's mum,
Kate's mum, Ceri's mother, Tracey's mummy'
we wave with hands scarred by groceries and too much
                                                washing up
catching echoes as we pass of old wild games

after lunch, more bread and butter, tea
we dress in blue and white and pink and white checked
                                                    overalls

and do the house and scrub the porch and sweep the street
and clean all the little terraces
up and down and up and down and up and down the hill

later, before the end-of-school bell rings
all the babies are asleep
Mandy's mum joins Ceri's mum across the street
running to avoid the rain
and Dave's mum and John's mum – the others too – stop
                                                    for tea
and briefly we are wild women
girls with secrets, travellers, engineers, courtesans, and stars
                                            of fiction, films
plotting our escape like jail birds
terraced, tescoed prisoners rising from the household dust
like heroines.

ANDREW MCNEILLIE

Andrew McNeillie was born at Hen Golwyn, Denbighshire, in 1946 and educated at John Bright Grammar School, Llandudno, and Magdalen College, Oxford, where he read English. His first job was that of news reporter with the *South Wales Guardian* and *Llwchwr Chronicle*, from which he moved to Liverpool and then London, where he wrote news bulletins for the BBC. He worked for a while for the Virginia Woolf Estate, editing the writer's diaries, and then for Blackwells. He founded Clutag Press in 2000 and, since 2004, has been Literature Editor at Oxford University Press. Besides a prose memoir, *An Aran Keening* (2002), which is based on a journal of nearly a year spent on Inishmore in 1968, he has published three books of verse: *Nevermore* (2000), *Now, Then* (2002) and *Slower* (2006).

DARK HORSE

Once, up there, before the stream, we found
A mountain pony's skull and jawbone
In the bog, and then the whole of it,
Just near the surface and dispersing
Like stars racing over the mountains.

On our way home we brought the skull with us:
To whinny in the dark of the outhouse,
And roll its eye, and show its teeth –
Its nostrils flared to scent the wilderness –
And dream like us of stars and mountains.

PISS

'He gave it the worst look he had left.'

John Berryman

A man must do more than come from somewhere,
sing the songs of his people and relate their stories

to warrant respect, still less earn praise: I'm bored by
the bravura bores parading their lack on their sleeve.

Their claim that where they come from it's pronounced
to sound like loss is neither here nor there to me.

I piss on their empty pride. I piss on their loss,
their folk measures, their hearty reminiscence and

sneering or sensitive superiority of demeanour, their
transparent manoeuvres to attract the limelight, and I piss

on the dupes who would atone for their want of purity of
being
by seeking to sample the nostalgia that dare not speak its
home.

I spit in their eyes for shysters. I piss in their repertoire.
I piss down their tin whistles and into their fiddles.

I fill the bladders of their bagpipes with the urine of bevies
of bevies of heavies and echter than echt drams.

608

I revile them for I know where they come from and why
they lack attention there, and how, should they dare

or presume to return, the locals will soon clip their wings,
cut short their tedious reminiscence, with sharp recollection
of their own

(piss on them too). Which is why the bastards won't go
home.
But still the call resounds, 'Have you no homes to go to?'

from PLATO'S AVIARY

xii

Cormorant (*Phalacrocorax carbo*)
for Iain McNeillie

I remember the day the old man shot one
high over the house and how it folded,
like a winded umbrella, and came down
in a thorn bush, stone dead, neck collapsed,
wings hooked up to dry for the last time.
But why still, the nervous, apprehensive wonder,
the word *skart* on my tongue for pleasure?
Why couldn't I settle to sleep that night
for thinking about it? I wasn't upset.
I didn't weep. It got what was coming to it.
It was the devil, the thief on the cross, of fish
that we might catch. Way out of range it swerved,
but the old man was a dead-eyed dick.

I'd seen him perform such miracles before.
And even if I smiled, when he laid it out
for my education in the life and death
of birds, and distinguished it from *SHAG*,
I kept my school-yard smirk to myself, so he had
no cause to curse me for a tom fool.
Perhaps it was just those three dabs,
the size of half-a-crown, that came
flipping from its gullet alive, alive O
O, O as moist as eyes? ... Maybe.

WISH LIST

The iceberg that makes it round the world.
The complete works of Anon.
A cape and stars above the sea.
The camel through a needle's eye.
The Life of William Shakespeare by Himself.
The first of day. Her louch look.
The sweetest fuck.
The nesting bird.
The omertà of old age.
The light at the heart of the pyramid.
The song you have by heart.
The harbour light at dawn.
The sound within the poem.
The curlew on the moor.
The wild-goose skein.
The raven rolling in a windy sky.
The world turned upside down.
Tête à tête avec Owain Glyndŵr.

Genius-in-waiting.
Winter lightning.
The last word of the old order and first of the new.
The Republic of Scotland.
The Republic of Wales.
Vision and revision.
Hindsight as foresight.
The reader read.
The people's voice.
The happy couple.
The oar's puddle.
The Tower of Babel.
The lighthouse bell.
A millpond sea.
The dune's crest in the moving air.
The tribe's oral tradition.
The other as me.
The one in B minor. The next line.
The coelacanth's mating ritual.
The girl who never returned your love.
The end of all that. The end of all this.
A new poetics. A new prosody.
The poet guilty as charged.

IN DEFENCE OF POETRY

Older than we are by however many ages,
it doesn't need defending against anything.
(Far more do air and fire, earth and water.)
Not even in our empty times. Neglected, it will
go underground, or into interstellar space.

Until out of somewhere someone calls it up,
like the Greek who cut my hair last week.
Where was he from? 'Spar-ta,' he said.
'You are a Spartan!' I exclaimed. 'Oh no,'
he said, 'there are no Spartans anymore.'

GONE FOR GOOD

How many more poems will you haunt,
old man? I know you won't say; but
don't pretend you're not keeping count.
I know you and I know you're not done yet.
As on those endless dour days you'd cast
and cast into the evening and keep casting
while I'd pray the next would be your last
not knowing then that faith is everlasting.

My mother said you just upped and left
but that was ever your way, if you could.
Given half a chance to fish I'd do the same.
There's nothing new except we are bereft
and now we say you've gone for good
which so far hasn't lived up to its name.

from GLYN DŴR SONNETS

x

When young Owain went to Bod Alaw,
the Welsh School in Colwyn (founded
in 1950), you'd think he was retarded,
and his parents thick. How could they allow
him to miss so much, fall behind forever,
in his rough flannel shorts, his pebble specs?
It made no sense. 'A language no one speaks,
except to the sheep and the weather.'

'Welsh-Welsh...' or 'thick Welsh', they'd say meaning both
twp and spluttering guttural Babel.
As to their poetry! It beggars belief
that it doesn't translate, they'd sneer. As if
they knew all about the art of the *Awdl*
and *Englyn*, and the rules of *Cynghanedd*.

DOUGLAS HOUSTON

Douglas Houston was born in Cardiff in 1947 and brought up in Glasgow. He was educated at the University of Hull and taught English in Germany before returning to Wales in 1981 to live as a full-time writer in Cwm Ystwyth in Ceredigion. He worked as an editor of internet-based information for use in government and education until 2003 when he joined the staff of the University of Glamorgan where he now edits on-line learning materials. He has published three books of poems, *With the Offal Eaters* (1986), *The Hunters in the Snow* (1994) and *The Welsh Book of the Dead* (2000).

TOMORROW NEVER KNOWS
i.m. John Lennon, 1940-1980

No guilt attaches to a hero's end;
Five bullets from a madman's gun defend
The right to sudden death that cities keep
For those whose truth disturbs official sleep.

There was blue sky unclouded by belief.
The clarity of daylight was enough.
A man was singing of the one relief
That life affords from death and he meant love.

'HERE'S TAE US ...'

This was my father's tankard,
Truncated cone of pewter, glass
Through which light strikes the bay of beer
At the bottom of which lies emptiness.
The handle's bow and his masonic fist
Were intimate where my mother served the beer,
In Cardiff in the old days when the trams ran,
Say 1945, before my time.

Out of retirement now, it holds home-brew,
A pint and a slop on top at a time,
And that passes well through the guts of a son
Who thinks as he drinks of a father months gone
Since the summer that suddenly turned on a funeral
Has itself been disposed of in due season,
And the norms of wetness, wind and cold
Are re-established in this muddy shire,
In which he died, that now assumes his flesh.

Comatose, he hung on till the doctor came,
Then punctually ceased to struggle for breath.
I have come into much since that day, his birthday,
When he ate his chocolates more thoughtfully
Than chocolates are usually eaten,
And though I regret not kissing the body
At my sister's request, for both of us,
Our lips meet out of time round this tankard.

615

DEAD MAN'S SHOES

The leathern strata of the best pair's heels
Had brought forth powdery sulphur-yellow mould.
But costly, sleek, of calf, I liked their feel;
His widow asked ten pounds; we called them sold.

It took eight months for grief to dissipate
Sufficiently to sell off his effects;
An invalid, the soles were in a state
That told his legs had fallen to neglect.

She'd said that he's been big, and I regret
His pants and jackets would have held me twice;
But bless his perished feet, a matching set
For my elevens, their cast-offs at a price

She took by cheque, accepting it post-dated.
The daughter fetched two more pairs from the shed,
While mother, in continuing, related
How on a snowed-up night she'd found him dead

On his return from going for a pee;
'*Ten for the brand-new casuals, two for these,*
Take three pairs and you'll have the slippers free.'
Furred arteries, it seems, were his disease.

I'm happy in my socks, but, *de rigeur*,
A man needs shoes to strut his stuff today.
I'm keeping those calf numbers to ensure,
If necessary, my feet will look O.K.

DAY IN, DAY OUT

Fine days in early winter are clear light
Down all the valley's long intricacies,
A distance of the river's meandering
Where adjoining vales occlude its curving
To the sea beyond the last range of hills.

Inside I study different fires by night,
The hues of various woods' combustion
Or metallic yellow of soft coal's flames,
Effulgent landscapes of the ember hells
And thin smoke clouding in the varnished beams.

Another weekend comes over the hill.
Saturday is perpendicular rain,
Soaking the woodchips from my hatchet work,
Weighting the countless leaves and blades of green.
The morning's eggs steam, breath mists the table.

They are sitting beside the dying fire,
A man and wife speaking softly in Welsh.
Upstairs I lie afraid of these shadows,
Who sometimes move an object carefully,
Recalling their rights to the mantelpiece.

The two stone sheds sag under the weather,
Their mortar crumbling, their beams going soft
In the percussion of insistent rain,
Each full drop bursting like a glass grenade
On the packed black mud of the rough pathway.

I look for optimism in the night
While urinating onto the dark earth,
Aimlessly gazing for falling meteors
That vary the fixed plan of heaven's lights.
I wish for success, and shrug at the sky.

As there is no thread or pattern in it,
Let us spend the day on the hill, my love,
With a fine view of the rain on our house
Some distance between its neighbouring farms
In the wet fascination of winter.

W. H. AUDEN IN CWMBRWYNO
(for Bruce Woodcock)

Since to discount the hereafter as a possibility
      Seemed at best rather unfeasible,
At worst irredeemable folly (though to imagine it
      Remained a poser limestone half solved),
It hardly amazes me, who became inured to surprise,
      To come to consciousness up here.
Indeed, I am delighted at whatever dispensation
      Has placed me amid this landscape
Like a locality I loved. Though the machines are gone,
      The derelict wheelpits, grey spoil-heaps,
And several crumbled buildings linked by the purposive
                      stream
      Announce *lead-mine* to one informed
In these matters from infancy. To me such uplands spoke

A code of love it took a life
To render into simple language of reciprocation:
    I held their desolation dear,
And their complete abandonment always made room for me,
    Whether the barren *Ding an Sich*,
Or in the privacy of space entered through memory's adit.
    The after-life advantages
The visitor, it appears. No guide book is necessary now
    The mood of place translates itself
Into particulars of what happened here – mostly labour;
    The delve and drainage, sorting rock,
Clean ore sent clattering seawards along the little railway,
    While, out of sight, a fortune grew,
Then faltered till silence took root in 1888.
    These hills do not care to impress,
Ancient and scraggy with ribs of stone breaking through the
                      thin green
    So slowly healing the mine's scar
(And certainly not interested in my sympathy
    In their dedolant emptiness).
Only the bones of sheep might be considered additions
    To what the paid-off miners left;
Beyond loss, what remains long since utility collapsed
    To irreducible aesthetics
Of rusted curves of rail, dejected masonry and peace,
    Is absolute to me, resisting
Even the colonisation of the imagination
    And silently insisting on
Its terms of barefaced honesty beyond alternatives.
    Though its poetic forms appealed

619

(Intimidatingly complex), Wales meant little to me
      After the early photographs,
Memorialising how at six I loved simple machines
      On holiday in Rhayader.
Here, however, I'm at home below the slouching mountains'
                           mist,
      Donated random mineral finds
Turned over by my foot – this algae fossilised on slate,
      A slow subaqeous holograph
Whose text is years in millions. Shattering a weighty chunk
                         of rock
      Against an unyielding boulder
Has introduced to daylight a good vein of galena
      Whose lustrous facets quite outshine
The subservient metal wept by these fractile crystals
      When smelting rends their bond with sulphur...
From what I gather, the Great Powers have not mended their
                         ways,
      Monied, immune, even more dangerous
In uncontainable Megalopolis, since foreclosure
      Deprived me of my mortal manor;
But to my list of sites least likely to be further robbed
      This nook some way below Plymlimon
Is added to become one of the irrefutable Prophets.

DAVID HUGHES

David Hughes was born in Bargoed in 1947 but has lived most of his life in Swansea. He trained as a teacher and taught for four years at schools in the West Midlands and Swansea. Since 1975 he has been a social worker, latterly in the Mental Health Services Department of the City and County of Swansea. He has published one book of verse, *Tidy Boy* (1998), which contains a number of poems in the demotic language of the city in which he lives and works.

FLOWERS

Let's hear it for the kids with the spray cans,
for Cheri, Fat Sam and Jack;
the kids who have gone off the rails
who live on the wrong side of the tracks.

They're the kids who missed the points,
who don't know their station.
They don't obey the signals,
they've got no motivation.

But their names blossom in this desert
of sidings, concrete and sheds
and the letters of their names
bloom in purple, yellow and red.

621

Scrambling over railway lines,
overlooked by high grey towers,
they have taken paint to a waste land
and turned their names to flowers.

TIDY BOY

We woz kids tgether, frommer same street.
I sat nex towim ry threw jewnyers.
Ewster goter play up iz ouse a lot,
iz mam never said nuthin much twus;
iz ole manad buggud off yurzago.
Air woz oney im an iz mam inny ouse.
E woz quiet like, butter tidy boy.

We ewster go onner mitch tgether.
Gowup iz cuzns farm, upper valley;
reel Welshy up air. We elped wither sheep
an after, iz cuzn took us shootin rabbits.
At woz great – I got one once.
E never bothered much, e cummerlong though.
E woz quiet like, butter tidy boy.

We went onnat YOP crap – snot much cop.
Sumvower mates woz lucky, ay did orrite;
me annim got bloody shitty jobs.
I ewster avver bitver go see
atter boss. E wozn mouthy like me
kepiz ed down, never lookedfer trouble.
E woz quiet like, butter tidy boy.

E never cumout much wither boys downer pub;
ewster stay inny ouse withiz mam
or go out byiself crosser commun.
Annen I wozonner piss wunight
an took iss car an smashed it up.
Got sent down forat. E woodnuv dunnit.
E woz quiet like, butter tidy boy

I yurd wot appentowim from my girl
wen she cum downer nickter see me.
Ay foundim up onner farm. Shotgun
inniz mouth, anniz brains blowed crosser field.
A screw seddy mustav been offiz ed.
Bastud. E wozn mad, e woz my mate.
E woz quiet like, butter tidy boy.

THE STREETS OF LLANDEILO

As I walked out in the streets of Llandeilo
I spied a Range Rover crashed into a tree,
slumped over the wheel in a waxed Barbour jacket,
a young man lay dying – as pale as fresh brie.

I saw by his wellies that he was a yuppie
and these words he did say as I boldly stepped by,
'Come sit down beside me and hear my sad story
for I've lost all my money and will soon have to die.

It was once in a Porsche I used to go blithely,
once in the Porsche all the girls would come fast,
first to a wine bar and then to my penthouse,
but that good life now is a thing of the past.

Get six crooked brokers to sort out my folio,
get six crooked lawyers to cover my deeds,
put the FT index on top of my coffin
with a picture of Fergie and my worry beads.

Switch on my CD player with the special sound system,
play Dire Straits as you carry me about,
take me to a priest for absolution,
my only sin was being found out.

Go gather around you a crowd of best yuppies
and tell them the story of this my sad fate,
tell one and the other before they go further
not to invest in west Wales before it's too late.

The people here all Godforsaken;
they don't want marinas to tie up our yachts,
they don't want tasteful little wine bars
to bring added lustre to their few beauty spots.

Go fetch me a cup, a cup of lemon Perrier
to cool my parched lips,' the yuppie then said,
but before I could think, where was the nearest Sainsbury's
he'd folded his filofax – the yuppie was dead.

624

So I drained off the diesel from his Range Rover
and I left the yuppie where he did die.
But as I cast for salmon on the banks of the Tywi
his waxed Barbour jacket keeps me comfy and dry.

PAUL GROVES

Paul Groves was born in Gloucester in 1947 and brought up at The Narth, a hamlet between Monmouth and Chepstow. He was a nurse for a year before training as a teacher at Caerleon College of Education, then studied at St. Michael's Theological College in Llandaf, Cardiff; he is an Anglican reader and part of a team ministry based in Coleford. Since 1989 he has taught Creative Writing at the Royal Forest of Dean College; he lives at Osbaston, near Monmouth. He has published four books of poems: *Academe* (1988), *Ménage à Trois* (1995), *Eros and Thanatos* (1999), and *Wowsers* (2002). Playful, formal, ironic, deadpan and elegant, his poems often explore the darker aspects of life, especially those associated with sex and death.

not starting from the top.
I hope you did not mind me
rising to a stop.
So this is how you find me –

feet, decanting woes.
that creep about on wary
and mean as much as those
Words can be light and airy

or sweep it from the room.
and symbol-ridden parlance,

the poet's sense of doom
now and then can balance

a little levity
unrelievedly serious;
   when poetry must be
I feel it's deleterious

and hardly something worse.
eliciting a snigger
   out of a page of verse,
an unfamiliar figure

a small attempt to cut
essentially it's harmless,
   and artificial, but
The project may seem charmless

On this what is your view?
a poem written backwards.
   rather than bend them to
One might be wise to lack words

while passing on his bike.
a vicar pulling faces
   perverse, perhaps, and like
Starting from the base is

TURVY-TOPSY

A LOOK AROUND NEW YORK

Grand Guignol. It is not enough to buy
Flowers on Sixth Avenue, or books
In Greenwich Village; nor is it enough
To see *Potemkin* for the zillionth time,
Odessa steps or not. No, what we love
Is something else. Forget the classy looks
Of Bloomingdale's and Macy's. Come, let's fly.
Welcome to the sanctuaries of crime.

He takes me to the barber shop where, in
Nineteen fifty-seven, Anastasia
Met his end. 'The bullets really flew!'
Gallo, his assassin, was rubbed out
Himself in April, nineteen seventy-two.
Umberto's Clam House. 'Don't let all this faze yuh
– They merely reaped the harvest of the sin
They earlier sowed. Enjoyable?' No doubt;

I am the guest, and must not be ungracious.
'Now here's one for the limey. 72nd
Street . December, nineteen eighty. Does
That ring a bell?' His Buick has the answer.
It always had. A teenager, he'd buzz
The town for hours each night – or so he reckoned.
I gravely nod. The formidable, spacious
Dakota block. I hope he dies of cancer

Or cardiac arrest, and not through being
Gunned down in the foyer of the Plaza
(Hardenbergh, its architect, designed
Lennon's landmark), or one day some brash
Murder freak might similarly find
Delight in such a guided tour. It has a
Grim appeal admittedly – like seeing
Stray dogs urinate, or windblown trash.

His duty done, we home to his apartment,
A bijou residence in Union City,
Old-ladyish, no hint of vile disaster.
We tackle sushi followed by a yokan
And green-tea ice cream, then we play canasta.
He lets me win. We smoke a little shit. He
Is human, too, and probably at heart meant
To honour me with his best social token.

MAGNUM OPUS

He had this house near Estremoz
in Portugal, beside the Tera
    — but not the 'tera' in literature.

He was writing a sort of Osborne play;
he'd seen *Look Back...* with Burton and Ure
    – but not the 'ure' in literature.

She stayed three days. It started well,
though he drank too much, and he wanted it
    – but not the 'it' in literature.

629

'No sex,' she said. 'You're here to work.'
His stateside brashness reached for the liter
    – but not the 'liter' in literature.

'This drama,' he boasted, 'will sweep the board.
A blockbuster. Start of an era.'
    But not the 'era' in literature.

Dusk left the sky a bloody mess
night sluiced away. Lamps were lit
    – but not the 'lit' in literature.

On the third day he said, 'Get out.
You're not inspiring me.' The rat!
    But not the 'rat' in literature.

THE BIG ADVENTURE

Jumbo and I set off for the Mound of Venus.
Nana bounded beside us down the path.
'I think it's in that direction,' Jumbo said.
I disagreed. He picked two blades of grass
and offered their green tips. I chose the shorter.
There'd been a shower. A rainbow graced the sky.
Nana chased a rabbit to its burrow.
We walked like chums towards the shining hill.
He gave me gum. I lent him my best penknife.
'It might well come in handy,' I exclaimed,
not knowing how. Nearby a blackbird sang.

'When we see the Mound of Venus,' Jumbo said,
'what do we do?' I shrugged in ignorance.
Nana was rolling over on the grass.
There were a million buttercups. The fields
were alive with growth. The ebullience of spring
had touched us in a host of subtle ways.
We almost felt like teenagers. The Mound
was only a mile further, Jumbo assured me,
though he'd never actually been there. Not yet.
Nana had found a flea. A brook ran by.
We would be home for lunch. Our appetites
would quite surprise our mothers. 'I've been told
it's just beyond those trees,' Jumbo announced.
We ran towards them, rapidly growing up.
We opened bedroom doors in separate cities.
The friendly dog was nowhere to be seen.

BOOSENING

(An old method of treating insanity
by immersing the patient in cold water.)

Mr Marquand, though slight,
had a vice-like grip.
He had the brows of a beadle,
a mark around his forehead
where the top hat fitted.

Souvenir Leslie, whose father
had been transported, was wiry,
tough as a bull terrier.

Nothing escaped his attention;
no one escaped his clutches.

It was a wet Friday, soon
to be made wetter.
Horatio Charles led in
the first inmate, shivering
in a shift. 'Time for

your baptism, my beauty.'
Brusquely disrobed, the emaciated
specimen stood, too stupid
to cover its pathetic manhood.
Its grin was chipped, irregular.

Mr Marquand and Souvenir Leslie
wore gloves of industrial leather,
stout trousers, and crushing boots.
Regimentally they stood, one
on either side of the wan exhibit.

They linked hands behind it.
The vat waited, round
as a witches' cauldron, chill
as the Northwest Passage.
They counted to three.

Mr Charles hit the patient
squarely, without rancour,
in the solar plexus.

It doubled up, squealing,
seeking lost breath.

In an instant the dis-
equilibrium was seized upon.
As the fool was lifted
and lowered into the depths,
displacement washed over

the institutional floor.
White tiles, white walls:
this was a snowscape.
Winter had come suddenly.
'Boosening, my boy,' Marquand

boomed. 'Never fails.'
Ice had been made and broken
since dawn, brought
from the kitchens, and added
to the vat. The patient

was too shocked to scream.
Its eyes lit up like coals.
'Christmas,' said Souvenir Leslie,
'is a week away, and this
– be assured – is your first present.'

A HIGH ROOM OFF SPITALGASSE

(In the eighteenth century, Dr Tissot told of a school
in Bern where a whole class masturbated during
the metaphysics lesson of a nearsighted teacher.)

The boys of Bern are beating their meat.
The *professeur* doesn't see them do it.
He writes on the blackboard, small and neat.
Metaphysics is driving them to it.

Down below in the busy street
a bright new morning is under way.
Here it is disciplined, discreet;
lofty parameters hold sway.

Over in Königsberg, Kant is thriving.
Leibniz is dead, but his words live on.
Hume is alive and well, and living
in Edinburgh. But here in Bern

twenty boys are cleaning their rifles,
buffing their swords, pounding their pork,
while the *professeur* is dealing in trifles,
vague abstractions, shadow talk.

Their eyes are glassy, their faces are set
in rapt attention, while under each desk
a gentle frenzy continues. Yet
all he sees is a picturesque

Spinozan equation that he alone,
among those present, can understand.
He turns, thick-lensed in his twilight zone:
'If you have a question, please raise your hand.'

Reflexively, ten hands go up.
They are all left hands. He turns again
to the crowded board, to his brimming cup
of obtuse wisdom, his regimen.

LINES FOR GEORGIA O'KEEFFE

I met you years after your death and fell for you. I've a lot
of photos of you beneath your husband's lens – the taut
smooth skin, the breasts, the hair – and that can never

age...
and your timeless work in colour, page after glorious page.
What more could I want? I've got your painterly life,

complete,

and can go through it any night. So I sit at your feet,
a devoted disciple. You keep me calm. You can't stroke my

hair

or speak to me or sleep by my side exactly, where
I'd sometimes want you to be, but your grace and humour

extend

about me like a country without borders, without end.

Though an average farmer's daughter from Wisconsin, you

were more

than human: you were clear water, light descending where
the eye takes in the vista. You were New Mexico,
a true alignment, a sister to that stone, that sunrise glow
over the mesa. Take these heartfelt verses now

as if you were living. Speak in the evening wind, in the
                                                    snow,
even the first snowflake, a sensitive pretty thing.
Slumber, and when you awake turn towards me and sing
the song of eternal morning lightly, so that the words
resemble the wind's moaning, the distant wing-beats of
                                                    birds.

THE CORDLESS HANDSET

Her garrulous mother phoned while we were screwing.
Penelope was cool, despite the action:
she told the lady how the lawn was doing;
the borders were a source of satisfaction;

the hedges needed clipping ... that would follow
fairly soon, she said. The bed was groaning
beneath our fraught exertions. We would wallow
in lust like this for hours; we'd take all morning

sometimes. Interruptions at this juncture
were something new: either an added thrill
or what could lend itself to a slow puncture,
both partners stalling, going off the boil.

Which would it be? She straddled me. I lay
under her urgent weight, her golden thighs.
If they got onto shopping, that would slay
all consummation, cancel paradise

with one abrupt cessation. Penny said
the only thing she could say. Nerves were humming;
our bodies were on fire. 'Look, I'm afraid
I'll have to call you back as someone's coming.'

PETER FINCH

Peter Finch was born in Cardiff in 1947. Educated at the Glamorgan College of Technology in Trefforest, Pontypridd, he worked in local government until 1973 when he was appointed manager of Oriel, the Welsh Arts Council's bookshop in Cardiff. From 1966 until it ceased publication in 1974 he was editor and publisher of the little magazine *Second Aeon*. Since 1998 he has been Chief Executive of Academi, the body which promotes the writers and literature of Wales. With Meic Stephens, he edited *Green Horse* (1978), an anthology of verse by young Welsh poets, and with Grahame Davies *The Big Book of Cardiff* (2005). He has also published a collection of short stories, *Between 35 and 42* (1982), and two books about his home city. His poems, boldly innovative and often exploring the boundaries between sense and sound, rely on wit, literary allusion and sheer gusto for their effects. Among his books are *The End of the Vision* (1971), *Blats* (1972), *Some Music and a Little War* (1984), *Make* (1990), *Useful* (1997), *Food* (2001) and *The Welsh Poems* (2006); his *Selected Poems* appeared in 1987 and *Selected Later Poems* in 2007.

THE TAO OF DINING

We go into the restaurant and the bill is thirty
before we sit. The waiter sells us three pound
Chardonnay for twelve. The menu reads like a
language test. Understanding creeps we go
limp and warm. I want a full plate three bread

638

rolls I get a biscuit and a pool of yellow in its centre a
centimetred fish. We are dining because this is
intimacy and the alcohol helps. I want life
it's here. Snazz blues in the backdrop the
waiter skips. "You enjoy, *monsieur*?" He's
Australian. The bill is already sixty I don't care.
The wine is a symphony I have no way of
judging. Crème Brulée makes our hair shine.
Our fellow diners glow like angels,
our souls are singing.
The bill is somewhere I have never been before,
read with joy, signed with ecstasy,
the whole restaurant is smiling.
Someone said dining is all experience.
Lao Tzu that only the one you are in right now
has any importance. Outside it's raining.

THE STUDENT HOUSE

We arrive through thin snow to
my son's student house where
no one has been for three weeks.
The ice has turned the air to knives.
I find a ketchup-smeared plate
frozen at 45° in the unemptied
kitchen sink. A river of lager
cans flows down the hall.
As I stamp into the lounge
keeping my feet alive the ghosts
of dust come up around me like
children. The stains across the

sofa look like someone has died.
Amid the wrappers and old news
washing against the skirting I
spot the letter I sent up six-months
back. It's up to you, I wrote,
you are on your own now,
no one can do this for you,
something like that.
He enters the room in his ripped
jeans and shrunken sweat-shirt
fingers locked in his arm-pits.
Do we clear this place? Can't be bothered,
the energy has been
frozen out of us. He hands
me the torch. I go to the basement
to see if I can fix the boiler, no
longer in charge but still trying,
the fallen king. I light the pilot
and the heat comes back,
a kind of love, pressing us softly
as we stand saying goodbye
amid the junk mail in the hall.

BLODEUWEDD TRANSLATED

I ws bldng n t lp f bsts
Pllng stffl t m lv. I hv t scmng
tht wnds mir n t mn. Grmnts f groc
dlt n clpp n t wnk f m il.

I m starrr f mgh mlssssss
wr tghtngngngn shot my moderness appalling
nasnasmast f I hd fop on fop on me
n t rbble f stirling I list m why

I ws bllll l l ll llls
Pllng ngngn n n ng. N ng n ngngng
tht thth t t th. Gthths yt thth
dlt o oooo o o ooo o o oo

I m storrr r rrr r mssssssss
wr starlight starlight starlight
starlight starlight starlight me
god gaths stir m m starlight why

I ss sssss sssss blod oak broom meadowsweet

ALL I NEED IS THREE PLUMS
apologies to William Carlos Williams

I have sold your jewellery collection,
which you kept in a box, forgive me.
I am sorry, but it came upon me
and the money was so inviting, so sweet
and so cold.
I have failed to increase my chest measurements
despite bar bells
and my t-shirt is not full of ripples.
I am sweet but that is no consolation.
Your hand is cold.
I did not get the job, your brother did.

641

He is a bastard I told him, forgive me.
The world is full of wankers, my sweet.
I have lost the dog, I am sorry.
He never liked me, I am hardly inviting.
I took him off the lead in the park and
the swine chased a cat I couldn't
be bothered to run after him.
Forgive me, I will fail less in the
future.
I have collected all the furniture I could find
and dismembered it in the grate, I am sorry
but I have these aberrations.
The weather is inclement. You have run out of
firelighters.
It's bloody cold.
Please forgive me, I have taken the money
you have been saving in the ceramic pig
and spent it on drink, so sweet and inviting.
This is just to say I am in the pub
where I have purchased the fat guy from
Merthyr's entire collection of scratch and win.
All I need now is three delicious plums.

Forgive me, sweetie,
these things just happen.

LLYWELYN GOCH AP MEURIG HEN AT SPEED

South heart like a birchtop woodsong
light and little proud ah
Lleucu heart broken

Merioneth
Machynlleth
Mawddwy

Deheubarth buggered

the barbs of longing the pain

You've been writing again, she said,
no it's just blisters on my fingertips,
and great caves in
the space inside me. Heart
thinks it's the soul. Full of birds.

Life has five plots:
rise to fame, fall from grace,
gain love, lose it
and death.

RNLD TOMOS (vcl, hca, some prse) aka Curtis Langdon.
1913-2000. Gospel. Austerity tradition. Jnd Iago
Prytherch Big Band (1959), gog, gap, bwlch, lleyn, tan,
iaith, mynydd, mangle, adwy – mainly on Hart-Davis race
label. Reissue Dent PoBkSoc Special Recommnd.. Concert
at Sherman support Sorley Maclean (gtr, hrt clutching) sold
out. Fire Bomb tour Sain triple cd for D Walford Davies
(vcl, crtcl harmonium) new century highspot. A pioneer of
dark wounds and internal tensions. In old age bird song
and reliable grouch. Stood, was counted, still no change. To
live in Wales is to become un-assailable. 'An angel-fish'
(Clarke). Expect retrospective, marvelling and statue.

GOD MOVES IN MYSTERIOUS WAYS

When the meter man came to
read the electric with his
data-capture Oyster, his long-life
torch and how are you mate
he opened the door to the dark
space understairs and found a fifties
jungle of boots and fox-furs and
my mother still in there fixing the
peeling paper with paste so strong
you had to trowel it, my sister
doodling on the organ wafting church
music – the stuff they play to keep
the congregation amused when the
vicar's late – and my old self too
like a hard rat with pretty cheeks
biting things and told to stop
keeping train numbers and
a scrap-book of breasts. We all
turned then, old me and them, winced at
the light with our anaemic eyes.
My mother had the right idea,
polishing the dials with Brasso,
tell them we're Catholic, she said,
and my sister did and old me shut
the door and sped off into the future
repeating the same lie over and over
for the rest of my life.
Bless you, mate,
the meter man smiled.
Sod off, I said.

644

GLENDA BEAGAN

Glenda Beagan was born in Rhuddlan, Flintshire, in 1948, and still lives there. Educated at the University College of Wales, Aberystwyth, she is Welsh-speaking. She has published two volumes of short stories, *The Medlar Tree* (1992) and *Changes & Dreams* (1996), and a collection of poems, *Vixen* (1996).

RHIANNON

find me
under the owl window
I smile
I am not what I seem
sat, clad simply carding wool

old woman at the edge of life
now, with time's loosening
how should it be other than this:
these palsied hands,
these shadows?

drowsy, I see
small smoke of bees
lift from the keps
at the orchard edge

pulse of the land
its coiled gold

645

its glimmering combs
its sweetness

bring me no bishop and his book
bring me no kindly simperings
cold piety would kill my worlds
of falcons, hounds
and steeds white as anemones

I let them think I have lost my wits
this way I keep my flickerings
the dappled harvest in my lap
the charmed birds on my sill

I am my past
not this dull shape
I am my loves
my laughing hair

bodies of heroes burn in me
wasps sing in ripe red air

BOUDICCA

I can be free
under the sky, washed
in bright air. I can
fly, canny falcon, over flanks
of long hills, shoulders
of windflexed barley.

Here, oak and lichen
mix with yellow carr.
Streams of sharp cresses
course in this land as blood
hums in my body. This is earth
I know and love as they never can.

A people of clarity,
their straight lines, their searing light
have shunned the smell of beast and byre.
Dung and mulch, the breath of horses, are part
of me, as much as the twittering of martins
in the thatch, the seep of spring water.

Their palaces of tile and brick
would thin our strength. Near them
I hunger soon to clothe myself in woodsmoke,
feel again warm loam under my feet,
drink the strength of mare's milk.
For some, not least the man I must call husband,

their softness calls,
but I have seen their flagons of glass
the colour of damsons, sipped tangy wine,
whitebubbled, stared them out,
returning to rough mead, the withy cart's
wild speed, the tearing blade.

MELANGELL

They call me saint.
They bless me and the hares they call my lambs,
here, in quietness of forest, fastness
of mountain wall.

Pennant is my place,
mellow paps the hills behind my home,
dappled cones sunlight plays upon,
with clouds dancing.

Fierce beasts were the waves
that tossed me, my landfall so
far west of here.Through winter's mire and frost
I struggled.

A carlin, hooped
in age gave me bowed wisdom, broth
in a dish of bone, simples and salves.
The body mends at last.

The spirit grows
to a glade's calm, chill of well water,
bannocks of coarse flour. I delve and hew,
Erin remembering:

Tanat rejoicing.
Then comes the summer of mallows and wild lupins

blue as streams on soft banks of seed,
the cry of the hunt,

the blare and wild
will of hounds, till through birches they come like a fire
running, a hare at my hem, a huntsman's horn singed
to his lips in a blister of sound.

They call it miracle,
and so it was, I, frozen in his prince's sight, never
having seen a man so like god, a flame. His name is Brochwel
and I, a bride of Christ …

My hares, my lambs
are sweet velvet nutmegs. I have seen them dancing
in moonlight. At the *prie dieu* I leave posies
of white broom.

Maidens flock here,
craving this rule, this life I blend. As years
mount the arch of the sky, I kneel and whisper,
plaiting staunch cords of peace.

ROBERT WALTON

Robert Walton was born in 1948 in Cardiff, where his parents kept a pub. He read English at the University of Exeter and taught at a comprehensive school in Bristol, where he still lives. He has published one book of poems, *Workings* (1979).

AIRING CUPBOARD

My mother folds sheets
And shuts them into darkness
Like pages of pressed flowers,
Their fragrance lost. I watch,
At a distance. That's
Her business with them now,
To sleep in a field of dreams
And then the cleansing and drying,
An inocent use. And though
Doctors have removed half
Her insides, there's still the ring
On her finger and a love
For the man, my father, to make
Pulse within her, like shoots
Out of ashes, an ache of blood.
The door's closed. The sheets
Air, I turn to words.
Petals unfold in the dark.

A WOMAN OF SIXTY CHANGED HER NAME

And why not, now you're sixty, Nancy,
change your name to Anne-Marie!

You won't retire to age in a nest
feathered with moulted memories without

some flare of colour, we know you well
enough. And how exotic the flourish,

this ruffled spread of flamingo plumage
your sobriquet conjures. All

the years of graft, Nancy, down
on your knees, arthritic, on the tiles

scrubbing the slops from last night's binge,
or bent at the bar, pressing your shoulder

to the swirl of polish darkening the grain
to a gleam, all the years you're proud of,

damn the grind, damn the virtue
of drudgery, recede, a shadow behind

a closed door's frosted pane,
and now emerges, imaged in the mirror

behind the bar where you sit, what
new self, what years of life

you lift your glass to cheer your dream of,
Anne-Marie? With a name like that,

you'd siren the salons and break the gallant
hearts on your debutante's whim, or grace

the court au fin de siècle, serene
in velvet and crêpe de chine, madame,

indulging your fancy. But you choose to do
otherwise, toothless and whiskey-voiced,

astride a stool in your corner of the saloon.
Standing a round for the boys in The Duke,

you toast the place you've worked your life in,
its follies and uproar, its feuds and laughter,

and leave the dreams untamed, unspoken,
on the wings of your name, Anne-Marie.

NIGEL JENKINS

Nigel Jenkins was born in Gorseinon, near Swansea, in 1949, and brought up on a farm in Gower. On leaving school he worked for four years as a newspaper reporter in England before taking a degree in Literature and Film at the University of Essex. He returned to Wales in 1976 and now lives in Swansea, where he teaches Creative Writing at the University. He was the first Secretary of the Welsh Union of Writers and co-edited the Academi's *Encyclopaedia of Wales*. His books include a monograph on John Tripp in the *Writers of Wales* series (1989), an account of Welsh missionaries in north-east India, *Gwalia in Khasia* (1995), and a selection of his essays, *Footsore on the Frontier* (2001); he has also co-edited a collection of essays, *Thirteen Ways of Looking at Anthony Conran* (1995). He has written plays, notably *Strike a Light!* (about Dr William Price, the pioneer of cremation) and *Waldo's Witness* (about the Welsh-language pacifist poet Waldo Williams). His books of poetry are *Song and Dance* (1981), *Practical Dreams* (1983), *Acts of Union: Selected Poems* (1990), *Ambush* (1998), *Blue* (2002), *Hotel Gwales* (2006) and a collection of haiku and senryu, *O for a Gun* (2007). Many of his poems address political issues, mainly from a left-wing Nationalist point of view, but are also by turns tender, celebratory, angry and scathingly satirical.

SNOWDROPS

I know what I am doing here,

come every year
in the iron first month

to seek them out.

I choose my time,
a day to freeze
the waters of the eye,
and I move through it

– primal caver delving in sign –

to link with light
of the living blood.

*

Last year too soon,

not a white word
in all the wood's deadness.

Home then speechless

to wait.

*

Sky grey and lowering

curtains the wood:

no money, no food: hush
of alone here, cold
of hunger,

last place of warmth
a hole in the head
that's known, I remember, as mouth.

*

A man in a coat
hunting flowers.

Sudden scatty cackle –
the waving of a branch:
a magpie, I trust, has left the tree.

Here, now
the blue gift amazing
of kingfisher flight

would not be believed.
I ask only

snowdrops,
a warmer world.

*

A warmer world?

*

And here they nod
in the cold and quiet.

In Bolivia the soldiers
broke glass on the ground.
They made the naked children
lie flat on the glass,
they made the mothers walk
on the children's backs.

Here snowdrops nod
in the quiet and cold.

If the bomb fell on Swansea,
fifty miles away in Cardiff
eyeballs would melt...

Can
        a flower?
Can
        the poem?

*

Brother dead in Paviland:

the first I pick
I pick in celebration

of the species that stayed
when all others fled

656

the coming of the cold,

species now trembling
through a darker season
of its own manufacture.

*

Feet gone dead, hand around the stems
some borrowed thing, a clamp
of frozen meat

but

tlws yr eira

blodyn yr eira

cloch maban

eirlys

lili wen fach

– a song in my fist.

*

The owl is with her
the day's length,
and she is sick
of the moon:

657

her winters are long.

I hand her snowdrops:
she grasps the primrose.

*

Inside from the cold
they boast no bouquet,

just green breath
of the earth's first things.

I find them a glass,
and on the worktable
scattered with papers
I place them.

It is enough.

*

Thin sun creeps
upon the afternoon

and the water warms,
bubbles sprout
on the earthpale stems.

They'll die early, yes,
and drop no seed:

the year may live.

THE LANGUAGE OF LOVE

walking down this fuckin street
I spies this fuckin bar
n feeling fuckin thirsty
I goes in for a fuckin jar

it's pretty fuckin lonely
for a Friday fuckin night
me n this fuckin woman
the only fuckers in fuckin sight

so I buys meself a fuckin pint
n her a fuckin stout
n we drinks for fuckin hours
till they kicks us fuckin out

then we takes a fuckin taxi
to this block of fuckin flats
n we rolls into her fuckin pad
as pissed as fuckin rats

what next? you're fuckin thinking
well yes of fuckin course
we took at last to her fuckin bed
and had sexual intercourse

WILD CHERRY

Tiptoe on wall-top, head in
clouds of white blossom, I
reached for the fullest, the
flounciest sprays, I travelled
many miles to give you them.

You placed them, smiling,
in a jar on your table,
and there was beauty between us,
between us too there were words,
white clouds of words ...

One of the sprays I'd kept myself,
and I'll know on what morning
you brush up the petals, you
toss out the twigs with the ashes
and empties, yesterday's news.

NEVER FORGET YOUR WELSH

I
& not the lingo

bland bitter brewed with Wales in mind
mad March hares even the gogs
2 to I against

April Fools' Day
white dragon

lifts the cup to our lips
drink to remember drink
Eurofizz
fond farmers fond miners avuncular ghosts

the Daily Mail
owns my
brain

Fe godwn ni eto yes but we
need more than
magic

'sweet snare of yellow mead'

II
bad eggs
tomatoes
articulate guitars

it is
good
to have
friends

it is
necessary
to have enemies

'of the three hundred only one returned'

Keith Joseph you're mad we
hate you

III
fifteen thousand
golden handshake
'for a year over mead great was their purpose'

we live
spectator lives
old bopa Max the white man's Welshman
wet eyes
wet nappies
drinks with Scarlets to
fascist apartheid

say it with baby grand
English theatrical space invaders
greedy halfers pushing for fame

museum
mausoleum

liquid plash of camera shutter

Roddy fucks royal in Bahamas
another first for Wales

662

IV

guten Morgen bonjour at
Hotel International
bore da what language is that
some of the happiest years of Petula Clark's life
were spent in Wales

land fit for
CB radio
hick schlitz twits
dressed to kill Yankee GIs
get drunk and screw
londonised droner disco duck spins
Yoko Ono
not too bad for a woman of 50

they
Country & Western
in Welsh too

'and after the revelling there was silence'

finalising light
USA genocide stations

V

Radio One is Swansea Sound
Jason meets Tracy in
glory estates'
amnesia bid

663

'and in their short lives were drunk on mead'

but
paid â phoeni
Wynford Vaughan Thomas
by appointment to
the sheep of Wales
will keep the people's memory
clean

arise
Sir Neddy Seagoon
arise Gerald Murphy
two years inside for getting caught
then HTV
scrubs the prison soup
from his chin

the people can't
read
history's a lovespoon
or the Duke of Beaufort's
class collaborationist
Banwen
miners'
foxhunt

they want to destroy us

VI

West Glam Welshes on Mumbles
replica individualists
anglo Langland perfumed hawks most
debonair and parlez vous
spraying a little
culture about
the beaux beaux arts so beaux for the soul
no objection to the language but

vultures of unthink
Thatcher their queen
came to the Patti and
told us
go
Maggie Maggie Maggie
Charles and Di
orgasmic grovel
glee-faced serfs no
tongue like a Taff's
for lavish licking of the royal arse

homo erectus
victim of magic
lonely thoughtful in bingo queue

200,000 & rising
'those fiery men from a land of wine'

every day the Tories
check it for bombs

AN EXECRABLY TASTELESS FAREWELL TO VISCOUNT NO

The Viscount of No, Wales rejoice, is dead.
White man's Taff
And blathersome stooge of the first 'Order!'
Orgasmic in ermine,
May his garters garrotte him.

O Death! For past misdeeds I almost forgive you
Now that you've lightened our land of this load,
The Lord of Lickspit,
The grovelsome brown-snout and smiley shyster
Whose quisling wiles were the shame of Wales.

Queen-cwtshing, Brit Nat, Cymro Da,
The higher he climbed the acider the rain
He pissed on his people
As he stuffed them with Prince shit
And cheered as the voice of Tryweryn was drowned.

Now he's a No-vote,
His goody-buckled-two-shoes dancing aflame
In his Hell of our Yes.
The hand that crossed that paper –
All power to its arm.

Fuck me to heaven in a bath of champagne,
The rending and gnashing of the Viscount's No,
His old 'Order! Order!''s sweet disorder
Is youth to my ears,
It's a cown' glee-bomb.

STEVE GRIFFITHS

Steve Griffiths was born at Trearddur Bay, Anglesey, in 1949, and brought up in Amlwch. He read English at Churchill College, Cambridge, and did various jobs until 1973, when he became involved in community work and welfare rights in north London; he is currently working as a freelance researcher in the fields of poverty, social security and health. He has published three collections of verse: *Anglesey Material* (1980), *Civilised Airs* (1984), and *Uncontrollable Fields* (1990); his *Selected Poems* appeared in 1993.

CROSSING LADY STANLEY, HERE, 1868

You are ensconced in your folly
on the cliffs. The wind would flatten
even your hair, Lady Stanley,
posed with your frilled infants.
Before dinner you imagined yourself
to be Byron, stripped of his laughter,
self-glorified in a sunset of madness:

the cries of seabirds fell on each other
as so many colours fall at the horizon,
not considering the one below
shivering and settling in the shadow
of its transformation.
Now giant winds and giant darkness
outpower the tinkling cutlery of a family feast.

Your eyes illuminate the fat candles,
a manservant attends, and a mason or two,
for you want us to know what you did with all that money:
your name is everywhere, benefactress of hospitals
and churches; purveyor of lasting graffiti,
Kilroy of the marble halls. Superseded
by Amlwch bootboys in rainy bus-shelters.

Last week, my friends probed your folly
and craned through your poor mock slits.
Lax feet turned the bean-tins in your monument,
half-curious, cameras in cases.
My face a necessary mask in a cutting wind,
I was laid flat in the heather; framed
in banks of cloud lay a lake of purest turquoise.

You stood at the edge of the colour, slight,
but there, as by the ballroom floor you might
have wanted to impress some well-lined beau.
Our minds moved together, a moment shared.
You would have shuddered at the intimacy.
You had bought this view. A carriage waited
on the mountainside, to remove it from you.

I carried our intimacy back to the van,
a fragment of eggshell,
a peasant savouring the illicit
with a little smile of gratification.
Your driver too was waiting,
with his patient, leathery face,
an impenetrable landscape.

THE MINES IN SEPIA TINT

A man beats his wife on the mountainside.

Their shouts pierce the copper drumskin
of the coming storm: the earth of copper
the heather, the copper sky:

everything rumbles round inside the drum.

The man in a grey suit, white-faced,
his eyes shifting fast and nervous
copper copper copper copper the woman
outraged by my witness of her beating

my warning shout as I passed
and my feet pounded the veins of copper
across country: then, poised on thin white legs,
doubtfully angry, wet hair plastered on my forehead,
sixteen, not knowing what to do.

They gave me silent, heated looks,
and I ran on.

Later I wrote a poem about the pylons on the horizon.

Often I have written the wrong poem.

CHILDREN IN A WALLED GARDEN

The dreams are rare visitors now,
haughtily enigmatic, they know

the horizon's cemented in, though flawed.
Last week, in an airless visitation, a pair
of vicious and jaded politicians caught me
measuring furtively how many sheep
rank with dried piss and fear
would fill the intolerant volume of their car.

I see how freely my two-year-old
abandons his buttressed cities of lego,
a cat forgetting a mauled fly.
The airy mistakes of unsupported walls
cave in like the shrugged-off catastrophe
of ants under the darkening sky
of a ribbed sole on the lawn.

What a cheated irregularity,
what a deception of that foam
in the high wind from the rocks
is my painstaking accumulation of poetry,
bandaging and crystallising, guiding
the bones of a last Emperor's
concubine's bound feet.

I notice how eagerly
I follow your tricycle
on the faulted pavement
like a seagull after a tractor
in my old wild mint days,
viewed through a rough hedge on the hill
when the future was an overlapping
of headlands fading to haze.

GLYNDŴR SUBDUED

Burned out, there was no way back,
and the flames of Sycharth brought Glyndŵr
dreams enough:
his home was a country now,
the revenges multiplied.
The helicopter's shadow,
a great hare
runs fleetingly across a field –
the grass panicking, flattened,
trying to disperse but unable.

Almost an experiment,
the disciplined ructions of the first raid,
the strained respect for brawny lives
a delicate line: Rhuthun settlers,

robbed and dishevelled, emerged
to a heady, bright, small Welsh triumph
reeking of sheepshit
and soot in the bright sun:

insults counted, it was a homely,
small, scared, village altercation
as shoving and grunting skirmishes
around slag once made history.

The victors clattered away
shod heavily with expensive curses

to where even the sparks on the hill
were drunk down by the mud and the dark.

Later the conscripts, cast-off and dangerous,
sported their rusted dream of omnipotence,
hacking for their neglected fields
and their friends cut down,

and then for the riven cold in their bones
women ran in the wet grass
brought down like deer with cries of triumph.
People ran blindly,

made his, the pervasive guerilla
reeking of smoke and prophecy,
the peaceloving fire
displaced in his rafters.

The banging of shields,
plastic and leather,
rang in his ears:

war war war sle sle sle
went the childish wailing of sirens
in the gusting wood,

and the night's drunken instruments
scoured the wet streets
for the Welsh doggis and their whelps.

An English city listens behind curtains
to the running and breathing, the slugging
thud of quarry cornered and floored:

the resistance is
that we will not turn the television up
in tribute to the night.

Divided loyalties, undermined
meal-tickets, sprouted on hillsides,
the weeds Indignation
twined with deep-rooted Ambivalence

picked for the same dish.
Drenched resisters sidled in droves
along valleys to give themselves up
to the straggling columns of troops and grain.

When the fighting is over, the land of dreams
is a table lit with unshareable faces,
a once-in-a-lifetime
remembered meal to the hungry:

a looted peacock under the arm
of some big, sharp-featured
father of mine
who dried his eyes at the flame of Sycharth.

Then the withdrawal to memory
of the fair people, walled in the clouds
of exile within, the retreat to mystery
of the fair times on their vague upland tracks.

Glyndŵr had to master this potent
trick of retirement, to the light
in a dolmen glimpsed rarely and late,
a light in the mind

where sometimes he lingers noisily in the grid of years
and the speed and charisma growl in him
to the applause of the shingle in the undertow,
old chimera whose wait has a tide's hypnotic

push still. It breaks
in like the sudden clatter of leaves
of a kneeling army

or a belief in the mountains upturned,
with mirrors,
lit from inside with our own light.

IFOR THOMAS

Ifor Thomas was born in Haverfordwest, Pembrokeshire, in 1949. He lives in Cardiff, where he practises as an architect; he is Welsh-speaking. In the 1980s he was a founder of the poetry groups known as Cabaret 246 and The Horse's Mouth. He has published six books of verse: *Giving Blood* (1985), *Giving Blood 2* (1987), *Bogwiser* (1991), *Pubic* (1995), and *Body Beautiful* (2005); his New and Selected Poems were published as *Unsafe Sex* in 1999. Many of his poems are meant to be read in public and some are 'performance poems' of a startling kind; one involves the use of cling-film and a chain-saw.

I TOLD HER I LOVED HER A LOT IN SPLOTT

I said I'd be sad if
she didn't come to Cardiff.

I called her a sensation
when I met her at Central Station.

I sang like a lark
when we walked in Roath Park.

I said I'd never met any one finer
in Rhiwbina.

I vowed I'd be her man
in Pen-y-lan.

I fell at her feet
in Oakfield Street.

I told her I loved her a lot
in Splott.

I said I liked having you
in Western Avenue.

But our love turned sour
over beer in the Glendower.

She called me a fool
in the Empire Pool.

She broke down and cried
in Riverside,

after I'd let her down
in Grangetown.

She shouted *YOU BRUTE*
in Bute.

So we called it a day
in Manor Way,

the next time, she said,
I'll get an A to Z.

BOMBER

After fifty-six years the aluminium is slate grey
and the ribs of the wings as light as bird bones.
Wind rattles through the remains of the bomber
that failed to clear the escarpment of Cwar y Cigfan.

The walkers rest here, throw a ball for the dog,
drink beer, share a bag of crisps, lean against the rough
                                          memorial.
The wreaths of last November have moulted their poppies,
there is a wooden cross jammed between stones.

It's a long way home for the five Canadians
whose names are now barely legible.
Above, a hang glider hovers on the edge of a thermal
then skitters into a mocking dive.

Clouds are solid enough to reach up and grab
like the craggy hands that pulled these airmen to earth
splattered their blood over the stones and sheep shit of
                                        Cwar y Cigfan
made them forever part of Wales.

UNCLE DEWI'S LUMP

Uncle Dewi was tough, ex-copper
won medals in the war killing Italians.
More than once he wiped
a dead man's breakfast from his bayonet.

Dewi nearly blew himself up
when he tossed a grenade back.
Got showered by bits of enemy
and had a lump on his head ever since.

Until one summer that is,
when we were on the train
going to Tenby. His head ached
and he was grumpy as hell.

Doris had a look,
pulled off the lump with her fingers.
Turned out to be the Italian's tooth.
Been carrying it around for twenty years.

'Can I keep it?' I asked
'What for you daft bugger?'
He tossed the last mortal remains
of the Italian out of the train.

'Pity,' said Doris:
'it was the only real tooth
he had in his head.'

HOTEL ROSSIYA – IN MEMORIAM

My ghost has a good choice –
Three thousand rooms and some to spare,
A shuffle across from Red Square.

I never felt at home in the mausoleum –
Lenin, pickled in pride and formaldehyde
Being no company for this fun-lovin' Georgian.

Even so, for that jumped-up clown
Who backed down when the going got tough
To dump my corpse under the wall, was a bit much.

Now I sometimes take a beer
In the south entrance of the Hotel Rossiya
Though it's hard to catch the eye

Of the girls behind the bar
They get bigger tips from the tourists.
I don't feel as if I'm made of steel, these days.

I met a football supporter from Wales
Who couldn't believe how much I've aged.
We both could smile looking back now.

The Rhondda was part of the USSR,
I said. Except for the gulags, he replied.
I waved that carping criticism aside.

Look at Solzhenitsyn, did wonders for his career!
We got on well and I fixed the result.
A bit of a bore, Russia / Wales a 0-0 draw.

Now I hear these guys from the Duma
Have agreed with Putin that the hotel
Is too reminiscent of the 'old days' –

Pah! Somebody's made an estimate
There is too much value in the real estate
For even a nod to history –

Biggest hotel in the world, socialist leaning,
First to introduce central vacuum cleaning.
Six thousand souls crated in peace

The very model of a society at ease,
Even if the paperwork is onerous.
Now the world's moved on, harder to please.

There's no place I can call heaven.
Even the Welshman had a mobile
Said he'd text me from Blaenavon.

Moscow is not the place I knew.
My ghost will rest with my bones
Under the Kremlin's foundation stones.

SHEENAGH PUGH

Sheenagh Pugh was born in Birmingham in 1950 and educated at Bristol University, where she read Russian and German. She came to Wales in 1971 to work in the Welsh Office, and now lives in Cardiff. She is Reader in Creative Writing at the University of Glamorgan. One of the most prolific of contemporary Welsh poets, she has published ten books of poems: *Crowded by Shadows* (1977), *What a Place to Grow Flowers* (1980), *Earth Studies and Other Voyages* (1983), *Beware Falling Tortoises* (1987), *Sing for the Taxman* (1993), *Id's Hospit* (1997), *The Beautiful Lie* (2002) and *The Movement of Bodies* (2005); her *Selected Poems* appeared in 1990. A selection of poems translated from French and German appeared as *Prisoners of Transience* in 1985. She has also published two novels, *Kirstie's Witnesses* (1998) and *Folk Music* (1999), as well as a study of fanfic. Her poems are compassionate, drily sardonic and meticulously crafted, and derive much of their subject matter from history, mythology (especially Norse mythology), and her fondness for Iceland and the Shetland Islands which she visits regularly. A selection of her poems is to be found in *What if this Road* (2003) in the Corgi series.

WHAT IF THIS ROAD

What if this road, that has held no surprises
these many years, decided not to go
home after all; what if it could turn
left or right with no more ado
than a kite-tail? What if its tarry skin
were like a long, supple bolt of cloth,
that is shaken and rolled out, and takes
a new shape from the contours beneath?
And if it chose to lay itself down
in a new way; around a blind corner,
across hills you must climb without knowing
what's on the other side; who would not hanker
to be going, at all risks? Who wants to know
a story's end, or where a road will go?

CAPTAIN ROBERTS GOES LOOTING

It's best when they surrender. No time wasted
on violence: just a few swift kicks
to the officers' groins, for luck, and straight on
to serious matters.

An ox-roar: Valentine Ashplant's voice;
he's found the rum. Young Bunce is slashing bales
of silk to bright shreds. And the captain strolls
to the great cabin,

682

pauses at the door; breathes in the musk
and sandalwood: these hidalgos do themselves well,
and there's the china. White, fluted eggshell
you can see through;

he strokes it gently. *We had some of this*
at Deseada: Val Ashplant smashed the last.
(He's bellowing again: found the sugar
to make rum-punch.)

Will Symson eyes a woman passenger
and meditates rape. But the captain has found
the tea, twisted up in papers. He crushes
a leaf; sniffs. Lapsang,

smoky-scented, and the next is Oolong,
with its hint of peaches. Ashplant's delirious;
found the moidores that'll buy more sugar
and rum. Later,

back on their own sloop, the men cheer
the fire; they love watching a ship burn.
They've hauled over a hogshead of fine claret
to wash the deck;

it's like spilled blood, catching the fire's glint.
Captain Roberts sips peachy gold
from a translucent cup, wondering how long
it'll stay whole.

ID'S HOSPIT

I look out from a 17 bus:
more letters gone: ID'S HOSPIT
it says now, and one 'I' hangs loose.
The stone front is like a film set,

nothing behind; no wards, just a waste patch.
Sunday car boot sales. No profit in land
right now, Danka; it doesn't pay them much
to build there yet... A man turns half around,

looks at me oddly, and I know I spoke
aloud; spoke to you. I see you wave,
from the window where I would look back
after visiting, not wanting to leave

you and Richard. You'd be holding him,
a white parcel: *my son*. I felt unreal,
dizzy with light. Never such a time:
each night that week, the lads from the mill

took me out drinking. *Ryszard's got a boy*,
they'd tell the Taff Vale, the Panorama,
the Globe, the Greyhound and the red night sky;
a steel-town sky: you remember, Danka?

Not any more; years since I would see
a steel sunset. Jobs have got scarce
for the lads, and their lads. It's a harder city
than you knew, but there are places worse.

684

Under the high roads of Waterloo,
– you won't believe, Danka – people have put
a town of boxes up. I saw a soup queue.
Old times come round again; who would have thought?

And who thought they'd sell the corridors
where you walked singing? The things I miss:
pubs have dress codes and names like Traders,
and I talk to myself too much these days.

Our saint has lost his head, and the healing word
is flaking off the wall, letter by letter,
and I can't recall behind which board
was her window. I suppose it doesn't matter;

and perhaps tomorrow I will go to London,
back to the poor shacks in the concrete shadow,
and see if I cannot find my son
huddled in black, his face a boarded window.

STONELIGHT

'Not the frailest thing in creation can ever be lost'
George Mackay Brown

Each stone happens
in its own way. One stands
true in a house-wall.

Anger quickens another: it flies,
fills a mouth with blood.

Shaped and polished, one shines
in the eyes of many.

One seems inert, earth-embedded:
underneath, colonies are teeming.

But the best are seal-smooth,
and the hand that chose them

sends them skimming, once, twice,
ten times over the ocean, to the edge

of sight, and whenever they brush the water's skin,
an instant is bruised

into brightness. The eye flinches. When they sink,
if they sink, the light they left

wells out, spills, seeds itself, prickling
like stars, on a field that never takes
the same shape twice.

ENVYING OWEN BEATTIE

To have stood on the Arctic island
by the graves where Franklin's men
buried their shipmates: good enough.

To hack through the permafrost
to the coffin, its loving plaque
cut from a tin can: better.

And freeing the lid, seeing
the young sailor cocooned in ice,
asleep in his glass case.

Then melting it so gently, inch
by inch, a hundred years
and more falling away, all the distance

of death a soft hiss of steam
on the air, till at last they cupped
two feet, bare and perfect,

in their hands, and choked up,
because it was any feet
poking out of the bedclothes.

And when the calm, pinched,
twenty-year-old face
came free, and he lay there,

five foot four of authentic
Victorian adventurer, tuberculous,
malnourished, John Torrington

the stoker, who came so far
in the cold, and someone whispered,
It's like he's unconscious.

Then Beattie stooped, lifted him
out of bed, the six stone
limp in his arms, and the head lolled

and rested on his shoulder,
and he felt the rush
that reckless trust sends

through parents and lovers. To have him
like that, the frail, diseased
little time-traveller,

to feel the lashes prickle
your cheek, to be that close
to the parted lips.

You would know all the fairy-tales
spoke true; how could you not try
to wake him with a kiss?

GRAFFITI MAN

Flint scratched a stick-man
into stone: *me*. A wavy spear
perched on its hand: *me hunting*.

He torched his way across continents,
Als'kander, Iskandar, Sikandar,
founding Alexandrias.

He wrote his name on diseases,
roses and children; scribbled it in neon
across skyscrapers;

spiked programs with its virus.
He sprayed it on ohms, sandwiches,
wellingtons, dahlias, hoovers.

White columns, grey stones, black walls,
heavy with names beyond number.
Such a one died

in war; of AIDS; from old age.
I, Kallaischros, lie
in the restless sea,

no-one knows where, and this stone
lies too, marking the place
where I am not.

Leningrad's gone, and Rhodesia,
scrubbed off the stone.
Ideas are harder

to clean: names won't come loose
from a phrase of music,
a story, a law, a faith,

but you need a keen edge
to carve them. Most settle
for a can of spray-paint.

On every stretch of sand
stick-swirled patterns,
waiting for the tide;

on every snowfield
the definition of footprints,
crumbling in the sun;

on every window
words, fading on the brief
page of mist.

Segunders are named each day,
and if you breathe on the window,
the words come back.

THE TORMENTED CENSOR

He sees what is not given to others,
the foreign magazines before they are made
fit for the faithful. He makes them fit.

All day long, he sifts indecent women.
Runner's World; his glinting scissors meet
and part; amputate bare legs and arms.

All through *Hello!* his soft felt-tip is busy
stroking a chador of thick black ink
over celebrity cleavages.

Even in *Woman's Weekly*, some minx
moistens her lips with the tip of a pink tongue:
he rips it out. The whole page.

They all get shredded, the silky limbs,
the taut breasts, flesh cut to ribbons.
He is devout, and keeps none back,

but after work, walking home, if a woman
should pass, decently veiled, all in black,
his gut clenches; he tries not to look,

as the little devils in his mind whisper
what they know; melt cloth; draw curves
on her dark shapelessness.

TOAST

When I'm old, I'll say *the summer*
they built the stadium. And I won't mean

the council. I'll be hugging the memory
of how, open to sun and the judgement

of passing eyes, young builders lay
golden and melting on hot pavements,

691

the toast of Cardiff. Each blessed lunchtime
Westgate Street, St. John's, the Hayes

were lined with fit bodies; forget
the jokes, these jeans were fuzz stretched tight

over unripe peaches. Sex objects,
and happily up for it. When women

sauntered by, whistling, they'd bask
in warm smiles, browning slowly, loving

the light. Sometimes they'd clock men
looking them over. It made no odds;

they never got mad; it was too heady
being young and fancied and in the sun.

They're gone now, all we have left of them
this vast concrete-and-glass mother-ship

that seems to have landed awkwardly
in our midst. And Westgate's dark

with November rain, but different, as if
the stones retain heat, secret impressions

of shoulder-blades, shallow cups,
as sand would do. The grey façade

692

of the empty auction house, three storeys
of boarded windows, doesn't look sad,

more like it's closed its eyes, breathing in
the smell of sweat, sunblock, confidence.

ROWAN WILLIAMS

Rowan Williams was born in 1950 at Gurnos, a small village near Ystradgynlais, and grew up in Cardiff and Oystermouth, near Swansea; he was brought up a Nonconformist. Educated at Dynevor School, Christ's College, Cambridge, and Christ Church and Wadham College, Oxford, he was ordained an Anglican priest in 1978. He has held a number of academic posts, including that of Lecturer in Divinity at Cambridge University (1980-86), and was Lady Margaret Professor of Divinity, Christ Church, Oxford, from 1986 to 1992. He became Bishop of Monmouth in 1992, Archbishop of Wales in 2000 and Archbishop of Canterbury in 2002. Besides theological works, he has published three books of verse: *After Silent Centuries* (1994), *Remembering Jerusalem* (2001), and *The Poems of Rowan Williams* (2002); the first of these contains his translations of poems by Ann Griffiths, T. Gwynn Jones and Waldo Williams. A characteristic of his poems is that they embody abstract ideas in vivid images and have a place for the visual arts and a social conscience; but above all, they are meditations on the Christian life.

OUR LADY OF VLADIMIR

Climbs the child, confident,
up over breast, arm, shoulder:
while she, alarmed by his bold thrust
into her face, and the encircling hand,

looks out imploring fearfully
and, O, she cries, from her immeasurable eyes,
O how he clings, see how
he smothers every pore, like the soft
shining mistletoe to my black bark,
she says, I cannot breathe, my eyes
are aching so.

The child has overlaid us in our beds,
we cannot close our eyes,
his weight sits firmly,
fits over heart and lungs,
and choked we turn away
into the window of immeasurable dark
to shake off the insistent pushing warmth:
O how he cleaves, no peace
tonight my lady in your bower,
you, like us, restless with bruised eyes
and waking to

a shining cry on the black bark of sleep.

ADVENT CALENDAR

He will come like last leaf's fall.
One night when the November wind
has flayed the trees to bone, and earth
wakes choking on the mould,
the soft shroud's folding.

He will come like frost.
One morning when the shrinking earth
opens on mist, to find itself
arrested in the net
of alien, sword-set beauty.

He will come like dark.
One evening when the bursting red
December sun draws up the sheet
and penny-masks its eye to yield
the star-snowed fields of sky.

He will come, will come,
will come like crying in the night,
like blood, like breaking,
as the earth writhes to toss him free.
He will come like child.

OYSTERMOUTH CEMETERY

Grass lap; the stone keels jar,
scratch quietly in the rippling soil.
The little lettered masts dip slowly
in a little breeze, the anchors here
are very deep among the shells.

Not till the gusty day
when a last angel tramples down
into the mud his dry foot hissing,
down to the clogged forgotten shingle,
till the bay boils and shakes,

Not till that day shall the cords snap
and all the little craft float astray
on unfamiliar tides, to lay their freight
on new warm shores, on those strange islands
where their tropic Easter landfall is.

PENRHYS

The ground falls sharply: into the broken glass,
into the wasted mines, and turds are floating
in the well. Refuse.

May; but the wet, slapping wind is native here,
not fond of holidays. A dour council cleaner,
it lifts discarded

Cartons and condoms and a few stray sheets
of newspaper that the wind sticks
across his face –

The worn sub-Gothic infant, hanging awkwardly
around, glued to a thin mother.
Angelus Novus:

Backing into the granite future, wings spread,
head shaking at the recorded day,
no, he says, refuse,

Not here. Still, the wind drops sharply.
Thin teenage mothers by the bus stop
shake wet hair,

Light cigarettes. One day my bus will come, says one:
they laugh. More use'n bloody prince,
says someone else.

The news slips to the ground, the stone dries off,
smoke and steam drift uphill
and tentatively

Finger the leisure centre's tense walls and stairs.
The babies cry under the sun,
they and the thin girls

Comparing notes, silently, on shared
unwritten stories of the bloody stubbornness
of getting someone born.

GETHSEMANE

Who said that trees grow easily
compared with us? What if the bright
bare load that pushes down on them
insisted that they spread and bowed
and pleated back on themselves and cracked
and hunched? Light dropping like a palm
levelling the ground, backwards and forwards?

Across the valley are the other witnesses
of two millenia, the broad stones
packed by the hand of God, bristling
with little messages to fill the cracks.
As the light falls and flattens what grows
on these hills, the fault lines dart and spread,
there is room to say something, quick and tight.

Into the trees' clefts, then, do we push
our folded words, thick as thumbs?
somewhere inside the ancient bark, a voice
has been before us, pushed the densest word
of all, abba, and left it to be collected by
whoever happens to be passing, bent down
the same way by the hot unreadable palms.

TOLSTOY AT ASTAPOVO

Off through the looking-glass he ran:
into the world of hedges, brooks, black and white
                                        cantonments,
the snapping Queen to urge him on, the fevers
rising and falling, painting black or white
the country of his choices. All around the iron lines
run to a point. Ahead of him strolls Platon,
not looking back; he runs till he is breathless,
burning, but he can't catch him. In the next-door squares
the pieces crowd, the journalists, the relatives, the
                                        hopefuls,

the *starets* in the ladies' loo, the script consultants,
newsreel men, police. Check.

Heat and smoke in the little squares; shivering,
he thinks of taking up a long-lost country skill
as quaint as thatching, complicated, unselfconscious,
the sort of thing you pick up in the hours
of glazed winter boredom, the absent-minded endlessness
of a poor childhood. *How do peasants die?*
Some things you can't get into at this age. He knew
he was too old to die, fingers too stiff for plaiting
the spiny ends. He put his head down in the straw.
Mate. All the words came tumbling
backwards out of his dream.

HILARY LLEWELLYN-WILLIAMS

Hilary Llewellyn-Williams was born at Pembury, near Tunbridge Wells in Kent, in 1951 and has lived in Wales since 1982, latterly at Waunfelin near Pontypool. Educated at Southampton University, where she read English and Theology, she is currently a tutor with the Open University. She has published five books of verse: *The Tree Calendar* (1987), *Book of Shadows* (1990), *Animaculture* (1997), *Hummadruz* (2001) and *Greenland* (2003).

REED NGETAL

October 28 – November 24

A wind rises up
from the wetlands,
carries the cry of the sea
in deepening gusts to my door.
I draw in my head, snail
in a stone shell, doubtfully.

Southwest sunset
catches the trees, splays
out their shapes like spread
nerves, webbed and strung
vessels of drowsy fluid,
warming dull stalks to a richer
brown, until the wind

701

lifts heavy wings and all colours
flatten out. A long note
sounds in our chimney: winter's flute,

blowing from the throats
of reeds in the waste ground
down by the river. The dead
once fished there, dragged their nets,
crouched in the sedge for duck
and plover, stole eggs in spring.
They sheltered under reeds
in these sodden hills;
reed roofs and low stone walls
tucked down to earth,
shut in from the flapping light.

Our fenlands, wastes,
moors, marshes and wild sloughs
are shrunken now, ploughed up –
but give them time. Decay
puts out its tendrils. Water
seeps upwards patiently.
Stands of reeds sing
high from behind clenched teeth,
knot their roots tight,
bow to the seasons, keep firm
and yielding. Lost souls
glint from the shallows.

All night the gale
scuds over us. Dawn
will be more naked still:
the trees will be peeled sticks.
I close my eyes and pull
the covers up, but lie
aware of blind movements:
small shift of the house
downwards, the closing in
of winter, thread of roots
through water – and here's
that noise again, that shrill
dark reedy whistling.

TO THE ISLANDS

Driving to Llanybydder from the hills
in sunlight, a clean blue sky
bathing us in its image: a light-pocket,
an open eye in all those weeks of rain,

we suddenly saw the sea in a strange place,
inland. We followed a new coast:
pale lucid water filled the low ground
to the west, and risen islands stood

netted with fields or thinly brushed
with trees, and shoreside cottages
whitewashed, perched over a harbour –
a landscape from the inner Hebrides

exact and stunning. Though of course we knew
it was only a trick of mist, sucked up
from unremarkable sodden earth, still
we cried out happily: 'Look at the sea!'

So it shall be someday, when the polar ice
melts, and expanding oceans lift
over the land again. Sea licking
these hills into islands and promontories

the Teifi swallowed into a sea-loch
and lush farms drowned, and hill-farms turned
into fishermen's cottages. We could see
the future in a bowl of clear water,

seeing the present too, scrying the land
that is always there but mostly invisible –
the land's other face, the place where boats
put out from curved inlets, and green fields

tilt down to the sea; where eels thread
their way between tall hedges. Sun low
behind us, as far south as it will go
as we ran into the outer blurs of mist

and the islands vanished. Above, we sensed
the summer colour of sky without seeing it:
and, turning west, we crossed the plain grey river
in silence, like driving through water.

THE SEALWIFE

One day I shall find my skin again:
my own salt skin, folded dark, its fishweed stink
and tang, its thick warm fat, great thrusting tail

all mine: and I'll take it and shake it out
to the wind, draw it over me cool and snug,
laugh softly, and slip back to my element.

I shall find my stolen skin, hidden by you
for love (you said) that night the sea-people danced,
stashed in some cleft in the rocks where I may not go

but used to go, and dance too, stepping free
in my new peeled body, the stalks of my legs in the moon-
light strange, my long arms shaping the sky

that have narrowed their circles down
to the tasks of those forked hands: lifting,
fetching, stirring, scrubbing, embracing – the small

stiff landlocked movements. In the sea
I plunged and swam for my own joy, sleek and oiled,
and I loved at will in rolling-belly tides.

Here love is trapped between the walls of a house
and in your voice and eyes, our children's cries;
whose boundaries I've understood, a language

learnt slowly, word by word. You've been dear and good –
how you would sing to me, those wild nights!
– and oil my breasts by firelight, and dip down

to taste my sea-fluids. I'd forget to mourn
those others then, trawling the flickering deeps.
Now I cry for no reason, and dream of seals:

an ocean booms in the far cave of my ear
and voices tug at me as I stand here
at the window, listening. Our children sleep

and by daylight they run from me. Their legs
strong, their backs straight, bodies at ease
on solid ground – though they play for hours on the shore

between sand and sea, and scramble the wet rocks
gladly. It won't be long now, the waiting:
they love to poke and forage in the cracks

of the cliffs; sharpeyed, calling, waving.

ANIMACULTURE

The gardening angels tuck their robes
into their belts, pull their boots on
cover their heads with haloes and set out

to cultivate the world. Each one
has hoe and sickle, spade and watering-can
and wings, and a small patch

to care for. They come in all colours:
dawn, rain or dusk, rose, marigold,
moss, midnight; gliding between

reflections, rarely seen. At three
years old, occasionally I'd catch
the flick of a wing, a glitter on the air

a tickle of warmth behind me, someone there
playing roll-in-the-grass with me
pushing my swing. And at night

my gardening angel laid her head
beside me, smelling of daisies,
and breathed with me. At my maiden flight

along our street, my feet grazing the privet,
past lamp-posts and garden gates, her voice
in my ear steered me and said –

This is the way to heaven, along here.
Since then, so many false choices:
knotted with weeds, I'm overgrown

and parched as dust. Who will open
the door to the garden, who will water
me now? Wise child, I trusted my own

right words, I knew the angel's name
and that death was part of the game.
I find it very hard to remember her.

The gardening angels prune and propagate
moving in secret through the soul's acres;
have I called on mine too late?

Whistling, she strolls in from long ago,
and she hands me the rake and hoe –
Your turn, she says; and I feel my wings stir.

A LAP OF APPLES

Looking for drowned apples
sunk in October seagrass
wet and salt with rot

I wonder what I'll find
in the rooty shade:

firm fruit just slit its skin
oozing white sugar-foam
bruised thumbprints still new,

drill-hole of a bird's bill,
all muddy but edible –

or pretenders laid
squat on a brown soft bloom
or a hollow woodlice home

or worse, those that lurk
under my shoes
blackened as leather balls

grenades in the dew.

A damp trawl nets some
sound ones, plus a few
hangers-on from the trees

to add to the store. Daily
the box fills, and the scent
of apple-ferment rises

cries *eat me* – peel, core,
make pies, make crumbles,
jelly rose glow, sweet
pulp to bag and freeze
and wine, wine...

But what if I don't have time
to deal with this glut?

I'm not the first to know
guilt over apples, regret
over all that's spoiled

all that tumbles into waste.
Did Eve and Adam lose
Eden the day they said

Such a pity this tree's unused!
Let's put this lot
to work for us – in their leafy aprons
bagging up windfalls?

Well if I know God she's no
housewife, she'd rather dance
than sit with a lap of apples.

Slattern, she'll let the mess
take care of itself; which of course
it does – the leaves, the fruit

the lives all fallen
into rich mulch.

ROBERT MINHINNICK

Robert Minhinnick was born in Neath in 1952 but grew up in Maesteg and Pen-y-fai near Bridgend. He read English at the University College of Wales, Aberystwyth and University College, Cardiff. In 1984 he founded Friends of the Earth Cymru and is still involved in environmental campaigns; he lives in Porthcawl. Since 1997 he has been editor of *Poetry Wales*. His essays have been published as *Watching the Fire Eater* (1992), *Badlands* (1996) and *To Babel and Back* (2006); he has also made English versions of the work of six Welsh-language poets, which appeared as *The Adulterer's Tongue* (2003). One of the most prolific of contemporary Welsh poets, he has published seven books of poems: *A Thread in the Maze* (1978), *Native Ground* (1979), *Life Sentences* (1983), *The Dinosaur Park* (1985), *The Looters* (1989), *Hey Fatman* (1994), and *After the Hurricane* (2002); his *Selected Poems* appeared in 1999. His work is complex, lexically rich and stylistically assured, his themes both local to South Wales and taking in wider environmental and political issues.

SALVAGE

Children of ten or twelve
Transfer a traditional skill with horses
To ancient lorries and cars. They go jousting
Over the Tremorfa moorland, loud with the privileges
Of their raggedness

And illiteracy.
Hidden in a smashed martello, out of range
Of the gaffer's cuff and loud harangue, they watch men
Salvaging the hulk of 'The Flying Fox',
A rusted naval craft

Gutted from deck to brine
Filled bilge, – while faint on the wind come sounds
Of the remote city, the retreating tide,
As the Channel shifts its immense cold acre
A little farther from

The shore, revealing a
Tundra streamered with weed, an obscene
Exposure of a city's sludge. Walking out of a job,
I end exile in a landscape of exhaustion:
And am happy to retreat,

But the hammering on
The iron hull, the hoarse windward singing
Of sea-carrion travel with me down a coast poisoned
By people, crossboned with shipwreck. And there is
No shaking off one's own defeat.

THE DRINKING ART

The altar of glasses behind the bar
Diminishes our talk. As if in church
The solitary men who come here
Slide to the edges of each black

Polished bench and stare at their hands.
The landlord keeps his own counsel.

This window shows a rose and anchor
Like a sailor's tattoo embellished
In stained glass, allows only the vaguest
Illumination of floor and ceiling,
The tawny froth the pumps sometimes spew.
And the silence settles. The silence settles

Like the yellow pinpoints of yeast
Falling through my beer, the bitter
That has built the redbrick
Into the faces of these few customers,
Lonely practitioners of the drinking art.
Ashtrays, a slop-bucket, the fetid

Shed-urinal, all this I wondered at,
Running errands to the back-doors of pubs,
Woodbines and empty bottles in my hands.
Never become a drinking-man, my
Grandmother warned, remembering Merthyr
And the Spanish foundrymen

Puking their guts up in the dirt streets,
The Irish running from the furnaces
To crowd their paymaster into a tavern,
Leather bags of sovereigns bouncing on his thigh.
But it is calmer here, more subtly dangerous.
This afternoon is a suspension of life

I learn to enjoy. But now
The towel goes over the taps and I feel
The dregs in my throat. A truce has ended
And the clocks start again. Sunlight
Leaps out of the street. In his shrine of glass
   The landlord is wringing our lives dry.

AFTER A FRIENDSHIP

Still clear, that morning his family moved,
The lorry carrying furniture and people
Towards Swansea. I never waved
But breathed at the window the sweet-stale

Air of the empty house. And walked home.
If there was grief I have forgotten it,
But from then on things were not the same.
Grammar-school, homework, rugby-kit

Filled my time. I learned to become
Invisible and wrote the days' timetable
In an exercise book. My uniform
Had a heart-shaped badge and its black wool

Steamed in the rain. We were all proud.
And seven years passed like the days'
Seven lessons and he slowly dwindled
From my mind, a small ghost who preys

Now suddenly but for good reason
On imagination and memory.
It was never repeated, that season
Of friendship: a ten-year-old boy

With mad eyes, a truant, a sleeper-out
In haystacks brought down his fist
With a cobble in it and a gout
Of blood like a grape into the dust.

Fear and learning; deliberate
Childish violence. Like steel and flint
We sparked each other to the great
Discovery of ourselves. And went

Our ways. Children with their tough minds
Would understand. Seeing my blood
Did not scare us. It ran for the parting of friends.
We both knew we were going away for good.

CHINA 1830

Across the hillside comes a line of men:
Dawn's extraordinary light like the cholera
Party moving through China, whitelime on the skin
Turning to ash in the dew of flickering Merthyr.

In the taverns the burnt men show their scars;
Lacerations of fire where the furnace spat.
It's bandit country that lives by its own law,
That snoring ale-stained giant its emperor.

And flourishing in Dowlais now the dialect
Of iron is more powerful than psalms;
The vocabulary of the engineer, industry's elect,
Has drawn the populations from the quiet farms,

Coal-hewers, turners, every creed and sect
Sleeping shoulder to shoulder on the tavern boards,
While the English language ravenous for words
Goes swaggering like a drunkard on the street.

THE BOMBING OF BAGHDAD AS SEEN
FROM AN ELECTRICAL GOODS SHOP

Eating was serious work.
I watched you arrange as an evening ritual
The hummus rough with lemonrind
And bread dusted with Jordanian thyme.

Every supper, you said, might be the last.
So maybe that's the way to live,
The way that we should read our books
Or view as now at home this notch of sea
Silvered and thunderstruck
Between the pillars of the esp,
A ladle of spelter hissing at the air.

Nazaar, I know the market place today
Must be quiet as the British Cemetery,
That field with headstones of forgotten boys
Who died of cholera and Baghdad heat.

There's no haggling with the smoke-seller
Or the women with switchsticks, flicking
Flies away from Tigris bream:
The honey and grapes and Syrian soap
Are stalled in convoys along the border road.

And I suppose that you're at home,
Because where else is there to be on a night like this,
Listening to the Cruise missiles, the only
Traffic out tonight on Palestine Street,
While here in the window of Edwards Electrical
Your city in the tracers' glow
Becomes a negative of itself.

ONE MOMENT ON THE AVENIDA

Save us mother.
I saw DNA's double helix
doing the lambada, the girl
from Santa Theresa in the red rubber sheath
– all hips and lips they said –
and her hands restless as mahogany flowers
in the wind that blows out of the backlands
and down the avenida.

Save us, mother,
as the samba reaches to the tropic of capricorn
I never knew existed in my blood,
to the equator that is an iron band around my skull,

save us, for the girl is so close now,
her dance a shimmy
in every shining molecule.

Save us,
for we are the peasants with broken hands;
the worms in our bellies have jewelled mouths,
and we march our milkeyed children
out of the backlands and down the avenida,
pushing over the barracas, stealing Pepsi from the
                                        lanchonettes,
because it's the time of the reckoning,
it's the judgement hour
on Ipanema of the dangerous wave.

So mother, save us.
Can you hear us shouting?
Take away, we shout, take away the drought and the
                                        chiggers
and the caatinga from our chromosomes.
Make us as rich as the pimps and the moneychangers
on the Avenida Princesa Isabel.

And mother, we will stay
at the Sheraton and feast upon
a river porpoise flown from the market at Belem,
and the army will not move us
nor the thunder in Minas Gerais
nor memoranda from all the laptops in the Centro,
and we will turn on the televisions in the celebrity suites

and the girl in red will dance for us,
the seductress of the genes, she will dance for us, mother.

And when at last
her spinning has ceased
and we have drunk the gold beer of Antarctica
in the minibars, she will cry with us,
for she is a peasant girl too,
and she will lead us the long walk home, rejoicing,
in her red shoes.

THE ORCHIDS OF CWM-Y-GAER

Now, disbelieving, I will go
down a road so narrow
I must travel sideways
though still the willows will swat me with their swags of rain
and my own sweat tighten under my arms
as once my father's fingers did.

Step carefully
for here they are,
newborn but already white with webs.
Once the superstitious thought
it was Christ's blood that mottled the leaves,
but now it's as easy to suppose
that these eruptions, under a shadow's anglepoise,
are uranium rods
broken through from the terrible core.

719

We build our legends;
    we build our gods;
but how does a people understand its gods?
    These might be such, thrusting up
like the pillars of the reactor,
their alpha-love kissing our skin,
their gamma-love passing through our bones
to leave their ghosts forever hidden in our chromosomes.

We are people who worships gods
whose mouths gasp electric,
                whose eyes
are a dull, totalitarian
gold, whose commerce is strange
as a rockpool's
          pornography.

    I pause one moment
    on this narrow road
with the light tipping out of a tree's tundish
and the spiders at their riot after rain.
    Already a thread hangs from my hair
    and ties me to this place.
So I open my hands to the orchids at Cwm y Gaer
    and count each breath.
How long before the welts appear?
How soon before the cradle of nightsweats,
or that deep, enriched delirium, dark as dew?

PASCALE PETIT

Pascale Petit was born in Paris in 1953 to a French father and Welsh mother. Although she has a French passport, she considers herself Welsh. She was brought up at Berriew in Montgomeryshire and Llanbradach in the Rhymney Valley. Trained as a sculptor at art colleges in Cardiff and Gloucester, and at the Royal College of Art, she lives in London where from 1989 to 2005 she edited *Poetry London*, a magazine which she co-founded. She has published four collections of poems: *Heart of a Deer* (1998), *The Zoo Father* (2001), *The Wounded Deer: Fourteen Poems after Frida Kahlo* (2005), and *The Huntress* (2005). She has travelled extensively in the Amazon region of Venezuela.

AS IF I WERE WINTER ITSELF

When I enter the hospital where my mother is lying

I will bring a flask of water collected from Lethe
and a flask from the Mnemosyne.

I will sip from each.
This will feel like swallowing shafts of sunlight.

I'll take deep breaths, hungry for canyon air.

A porter will rub fox-fire on my face
for the ride in the luminous lift.

Corridor walls will be translucent,
I'll see the trees imprisoned inside –

blue branches with old wounds as leaves,
red trees with raptor-roots.

Are you ready for the truth?

Ward Sister will ask, releasing
lemon-yellow and saffron butterflies.

They are the first flurry of winter
I'll reply, addressing

Mother's forgetting eye
and her remembering eye.

Then I'll say everything I always wanted to say to her.

The butterflies will mass on her bed,

rays streaming through the window
will wash us both.

Her hands will shake but that won't stop me.

SELF-PORTRAIT WITH FIRE ANTS

To visit you Father, I wear a mask of fire ants.
When I sit waiting for you to explain

why you abandoned me when I was eight
they file in, their red bodies

massing around my eyes, stinging my pupils white
until I'm blind. Then they attack my mouth.

I try to lick them but they climb down my gullet
until an entire swarm stings my stomach,

while you must become a giant anteater,
push your long sticky tongue down my throat,

as you once did to my baby brother,
French-kissing him while he pretended to sleep.

I can't remember what you did to me, but the ants know.

THE STRAIT-JACKETS

I lay the suitcase on Father's bed
and unzip it slowly, gently.
Inside, packed in cloth strait-jackets
lie forty live hummingbirds
tied down in rows, each tiny head
cushioned on a swaddled body.
I feed them from a flask of sugar water,
inserting every bill into the pipette,
then unwind their bindings
so Father can see their changing colours
as they dart around his room.

They hover inches from his face
as if he's a flower, their humming
just audible above the oxygen recycler.
For the first time since I've arrived
he's breathing easily, the cannula
attached to his nostrils almost slips out.
I don't know how long we sit there
but when I next glance at his face
he's asleep, lights from their feathers
still playing on his eyelids and cheeks.
It takes me hours to catch them all
and wrap them in their strait-jackets.
I work quietly, he's in such
a deep sleep he doesn't wake once.

THE ANT GLOVE

Dear Father, after Mother's death, after I'd read
    all your letters to her and her letters to you

and finally understood that I was the fruit of her rape,
    I walked into the forest.

The tribe I met there helped me write this letter
    preparing me as they would prepare a boy

who wanted to become a man.
    The elders raided nests of giant hunting ants

for three hundred shining black workers
    which they wove into the palm fibres of a glove,

their stinging abdomens pointing inwards.
   They blew on them to enrage them.

They painted my writing hand with black dye
   from the genipap fruit and thrust it into the glove.

I had to remain silent while the ants attacked.
   Can you smell the lemony scent of formic acid?

These words are dancing the Tocandeiro.
   I hope you're dancing as you hold my letter,

as I had to dance wearing the ant glove
   stomping my soles hard on the ground.

Afterwards I cut the stones from my feet.
   Afterwards I celebrated with a feast

biting off ant-heads to suck blood from their bodies
   until my lips and tongue were numb.

I hope you've sucked the blood from the words
   that stung you. My hand is still swollen.

Are your fingers swelling as they stroke my signature?
   Are your lips and tongue numb from kissing my kisses?

My hand is always in the glove, writing goodbye,
   red and blue feathers flutter from my wrist.

SELF-PORTRAIT AS A YANOMAMI DAUGHTER

I've built a rainforest shelter,

painted *hekura* on the walls –
my only visitors, these helper-spirits.

I haven't been out since you died.
Like a good Yanomami daughter

I've kept our fire alight.
Your body made it burn so fiercely.

My hair singed as I raked
the embers for all your bones

to grind to a black powder.
When I finished, the hekura spoke.

They told me to shave my hair
and braid it into a belt,

bind it tight around my waist
the way you used to hold me, Father,

when you turned into a demon
and tore me with your penis.

This is how Night was made,
my thighs sticky with star-blood,

my mouth flooded with moonseeds.
Now, I wear a child's necklace

threaded with toucan beaks.
I shake my rattle,

stamp my clapping stick.
I pour your ashes into plantain soup.

The first sip makes me retch,
then I learn to like the taste.

THE DEN

In the silence of my own home
I hear the buzz like a shivering of icy leaves.
The back of my neck tickles
and I glimpse the rattler's tail
disappearing under the floorboards,
its skin faded as old documents.
And I lift the boards
while still sitting in my chair.
The nails pop out as if with a claw-hammer.
Then I see the den my visitor
keeps returning to –
hundreds of ancestor-snakes
hibernating. I don't move
in case one feels the vibration
and wakes the others.

I don't want them roused like a beehive.
I wait calmly, then blink once –
that's all I allow myself.
Just as when I sat with you Mother,
I let my ophidian mask
slip down my face
and blinked no more, its eyes lidless.
I don't let my forked black tongue
taste the air for wind jewels
of your scent, three years after your death.
I look through the renailed floorboards
and see our letters rolled tight
where I have hidden them,
a bolus of papers
seeking warmth from each other,
scrolled like ancient codices.
Each letter sleeping with its venom
tucked in the fold.

MY MOTHER'S PERFUME

Strange how her perfume used to arrive long before she did,
  a jade cloud that sent me hurrying
first to the loo, then to an upstairs window to watch for her taxi.
  I'd prepare myself
by trying to remember her face, without feeling afraid. As she drew
  nearer I'd get braver
until her scent got so strong I could taste the coins in the bottom
  of her handbag.
And here I am forty years on, still half-expecting her. Though now
  I just have to open
the stopper of an expensive French bottle, daring only a whiff of
  Shalimar
which Jacques Guerlain created from the vanilla orchid vine.
  Her ghostly face
might shiver like Christ's on Veronica's veil – a green-gold blossom
  that sends me back
to the first day of the school holidays, the way I used to practise
  kissing her cheek
by kissing the glass. My eyes scanned the long road for a speck
  while the air turned amber.
Even now, the scent of vanilla stings like a cane. But I can also smell
  roses and jasmine
in the bottle's top notes, my legs wading through the fragrant path,
  to the gloved hand emerging
from a black taxi at the gate of Grandmother's garden. And for a
  moment I think I am safe.
Then Maman turns to me with a smile like a dropped
  perfume bottle, her essence spilt.

MIKE JENKINS

Mike Jenkins was born in Aberystwyth in 1953 and educated at the University College of Wales in his hometown. He taught English in Northern Ireland before settling in Merthyr Tydfil; he was for many years a teacher at a comprehensive school on the Gurnos estate but now teaches in Radyr, Cardiff. He is a prominent member of the Red Poets Society and was editor of *Poetry Wales* from 1987 to 1992. As well as two volumes of short fiction, *Wanting to Belong* (1997) and *Child of Dust* (2005), he has published ten books of poems: *The Common Land* (1981), *Empire of Smoke* (1983), *Invisible Times* (1986), *A Dissident Voice* (1990), *Graffiti Narratives* (1994), *This House, My Ghetto* (1995), *Shirley Egg* (1997), *Coulda Bin Summin* (2001), *The Language of Flight* (2004) and *Walking on Waste* (2007); his *Red Landscapes: New and Selected Poems* appeared in 1999. His poems are primarily concerned with the post-industrial valleys of south Wales, in particular Merthyr, the Radical history and present realities of which he has made a central theme of his work; he is among the very few Welsh poets who have successfully used demotic English for the purposes of poetry. A small selection of his poems is to be found in *Laughter Tangled in Thorn* (2003) in the Corgi series.

CHARTIST MEETING
Heolgerrig, 1842

The people came to listen
looking down valley as they tramped;
the iron track was a ladder
from a loft to the open sea –
salt filling the air like pollen.

Each wheel was held fast
as you would grip a coin;
yet everything went away from them.
The black kernel of the mountains
seemed endless, but still in their stomachs
a furnace-fire roared,
and their children's eyes hammered
and turned and hollowed out a cannon.

Steam was like a spiral of wool
threaded straight down the valley,
lost past a colliery.
The tramways held the slope
as they were wood of a pen.
Wives and children were miniatures
of the hill, the coal engrained
in enclosures on their skin.

They shook hands with the sky,
an old friend; there, at the field,
oak trees turned to crosses

their trunks bent with the weight
of cloud and wind, and harsh grass
from marshes that Morgan Williams,
the weaver, could raise into a pulpit.

A thousand listened, as way below them
Cyfarthfa Castle was set like a diamond
in a ring of green,
and the stalks of chimneys
bloomed continuous smoke and flame.

The Welsh that was spoken
chuckled with streams, plucked bare rock,
and men like Morgan Williams
saw in the burnt hands a harvest of votes.

MEETING MRS BERNSTEIN

Mrs Bernstein, the dogs sniff suspiciously
in your plotted neighbourhood,
while you open your door and your life
to strangers: trying to sell us your house
when we came for a piano;
sprightly body nudging a doddering mind.

You introduce us to your husband
who, impassively from the sideboard,
remains your dear boy.
With your father, the town's last rabbi,

your pride is framed.
In a small drawer
is tucked away your profession.

'Here they all are!' you say.
On a table's planet
the seas and cities defined
in pictures of your family.
Confident fathers and dark-skinned
daughters explained by qualifications.

Incongruous amongst a trilled dresser
and desk where you drum out the past
are Harvard and Yale pennants:
two sails beckoning your sight
beyond the whispering walls.

Mrs Bernstein, we listen to your playing:
Rachmaninov's chords bluster to America
where your anger declares itself;
during Chopin's night you commune
with your restless dead.

Down the garden steps you grip my hand
with a ring of bone. We cannot buy
this instrument of emotions
only your fingers know.

MOUTHY

Sborin, sir!
We're always doin racism.
It's that or death, sir.
Yew're morbid, yew are,
or gotta thing about the blacks.

But sir mun! Carn we do summin intrestin
like Aids or watch a video o' Neighbours?
Mrs Williams Media upstairs ave got em.

Oh no! Not another poem!
They're always crap, rubbish
not enough action, don' rhyme.

Yer, sir, this one's got language in it!
It's all about sex!
Yew're bloody kinky yew are!
I'm getting my Mam up yer.

Sir! We aven done work frages,
on'y chopsin in groups.
We ewsed t' do real English
when we woz younger,
exercises an fillin in gaps.

Sir mun! Don' keep askin me
wha we should do,
yew're the bloody teacher!

from MERTHYR PEOPLE
for Steve Phillips, photographer

Waltzing Eyes

She's framed by the Zimmer, knits her arthritic fingers into
each other, the crotchety texture of her pain.

The present is a tea-cup (no saucer), the stump of a candle,
an egg-cup full of pins.

Further along the mantelpiece the dice are all on one, a
photo of her grandchildren burnt white by her cataracts.

It becomes darker: her hubby's trophy, his leather-bound
portraits a modest library.

Her skin is falling. At her feet are neatly-chopped logs. If
she should rub her bones much harder, then a spark...

There's smoke from her grey hair. If only her flesh were
grained like wood.

Behind her shoulders the plant has turned to soot.
You won't see her waltzing eyes till the flames begin.

Wolf Hour

It's wolf-hour in the precinct: pack of dogs, pack of boys. The
mirror can't be seen. They reflect and swop
features, triads with sharpened fangs.

Leaders face nose to snout, staring each other out.

Three concrete blocks where winners would stand to
receive a battered coke-can cup.

The dogs are more patient: paw-leafed pavingstones
are their horizons.

735

The boys have blurry feet. One jerks in incredible
contortions, head taking off over the binned estate.

Hip-hop away, their leader's flung a can – 'Fuckin mangy
strays! Don't shit yer!' His hair thick as an alsatian's coat.

It's wolf-hour in the precinct: the Shop Boys lurk in the
background, from a ridge of reputation. Night comes,
they'll snap up and pocket the silver moon.

Shadow without Sun

Perched on a black and white pillar, call him 'Piggy', he
doesn't care. His head's two stories above his sister.

His knee jabbers for him, saying: 'I'm loud 'n' dirty, I'm
bloody mucky, open t' the air.'

Arms folded, captain of a team of one, holding the match
ball, his cheeks blown up.

He's casting a shadow without the sun. She's in it, clutching
her check skirt in case the wind... Her hair's the shine of a
plastic bucket.

Her face conceals a window. His hair is curtained,
tousled, already drawn.

GWYN ALF

Never bin one f'r istree
lines o' dates
them kings an queens,
my memree no ware'ouse
f' such thin's, but ee...
ee spoke like one of us

736

took me back in them talks
I wandered to at first.
Ee brung it up t' date,
constructin a buildin
o' sights an smells
is stammer a-drillin
ands framin windows,
is fag the chimlee.
An oo owns 'is ouse?
ee seemed t' say.

Never bin one f' politics, mind,
them politicians on'y come
'lection time buyin ower votes,
I know enough t' know
a cross is thin as ink,
once 'ey get in
'ey'll all forget, but im...
ee wuz always from
round yer, no matter ow far
ee went, Russia or America,
ee laid a track
f' tram or train, is spinnin brain
'maginin a future town
where we'd get off, t' larf
an eat an sing under-a roof
of-a place we'd made.

Ee coughed his guts out...
death? never bin one t'say

737

tha much about it.
but when I yeard 'bout im
I couldn elp it,
my missis sayz, "Don't talk soft!
Yew never even knew im!"
But I felt-a cement
dryin my throat, my ead
poundin' with-a wheels turnin.

CHRISTOPHER MEREDITH

Christopher Meredith was born in Tredegar in 1954 and educated at the University College of Wales, Aberystwyth, where he read English and Philiosophy. He was a teacher in Brecon, where he still lives, before his appointment as a lecturer in Creative Writing at the University of Glamorgan in 1993; he is now Professor. He has published three novels: *Shifts* (1988), *Griffri* (1991), and *Sidereal Time* (1998), and a novel for children, *Nadolig Pob Dydd / Christmas Every Day* (2004/2006); having learned Welsh, he has also translated a novel by Mihangel Morgan, *Melog* (2005). His books of poems are *This* (1984), *Snaring Heaven* (1990) and *The Meaning of Flight* (2005).

DESK

I rescued you, splinted your broken legs.
Forty years or so had scummed you dark
With ink, dead skin, the rain of dust, the grease
Of knees and cuffs and fingertips, with work

Done routinely by the bored but paid.
I unlidded you, cut wedges, made true
The skewed split joints, machined human gluten
Off the boards. My carpentry of nails and glue

Fell short of craft but was informed by love.
I plugged you, cleaned your handles, planed

Saw purity of copper and the packed white grain.
Some wounds were healed, the depth of others learned

– No restoration ever is complete.
People at work, the children and the staff,
Gave you their own disfigurement –
Not inborn malice but the hurt of graft

That rubbed a hole in their humanity.
And I played samaritan out of guilt
Of sorts. Worked out, I was looking for my
Small re-creation as you were rebuilt.

Relidded, drawers eased, your eight legs firm,
Beeswax bringing alive the fans and bars
Of tan and yellow grain, you are a place
For another sort of work. We're both scarred

But the worm in each of us is dead.
I'm not paid much, but neither am I bored
Nor hurt by work's attrition as we go
To real work. This page, this silence, these words.

ON HAY BRIDGE

8.00pm in a belated spring
in still air under marbled sky
trees stand foot to foot on their reflections.
The river dimpling only over stones
goes glassy at its edge,
is clear beneath me.

A salmon a yard long, dark slate
blotched with sour milk,
twitches against the flow,
sways, mirroring the ropes of weed,
sidewinds, sideslips, tacks upstream.
Gerallt saw her eight hundred journeys back.

The banks no doubt were greengorged then in spring.
In clearings spent homesteads smouldered.
Wooden towers, slowly, were rebuilt in stone.
Castles studded conquerors' intent,
stitched the sleeve with rock.
Lords dead in Gwent. A headless corpse in Cwm Hir.

Three hundred years of gradual collapse
and Bedo Brwynllys near here
sang sweet and politic of loving girls
and how their eyebrows curved
like rainbows or like squirrels' tails.
Namesake, let me not be you.

Eight hundred years and still we say
you lose less by retreat.
Some martyred hero and a moving song
will do to warm an evening perhaps.
In daylight, let the current inch you back
against yourself.

The light, waning, cools mirrored greens
to lave thought, blooms the river with
a promise of opacity. Swallows,
openthroated, trawl the air for flies
beneath the bridge, drive on like the salmon
and let their element wash through.

She, slatemilk, edging out of sight
slides under the reflected trees.
Come back, I think. Come rain
to puncture all reflection.
Give me that pied yard of muscle
to inch against what pushes me from home.

SHE PLANS A PURCHASE

Across the table came her photographs.
'This is the garden. This, the view.'
She faltered then, expected us to scoff.
We looked up from the snaps and she
Dropped her eyes defensively.

Dream home. The roseframed door. All that stuff.
For such sophisticated folk
I'd thought coffee, talk and books would be enough.
'And here, in the garden, a well.'
'No gnomes?' Still irony's the rule.

And 'Heaney's got a poem about wells – '
I bit my tongue. It's not done to

742

Be so showy. Literate types don't spell
   Out allusions. Even so, I'm
   Forced to think how place gives way to rhyme.

But her pictures try to fill an aching space,
To hold a certain, living self.
   A hole sunk to the lifesource of a place –
     Or some such phrase – helps her get by.
     These rhymeless ones need places more than I.

RED ARMCHAIR

I like to sit in my red armchair
that's rumpled in the morning sun.
I love the bashedup faded warm
of her scuffy terracotta arms
the foursquare squat untippable
strong give of her
the vivid brickred tongue
of her squashed squab
under my lazy arse.
Her fat red cushions are the daily press
that speak of falls and squeezes and slumps.
I throw myself into her
like I've never done with any job
and realize a little late
that the others – the bentwoods, the swivellers,
the ones that claimed to be adjustable,
the tubular sprung steel Bauhaus numbers,
the leggy backless types I've rubbed against

in midnight bars – they all mean nothing
come sober morning in the sun
to this my love, my bearer, my vocation.
She never trod a catwalk or did cool
has not declined from chic to dowdy churl,
was always strong and squashed and firm and giving
and fat with adjectives and never gave a shit
and never so cheap as to yield
to any of my metaphors
but always was is just my red armchair.

MY MOTHER MISSED THE
BEAUTIFUL AND DOOMED

My mother missed the beautiful and doomed
by a few years.
Where Waugh, hot for some pious ormolu,
dreamed Brideshead
she swept carpets, cleaned grates.

Sepia expects a tear
but none comes. She holds
the yellowed postcard of the House
at arm's length, beyond her two dead children,
two atom bombs ago.

'It was like that film. You know, *Rebecca*.'
She smokes.
Echo of casual elegance in the wrist, the gesture,
masks slow scorching of the fuse.

The drag of air
accelerates a hundred small ignitions.
'The drive and all. They had a maze.'
Ash hardens into brightness
small flames eat the paper
worming back along tobacco galleries.
She frowns and jewels, salvers, gleam the harder.
'Her Ladyship 'ould doll up to the nines
come dinner, like a filmstar.'
The mind drags air through fifty years of fading
burns off the filmdream, comes to other stuff,
makes it glow again.

Through half open doors
down perspectives of the glassy rooms
she hears them.
Iw. Mmn. Yiss. Tongues all twangs and daggers.
The Foreign Secretary stands in the hall
his collar of vermiculated astrakhan
flawed with sparkling rain.

She kneels by the scuttle with
an egg of coal in either hand.
His chauffeur in doublebreasted rig
loiters, one glove removed, ruffles her hair,
sets her neat white cap awry.
'Little Cinderella' he says.

She frowns to brighten memory's fuse,
looks down the maze of galleries where

745

her people cut the coal.
The hand that rained a blow or a flirtation,
the words half flattered her
and kept her down.

She glances sideways at the tight black boot,
the echo of the bentarmed cross.
Krupp's bombs rain now on undefended children
glimmer through smoking Barcelona.

Unwilled complicity can hurt so much.
She clutches at the deaths of millions.

'A skivvy all my life' she says
and strikes another match.

OCCUPIED

Shy Ghurkas walking from the camp
smile at my children,
like to say hello.

The young Scot who lives across the road
drinks cans of lager in his livingroom
and, out of battledress,
wears shorts patterned with a union jack.

Doveflutter deepened on an endless loop
is helicopters
some bulbeyed and filmy
others heavy, hung on glimmering blades,
gundecks slung over the Usk,
pinched up at either end
like a canoe.
They name them after beaten people.

Apache. Iroquois. Chinook.

HUW JONES

Huw Jones was born in Birmingham in 1955 but brought up Welsh-speaking in Welshpool, Montgomeryshire. Educated at the University College of Wales, Aberystwyth, where he read Theology, he was a teacher at schools in Newtown and Llandrindod, then taught Welsh to adults at the University College of North Wales, Bangor, before spending two years teaching in Botswana and three in Zimbabwe. Both he and his wife are ministers in the Presbyterian Church of Wales; since 2006 they have been based in Rhosllannerchrugog. He writes in both Welsh and English. A selection of his Welsh poems has been published as *Lleuad y Bore* (1994) and a bilingual volume as *Ceiliogod Otse: The Cockerels of Otse* (1996), which is about the time he and his wife spent in Africa. His English poems are to be found in *A Small Field* (1985).

HORSE CHESTNUT

Under sticky twigs
and tiers of candles
I sought the friendship
of your shade,

split open
your prickly presents
of glossy chestnuts
to soak in vinegar.

I went to school
with pockets bulging,
a year older, hardened
for the daily blows.

FOR THE QUAKERS OF MONTGOMERYSHIRE

I

We are a people
cold with creeds,
harried prey
of hireling priests.

In a broad white hat
and leather breeches
a preacher rides
from crowded fells,
his followers, like ferns,
shaking in the wind.

II Meifod

Brethren,
a Fox in sheep's clothing
leads our flock astray.

Trust not those
who go naked for a sign,
set sacrament aside
and boast of inward light.

749

At Coed Cowryd
cobblers, blacksmiths
and even women preach.
Pray for their salvation.

III Welshpool

Snow on the mountain
sills barred with ice.

We sleep in straw
and dirt, snared
for refusing the Oath,
dragged from our beds
to lie with robbers,
walked in chains
to Quarter Sessions.

Our allegiance is to one
who has no need of oath
nor tithe, nor sermons blabbed
like ballads at a fair.

Now we, like Paul, must wait.
The day is coming
when the faithful will be
as snow on the mountain.

IV Dolobran Hall

Spiders case
this secret kingdom,
moonlight flirts
with boarded windows.

Breathless now
the Foundry bellows,
slack and mute
the heavy chains.

Empty paths that led
to grace, man's estate
lost in the grass.

V Esgairgoch

They came to claim
the common land,
left open gates
paths cut back.

In a steep half-acre
pitted by cattle,
their bones were planted
under clouds of hawthorn.

A small field, lost
among the nine and ninety.

CYMMER ABBEY

Bees among the heather,
red glare of sorrel
in open cloister.
O, miserere, Domine.

Blasts for a new road
spoil again the peace
of Cymmer, echo a storm
of crashing stone.

Men who served another
king, lit the powder,
pilfered nectar
for the Tudor hive.

Bees among the heather,
red glare of sorrel
in open cloister.
O, miserere, Domine.

WORLDS

It is a month of birthdays,
parcels from Wales, candles lit.
Days when our shadows hide
from the sun. A Barbet

clinks at its anvil for hours,
dust drifts through the village.
Prayers at the Kgotla plead
for rain to rescue the maize.

We make love during a storm
our bodies lit by lightning;
dreams disturbed by thunder
the house too hot for sleeping.

You are the twinkle in our eyes
lodging in the womb's alcove,
lone survivor of a journey
from Adam to Eve.

You are a new creation
small as the letter O,
claiming our conversation
as Jupiter rises with Leo.

We plot your path together,
your existence a secret.
With each week we grow hopeful,
certain of your will-to-live,
to visit terra firma
beneath its blanket of air.

Tonight, Sirius heralds
another clear veld of stars

over a tense continent.
Here, crossing the savanna,
our ancestors played with fire,
baited traps, sharpened their minds.

Crickets retell their legends,
a baboon barks on the hill,
the new moon, an ark resting
on Ararat. Our daughters
sigh in their sleep, their breathing
the sound of darkness ebbing.

The scan confirms our fear –
your life-support system failed.
A probe relays pictures
of your crumpled space capsule.
You left recently
in small clots of blood.

Your placenta is examined
for signs of malfunction,
its network of villi
a pattern of galaxies.
You were a meteor
crossing the cold, desert sky.

RICHARD GWYN

Richard Gwyn was born in Pontypool in 1956 and grew up in Crickhowell. He studied Anthropology at the London School of Economics, then spent ten years travelling around the Mediterranean. He taught Creative Writing in the School of English, Communication and Philosophy at Cardiff University until his retirement in 2006, and has lived in the city since 1990. He has published five books of poetry: *Defying Gravity* (1992), *One Night in Icarus Street* (1995), *Stone Dog, Flower Red* (1995), *Walking on Bones* (2000), and *Being in Water* (2001); and two novels, *The Colour of a Dog Running Away* (2005) and *Deep Hanging Out* (2007).

EINKORN, SPELT AND EMMER

Were the staple cereals
of the old Celts. Rich
in protein, yielding

tonnage three times
greater than subsequent
generations can muster

with crops of half
the nutritional value.
Why is this so?

The soil, the grain itself
and perhaps the moon
contain the answer

But the ploughman's
fugitive memory
prefers to chase digits

on a space invader screen.

LA VENDANGE

Damn this town and my idleness
and the free availability of wine
and the wretchedness of man's estate

I came here to work
but barely off the train I met Peter
and soon reverted to old customs
and sleeping in the park

Damn the work
It is easier by far
to sit with Peter and a gallon of wine
and talk bollocks
in the autumn sun

MODES OF TRAVEL

Serge travelled the pilgrim's way to
Compostella with his crippled dog

the dog had two broken legs
from two separate motor accidents

Serge loved the dog and travelled
with a push-cart on wheels

into the cart went blankets
food and clothing

into the cart went the dog when his
two good legs would not take him further

On Ithaka I met a man who travelled with a coffin
he'd fixed the coffin onto bicycle wheels
and carried his possessions inside

at night he slept in his coffin
if it rained he pulled down the lid

he was prepared for any eventuality

NEW YEAR'S JOURNEY

My wish that New Year's Day – to ride wild horses
over sunlit hillsides. What I got was misery, abandonment,
and chaos. I loved it, all the suffering and heartbleed,

Humbling moments in the shadow of the god: and pain,
the haloed pain of tragedy – there was not enough that was
enough;
it was never quite enough. And then you wanted more.

Trips through winter islands, marooned on Amorgos,

the ferry anchored to the island for a fortnight's storm,
and when we leave, young Nelson told us,

So long waiting, we will drag the island with us.
Islands, islands, each one with its secrets; each one viewed
through rain-swept glass in sea-lashed ports.

Kasia, Nelson, Declan and myself, with Kasia's babies
made a crew of six; the travelling winter circus.
Set a precedent, I told the others as we started out from
                                                    Athens:

You see, a lot had happened in a little time, our heads were
full of Kasia's kidnap, articles of occult interest,
Artaud's madness, a girl who danced when she was sad,

And other ceremonials observed in a sprawling cemetery
at the city's edge, where the crimson paint shrieked
on the marble of her family vault: Antigone, Antigone.

On the boat to Paros, Kasia called for brandy 'to feed my
Slavic soul'. I sniggered at such self-parody, as the ship
pitched like a drunkard through the January swell.

On Amorgos we slept rough, the Wicklow boy and me:
he had to cut his sleeping bag to make a spread for two.
I was wakened by a crone who screamed 'You'll die you'll
                                                    die' –

And realised that we were buried in a snowfall. Frozen, we
huddled by that widow's woodstove, numb to any world
                                                    beyond

758

our island, yet we had a mission raging in our blood.

In Paros on a toilet wall I found more evidence, this time
attributed to Lorca: 'I come from the countryside and refuse
to believe that man is the most important thing alive.'

And there it ended. Or ought to have. The final boat trip,
ticketless, we spent below decks, boozing with the crew,
and then returned to freezing Athens. Night that followed

sleepless night. What passed for mind so brandy-stained
there were submerged cathedrals in my eyes, songs
of drowning women in my throat. And then, one afternoon

I crossed Syntagma, and stopping at a signal felt a tug
upon the sleeve; an instant of impossible reflection.
I shuddered, knowing that my call had come before

My time, and then moved on. The rounds of energy
that reckless travel requires were seizing up, and I retired
to a gloomy hostel, stayed in bed, read cold war thrillers,

Evenings talking with a schizophrenic Samiot named George
who worked in a biscuit factory with forty Cretan women.
'Barbarians!' he sneered, 'they all the time make play with
me.'

Kasia and Nelson married, live in Warsaw, have six kids.
I passed the Wicklow boy years later, playing whistle in the
metro.
His eyes were gone; what lay behind them also.

CATHERINE FISHER

Catherine Fisher was born in Newport, Monmouthshire, in 1956, and still lives there. Educated at the Gwent College of Further Education, she is a teacher in her hometown. As well as books for children, including *The Conjuror's Game* (1990), she has published three collections of verse: *Immrama* (1988), *The Unexplored Ocean* (1994), and *Altered States* (1999).

SEVERN BORE

Somewhere out there the sea has shrugged its shoulders.
Grey-green masses slip, rise, gather
to a ripple and a wave, purposeful, arrowing up
arteries of the land. Brown and sinuous, supple
as an otter, nosing upstream under the arching
bridge; past Chepstow, Lydney, Berkeley where a king
screamed; Westbury, where old men
click stopwatches with grins of satisfaction;
slopping into the wellingtons of watchers,
swamping the nests of coots, splashing binoculars.
And so to Minsterworth meadows where Ivor Gurney's ghost
walks in sunlight, unforgotten; past lost
lanes, cow-trodden banks, nudging the reeds,
lifting the lank waterweed,
flooding pills, backwaters, bobbing the floats
of fishermen, the undersides of leaves and boats,
and gliding, gliding over Cotswold's flawed

reflection, the sun swelling, the blue sky scored
with ripples, fish and dragonfly, stirred
by the drip and cloop of oars; and finally, unheard,
washing into the backstreets of the town to lie
at the foot of the high
cathedral, prostrate, breathless,
pilgrim from a far place;
refugee
from the ominous petulance of the sea.

IMMRAMA

First there was the island of the darkness.
When we rowed from there
the light was desolation for us.

And I remember a house with a golden chessboard
where we played too long.
What we lost I cannot remember.

As you go on it gets harder. Each landfall
an awakening of sorrows,
guile or treachery, the enticement of pleasures.

I lost my brother at the house of feathers,
good men at the harper's table.
There are always those who would hold us back;

you get used to the voices, the clinging fingers;
in every port the warning
'Beyond here is nothing but the sea.'

Islands of glass, islands of music and berries,
the isle of the locked door,
citadels and beaches where we dared not land,

these are behind us. Daily, the delirium rises;
it may be that smudge
on the horizon is a trick of my eyes.

And would we know that land if we should find it?
They say the scent of apples
wafts on the water; there is honey, hum of bees,

salmon leap into the boat. They say the others,
the lost ones, laugh on the sand.
But behind them, who are those strangers crowding the cliffs?

POEM FOR DAVID LEWIS
(d. 27 August 1679)
... I believe you are met here to hear a fellow-countryman speak...

You spoke Welsh on the scaffold;
the Usk men understood you.
They would not now.
The local executioner locked his door;
it was a stranger who tightened your
tourniquet of rope,

and then they held him back till you were dead;
would not let the worst be done.
They created saints in their own image;

small men, cunning and discreet,
saints of the kitchen and the gentry's table,
compassionate, unassuming.

David Lewis, priest, Welshman,
wearer of disguises,
look at your grey town and swollen river,
the churches and the muddy lanes,
the houses whose dark hiding-holes you knew.
Look at your people, David,

the women and the young men who still kneel
and kiss the cold unchiselled granite
that marks your March, your borderland,
the bruising ground of language gainst language,
where the rough rope necklace dropped,
and strangled speech.

GWERN-Y-CLEPPA

There's a squall prowling up the estuary,
piling clouds on the moon.
The wood is a black promise,
an emptiness.
Here's a place where everything's uneasy.

In its tangle of branches I'm a shadow
fumbling foot by foot
down aisles of alder;
a stumbler
in a room of roots and hollows.

763

I hold the moment with both hands,
but it's gone in the
rustle of leaves, the roar
of the cars
in the cleft below Graig-y-Saeson.

Now you, Dafydd, would have known
how to keep it, how to hammer
an armour from such nothings, the bright
hard words
intricately linked; the chain

that stops no sword. I wonder
how you'd recognize it,
all your green Wales, its welcome
of a poem
with a coin and some honour.

Darkness itself is not the same;
the hill sliced deep
to its red heart. And the moon
brings rain,
and even that has the touch of the betrayed.

Still I've come, to the hall of stems,
to ask whatever you can give.
Image of earth and leaves, a rhythm,
a word or two, I'll take them,
carry them home, hidden,

with a rueful kind of pride;
my gifts from a generous patron;
as the moon floods lost windows
with its silver,
lighting the way through the wood.

THOSE WHO MAKE PATHS

Here's a song of praise for all those people
who live at the forgotten edge of things;
who come out at night and take long walks
under the lamp-posts, remembering;
women who stay behind to clean old churches,
rubbing the shining faces week by week,
speaking their thoughts to angels and the dead,
a silent congregation at their back.

Men who go out in the early morning
to gather sticks from urban river banks;
old men with allotments, or with bikes
piled with panniers of spuds;
women who push home-made carts or carry
wood on prams, grandchildren riding high
and sucking kaylee. Where are they
in the world's eye?

And those who make the paths that run through hedges,
through the corners of fields, who leave charred
sticks and charcoal deep in hidden copses;
kids who dream in corners of the yard;

anglers, and cyclists going nowhere really
but away, happy to be alone;
those who live beneath the world's dignity;
those who've been poets, and have never known.

OLIVER REYNOLDS

Oliver Reynolds was born in Cardiff in 1957. Educated at the University of Hull, where he took a degree in Drama, he worked for a while in his home city as a pantomime director but now lives in London where he works as an usher at the Royal Opera House. He has published four books of poems: *Skevington's Daughter* (1985), *The Player Queen's Wife* (1987), *The Oslo Tram* (1991), and *Almost* (1999).

SMILE, PLEASE

Track it through the pages
Back to its first appearance

Some time after her parents died
Within months of each other

When she was
Still only sixteen.

That's when it stopped
Having anything to do with happiness

And started being something
Laid on top of her face.

That's when it started
Being conscious.

That smile was there to be recorded,
As neutral as her clothes

Or the shine of her brother's hair-oil
(Next to her in the garden at 'Rosewood').

She smiled formally, in the way
An old man might tip his hat.

Each decade tightened it
Into the rigor of the living,

But occasionally there was
A second's pleasure,

A hint of a suburban Gioconda
Framed by the rockery

And the 2.10 from Coryton
Rattling by in the background.

Orwell said we all at fifty
Have the face we deserve.

Some of us though
Disclaim responsibility,

Ducking the sentence for a moment
As stretched lips plead our innocence.

Smiles lodge our appeal
Before we return to the face's lock-up.

But not hers.
Her smile is a frown on bail,

The mouth led astray
By the hunched brow.

SELF-PORTRAIT

You need regular brushing
Of the whites of your eyes.

(Pecker is maintained
By talking to oneself
In assumed voices.)
I have a beard now.
I stand against a window.

Stomach in, chest out.
No more pocket billiards.

Next to the back of my head,
Reflected in the top pane,
A squat shadow
Lifts a small box to its face.
A stranger at the feast.

Watch the birdie, darlings.
Eyes and teeth, eyes and teeth.

I squint into sunlight,
Afraid of posterity
Holding me responsible
For the way I look.
I look askance.

No take click-picture me.
Him kill my spirit.

Lop-sided truculence,
I am the Hunchback
Of Rhiwbina Garden Village.
The shadow in the window
Crooks its finger.

DYSGU

After two months in earphones
We can cope with the mundane
So long as it's slow.
But we're in mined territory:
'Are you near- or far-sighted?'
'I live five minutes away.'

In the coffee-break
Maxwell Sirenya

Reads the overseas news.
An exile from South Africa,
He speaks Welsh
With a Xhosan accent.

Newland, the oldest, remembers
Cycling home alongside
The Glamorganshire canal
When it was still a canal:
A cone of light moving into dark
And the regular plop of frogs.

Each has his reason to be here
Speaking through declenched teeth:
I'd thought it time to stop
Welshing on the language
And learn about roots,
If only etymological ones.

DAEARYDDIAETH

The land was always worked
It was what you lived on.
So the feelings were strong:
The land was in your heart;
The land was underfoot.

It's still farmed, flat and hill,
Some of it good, some bad.

Cash crops may oust *hiraeth*,
But it's still praised: *Gwlad, gwlad*
With the ball hanging air.

And many of the poems
Carry the smack of loam,
In books of earthy style
Whose pages you leaf through
Like someone turning soil.

It wasn't long before
Love and the land were one.
Sweethearts had their contours
While streams grew feminine.
Desire and greening joined.

The genre pullulated.
Venus came on vernal.
The body pastoral
Was sung or lamented
As was Arthur's, grass-graved.

What though of city loves?
Hamlet's country matters
Aren't foreign to the town:
We've enough to ensure
Cupid stays urban.

Poets of the precincts
Lacking parallels

Instinct with the instincts
Should exchange Arcady
For the brick of Cardiff.

Fingers that divagate
Along the vertebrae
Assume Sanquahar Street,
Sesquipedalian
Way to the timber yards.

The gasworks surplus burns
Beyond Jonkers Terrace.
Wind flutes and twists the flame,
The gold column broken
Into plaits and tresses.

The path to Thornbury Close
Dwindles into Thornhill
Where tight dawn is seeping
Bit by bit into day:
Someone slowly waking.

At the side of the path
Is an old lamp-standard
Whose bulb is lit but pale
Above the base's stamped
And simple avowal:

D. Evans   Eagle Foundry
Llandaff 1911.

TO WHOM IT MAY CONCERN

In strictly economic terms it could be said the valleys
no longer have a reason for existing.

Welsh Office Report

Dear Jones/Jenkins/Rees/Roberts
(delete whichever is inapplicable)
as your Secretary of State
let me fill you in on your future:

you don't have one
(not if you stay where you are).
Sorry not to beat about the bush,
but that's Economics for you.

The last few jobs will soon be gone:
women making tellies for the Nips and men
taking tourists round the mining museums
(ex-NUM members need not apply).

So it's the dole for the rest of you.
But I don't want you to think
we'll be shelling it out for ever.
After all, this is Government, not Oxfam.

No, what's needed is some initiative,
some oomph, some get-up-and-go.
Well, we'll take care of the initiative,
just so long as you get up and go..

774

(Anyway, who wants to stay in the Rhondda
with its 30% of pensioner households
without inside toilets – I mean
who'd be old with piles *and* chilblains?)

The obvious answer to all this
is something that combines
maximum security for your future
with investment on a large scale.

Led astray by red rabble-rousing,
you might think this Government
would never offer such a thing.
Well, you'd be wrong. We would and we do.

We have endeavoured, at great expense,
to find an area rich in those qualities
recognized as quintessentially Welsh:
lots of rain and lots of sheep.

Sufferers from *hiraeth* (I trust that's right)
needn't fret: Patagonia's just hours away
and there are echoes of home in your Islands'
new name – Falkland Fawr and Falkland Fach.

CAVEAT

Lovers are often blind
And poets lie on oath:
You're in a double bind
Trusting those who are both.

GWYNETH LEWIS

Gwyneth Lewis was born in Cardiff in 1959 and brought up Welsh-speaking. She read English at Girton College, Cambridge and, as a Harkness Fellow, took courses in Creative Writing with Derek Walcott and Joseph Brodsky at Columbia and Harvard, before writing a doctoral thesis on literary forgeries at Oxford. After a while as a journalist in New York and the Philippines, she returned to Wales to work as a television producer with the BBC. She writes in both Welsh and English, and has published six books of poems. Her English poems are to be found in *Parables & Faxes* (1995), *Zero Gravity* (1998), *Keeping Mum* (2003), and *Chaotic Angels* (2005). She is also the author of *Sunbathing in the Rain: A Cheerful Book about Depression* (2002) and *Two in a Boat: A Marital Voyage* (2005). In 2005 she was appointed the first National Poet of Wales. It was she who wrote the inscription now to be seen on the front of the Wales Millenium Centre. She lives in Cardiff.

THE HEDGE

With hindsight, of course, I can see that the hedge
was never my cleverest idea
and that bottles of vodka are better not wedged

like fruit in its branches, to counter the fears
and the shakes in the morning on the way to work.
Looking back, I can see how I pushed it too far

when I'd stop in the lay-by for a little lurk
before plunging my torso in, shoulder high
to the hedgerow's merciful root-and-branch murk

till I'd felt out my flattie and could drink in the dry
and regain my composure with the cuckoo-spit.
Then, with growing wonder, I'd watch the fungi,

lovely as coral in the aqueous light.
Lovely, that is, till that terrible day
when the hedge was empty. Weakened by fright

I leant in much deeper to feel out which way
the bottle had rolled and, cursing my luck
(hearing already what my bosses would say

about my being caught in this rural ruck),
I started to panic, so I tussled and heaved
and tried to stand upright, but found I was stuck.

I struggled still harder, but you'd scarcely believe
the strength in a hedge that has set its mind
on holding a person in its vice of leaves

and this one was proving a real bind.
With a massive effort, I took the full strain
and tore up the hedgerow, which I flicked up behind

me, heavy and formal as a wedding train.
I turned and saw, to my embarrassment,
that I'd pulled up a county with my new-found mane,

which was still round my shoulders, with its tell-tale scent
of loam and detritus, while trunk roads and streams
hung off me like ribbons. It felt magnificent:

minerals hidden in unworked seams
shone like slub silver in my churned-up trail.
I had brooches of newly built housing schemes

and sequins of coruscating shale;
power-lines crackled as they changed their course
and woodsmoke covered my face like a veil.

Only then did I feel the first pangs of remorse.
Still, nobody'd noticed so, quickly, I knelt,
took hold of the landscape, folded and forced

it up to a chignon which I tied with my belt.
It stayed there, precarious. The occasional spray
of blackthorn worked loose, but I quickly rebuilt

the ropey construction and tucked it away.
Since then I've become quite hard to approach:
I chew mints to cover the smell of decay

which is with me always. Food tastes of beech
and I find that I have to concentrate
on just holding the hairstyle since it's started to itch

and the people inside it are restless of late.
Still, my tresses have won me a kind of renown
for flair and I find my hair titillates

certain men who want me to take it down
in front of them, slowly. But with deepening dread
I'm watching my old self being overgrown

while scruples rustle like quadupeds,
stoat-eyed, sharp-toothed in my tangled roots
(it's so hard to be human with a hedge on your head!).

Watch me. Any day I'll be bearing fruit,
sweet hips that glint like pinpricks of blood
and my dry-land drowning will look quite cute

to those who've never fallen foul of wood.
But on bad days now I see nothing but hedge,
my world crazed by the branches of should,

for I've lost all centre, have become an edge
and though I wear my pearls like dew
I feel that I've paid for my sacrilege

as I wish for my autumn with its broader view.
But for now I submit. With me it will die,
this narrowness, this slowly closing eye.

from WELSH ESPIONAGE

V

Welsh was the mother tongue, English was his.
He taught her the body by fetishist quiz,
father and daughter on the bottom stair:
'Dy benelin yw *elbow*, dy wallt di yw *hair*,

chin yw dy ên di, *head* yw dy ben.'
She promptly forgot, made him do it again.
Then he folded her *dwrn*, and calling it fist,
held it to show her knuckles and wrist.

'Let's keep it from Mam, as a special surprise.
Lips are *gwefusau*, *llygaid* are eyes.'
Each part he touched in their secret game
thrilled as she whispered its English name.

The mother was livid when she was told.
'We agreed, no English till four years old!'
She listened upstairs, her head in a whirl.
Was it such a bad thing to be Daddy's girl?

ADVICE ON ADULTERY

The first rule is to pacify the wives
if you're presented as the golden hope
at the office party. You're pure of heart,
but know the value of your youthful looks.

Someone comments on your lovely back.
Talk to the women, and avoid the men.

In work they treat you like one of the men
and soon you're bored with the talk of the wives
who confide in you about this husband's back,
or that husband's ulcer. They sincerely hope
you'll never have children... it ruins your looks.
And did you know David has a dicky heart?

You go to parties with a beating heart,
start an affair with one of the men.
The fact you've been taking more care of your looks
doesn't escape the observant wives
who stare at you sourly. Cross your fingers and hope
that no one's been talking behind your back.

A trip to the Ladies. On your way back
one of them stops you for a heart to heart.
She hesitates, then expresses the hope
that you won't take offence, but men will be men,
and a young girl like you, with such striking looks...
She's heard nasty rumours from some of the wives.

She knows you're innocent, but the wives,
well, jump to conclusions from the way it looks...
In a rage you resolve she won't get him back,
despite the pressure from the other wives.
They don't understand... you'll stick with the men,
only they are *au fait* with affairs of the heart.

781

You put it to him that you're living in hope.
He grants that you're beautiful, but looks
aren't everything. He's told the men,
who smirk and wink. So now you're back
to square one, but with a broken heart.
You make your peace with the patient wives.

Don't give up hope at the knowing looks.
Get your own back, have a change of heart:
Ignore the men, start sleeping with the wives.

MOTHER TONGUE

'I started to translate in seventy-three
in the schoolyard. For a bit of fun
to begin with – the occasional 'fuck'
for the bite of another language's smoke
at the back of my throat, its bitter chemicals.
Soon I was hooked on whole sentences
behind the shed, and lessons in Welsh
seemed very boring. I started on print,
Jeeves & Wooster, Dick Francis, James Bond,
in Welsh covers. That worked for a while
until Mam discovered Jean Plaidy inside
a Welsh concordance one Sunday night.
There were ructions: a language, she screamed,
should be for a lifetime. Too late for me.
Soon I was snorting Simenon
and Flaubert. Had to read much more

782

for any effect. One night I OD'd
after reading far too much Proust.
I came to, but it scared me. For a while
I went Welsh-only but it was bland
and my taste was changing. Before too long
I was back on translating, found that three
languages weren't enough. The 'ch'
in German was easy, Rilke a buzz...
For a language fetishist like me
sex is part of the problem. Umlauts make me sweat,
so I need a multilingual man
but they're rare in West Wales and tend to be
married already. If only I'd kept
myself much purer, with simpler tastes,
the Welsh might be living...
                              Detective, you speak
Russian, I hear, and Japanese.
Could you whisper some softly?
I'm begging you. Please...'

ANGEL OF DEPRESSION

Why would an angel choose to come here
if it weren't important? Into stuffy rooms
smelling of cabbage? Into the tedium of time,
which weighs like gravity on any messenger
used to more freedom and who has to wear
a dingy costume, so as not to scare
the humans. Wouldn't even an angel despair?

Don't say it's an honour to have fought
with depression's angel. It always wears
the face of my loved ones as it tears
the breath from my solar plexus, grinds
my face in the ever-resilient dirt.
Oh yes, I'm broken but my limp
is the best part of me. And the way I hurt.

from ZERO GRAVITY

I Prologue

We watched you go
in glory: Shuttle,
comet, sister-in-law.

The one came back.
The other two
went further. Love's an attack

on time. The whole damn thing
explodes, leaving
us with our count-down days

still more than zero.
My theme is change.
My point of view

ecstatic. See how speed
transforms us? Didn't you know
that time's a fiction? We don't need

it for travel. Distance
is a matter of seeing;
faith, a science

of feeling faint objects.
Of course, this is no
consolation as we watch you go

on your dangerous journeys.
This out of mind
hurts badly when you're left behind.

Don't leave us.
We have more to say
before the darkness. Don't go. Stay

a little longer. But you're out of reach
already. Above us the sky
sees with its trillion trillion eyes.

VI

Last suppers, I fancy, are always wide-screen.
I see this one in snapshot: your brothers are rhymes
with you and each other. John has a shiner
from surfing. Already we've started counting time
backwards to zero. The Shuttle processed
out like an idol to its pagan pad.
It stands by its scaffold, being tended and blessed

by priestly technicians. You refuse to feel sad,
can't wait for your coming wedding with speed
out into weightlessness. We watch you dress
in your orange space suit, a Hindu bride,
with wires like henna for your loveliness.
You carry your helmet like a severed head.
We think of you as already dead.

PAUL HENRY

Paul Henry was born in Aberystwyth in 1959 and spent his early years in the village of Waunfawr, but his family moved to Llangynidr in rural Breconshire when he was a teenager; he is Welsh-speaking. After taking a degree in English and Drama at Rolle College in Devon, he had a variety of jobs, including that of arts administrator with the Association of Artists and Designers in Wales. He now lives in Newport. He has published five books of poems: *Time Pieces* (1991), *Captive Audience* (1996), *The Milk Thief* (1998), *The Slipped Leash* (2002) and *Ingrid's Husband* (2007); a selection of his work appeared as *The Breath of Sleeping Boys* in the Corgi series in 2004.

DAYLIGHT ROBBERY

Silent as cut hair falling
and elevated by cushions
in the barber's rotating chair
this seven-year-old begins to see
a different boy in the mirror,
glances up, suspiciously,
like a painter checking for symmetry.
The scissors round a bend
behind a blushing ear.

And when the crime's done,
when the sun lies in its ashes,

a new child rises
out of the blond, unswept curls,
the suddenly serious chair
that last year was a roundabout.

All the way back to the car
a stranger picks himself out
in a glass-veiled identity parade.

Turning a corner
his hand slips from mine
like a final, forgotten strand
snipped from its lock.

THE VISITORS

The women of my earliest years
fill this room's empty bay
without warning –

Brown Helen
Catrin Sands, Gwyneth Blue,
Nightingale Ann...

Their songs
return to a stranger's hand
the keys to all past tenancies,

Heulwen, Dwynwen, Bron y Llan...

I lie back, let them haunt,
the soft pulse of their lips
against the stone wall I've become,

Heather, Geta, Prydwen Jane...

listen hard across the dark
as their voices fade again,

Edith Smart, St. Julia...

sleep with the bedroom door ajar
in case they should drift back in.

HOLIDAY HOME

This house, built on clay, the last
to slide into the sea,
splits its sides with parting cracks
by those who signed the book:

the Burns of Slough, 1959 –
'This Shangri-La of Wales must never die!'...

Dunkirk's very own
Dot & Ken, June '65 –
'Flymo broken. Shears first class!'...

and, lest we forget, *'Rex The P-o-ET!'*
whose pawprint authenticates
some doggerel from 1972…

The Burns return in '86, retired,
smug, children's professions listed
as if it counted – Accountant, G.P.,
Lawyer and … one missing
from *'Our Infamous Four!'*

Thirty-nine summers

assembled and folded away
neatly, into a fractured box,
like jigsaws, cards or dominoes

lined up purely to be felled
by the tide, which raises the stakes
with each turned over wave.

Here's the owner, Spring '98:
Hilary B – *'Down for repairs,
to keep this place afloat!'*…

I take in her skewed watercolours
and books, half-comforted
that someone still flies with Biggles,
pedals, bare-kneed, to Smuggler's Top
up the stairwell's 1 in 1.

Sunday Englishman, I sleep
almost imperially
on these suspect foundations,

happy to dream the same dream
as those who signed its sheets
without thinking, with love,

whose breakages, like mine,
are paid for by the sea's refrain –

Come back... come back... come back...

COMINS COCH

Coming in from the yard, we unlearnt
the natural dance of play, stiffened
into rows, one for each class, hands
reaching to touch the shoulder in front,

to establish neat spaces. Miss Jones,
our referee, after the shuffled pack
took order, would double-check
her game of patience on the linear stones.

She once broke the cane on Emyr Brees,
set him homework to cut another
from his father's hedge. Quiet Heather's
tears ran down her knees.

On the canteen wall, Sir Ifan ap
Owen M. Edwards, above the sprouts
and gooseberries, turned away, motes
of the alphabet caught in his sun-trap.

Time spelt us right. We got xylophones,
slide-rules, projector-screens,
trips to Chester Zoo and St. Fagans,
a topic on Ghana's coffee beans.

Miss Jones started to smile. The smell
of swede from the kitchen grew tame.
I pulled on the ring of the steel frame
so the field hung at an angle

in the huge window all afternoon,
waiting for the bell. We discussed,
in English: Carlo, George Best
and the next Apollo. The blackboard spun.

With her back to us, that last Friday,
with her bucket, her housecoat over her dress,
she might have been polishing glass,
not square, chalk-marked infinities.

THE BREATH OF SLEEPING BOYS

Something is about to happen.

Legs are crossed fingers.

A cup falls from its handle.
A wall crumbles into the road
under the weight of a flower bed.

In their dreams
something is about to happen.

Saved and damned, saved and damned –
the breath of sleeping boys.

One wave breaks, another inhales
and something is about to happen.

Shrubbery trembles, blatantly.

November the 5th in Lilliput Road.
The introvert is out of its lid,
reads and repeats the word BANG

until the tarmac sky translates
madness back into stars, a life
into mute, mouse-like slippers.

Something is about to happen. *Sh.*

Here is the sound (let it pass)
of young blades, wading through grass.

The town's terrarium anticipates
that something is about to happen.

The wind adjusts its volume.

Peace carries a wicker basket.
Her dress takes in the new breeze.

With each step she's moving out,
stork on her heels, almost in flight.

Something is about to happen.

Winged eyes in a blameless dark
beat inside their hemispheres.
Their lashes are feathers dipped in oil.

Deeper than ocean beds, their dreams
rebuild Atlantis in domed air.

Saved and damned, saved and damned –
the breath of sleeping boys.

FOR *X* AND *Y*

God love the zimmer-frame,
the Social Worker's absorbent smile,
the hand-rail, detachable limb,
smoke-alarm, peep-hole,
the nest egg, the ancient fruit
still caught by Titan's chariot
in X and Y's maisonette,
the spats and the flimsy white hat.

God love their sallow babies
tucked away in a cradled bag,
the melanotic leaf on a bough
about to snap, the oblique wig,
bread and wine on wheels, the prayer,
the Dental Technician's pride, the crust,
the limpet-like corn plaster,
the seaside town Chiropodist.

God love the adapted plug,
the bath tub's elevating chair,
the cure for heartburn, the box of figs
unopened since 1964,
the sleeping pills, the rack of pipes,
the one tot of sherry, the lie.
God love the flutter, the papers,
the reading glass and new sky.

God love the Daycare Nurse,
the old songs, the incontinent tales,
the monologues and the listeners,
the rain that brings out the snails.
God love the hearing aid –
THE HEARING AID! – the view of the bay,
their shells and their sugary blood,
their stitches in time, their silver days.

And God love the wedding they wore
that hangs in a blind must

                              that waits
    for a hand on the difficult door
    and then

                          for a chime of light.

HOUSE

    Something keeps this drainpipe
    clinging to the wall,
    these rags to their line,
    this roof to the felt interior.

    It might be the boys
    racing snails
    in the back yard, or the sun

    casting you in your past,
    or this holiday,
    or the first ice-cream van,

    or the last, or the breeze
    plucking the blinds,
    humming inside a sound-box.

    I watch the pegged out marriages
    grow and retract,
    grow and retract,

love's deep-breathing exercise
in time with the wind.

*

A blue curtain
by an open window
is the summer's concierge.

It carries your love
up to an airier room,
where Rodin's *Clouds*,

the sole exhibit,
moves you to sighs.
(In a dark annexe,

the moon jangles its stars).
Holding on to the frame
I watch you fly,

the trees rejecting
countless drafts
and ending up with sky.

*

The snow has built
a village out of the town.
Strangers pick up words,

mould them again,
pelt each other
with persiflage.

The face on the glass runs.
Under the giant quilt
there's talk of peace,

two cold noses kiss,
cars are dumbfounded,
neutralized.

All two feet are
equal except for
the sizes of their shoes.

*

Look down from your silence,
your fine, Roman nose.
Here, in an unmade garden,

the dead have floated
up to their branches
and back into their buds.

Hold your breath.
Something now.
Habitually.

Spring.

FIONA OWEN

Fiona Owen was born in 1959 in Whitehaven, Cumberland, and brought up in the Middle East. She has degrees from the Open University and the University of Glamorgan. Since 1974 she has lived in Wales, latterly at Llanfaelog in Anglesey. She has learned Welsh, writes music, sings with her husband Gorwel Owen and runs Rhwng, an interdisciplinary arts group at the Ucheldre Centre near Holyhead. Her poems have been published in *O my Swan* (2003) and *Imagining the Full Hundred* (2005).

BOXING WITH SHADOWS

Tonight, the Queen of the Night sings
her wild staccato aria at full blast while I fling

my arms at gargoyles that wink and leer:
Edward Scissorhands has arrived with queer

pincer insect hands. He can slice you in two
meaning to caress. The room is scarcely blue

lit by the cool blue winter moon and still I whirl,
boxing with shadows, feeling myself uncurl

from where I hid, under the covers,
where it isn't safe after all; even lovers

are really on their own and must face alone
the hammering of that top F on frail bone

and skin that dries to dust. There's no one here
but the Queen of the Night, singing a clear
top F (is for Fear). I have perfect pitch, a perfect ear.

ANOTHER ANNUNCIATION

Perhaps if Gabriel came again to Mary
it would happen at the kitchen table,
in front of her husband, while they were
each sipping tea. Only she would see

the blaze of gold, feel the air waft around her,
so she must shiver at the spread of white wings
and the glory of The Perfect. She would first
feel her heart centre ignite, then the light

would melt lower, until her womb swelled
bright. *My Child* she would cry,
as the flame spread glorious through her
and she would cast her eyes to Heaven.

Joseph would see only her face strange,
shudders of tears then sudden laughter, eyes
changed, magnifying something that was not him.
He would grow afraid of her babblings,

thinking her mind gone. He would tell her
to stop, maybe try to shake her back to him.
My Love she would say, but her words
would fall into cliché. And the Archangel's wings

would whisper away, the tea in the cups gone gold.

STEPHEN KNIGHT

Stephen Knight was born in Swansea in 1960. He read English at Jesus College, Oxford, and now works as a freelance theatre director in London. Besides a novel, *Mr Schnitzel* (2001), he has published four books of poems: *Flowering Limbs* (1993), *The Sandfields Baudelaire* (1996), *Dream City Cinema* (1996) and, for children, *Sardines and Other Poems* (2004); the poems in the second of these are written in demotic Swansea English and are meant to be read aloud.

DOUBLE WRITING

Sea View, Water's Edge, Atlantis,
lugubrious Guest Houses welcome the tide

after dark, from the opposite side of the road.
Their windows are lit with VACANCIES.

At closing time, Covelli's chips do a roaring trade
though his name has flaked from the side of the building.

Tighter than fists in the gaps in wooden benches,
pages of the local paper soak in vinegar.

Wind sizzles through trees
while, from the promenade, waves reach for the last bus

back into town. Ticking over in the back seat,
somebody sleeps it off. His thumb is in his mouth.

The timetable never works
and graffiti spreads through the shelter like wires –

refinements of a thick, black autograph
above the spray of glass, below the one-armed clock.

In West Cross garages, drums, guitars and microphones
huddle together, waiting to be famous.

Things go quiet. Things are unplugged.
Cutlery is laid out for the morning.

THE HEART OF SATURDAY NIGHT

IssFair wuz-honourCaw-munlarzSatdee:
doorjums, toff yapples, goalfish. Lie kytowld,
wee wenhonourGhosetrayn, mean Bare vully –

z'krap. Unwenchy wear gnome twavver-tee,
try duhWallsuz. Brill! Addter-reely old.
IssFair wuz-honourCaw-munlarzSatdee.

Ease werkinnerWallsuz awlnite wunny,
issgeezerKev eyesoreAir. Ease reel ye'owld.
Wee wenhonourGhosetrayn, mean Bare vully.

WenairwuzzerwindblowinoffaSee
izzreelyNoblin...Jeezus, *coarse* eyezcold –
IssFair wuz-honourCaw-munlarzSatdee,

803

caw-munzfuhkinfree zin!...Ease twennyfree,
Kev: why tandzAnna chaynmaydoubter-gold.
Wee wenhonourGhosetrayn, mean Bare vully.

Kev addSmak (whytes tough) asswaddyshowdme
Om-eye-life! Sed easegoneergerrit souled.
Issfair wuz-honourCaw-munlarzSatdee.
Wee wenhonourGhosetrayn, mean Bare vully.

THE BIG PARADE

Here they come past High Street station, everyone I've ever
known
and some I've only seen on television, marching three
abreast,

my Junior School headmistress at the front – Miss Morgan
with her bosoms now as much a shelf as when I saw her last

it must be thirty years ago – hurling to the sky a silver baton
(twirling up it tumbles earthwards like the prehistoric bone

in Kubrick's *2001*): turning at the Dizzy Angel Tattoo Studio
down Alexandra Road then into Orchard Street they go,

my other teachers – Grunter, Crow and Mister Piss on stilts –
juggle furry pencil-cases, worn board-dusters, power balls,

there's Adam West, his Batman outfit taut around his waist,
and then the Monkees, Mickey hammering a drum the others

804

blowing on kazoos: they navigate the Kingsway roundabout
to pass the Odeon where everyone is dropping ticker-tape

a storm of paper falls on Malcolm in a stripy tank-top, John
and Hugh and catches in the hairnet of our loony neighbour

Nestor – keeping up despite an ancient Zimmer frame –
and Bill the communist and Mister Shaddick, hirer of skips,

his brown bell-bottoms crack and snap around his platform
shoes,
the collar of his paisley-patterned shirt's two giant set-squares

look! a girl from Pennsylvania who kissed me once, still
thirteen
after twenty years, I shouldn't recognise her smile and yet
I do,

I call to her but she's too far away, atop a jewelled elephant
she's waving to the crowd like someone fresh from outer
space:

travelling along St. Helen's Road towards the sea, the cheers,
the noises of the instruments resounding through the city
centre

out, past vinyl three-piece suites and lava lamps in
Eddershaws
go Mary Dorsett, Julie Dolphin, Tony (very much alive),

Rhiannon then a row of faces I can't put a name to now
but still I wave and shout and watch them disappear,

the boy who butted me one break-time skulking at the back,
the music fading, blurring with the gulls, the sea, the sounds

of people going home, till everywhere I look
the streets are quiet as a fall of snow.

DAEDALUS
(for my father)

The sink is choked with dirty plates,
  Dead leaves, twigs – the tree
Outside the house disintegrates

  But Daedalus could be
No happier now he's begun
  To build his dream. To me

The watery autumnal sun
  Is cold and yet he sings
Out loud he's having so much fun.

  Obscured by coffee rings
& marmalade, his drawings flap
  Among the breakfast things

When breezes lap
  Doors and walls, our dripping tap.

*

Although he's working with antiques
    His father owned (the saw,
Flaked with liver spots, stalls & squeaks;

    The chisel fails to score
The softest wood; nails snap or fold)
    Still, shavings crust the floor

And clouds of sawdust fall like gold
    All afternoon: drifts grow
In saucepans. Sometimes, when that old

    Paint-speckled radio
Beside the kettle plays a song
    He used to know

He sings along –
    Every other word is wrong!

*

He works all day, intent, absurd,
    Narrowing his eyes
Because his pencil marks have blurred

    And nothing's cut to size.
At sunset, when a sudden wind pours
    Through every room then dies

Away, he's there still, on all fours
    To improvise with string
& strips of Sellotape. Though doors

    Slam shut, though feathers cling
To him – his gluey hands, his hair,
    His clothes – he's whistling

Without a care.
    Feathers falling everywhere.

ELVIS

He's out there somewhere, in the dark –
a pair of oil-stained overalls,
a monkey wrench. When drivers park
to stretch their legs and scratch their balls

he appears with a chamois leather
in a pail of suds. He doesn't pass
the time of night, curse the weather
nor laugh; he only cleans the glass.

Bored, tired of counting off the states
they've spanned, they can't see how odd
he is, the man who never talks;

the tubby, balding guy who waits
for tips, then shrugs.
                    The one who walks
across the forecourt like a god.

AFTER LESSONS

The classrooms are as dead as winter trees.
You hold your breath along the corridor –
Your plimsolls creak. There is no other noise.

A single light ices the polished floor.
You turn and, somehow, end up in The Boys,
A row of basins level with your knees.

You shouldn't be inside this place so late.
I wonder what you thought you might achieve
By squinting at the blackboard. What, and how?

In the dark, you wipe your nose across your sleeve.
It's much too late to put your hand up now.
There's someone outside, waiting at the gate.

ANNA WIGLEY

Anna Wigley was born in Cardiff in 1962 and still lives in the city. She read English at Cardiff University and currently works for George Thomas Hospice Care. Her two collections of poems are *The Bird Hospital* (2002) and *Dürer's Hare* (2005); she has also published a book of short stories, *Footprints* (2004).

IN THE CASTLE GROUNDS

Gaudy as transvestites
the peacocks float

their long torpedoes
of petrol blue,

opera singers' eyes
painted for twilight

sightings
from turreted rooms.

Haughty and rapt
as Sitwells in smoking suits,

bold from the pages
of Beardsley and Wilde,

they pace the lawns
like dowagers,

last exhibits of an age
of disdainful indolence,

when their high-strung cries
were thrown like banners

over the ramparts,
and the coffers of their tails

opened idly to amaze
with a sunburst of coins.

DÜRER'S HARE

Still trembling, after five hundred years.
Still with the smell of grass
and the blot of summer rain
on her long, thorn-tipped paws.

Look how thick the fur is,
and how each thistledown hair
catches the light
that glistens even in shadow
from the trimmed plush of the ears.

How did he keep her still?
She was crouched there long enough
for him to trace the fragile hips
and ribs beneath the mink,

811

to feel the pale edges
of the belly-pouch,
the sprung triggers of the flanks.
The nose shimmers
where the short hairs grow in a rosette.
Go on, touch it.

For she's only here for a moment,
Dürer's hare;
the frame can barely hold her.
Her shadow is a shifting thing,
slippery as a raincloud in wind,
and even as you look,
twitches to be gone.

THE BLUE SKIRT

Today you bought a blue skirt,
wandering small among the shop rails
that after twelve sequestered months
were exotic as Tibet.

Feel it, you said,
holding up the sheeny petal of the cloth,
then letting it float.

It was no ordinary blue,
and as you moved
it also moved through many hues,
as if the blue of forty fields

where speedwell and forget-me-not
grow thick as thistles,
was cropped and threaded in its folds.
You swung it like a gorgeous girl

and later wore it full and loose
with silk and downy wool.
Under it, your burning hip
half-eaten, hardly showed.

THE COMB

My blue comb fell out onto the grass
and lay there like a traitor's kiss.
Both of us stopped and stared at it.
Soft rain began to fall, the graves
were leaning their white-rusted heads,
and in the deep grass my blue comb glowed.
I want to look nice for you, it said.

PATRICK JONES

Patrick Jones was born in Tredegar in 1965 and educated at Swansea University. He earns a living as a writer and lives at Brynawel, near Blackwood. He has published six books of poems: *the guerilla tapestry* (1995), *the protest of discipline* (1996), *mute communion* (1997), *detritus* (1997), *commemoration and amnesia* (1999), and *against* (2003); a selection of his verse and plays appeared as *fuse* in 2001.

DEMONSTRATIONS FOR EXISTENCE

a. the unification

'I won't call it a strike. I would call it a demonstration for existence... the miners in South Wales are saying, 'We are not accepting the dereliction of our mining valleys, we are not allowing our children to go immediately from school into the dole queue. It is time we fought.'

Emlyn Williams 1981

tomorrow

filed away into the redtaped self assurance of office
                                                          regulations
newlaboured toried amnesia
of the gutwrenched days of dust and blackened blood –

this be the verse of commemoration

of

swallowing servility
spitting our dignity
making miracles from everydayed work in the belief of a
                                                       better place
through education
from a blacked out face
for emancipation
of a solaced smile
from walking underground miles
of creating a life to be
of communal obligation
of paying for the books in the library

this be the verse of commemoration

through the lies of this fucking century
first
thatchered denial of our fragiled history
now
blair
sits in socialist splendour
ignoring this struggling community
YOU
can call it politics blind us with statistics
starve us with your economics
lie to us with your campaign rhetoric
loud hail about your humanity
BUT
now   now   now

today

as the breathing blisters and lungs cough black
you imprison us with the degrading foreign factory
preach to us about common decency
but as
the eyes and hands that wait for the post to drop
but what about fucking morality
£6000 for a life underground?
your silence is like bedwellty cemetery
but without the stuttered dignity
without the sense of urgency
of 80,000 souls waiting to be heard

this –   this has to stop

and   as

tomorrow

breathes through the green haze of an oxygen mask
let us remember the mountained fresh

yesterdays

of labour, family, dignity and meaning
                              and let us, through
these voices
these truths
these histories
these eyes

these lungs
in unity in hope in disgust
exhale
and
let them hear HERE our screaming
let decency prevail
and allow

today   today   today

to be to be TO BE

still breathing

still   breathing –

tomorrow
to;   tomorrow

SAMANTHA WYNNE RHYDDERCH

Samantha Wynne Rhydderch was born in Aberystwyth in 1966. She read Classics at Newnham College, Cambridge, and studied Creative Writing at Cardiff University; she lives in New Quay, Ceredigion. She has published a pamphlet of poems, *Stranded on Ithaca* (1998), and *Rockclimbing in Silk* (2001).

ROCKCLIMBING IN SILK

wasn't something she'd intended
from the start.
The castle's finger
beckoned jaggedly.
I blame the sky
or the unconsoled sea,
the wind bandaging
the towers.

The seagulls, disenchanted
with the penitentiary,
mimed agony,
fought off the sun
that forced her down
among the irises,
the uncertain air
in her throat.

THE X-RAY ROOM

I am dismantled in monochrome
on the screen opposite the student doctors,
their gaze moving from me here to

me translated into porcelain
there. I am Exhibit A, my symmetry
unmasked by this cut and paste version

of my guts hermeneutically sealed
in negative. I stand by my parallel
text as if to elucidate

evisceration. My bones
in triplicate have nowhere to hide.
Their fragility becomes heraldic

when these exegetes invoke them
in Latin. You see, my other
has been deceiving me all along.

FIRST AID CLASS

I kneel with the head gardener in my arms,
feeling the pulse in his neck the way he touches
leaves in real life, his skin a series of impressions
on calico beside me. Everyone an iridologist
dressing head wounds with the enthusiasm
of the starched in field hospitals before 1915.

We learn that fainting is merely the rearrangement
of blood, my bronchial tree simply a cameo of me,
but more vitriolic. I am eager to see the cyanosed
around the edges, intuit a cardiac arrest.
Now and then I hear the thrum of a defibrillator,
arterial gestures from the past. Handling a rib-cage
over lunch I have a sense of ornament.
Finally we study a handout of unconsciousness,
poison ivy groping at the window panes.

I imagine us meeting under other circumstances,
coy about our intimacy. Then I begin to understand
the way surgeons avoid the resuscitated
in *The Lamb & Flag*, the gardener playing cribbage
something too abstract, why terminology matters:
'terracotta' to 'red', 'episode' only a dot
on a screen.

We are asked to elevate a limb: the rituals of a sacrament,
the illustrations in the manual mute in savagery
as my hands around those open veins.

FARMYARD MIRRORS

They will take you by surprise on backroads,
bereft of dressing tables, lurching from hedges,
rejected, astute, crucial at bends, luring
tractors out of lanes, blotched with mildew.

The glamour they once absorbed whole, glints
tarnished. How they long to hold the glow inside
a bedroom window, feel the heaviness of drawers,
be polished, strung with necklaces,

not nettles. Indisputable, ever-admiring at dusk,
frowning at dawn, their loyalty always presumed
upon. Such fall from grace would be unthinkable
to those who carved their fluted legs,

to the organdie runners pressed
under a thick rectangle of glass, stains of
L'Air du Temps officials as the bindweed is now.
How could the spectrum of reflection

invite such a betrayal? Weather permitting
the farmyard mirrors will survive two more
decades of deterioration, deflection on location,
before a recognition scene disappears forever.

WINDOW DRESSING

The frame large as my picture window at home
with its acre of sea, here in Amsterdam
we look in at her combing pale hair, curtained

by a drape plush as blood, a huge bed untouched
and pure as a museum piece, six dildoes
lined up on the mantelshelf like school prizes.

In the shop next door artificial fingers
point to a sky clear as the canal waters
that hold seven-storey houses upside down.

I enter a tulip stall, in awe and bound
by the glamour of the petals. When I come out
I am holding a bunch of wooden flowers.

They will never die, unlike he whose tombstone
I lay them on now, his fibreglass leg gone cold.

WILLOW PATTERN

When you dropped the plate, the bridge broke
in two and the tiny blue ferns were torn.
Like us they would not mend. They spoke
in their dismembering; we could not mourn.
I wrote your name in willowy
handwriting on a scrap of paper, dropped
it in a jar of jasmine tea
which three hours in the freezer turned to rock.

On our first walk I plucked a fern,
arranged it in a cast full of hot wax.
Now the candle is almost burnt
away, a hard miniature pool acts
as evidence on a plate, a spell
cast and lost on a pagoda shell.

DERYN REES-JONES

Deryn Rees-Jones was born in Liverpool in 1968; as a child
she spent her summers with grandparents in Wrexham.
Educated at Bangor University and Birkbeck College,
University of London, she teaches Creative Writing at
Liverpool Hope University. She has published three books of
verse, *The Memory Tray* (1994), *Signs Round a Dead Body*
(1998) and *Quiver* (2004). She is also the author of a
critical study of women poets, *Consorting with Angels*
(2005), and editor of *Modern Women Poets* (2005).

LARGO

Each week, our great Aunt Doris came to teach me piano,
rattling her strings of purple plastic beads, and smelling of
carbolic,

her emerald boa draped around her like a mutilated treble
clef,
her loose false teeth clacking like a metronome

as she pointed with a knitting needle to the notes of
Dvořák's *Largo*
with which I soon grew bored, and played too quickly, and
too loud.

Sometimes she'd tell me stories as I played
about the man she loved before the war, the telegram

they sent to let her know that he was killed
in action at the front. And by the end of half-an-hour

I was so proud – my fingers aching from such speed
and was left breathless. Both our eyes were full.

I never really learnt to play the piano, but for that
one inimitable tune, and not long after

great Aunt Doris died, from a tumour leaving her first
stone deaf, then blind. Years later, now, on empty afternoons

I play the *Largo* sometimes, the way that she had wanted it,
smoothly, and slowly, as if somehow those belated sounds

could compensate for all the sad percussions of her life,
the palpitating gaps, the ill-struck chords.

MAKING FOR PLANET ALICE

You stand on a chair with a wrinkled nose
In your glittery tiara. Queen Alice and her Queendom!

The room is full of ordinariness
And your laughter like a tossed coin

Spins into the air. Take me to that place, I say,
Where the trees grow upside-down and their thick bright roots

Explore the sky. Take me to that place
Over the backs of houses, past the forgotten railway,

Across the continents by rickshaw
Where the sun sets in a moment, then slowly rises

Like a blush. Where the door in the wall opens to yards
Of purple strawberries, a yellow field of grasshoppers –

Their low sweet hum. Where the green pool of your
                                                    imagination
Laps the edges of your head like sleep, its yawning
                                                    mountains

Rock like lullabies and clocks, and pampas grasses
Stroke your forehead in the winds. Quietly, quietly

Take me to that strange safe place, by bus, by unicycle
Helicopter, aeroplane. Let me sail to Planet Alice in my heart,

My leaky coracle; let me circumnavigate the moon,
The foam of snow white stars. Take me to that strange place

That hurts me. That we both knew once upon a time.
Which I've not only lost, but forgotten how to say.

JIM

The way she loved him was the colour green –
Not some blue china Wednesday in the sky;
Her body took him for the mountains, lay in him

825

To suckle him with flowers. Perhaps she loved him
Like tomorrow, though her head was lacking
In particulars – such things as names and dates
Eluded her, he knew. But looking for the snow

The weatherman had promised her, it was something
The rain implied, migrating to her eyes as she grew wary
Even of the female authors on his bookshelves
Lining the orange of his bedroom wall
With hardbacks, broken paper spines.
Walking alone one afternoon in early Spring
A passing friend asked where she lived. She smiled,

The clouds reflected in her eyes: her mouth
Was thinking of the taste of hills, and
Efo cariad, she said, remembering the sound
His brink-of-love would make, allowing
Her forgetfulness this time, the pattern
Of his single syllable, abbreviated name.

LOVESONG TO CAPTAIN JAMES T. KIRK

Captain. I never thought we'd come to this,
but things being what they are, being adults,
stardate '94 it's best to make the best of it
and laugh. What's done is done. Perhaps
I'll start to call you Jim or Jamie, James...

No one was more shocked than me when I arrived
(*the lady doth protest*) to find

my bruised and rainy planet disappeared
and me, materialised and reconstructed
on board the Starship Enterprise, all 60s
with my lacquered bee-hive and my thigh-high
skirt in blue, my Doctor Marten's and my jeans
replaced by skin-tight boots
and scratchy blue-black nylons rippling-
up my less-than-perfect calves. Sulu
looked worried. Spock cocked up one eyebrow
enigmatically, branding my existence
perfectly illogical. How nice, I thought. His ears.
Uhura smiled of course, and fiddled
with her hair. *O James.* Truth is
I loved you even as a child …

O slick-black-panted wanderer holding
your belly in, your phaser gun
on stun, and eyes like Conference pears! You're not my type
but I undress you, and we fuck
and I forgive your pancake make-up and mascara,
the darker shadows painted round your eyes.
The lava-lamp goes up and down. We're
a strange unison. Politically
mismatched. Our mutual friend
The Doc takes notes. *Go easy Bones!*
Scotty is beaming and shouts *Energise*,
and all of a sudden you remind me

Of my Dad, my brother and my mum,
my body rising like a shadow from the past

on top of you. As I press your arms behind your head
I drape my breasts so that you
brush my nipples gently with your lips almost
involuntarily as we boldly go. Come slowly, Captain,
and we do, with both our pairs of eyes tight closed.

FROM HIS COY MISTRESS

Some days I think I will become a nun,
book in a convent miles away,
cut off my hair, and dress in black
wanting to purge myself of men.

I'd kneel and pray and chant a lot,
lie in a narrow bed,
devising titles of unwritten books:
A Semiotics of Flirtation. Love:
Some Concepts of the Verb 'To Sin'.

One thing's for sure. By wanting you,
I'm not the woman that I think I am.
I cannot eat or sleep at all,
just think about your lovely mouth

the eerie moonlight and the Northern seas.
And hope my body's still the temple
that you'd come upon, by chance,
to excavate, a hundred years from now,

burn incense in, and dance and sing,
oh, yes and weeping, worship in.

FRANCES WILLIAMS

Frances Williams was born in Bridgend in 1968. She studied
Fine Art at Liverpool University and Sculpture at Chelsea
College. A former editor of the magazine *Diva*, she is now a
curator at Tate Britain. She has published three books of
verse: *Flotsam* (1987), *Wild Blue* (2000), and *The Red
Rubber Ball of Happiness* (2003).

ISAAC NEWTON

He told the time of day from
The shadow of his chair: dials
Thrown off its legs were minute
Accurate. Four pegs glowed solid
Trailing their tails of absence,
The static comets in
A wheeling room. While ants,
Insistent and agitated, crossed
Through the ribbed light
Busied with gathering.

It came to him, he said, because
He held the puzzle at the centre
Of his black circle. Could the earthly
Drag of gravity pull the heaven's
Looped motions? He took every
View of it, riding haloes to gaze
At the heads of saints, his satellite

Rimming the bald earth – a monkish
Contemplation, fathomed in silence.

This mind was alien as a moon
To his limp limbs. His hands hung
Useless, pale and thin, baboon mittens
Bereft of the vigour of trees. Flesh
Betrayed him – his pricks of sweat itching
At the sinful thoughts he sought to quell,
Keeping the pulse throbbing in the
Abstract darkness of his cranium.
All around him, a leprosy in touch.

He fled from plague to an orchard brim
Heavy with red pippins, a wind juggled crop.
Here was his wealth. In his pockets
He counted coins like discs of sun, touching
Them with a curious patience
Born of passionate detachment.

In a frowsy stupor, his apple dropped,
Wormless and perfect into
His aching lap. He did not pick
The fruit. It picked him, faithful
And flushed in his virgin palms.

OYSTER EATING

Luxury doesn't get more
Astringent. Plucked from
Cloudy depths, my plate

Of oysters wait for their
Moment, little glaciers
In silky cups. I suck

An avalanche of flesh.
Then clear my throat
Of their strange salt
Swallow, more touch
Than taste. Out of these
Rocky skulls, the brains

Come slippery as sex.
Each one tips over the
Rugged callused lips of
Its single shoe to speak
Only with the one tongue,
A probe both first and

Last. Such rash
Adventurers. Jonahs
In my whale. And also
Something sad in our
Hurried consummation.
A dozen down, I reach

A check-mate moment
In this game of numbers.
As Casanova, on a lucky
Night, might break a line
Of kisses, to pause for breath
On heaven's racing staircase.

EINSTEIN'S EYES

They stole your eyes – some Sicilian
Scientist making a bounty of your pharaoh
Sight. No longer lens conductors

Of the light, they float, oyster soft,
Locked in a pungent jar, slippery
As coddled eggs. Vision unstalked,

Your plucked jellies joke with horror
Unsavoury as Lenin's crumbling nose
Or the silver crested femur of a saint.

I half expect a spiral coil to bounce
Them back, droop from glasses with
A clown's sprung pounce. Or when

On Halloween, we turned off the lights
And passed peeled grapes from hand
To hand, shrieking at the witches' brew.

But these were you. Your orbs are ripe
For picking by Picasso, rolled to the edge
Of a diamond portrait. He would not

Be so cruel as the scalpel wielding
Doctor who saw fit to lift your closed
Lids, prising out this foul trophy.

832

No wit or purpose other than a quack
Science, pretending an empirical method.
Spawn of your own cold universe,

You swill in an ocean soup
Of serious portent, formaldehyde's
Ethereal hue working its dull miracle.

Your blood is blue, a glue of sticky
Tears, as though the juiced sky
Had filled up the cups that once eyed

Its wide expanse. Your white moons
Have fallen out of orbit. No glory
In their mucus membrane sight – your

Stars, your universe, are neither seen
By day nor night, but in unblinking clarity –
The bald slime of your clearest gaze.

DOPPLEGÄNG

All through February I hoard words,
Food for the famine, and comfort eat,
Porridge after bowl of mash. Stuff
Is the only thing between me

And extinction. I make room for every
Full spoon. I excavate everything
Lay it on white sheets for labelling
Into my sack of porcelain skin I fill

The bulky stash, shore up against
Absences that press against every
Window in netted frost. All stories,
By way of explanation, don't suffice,

Grow fat and full, meander with slow
Imponderables. What is it to know?
I wake in a room I've remembered
Whose shapes I cannot shake, walk

Into walls like a solid ghost. Outside
There's been a fall of snow. The trees
Thrill in the sudden nakedness. Breath
Wrestles with the air. I am a dragon

Spilling from wide nostrils. Isn't
Talking to yourself the first sign
Of madness? See how my hands
Shrug, miming their suggestions,

Magician gloved: I'm spelling out
A sculpture of expediencies, moulding
Air, fitting it to exhalations of spoken
Word. The hill rises, opens its crystal

Pathways of infinite variation. I soak
A line of prints, the glazed grass
Like needles underfoot. I pass,
Heavy as a dinosaur. I'm leaving

My own trail, the miracle seconds of
History In The Making. Someone
Treads behind me, stepping up, person
I used to be, and won't stop following.

LLOYD ROBSON

Lloyd Robson was born in Cardiff in 1969. He has lived in the city most of his life and earns a living as a writer, visual artist and workshop tutor. Among his books of verse and prose (he deliberately mixes the genres) are: *edge territory* (1996), *city & poems* (1994), *letter from sissi* (1997), *cardiff cut* (2001), and *bbboing! & associated weirdness* (2003).

from CARDIFF CUT

best known little known i shake myself in sleep; yagged shagged & stereotyped
i sustain my recovery position til the cold water wakes me (feel pins&needles then the next sharp *ping!* realise water now freezing)

& sudden there's half the council workforce in me street/bath/ears & there's roadworks fuckin everywhere all thro adamsdown right outside my window all for the sake of beaming an extra thousand channels to me screen. there is nothing in life can shift me arse as fast as roadworks & a cold tub of water to sleep in/the remnants of hallucinogens losing their power/my vision flicks between grey & colour (the vision of the killer burnt on the victim's retina/in my eyes there are admissions to no thought bar silence & sleep).

blue sky outa bah throom window

it ties me. this inability to tell real from reality, i know what i think i know but the real leaves me panicky (rapid fade to black&white...)

(*luck? what did i do with it?* i did what most would do: i pisst it up against the wall) & now i know i recognise the meaning of life as survival, i don't like but who the fuck askt for my opinion...

& all i can think of is smashing thro windscreens.

        ....

look forward to a 4.30 breakfast at tony's/a wet salty yoke of a satdee morning delayed til the afternoon if i'm sharp before football (finalscores, not kickoff); look forward to the earlymorn knock of godbotherers come sunday (satdee written off, all i'll do today is smoke, shit & coff stuff up) i'll burn their fuckin ears off if they ever come near me but

i refuse to accept my social limitations
i refuse to be tied to being only one person
i am a myriad a myriad my raid a myriad
i am
    dj tabloyd
    (aka cohort for uncle weirdness & the defenders of
                                        dublov)
i am
    el throbbo

837

        (*I thank yaow*, & all derivatives of)
i am
        nifty leftwinger too fuckt to run
i am
        sensitive poet & occasional cunt
i am
        experienced in champagne & swimming pools
        dolequeue headslum fodder thug
i am
        model employee
        for the first two months
i am
        fotograb
        donut maker *par excellence*
i am
        (button up)
i am
        memories of dreams & escapee from nitemare
        somebody's visible friend (speak only in private)
i am
        creator
        offspring
i am

(who begat *who came from* isn't up for the task)

i am
        brother
i am
        AX10

i am

      card carrying member
      rep for the union
      (subs up lad)

        ('it is better for a man to conquer himself
        than for a king to conquer & capture many cities')

i am

      spokesman for myself alone
      (myself meself MESLEF: a union of one)
      '1001 questions to ask of your city'

& i have none.

    ...*
      grasp nettle.

          find myself

            no longer
         compliant

sick from the taste of tobacco

&
i feel like
feeling

freeform

or

i feel like
feel like
freeform

or

i feel like feeling
freefall

or

i feel like feeling
feel like feeling feel like feel like feel like feeling like feeling
feel in freefall
feel like freefall

(i gotta turn the tape ove
rrrrrrrrrrrrrrrrrrrrrrrrrrrrrrrrrrrrrrrrrrrrrrrrrrrrrrrrrrrrrrrrrrrrrr
                                    or so people tell me)

& what's this?
you may ask yourself/ask me when the sun is up
i need some distance to crash out
(it is already)

(the great celtic *what goes around comes around* research
grant juss ran out/sponsored by the donut makers of cardiff)

the crash bang wallop of intentions
the uh, u wat? of shortterm memory problems
the miniature microdot of truth

     'poetry: the oil of the universe'

bending it in

(sometimes I hafta disappear off the face of the earth,
                        sometimes for years)

& the splash awake

& by the time we see the sky it's already out of date

(aark at that!
     there were priests on strike it lucky tonite!)

     & sim city sez it's time to build a powerstat
     & syndicate sez it's time to assassinate

the world is yours is yours is yours

     'it takes courage to enjoy'

(energy: nothing! without structure).

    ...*

i stopt learning when i began taking sides
(doan wanna make excuses i was multisubstanced at the
                                                    time)

my increasing hard colon & soft underbelly
i see all this in the water around me

asea on the float of tea & fags
living on the hoof/
                    off the cuff

i see all this in a cold cup

        (how do i feel?
                        like i wanna stop my mouth a month...)

aetiology

splenetic *tang*

                    (i can hear myself)

phazed & dysfluent

(i may have to go visit
my homelands)

        life is

'cashflow & lifestyle'

(charm is a con)

(*drowns in a steamd human chillum bong*)

(fadeout
      at long
        laaasst ...)

KATHRYN GRAY

Kathryn Gray was born in Caerffili in 1973 and brought up in Swansea. She read German at Bristol University and took a master's degree in Medievalism at York. A selection of her work appeared in *Anvil New Poets* in 1991 and her first collection as *The Never-Never* in 2004. She lives in London as a freelance writer.

THE ITALIANS IN THE RAIN

You could almost see them down the backstreets
as it bucketed on a Saturday night, the purr
of a Vespa, his right foot pressed on the kerb,
as he leans over, calls to a girl, and she parleys
a while, then hops on, wraps herself around him.
Or along the sea front, in the mirrors of Sidoli's
where a couple share a Neopolitan with one spoon,
the crest of biscuit between them, fight out
who gets the strawberry and who the chocolate.
You think it's just possible that she always knew
what he'd done with her best friend and sister.
Quicker than the grabbed coat and clipped heels,
from Landore to Y Crwys, now you hear
the parked Fiats as they creak at the beauty spots,
slapped faces and the smashed bottles outside the bars.
And maybe you see there is a man who lifts up
the fryer with its welded batter or does the books

on a stool by the till, the packets of coffee on the shelves
behind him. There's a watercolour of St. Mark's
or the Trevi fountain under the arrow to the toilets,
and as this rain shows no sign of stopping, he looks on
it all, gestures at two passers-by who try the door
a WE ARE CLOSED, returns to his work, forgets where he is.

METEOROLOGY

And, passing through only, it was then I thought of you,
how once you'd said it was that I opened up to you
as a cleft in the clouds can speak of a heat, a dry spell,
as a tumble of nimbostratus can come at us from a slouch
of any horizon. And I thought of that very afternoon,
terraced gardens strung with the swings of pegged lines,
which were, in fact, the isobars on which the *smalls*
of our lives were hung; and then it was I saw, here
and there, the woman with the basket, pulling down
each of the ephemera, a damp cotton corner of bedsheet,
while tarpaulins were drawn across a court in Wimbledon.
And then light occurred, as if an idea, over someone's
kitchen lino. I thought of telegraph wires running
relays from county to county in a slip and grip of hands,
while a motorway sped and brought to us an onwards,
a loss, and everything everywhere as weather, and I looked
out to a lopped half of sun dropped upon an arable land,
before returning again to where the convex rain held
steady the tremens of the window and, for the moment,
there was a yard, tilted right hip, a woman with a basket.

ASSIGNATION

Strangers come and go and come, and true, we only just
hear them
through these walls – but enough – as they've heard us by
the hour,
while a typical afternoon's light falls half-hearted on a
corded kettle,
thimbles of milk, the crisp sachets of sugar, the PG Tips,
Nescafé.

It's what we've done with time, not wanting to be that
much alone
(or so it goes), and I've filled in each moan, the intervals
between
conversation, stung by the heat of their drawn-curtain
futures
and uniform fumble for the alias and explanation. *It's not
me, it's you.*

But they're not us, you've said, pressed the point so many
times
I repeat it in your absence like a joint signature we might
have penned
elsewhere, but then we didn't; everything being settled in
advance
and cash, the faux-leather reception register's long become
defunct.

But whenever it is that we walk the familiar, bald-carpeted
corridors,

curled from the chipped skirting, appalled by their own
                                          frank horror,
and on whichever floor, it's fear keeps my head down,
                                          moves me fast,
in case my love and I were to find ourselves in the arms of
                                          another.

GUILT

It can seem like history, ad hoc, Imperial Leather
lathered away to the gold leaf sticker,
the coal tar smoke through a fist of water.

In a B&B in Colwyn Bay you wake to find the old brand
and feel morning spread from sea to land
or think of your father from nowhere, understand

how a workday morning for years was little more
than the end-of-terrace billboard's just post-war
Lifebuoy carp of *down there, behind the ears,*

Now Wash Your Hands in the raw. The filth
of an inside-collar Saturdays at dances. The *Macbeth*
you read when you were twelve. Hold your breath.

You spell out that word against a mirror. *Cunt.*
Remember how she gave you a clout,
dragged you to the basin to clean your mouth out?

We're better than that, you cant as of old; the Lux
slapped against the beige flannel, the knucks
she lathered up babbling to the Armitage Shanks.

DETTOL STINGS

Before you know it, you're walking the appointed corridor,
a dark vinegar or urine colour and, of course, there's the
                                                          bucket
left outside 3B; inside it, noises, a canon of playing field
                                                          voices.
From nowhere, schoolyard concrete rises up to meet your fall

and as a ball careers down a verge and a girl chalks numbers
at the paving, a stone is thrown, tears, and you follow
                                                          through
to the same room, bleeding as if it were not all years before,
where she will turn to you, a studied look of *What's the*
                                                          matter

(you forget she died of cancer) and now, from the wad, balls
a squeak of cotton wool between her thumb and finger. Still,
                                                          you
can't say where it hurts, but here is your knee, a pomegranate
red in the yellow, the ball pressed to the mouth of the bottle,

and the gulp, as always, will fill the seat of a chair at the back
of a class and drip to a spread of hot piss across the polymer
                                                          floor.

Once more, you choke on flecks of black, stones scoured
to chalk, feel stings enter the open; the high window's flung

out somewhere, someone calls; an Elastoplast snags and
snaps
away from a scab and, for that lag, it might easily be summer,
but there happens again a sharp stink of something, not
flowers,
and the corridor stops running now. You stand before the
door.

OWEN SHEERS

Owen Sheers was born in Suva, Fiji, in 1974, and brought up from the age of nine at Llanddewi Rhydderch near Abergavenny. Educated at New College, Oxford, and the University of East Anglia, he lives in London. He has published, besides the travel narrative *The Dust Diaries* (2004), and a novel, *Resistance* (2007), two books of poems, *The Blue Book* (2000) and *Skirrid Hill* (2005).

FEELING THE CATCH

It is four in the morning, and one lamp strobes me in its
                            stutter,
the only sound, its filament fizzing, popping, fizzing
as last night's rain slugs by in the gutter.

I am by the pub where things happened first:
the hot flush of whisky down the back of my neck,
the quick release in the alley out back.

There is a body shifting on the step of the doorway,
deep in its sleeping bag, a draft excluder caught the wrong
                             side;
a dirty blue chrysalis of dreams and cold.

But all I can think of is the heat in there,
the press of dancing bodies, the sheen of sweat,
piss steaming in a full ceramic sink,

three men round it, looking down, hands in front,
like picketing workers round a brazier
or bowed head mourners at a funeral sermon.

And of Dai, doing his flaming Drambuies,
head back, eyes to the ceiling, mouth open wide,
singing hot notes of blue flickering flame.

How he used to make us lower the match
that lit the pink, ribbed roof of his mouth,
before it caught and he felt the catch;

a flame from nowhere,
hot on his lips, which he would shut with a snap,
careful not to burn himself on his own blue breath.

And then his gasp, his long outward sigh,
and the shake of his head, like a horse,
bluebottles caught in its eye.

*

And now here, on this hill, where I came with you,
the girl in the red dress whose name I can't remember,
on the only night we ever spoke.

Lying back on the bonnet of your father's car,
watching the house lights strike off,
shrinking the town to its tight centre.

851

Then looking up, constellations growing on the night sky;
following the curves of slow satellites
or the quicker release of meteorites: eighteen that night.

I never did see that dress, or you again.
Some told me it was because you were with Dai,
although I never knew and you never said,

but still I like to think I made an impression,
or at least left a reminder in the shallow dent
in the finish of your father's car –

right where it's hardest to beat out.

*

This was where Dai came too, eighteen that day,
stopping above the valley's river of lights.

Unscrewing the cap like a bottle of squash,
and pouring it out over his thighs,

lifting it, so it ran, thick over his head,
hair slicked down, an otter rising through water.

Then he must have lowered the match, careful,
waiting for the quick release and the catch,

which when it came set his body alive with fire,
flames quick at his finger tips, hot on his lips,

peeling at his skin, turning his hair to magnesium strips,
which fizz, then pop, then fizz.

The car windows shatter,
shooting stars out,

glass constellations growing on the dark tarmac
with each pane's crack and burst,

while Dai, head back, mouth open wide,
burns himself on his own blue breath.

HEDGE FOAL

At first we saw just the mare,
her swollen stomach deflated,
the wax on her teats broken,
standing, head low, by the hedge,
waiting for something to happen.

Then the afterbirth, discarded by her side:
a jelly fish placenta,
its bloody tentacles and loose, clear skin
slick over dock leaves and nettles.
The bitten umbilical cord like red steel rope.

And then finally, the foal,
cast deep in the hedge,
where it had rolled down the slope,

finding its all-hinge legs too collapsible
and its pulpy hooves too soft.

Suspended in blackthorn,
hung by bindatwine round its lips,
pulling them forward to a pucker.
Still and patient; an embryo
awaiting its birth back into the field.

NOT YET MY MOTHER

Yesterday I found a photo
of you at seventeen,
holding a horse and smiling,
not yet my mother.

The tight riding hat hid your hair,
and your legs were still the long shins of a boy's.
You held the horse by the halter,
your hand a fist under its huge jaw.

The blown trees were still in the background
and the sky was grained by the old film stock,
but what caught me was your face,
which was mine.

And I thought, just for a second, that you were me.
But then I saw the woman's jacket,
nipped at the waist, the ballooned jodhpurs,
and of course the date, scratched in the corner.

All of which told me again,
that this was you at seventeen, holding a horse
and smiling, not yet my mother,
although I was clearly already your child.

ANTONIA'S STORY

She told me how she fell to sleep with the sound of his fists
on the door.
Dull thuds that echoed on the stairs,
that became the beat of her heart on the sheet,
the rustle of blood in her ear on the pillow, then sleep.

Of how she slept a dark sleep with only one dream,
of an apple ripening, then falling a fall.
Its loud thud echoing on in the night
in the beat of her heart on the sheet.

And how she woke to the sound of fists on the door
and how she was surprised by the persistence of love.

She told me how she answered the door, and how she
saw him over the policeman's shoulder, lying on the lawn,
and how she thought why is he lying on the lawn, so pale
and quiet?
Why is he lying asleep and covered in dew?

And then how she saw the broken drainpipe he had tried
to climb,
and how she knew he had fallen, ripe in the night,

from the broken drainpipe, which still swung wild,
a madman's finger preaching in the wind.

And then she told me how each night she unlocks the door,
which sometimes gets blown, wild in the wind.
How her feet echo, dull on the stairs, as she climbs to bed
where she falls to sleep, the rustle of blood in her ear.

And how each night she sleeps a dark sleep with only one
dream,
of an apple, which falls, ripe in the night.
And how she wakes with the beat of her heart on the sheet,
surprised by the persistence of love.

A TRUE STORY

You have the truth tattooed on your back.
At least, that's what you told me it meant,
a single Japanese symbol
in blue-green ink, high on your shoulder blade,
a spider pretending to be dead.

Sometimes it looks like a mistake,
part hidden by the strap of your dress.
Does that make it a half-truth?
A white lie on your shoulder
ready to whisper into your ear.

Once, when we had argued,
and you had played dumb all day,

you turned your back to me in bed;
forcing me to face the truth,
in a language I will never understand.

ECLIPSE

We watched it apart, and perhaps that was my mistake,
letting the half-darkness fall over you in the city,

while I traced its spreading hand across the fields,
following the rooks, flying in threes to roost.

But as the sun became quarter, then half moon,
it unlocked in me, and I saw us connected again,

by the day's slowing to monochrome, by the mid-day
                                    midnight breeze
and by the moon's shadow passing over and between us.

It was, however, just a trick of the light,
as I learnt, on returning and calling you that night;

listening to your voice down the line,
cooled by his presence, eclipsed and clipped.

And then, on going to sleep, the dream –
his shadow falling across your up-looking face –

his shadow, falling across your memory of me.

857

Index of Titles

Index of Poets

Acknowledgements

Parthian would like to thank all the poets, estate holders and publishers for their cooperation in the preparation of this volume. We would also like to thank the editor, Meic Stephens, for his energy and enthusiasm.

The editor and publisher are grateful for permission to include the selected poems in this collection.

Although every effort has been made to secure permissions prior to printing this has not always been possible. The publisher apologizes for any errors or omissions but if contacted will rectify these at the earliest opportunity.

Further acknowledgements

The publishers would like to thank Mick Felton for his assistance in obtaining permissions for poetry published by Seren Books.

The publishers would like to thank Michael Schmidt for his assistance in obtaining permissions for poetry published by Carcanet.

The publishers would like to thank Gomer Press for assistance in obtaining permission on poems published.

All poems by Dylan Thomas from *Collected Poems*, Dent.

All poems by Dannie Abse from *New and Collected Poems,* Random House. Reprinted by permission of The Peters Fraser and Dunlop Group Limited on behalf of: Dannie Abse.

Poems by R. S Thomas in *Selected Poems 1946-1968* (Bloodaxe Books, 1986).

Poems by R.S Thomas in *Collected Poems 1945-1990* (J.M. Dent, a division of the Orion Publishing Group).

Poems by David Jones and Oliver Reynolds by kind permission of Faber and Faber.

Poems by Robert Minhinnick by kind permission of Carcanet and Seren.

Poems by Gillian Clarke by kind permission of Carcanet.

Poems by Gwyneth Lewis by kind permission of Bloodaxe.

PARTHIAN Library of Wales Trinity College Carmarthen SA31 3EP
email parthianbooks@yahoo.co.uk www.parthianbooks.co.uk

Parthian Books Ltd Registered Office: The Old Surgery Cardigan SA43 1ED

Parthian is an independent publisher that works with the support of the Welsh Books Council.

With additional support from Go Wales, Wales Trade International, The Paul Hamlyn Foundation, Ceredigion County Council, Trinity College Carmarthen.

Preface by Dafydd Elis-Thomas

Dafydd Elis-Thomas, the former Plaid Cymru Member of Parliament for Merioneth (later Meirionnydd Nant Conwy), has been a Member and the Presiding Officer of the National Assembly since 1999. Born in Carmarthen in 1946, he taught at Coleg Harlech and the University College of North Wales, Bangor. He took his seat in the House of Lords as Lord Elis-Thomas of Nant Conwy in the County of Gwynedd in 1992. From 1993 to 1999 he was Chairman of the Welsh Language Board. Among his many interests are film, contemporary literature, the visual arts, broadcasting, the theatre and hill-walking.

Editorial note by Meic Stephens

Meic Stephens was born in Trefforest, Pontypridd, in 1938. Educated at the University College of Wales, Aberystwyth, where he read French, and the University of Rennes, he taught in Ebbw Vale for several years before becoming a journalist with the *Western Mail*. He founded the magazine *Poetry Wales* in 1965 and was its editor for eight years. From 1967 to 1990 he was Literature Director of the Welsh Arts Council. He joined the staff of the University of Glamorgan in 1994 and was given a chair as Professor of Welsh Writing in English in 2000. He is the author, editor and translator of about two hundred books, including a number of anthologies, *The New Companion to the Literature of Wales* and the *Writers of Wales* series.

The cover image by Ceri Richards

'Do not go gentle into that good night', is by Ceri Richards (1903-71), a native of Dunvant, Swansea. Among the works which brought him an international reputation as one of the most important British painters of the 20th century was a series of paintings based on the poetry of Dylan Thomas and Vernon Watkins.

877

LIBRARY OF WALES

The Library of Wales is a Welsh Assembly Government project designed to ensure that all of the rich and extensive literature of Wales which has been written in English will now be made available to readers in and beyond Wales. Sustaining this wider literary heritage is understood by the Welsh Assembly Government to be a key component in creating and disseminating an ongoing sense of modern Welsh culture and history for the future Wales which is now emerging from contemporary society. Through these texts, until now unavailable or out-of-print or merely forgotten, the Library of Wales will bring back into play the voices and actions of the human experience that has made us, in all our complexity, a Welsh people.

The Library of Wales will include prose as well as poetry, essays as well as fiction, anthologies as well as memoirs, drama as well as journalism. It will complement the names and texts that are already in the public domain and seek to include the best of Welsh writing in English, as well as to showcase what has been unjustly neglected. No boundaries will limit the ambition of the Library of Wales to open up the borders that have denied some of our best writers a presence in a future Wales. The Library of Wales has been created with that Wales in mind: a young country not afraid to remember what it might yet become.

Dai Smith
Raymond Williams Chair in the Cultural History of Wales,
University of Wales, Swansea

LIBRARY OF WALES
FUNDED BY

Llywodraeth Cynulliad Cymru
Welsh Assembly Government

CYNGOR LLYFRAU CYMRU
WELSH BOOKS COUNCIL

Dannie ABSE

Ash on a Young
Man's Sleeve

Ron BERRY

So Long,
Hector Bebb

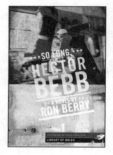

Gwyn THOMAS

The Dark
Philosophers

Lewis JONES

Cwmardy & We Live

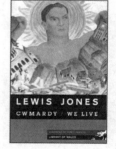

Alun LEWIS

In the Green Tree

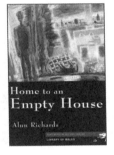

Alun RICHARDS

Home to an Empty House

Raymond WILLIAMS

Border Country

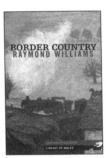

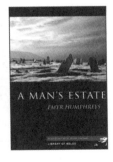

Emyr HUMPHREYS

A Man's Estate